ON CIVIC FRIENDSHIP

SIBYL A. SCHWARZENBACH

ON CIVIC FRIENDSHIP

Including Women in the State

COLUMBIA UNIVERSITY PRESS
NEW YORK

COLUMBIA UNIVERSITY PRESS
Publishers Since 1893
New York Chichester, West Sussex

Library of Congress Cataloging-in-Publication Data
Schwarzenbach, Sibyl A.
On civic friendship: including women in the state / Sibyl A. Schwarzenbach.
p. cm.
Includes bibliographical references and index.
ISBN 978-0-231-14722-4 (cloth : alk. paper)
ISBN 978-0-231-14723-1 (pbk. : alk. paper)
ISBN 978-0-231-51948-9 (e-book)
1. Women in politics—United States. 2. Women's rights—United States. 3. Feminist theory—United States. 4. Liberalism—United States. 5. Democracy—United States.
I. Title.
HQ1236.5. U6S39 2009
320.973082—dc22
2009000815

Columbia University Press books are printed on permanent and durable acid-free paper.
Printed in the United States of America

c 10 9 8 7 6 5 4 3 2 1
p 10 9 8 7 6 5 4 3 2

Permission from the publishers to reprint parts of the following articles is gratefully acknowledged: "On Civic Friendship," *Ethics* 107 (1996): 97–128; "A Political Reading of the Reproductive Soul in Aristotle," *History of Philosophy Quarterly* 9, no. 3 (1992): 243–64; "Locke's Two Conceptions of Property," *Social Theory and Practice* 14 (1988): 141–72; and "Rawls and Ownership: The Forgotten Category of Reproductive Labor," *Canadian Journal of Philosophy*, suppl. 13 (1987): 139–67.

Designed by Martin N. Hinze

IN MEMORY OF MY FATHER
Robert Maximilian Schwarzenbach (1917–1988)
my first civic friend

AND FOR
Jeff

CONTENTS

PREFACE: A PARADOX OF DEMOCRACY

The term friendship ought to inspire respect.
IMMANUEL KANT

One motive may still be capable of competing with the all-pervasive profit motive in our advanced capitalist society, and this is the motive of friendship. The dictates of tradition, of religious duty, and even of morality, it seems, are losing ground in the popular view to calculations of self-interest, to the desire for ever greater material goods, personal happiness, or individual pleasure. Loyalty and goodness—even justice itself—are frequently laughed at in the face of the almighty dollar, commercial success, or the fame afforded by the wielding of brute power. When it comes to the consideration of friends, however—and I here include lovers and family members as well—these others make us stop and think. For we all want genuine friends—the mere appearance will not do—and we all know what it is like to have someone we believed to be our friend betray us: to treat us not for our own good, but for theirs alone.

From this most fundamental impulse toward others, moreover—together with our own deep vulnerability and the profound hurt these others can cause us—may emerge the awareness of reciprocity, the need for self-limitation in the face of the other, and even the concept of duty itself. From within this intelligent conflict of desiring the presence of another, of wanting to be understood and cared for "for our own sake," and of otherwise fulfilling our most selfish and private desires, the problematic of morality is born. Further, such an awareness of the presence of others, of wanting to be near them, as well as a consciousness of our own limitations, may come about without the threat of eternal damnation or the promise of heavenly reward. The profound desire to be loved and cared for by one's moral equals for our own sake naturally imposes on a reflective being a duty toward them of like affection.

If one has never known genuine friendship, one cannot be good. This is the profound and fundamental insight of the ancient philosopher Aristotle, with which I begin this discussion. For Aristotle, friendship (*philia*) is not a mere personal phenomenon, however; it is also of great political importance (*politike philia*). In the worst regimes, such as tyranny, Aristotle notes in the *Nicomachean Ethics*, there is the least amount of political friendship (1161a31); in tyranny suspicion among citizens, corruption, exploitation, and betrayal reign. The following work argues for a version of this original insight of Aristotle's: that a form of political or civic friendship between citizens emerges as a *necessary condition* for justice in the *polis* or city-state. Not only is Aristotle's insight essentially correct, but I shall argue that a version of it applies even today to our far larger, modern nation-state. All talk of a social and political justice without the consideration of a prior civic friendship between citizens remains empty and a sham. Further, I shall aim to reveal the intimate connection between a political or civic friendship and the political form of *democracy* in particular—a connection, paradoxically, that has been all too often neglected by political philosophers in the modern period. Such are the central aims of the present book.

I say it is paradoxical that modern political philosophers rarely, if ever, mention friendship as a central element of democracy, because the connection between the two concepts, once recognized, not only appears obvious, but was acknowledged by many philosophers in the ancient world. Aristotle notes that the just *politeia* (the mixed polity) embodies the value of political fraternity between equals to a greater extent than other forms of regime (*NE* 1161b9–10). It turns out that his criticism of the polity's "perversion"—that is, his criticism of Greek democracy—lies not with democracy's emphasis on friendship, which he views as its strong point. Rather, Aristotle's criticism lies elsewhere: on ancient democracy's insistence on an "extreme" version of equality, on its form of mob rule and decision by lot, its emphasis on individual freedom conceived as mere license, and on its neglect of the education of its own citizens. In short, Greek democracy did not (and could not, in Aristotle's world view) live up to its own potential for a civic friendship between equals.

By contrast, the dominant political theory of the last four hundred years—political liberalism—has little or nothing to say about the friendship between citizens (at least until recently), and this is the case in an ostensibly democratic regime. Indeed, the vast majority of contemporary democratic theorists still try to account for the superiority of democracy as a political form in terms of the value of freedom or equality, or some combination of these two values.[1] Hence the paradox; ancient philosophers stressed the friendship between equals as a central value of democracy, while modern democrats largely ignore it and instead view "friendship" as unfit for political purposes. Thus my claim here is that the problematic of a civic friendship between citizens is *the* forgotten problem of *modern* democratic theory.

In this book I will argue that a third critical value of democracy is not "fraternity," since I reject the male implications of the term, but what I call *civic friendship*. To avoid confusion, it may be helpful from the start to distinguish "civic friendship" preliminarily from other, related terms. As I develop the notion, "civic friendship" emerges as that more specific form of political or institutional friendship (Aristotle's notion of *politike philia*), which essentially embodies, not just the rule of law, but now a modern doctrine of individual rights as well (3.1). So, too, I distinguish civic friendship from the older notion of (male) "fraternity," because civic friendship explicitly now entails not only the political recognition of women as equals but also the embodiment of their traditional form of labor and activity in public and state institutions. This form of labor and activity I call ethical reproductive *praxis,* and it aims at relations of friendship for their own sake and in the best case (2.5).

In a similar vein, I distinguish civic friendship from Marxist notions of the relations between "comrades" and from the idea of "solidarity." The concept of "solidarity" is far more general and vague—it can connote the common binding interests of *any* group, no matter its questionable ethics and aims (7. 5)—and in the original Marxist tradition, at least, it tends (again) to be conceived as primarily male. The history of the notion of solidarity misses the distinctive feminist ring that our notion of civic friendship will hopefully acquire. Finally, I distinguish civic friendship from recent feminist calls for "public care" insofar as I argue that friendship, unlike care, is not only necessarily reciprocal but essentially has the aim of equality at its heart (7.3). Indeed, I argue that care theorists must develop an adequate *normative* notion of public care: as with the older notion of sympathy, care is often paternalistic or parochial; one can care merely for oneself for one's own, or even for deluded demagogues. The notion of a civic friendship between equals, it turns out, can play this role of normative guide.

A central claim will thus be that the richer notion of friendship as *philia* (and not merely a political version of "care" or "solidarity") may aid in determining the limits of legitimate freedom and equality in a genuine democracy (7.5). Why? Because many, if not all, of the other criteria that are typically cited as distinctive of democracy can be understood to flow from this central value. Democracy, for example, literally conceived, means "rule of the people," but such rule presupposes not only that these "people" are in some sense my equals, but also that they are not my fundamental and ineluctable enemies. For, if this were the case, how could I sincerely be a democrat? I cannot genuinely wish my enemies to rule over me. Similarly, various theorists see the central point of democracy to consist in, say, the rejection of hereditary and unearned privilege (as in the theory of Ian Shapiro), or as the end of the domination of some by others (as for Carol Gould), or as the institutional embodiment of reason and discourse over force and fraud (as for the various deliberative democrats).[2] But all these criteria, we must note, are distinctive of the ideal relationship between genuine friends as well.

Finally, I will argue that if one accepts the centrality of the value of civic friendship for the realization of justice in a genuine democracy, then such an interpretation will *centrally* include women and their traditional characteristic work in democracy's historical realization. For, as Aristotle already recognized—and as the women's movement is again bringing to our awareness—it is women who traditionally perform much of what may be called *the friendship-labor* in society (2.5). On such an interpretation, women will not be conceived as mere "afterthoughts" to a conception of democracy in which the model of the political person remains essentially male. To the contrary, a version of their historical activity emerges at the very heart of this governmental form.

In sum, our topic is the necessity of a form of civic friendship between citizens today as a requirement of true justice in the evolving democratic state, as well as the nature of the conditions of its possibility. My task now is to delineate what this might mean at the dawn of the twenty-first century.

June 2008

ACKNOWLEDGMENTS

Over the numerous years of writing this book, I have incurred many intellectual (and otherwise) debts—some going way, way back in time. For helpful discussions, comments, criticisms, or textual aid, I would like to acknowledge as many of them as I can (the others, hopefully, will be acknowledged in the text). Thus I wish to thank Joanne Abed, Kristana Arp, Annette Baier, Philippe Balzer, Jeffrey Bliss, Stanley Cavell, Birgit Christianson, Gerald Cohen, Omar Dahbour, Gerald Doppelt, Ronald Dworkin, Gertrude Ezorsky, Carol C. Gould, Alan Grose, Virginia Held, Sylvia Law, Paul Miller, Paula Moya, Tom Nagel, Martha Nussbaum, Summer Pierre, Frances Fox Piven, Thomas Pogge, Hilary Putnam, Peter Schaber, Yegane Shayegan, James Sterba, Joan Tronto, Jami Weinstein, Allen Wood, and the late Marx Wartofsky. The expression of my thanks, of course, hardly means that these thinkers would agree with what I have written here, nor that I have satisfactorily answered their many objections.

I would also like to thank Myrna Chase, former dean of the Weissman School of Arts and Science at Baruch College, City University of New York, as well as the college itself and the CUNY Graduate Center for their support over the years; the Stanford Humanities Center, where chapter 7 was written; the Center for Place, Culture and Politics, where many insights were honed; and my many undergraduate and graduate students in my (by now) myriad lectures and seminars over the years, whether at City University, Princeton University, or (going even farther back in time) Harvard University. So, too, I am most appreciative of all the hard work performed on this manuscript by the editorial team at Columbia University Press. Finally, I would like to acknowledge my deepest debt and gratitude to one who influenced my thought like no other, with whom I disagreed over and again throughout the years, but from whom I also learned a great deal: the late John Rawls.

ON CIVIC FRIENDSHIP

1 INTRODUCTION
Metaphor and Theory Change

Women's labor is considered a natural resource,
freely available like air and water.
MARIA MIES

1.1 THE PROBLEM OF SOCIAL UNITY

This work attempts a novel answer to the time-honored question of "social unity" or, alternatively, of "community": the problem of what holds a good and just society together. Since ancient times the question of that which ultimately binds people together in a *polis*—whether fear or friendship, religion or self-interest, a shared interest in liberty or justice, a common ethnic identity, or something else altogether—has preoccupied political theorists as well as sharply divided them. In our own time, the problem of social unity is experiencing a resurgence of interest for reasons that are not difficult to fathom. In the United States, at least, we are witnessing ever growing disparities in economic wealth, persistent violence, mounting religious and racial tensions, the disintegration of traditional (bourgeois) family relations, as well as staggering rates of systemic homelessness, drug dependency, illiteracy, and so forth. Such phenomena are also on the rise in Europe, including a burgeoning xenophobia, chauvinistic nationalism, as well as the myriad difficulties involved in the aim of a unified Europe. This is not even to mention (yet) the expanding global inequities, growing world hunger, precipitous environmental destruction, international terrorism, and war. Despite such evident and critical social problems, however, political liberalism—the dominant political theory of the last four centuries—has historically concerned itself with other issues.

By "political liberalism" I intend that tradition of Western, political thought and practice that has its roots in at least three momentous developments of the modern period. The first of these was the Reformation, which led to the acceptance, at first reluctant, of the principle of liberty of conscience, and eventually to religious toleration more generally. Politically speaking, the liberal argument runs, we can no longer demand of all humans one and the same comprehensive view of the good life (or of God); happiness is no longer seen as something that can be imposed on the individual from above or from without, but rather as something that must be "self-chosen." This acknowledged absence or lack of a comprehensive political conception of the good has come to be known as the modern "fact of pluralism."[1]

The second, momentous development of the modern period, beginning in the sixteenth century, was the centralized nation-state. Centralization—including territorial dominion with an internal police and external control (army) in the name of security, regulation of competition and material production, and consolidation of collective cultural identity (the "nation"), as well as administration of the private civil realm—was accomplished first under the direction of the crown. This development gave rise to attempts to limit the sovereign powers of monarchy: to subject monarchs to the rule of law and often to the constraints of a bill of rights (stipulating a set of individual rights and liberties applying, in principle at least, to all men).

Finally, a third historical development was the rise of the free-market economy. It is often overlooked that on any liberal view—from the work of John Locke or Adam Smith to that of John Rawls—certain measures are always specified to assure that citizens have adequate material means effectively to use their basic liberties and opportunities. Traditionally, such measures have ranged anywhere from free-market distributive mechanisms, to laws of inheritance and bequest, to the direct provision of public goods and services. And, at least historically speaking, a liberal economic reign at home was fully compatible with political or economic empire abroad, even if the normative ideal remained that of peace and trade between nations.

If this brief characterization of political liberalism is correct, it soon becomes apparent that the central problems that early liberal thinkers grappled with for centuries gained their original significance against the backdrop of medieval feudal life; liberal theories gained prominence in criticizing the political doctrine of royal absolutism as well as late feudal economic policies, such as mercantilism. Liberal concerns, that is, typically focused on how to avoid abuses of royal power and of the state; on a new, positive determination of the nature and extent of legitimate political and economic authority; on questions of the new citizen's obligation (now grounded in either consent or utility); and on the clear delineation of a basic set of equal rights and freedoms of individuals. The primary focus of liberal theorists' attention, in other words, was not on what ultimately binds people together in a just community. Concern with issues of social unity, trust, or civic friendship, or with the social and material conditions of human communal existence, lay further from the traditional liberal's heart. And the reason is, again, not difficult to fathom. The positive relations between men and the ordering of the human social community were generally perceived to be governed still by a "natural" (if no longer by a divine) order. Such things ought by all rights to take care of themselves.

On all three of these characterizations of liberalism, John Locke emerges as the paradigmatic liberal. Locke's *Letter of Toleration* (1689) is an important philosophical statement of the principle that each person must be free to conceive and to seek his good in his own way; his *Second Treatise of Government* (1693) argues not only for a basic set of natural rights of individuals derivative from natural law (the law of reason) in the state of nature, but also for that arrangement of social institutions (such as that of private property) which arguably makes all "better off" (3.3). Finally, the view that the positive human social community—for example, the relations between the sexes or of those within the family—was governed not only by a natural (reasonable) order, but even still by divine law, is clearly visible throughout both of Locke's *Two Treatises of Government.*

Already by the end of the eighteenth century, however, the problem of social unity as a primary political concern once again surfaces. We see this reflected primarily in the work of Rousseau, Hegel, or such socialist thinkers as Karl Marx. And in spite of the differences that might today distinguish many continental thinkers, socialists, Marxists, feminists, civic republicans, contemporary communitarians, and even conservative, religious fundamentalists from one another, one thing at least appears to unite them: the common belief that traditional liberalism has an "inadequate conception of community."[2] Even so good a liberal as John Rawls himself admits that, in comparison with the ideas of liberty or equality, the idea of fraternity has (at least until his own theory) held a lesser place within the tradition.[3] And Ronald Dworkin, that champion of individual rights, has been hard at work developing an adequate conception of "liberal community."[4] Finally, in the last two decades, a plethora of works on the issue of liberalism, community, and civic virtues have burst upon the philosophical scene.[5] At the same time a whole new movement has emerged, known as the feminist ethics and politics of care.[6] If all these thinkers are correct, a lacuna exists within our dominant political tradition of the last four hundred years—and, by extension, within our public conception of our selves.

It was undoubtedly Thomas Hobbes who, at the dawn of the modern period, attempted the most trenchant defense of fear and enlightened self-interest as the sufficient political glue, while Locke emphasized security, property, and a shared interest in freedom.[7] David Hume, in criticizing the parochial and militaristic citizenship of the ancient republics, proclaimed the new peaceful bond between men to be commerce.[8] More recently, John Rawls (although at one point calling his difference principle a "principle of fraternity") primarily argues in terms of a shared conception of justice and its habituated practice as the unifying force in his well-ordered society,[9] while Jürgen Habermas calls for a new "constitutional patriotism."[10]

The position on social and political unity put forth here, by contrast, will distinguish itself from all these views (including those of dominant care theorists) by arguing a version of a much older and essentially Aristotelian claim: not only social but political unity has always included, and must again be acknowledged as including, *philia*, or friendship in its civic form. As Aristotle writes in the *Nicomachean Ethics*: "Friendship (*philia*) seems too to hold states together, and lawgivers to care more for it than for justice. For when men are friends they have no need of justice, while when they are just they need friendship as well, and the truest form of justice is thought to be a friendly quality" (*NE* 1155a2224).[11]

Aristotle's claim strikes the modern reader as highly implausible, however, not only because it refers to the ancient *polis* (whose inhabitants typically numbered between 40,000 and 50,000), but also because it omits the claims we are long accustomed to hearing: that the human entered the modern social compact and political society out of fear, rational self-interest, the desire for freedom and a commodious living, or to secure law and order. Certainly, our contemporary lawgivers appear unconcerned with friendship—they hardly even mention the term. On the contrary, the modern standpoint is better captured, I believe, by the words of G. W. F. Hegel, who criticizes the romantic sentimentalism of his contemporary, Jakob Friedrich Fries. Although acknowledging the role friendship and even love played in the ancient *polis*, Hegel jettisons them as a possible basis for the larger, far more complex, modern nation-state. He writes in *The Philosophy of Right*: "Love, however, is feeling, i.e. ethical life in the form of something natural. In the state, feeling disappears; there we are conscious of unity as law; there the content must be rational and known to us."[12] As for so many of his liberal predecessors, "feeling" disappears in the state for Hegel, who views a shared interest in law, reason, and (positive) freedom as the sufficient political mortar binding citizens together.

Although Hegel's words generally ring true to contemporary ears, I shall argue that this dominant modern position emerges as untenable; *philia* must again be acknowledged as an essential factor unifying even the just modern state. This is the case, I shall maintain, because political friendship emerges as a necessary condition for genuine justice. As I shall show in chapter 2, without a reciprocal awareness between citizens of their (moral) equality, without a basic good will between them, and without a willingness practically to do things for one another, genuine justice becomes impossible.

There is a further important reason why the dominant modern position on state unity emerges as untenable, and a version of Aristotle's view as still correct. This further reason is that much of the activity of friendship that de facto binds people together in modern community—an activity I shall here refer to as "reproductive activity" in an extended ethical sense—has continued to be performed over the centuries, but it has been performed outside the official version of the state, as well as beyond the eye of the traditional philosopher; that is, it has been performed primarily, though not exclusively, by women. In slightly different words, my argument runs that the traditional, ethical reproductive practice of women not only embodies and consciously aims at *philia* in the best case (something Aristotle already recognized) but also contributes greatly toward binding even the modern state together (granted, in a hitherto unacknowledged fashion). At present, moreover, the time is ripe for the implications of such ethical reproductive activity, as well as its proper aim of *philia*, to be acknowledged once again for public, political life.

1.2 LOCKE'S METAPHOR OF MIXING ONE'S LABOR

In focusing almost exclusively on the issue of civic friendship, this book attempts nothing less than a fundamental shift in the dominant political problem to be analyzed. In contrast to traditional liberal concerns with the protection of individual rights and obligations, or with the limits of state power and authority, we are here engaged in a new problem setting after hundreds of years. Such a departure from liberal orthodoxy is easier said than done, however. How, for instance, are we to succeed in keeping problems of social trust, friendship, or community in the foreground without overlooking the fact that we wish to do so now in a political and state context? How are we to do so without simultaneously neglecting such traditional liberal issues as individual rights, or the extent of legitimate state power or the use of force, as it seems all too many Marxists, communitarians, religious fundamentalists, and even feminists have done?[13] For one thing is certain: we wish here to focus on a civic friendship at the same time as we distinguish ourselves from the illiberal imposition of a Soviet-type "comradeship" from above, or from the views of a Carl Schmidt, who saw the friend–enemy distinction as *the* criterion of "the political."[14]

Problem settings, it has been argued, are mediated by the "stories" people tell about troublesome situations—stories in which they describe what is wrong and what needs fixing.[15] When one examines the problem-setting stories told by any number of early modern political thinkers, it becomes apparent that the framing of the issues often depends upon metaphors underlying such tales; these metaphors not only generate the problem setting, but also can set the direction of problem-solving. One such powerful metaphor—one that I believe underlies the whole of the modern liberal political tradition—is that presented by John Locke in the chapter "Of Property" in his *Second Treatise of Government.* I refer to Locke's famous metaphor of the individual in the state of nature who originally "owns" that with which he has "mixed his labour" (*ST*, para. 27). Let us focus for a moment on this powerful metaphor, which has so profoundly influenced our political vision for the last few hundred years.

In general, the cognitive potential of metaphor is again being appreciated by philosophers, after centuries of metaphor being considered a mere "ornament" or "embellishment" of language. In a series of famous articles, for example, Max Black claimed that metaphor carries with it a "tacit implication-complex"; every metaphor, he wrote, is "the tip of a submerged model."[16] So, too, Nelson Goodman describes a new metaphor as being capable of, among other things, "a re-organization of our familiar world"; it is a mode of "re-cognizing" things.[17] Richard Rorty has gone so far as to claim that metaphor is "a third source of truth," because it suggests that cognition is not always "re-cognition," that the acquisition of truth is not always a matter of fitting data into a preestablished scheme. In Rorty's view, a creative metaphor actually challenges the established scheme itself: "A metaphor is, so to speak, a voice from outside logical space, rather than . . . a logical-philosophical clarification of the structure of that space. It is a call to change one's language and one's life."[18]

Whether or not a metaphor is a voice from "outside logical space," a novel metaphor may certainly change one's vision, one's language, and even one's life. Certainly, the introduction of Locke's mixing metaphor in the seventeenth century captured something important and encouraged a radically new way of looking at things. This new metaphor not only set the parameters of a new political problem, but also, simultaneously, set the direction of problem-solving for hundreds of years to come.

As one author notes, before Locke's *Second Treatise,* few thinkers understood that man had a natural right to property created by his labor; after 1690 the idea becomes a near axiom of social science.[19] That is, in contrast to older criteria of ownership, criteria such as nature, custom, conquest, or first occupancy, few thinkers before Locke had dared claim that individual labor was a leading criterion of property acquisition (with gift and contract as derivative modes). Many scholars of Locke have emphasized the degree to which Locke's property theory—as a sub-part of his more general critique of royal absolutism—was designed to tread a fine line between Tory and Leveller positions.[20] In the face of the abuses of the reign of Charles II, and in the midst of the so-called Exclusion Crisis, Locke was led to emphasize the people's right of resistance to an arbitrary and absolutist government, and to deny the Tory position that either tradition or property could be the rightful basis of political authority. For this purpose, Locke needed not only a new justification for legitimate political power (which he now argued lay in the realm of individual consent), but also a new justification for the rights and property of individuals prior to and independent of government. In light of these aims, Locke, appealing to both Scripture and natural reason, begins his famous chapter "Of Property" with the notion of the earth as original common property, in explicit contrast to Sir Robert Filmer's *Patriarcha* (reprinted in 1680), in which the earth was seen as a divine gift to a patriarchal head. Since Locke simultaneously wished to distance himself from such radical positions as that of the Levellers (who argued against all private property on biblical grounds), the task he explicitly sets for himself in this chapter is to show "how rightful individuation of the common gift is possible," and this prior to "any express compact of all the Commoners," that is, prior to the formation of government (*ST*, para. 25).

Locke's task was thus to ground legitimate political authority on individual consent at the same time as a basic set of individual rights (to freedom, political equality, property, and so forth) was justifiable independently of the need for consent. Surely, a part of the solution to this dilemma is Locke's famous labor theory of property. With the introduction of the mixing metaphor, Locke answers the question of how the earth, originally given to men in common, comes to be unequally divided among them, and this prior even to the formation of government. In Locke's words, "different degrees of labor, industry and ability were apt to give men legitimate possessions in different proportions" (*ST*, para. 48).

Locke's mixing metaphor may appear to express the most obvious, self-evident truth. That labor in some sense fashions a right to property—and ultimately "property" in its private form—was a premise conceded by nearly all and for centuries to come: by natural rights theorist and utilitarian alike, as well as by the average man or woman on the street. And yet the ancient and medieval world never thought to establish this truth as a general principle. In the case of both classical Greece and Rome, the reason seems quite clear: in both societies, a highly significant portion, if not the majority of labor, was performed by slaves (precisely those who owned no property).[21] As Hannah Arendt notes, labor tended to be viewed by the ancients as the consequence of poverty, never as a creative means to poverty's abolition.[22] Indeed, among the ancients one finds extensive discussions on whether it is natural for citizens to own equal portions of land or to hold land in common, whether ownership should be attributed to the virtuous or to those of long occupancy—the normal assumption being that the land would be worked by others. Thus Aristotle is able to view property as a "provision from nature" like milk to offspring: "Property of this order (that is to say, for the purposes of subsistence) is evidently given by nature to all living things, from the instant of their first birth to the days when their growth is finished" (*Pol* 1256b). Similarly, under serfdom in the medieval period, labor as a justification for ownership played a negligible role; the serf worked the land of his lord by custom and so too were its fruits divided. Thus, in contrast to the tradition, and like all new and powerful metaphors, Locke's mixing metaphor entails a rule violation; it firmly weds the notions of "labor" and "ownership," hitherto kept quite distinct.

A more careful scrutiny of this mixing metaphor reveals further implicit assumptions. Clearly, "the individual" to whom Locke refers in his mythical state of nature is neither a slave nor a serf, for neither of these possessed the recognized power of "free personhood" ushering in private property. In the case of the slave, both his labor-power and its fruits belonged exclusively to his master, while in the case of the serf, custom divided the time, amount, and results of the serf's labor between himself and his lord. It emerges that for a man privately to "own" that with which he has "mixed his labor," he must already exclusively *own* his actions and labor-power to begin with.

Thus, not only must Locke's "individual" be a free political person, who possesses exclusive rights to his own limbs, actions, and labor-power, but he cannot fully own (in the sense of private property) that with which he mixes his labor unless the instruments and the raw materials worked upon are already "his" to a certain extent as well. Locke's images are all agricultural ("to mix" originally meant "to manure"), but the metaphor quite nicely extends to craft and artisan work, as well as to other forms of social and wage labor. Thus, if the material instruments belong to the guild or to another (perhaps they are rented from a neighbor), the laborer must partially reimburse this other. If the laborer is employed by a capitalist (as Karl Marx most famously pointed out), the laborer normally receives none of the products made but merely a "wage." And if the tools and fields should be collectively owned, the laborer must share a part of the produce with the other co-owners. Even the colonial farmer hacking away at the wilderness in America (perhaps the closest analogy to Locke's original state of nature) typically used his own tools and first needed to drive off the original inhabitants from the land.

We thus find that Locke's famous claim that man originally "owns" that with which he has mixed his labor in reality presupposes the institution it is meant to justify—the institution of private ownership.[23] The metaphor paradigmatically pertains to the small, private landowner, who already rightfully possesses his own person, labor, and land, and who then works his fields (either by his or his family's own hands, or through hire), or it refers to the craftsman who already owns his own labor, tools, and raw materials. Far from "grounding" the institution of private property, the metaphor merely helps focus our attention in this new institution's direction.

Further, the mixing metaphor directs our attention toward a particular form of property ownership and to a now "free" form of individual labor, but not even to all free forms of labor at that. It implicitly assumes, for instance (something Locke later explicitly argues), that the free labor ushering in rightful fruits must be *productive*; morally speaking, such labor must create "value." If the individual spends his time and energy, say, *destroying* the resources of the originally common earth, no ownership rights follow. For Locke, men *gave up* their common right to the land, but only in exchange for the more commodious living that would result from the heightened initiative of private ownership, and from the institution's resulting greater productivity and wealth for all (*ST*, paras. 41–48) (3.3).

Finally, Locke's mixing metaphor does not apply to the labor of women, and for at least two important reasons. First, although women in the seventeenth century were considered neither slave nor serf, they did not yet fully "own" their own persons and labor-power. The labor-power of women (as well as its fruits) was typically considered the legal property of their father or husband under Blackwell's doctrine of unity of personhood.[24] Indeed, women did not privately own their own labor-power (or wages) in our tradition until well into the nineteenth century—and in many parts of the world not even today.

There is a second and equally important reason, however, why Locke's mixing metaphor does not apply to the traditional labor of women. Even if women did legally own and control their own labor-power (much as in our society today), the *form* of labor they performed appears particularly ill suited to the ushering in of private property rights. That is, beyond their work in the fields, in gathering, weaving, and so forth, women spent an inordinate amount of time "mixing their labor" in caring for their children and other family members, maintaining the household, and even aiding others in the neighborhood. They washed, cleaned, attended to and nursed others, cooked for and served them, sewed their clothes, and so forth. And yet this form of daily *reproductive* labor—in explicit contrast to the category of productive labor—ushers in no private property rights at all. And for good reason.

To drive this point home, let us note the distinguishing features of the modern institution of private property. Private property is distinguished from common use rights, private possession, stewardship, or communal ownership by the fact that the owner not only exclusively has the right to use and control the property (so long as he infringes on no rights of others), but he even has the right to *alienate* (sell) the property if he so wishes.[25] Among the eleven standard incidents of the full-blown institution of private property, eight are liberties and three are prohibitions: (1) *the right to possess* (exclusive physical control); (2) *the right to use* (personal enjoyment of); (3) *the right to manage* (decide how and by whom); (4) *the right to income*; (5) *the right to capital* (power to alienate, modify, waste, or destroy the thing); (6) *the right to security*; (7) *the power of transmissibility*; (8) *the absence of term* (indeterminate length of one's ownership rights); (9) *prohibition of harmful use* (to others); (10) *liability to execution* (to have the thing taken away for the repayment of debt); (11) *residuary character* (existence of rules governing the reversion of lapsed ownership rights). That this form of private ownership is an inappropriate reward for the traditional labor and activity of women should be clear from the following considerations.

First, the children and other members of the family with whom the woman directly "mixes her labor" are not private property, for the simple reason that persons in the modern period are increasingly viewed as inappropriate objects of private ownership.[26] A woman's labor with (and upon) other family members hardly gives her a recognized right to do with such persons "as she wills"; these other persons are "hers" only in the sense that much of their health and well-being remain her *responsibility*. So too, the household worked upon or the objects produced by the women within and for it—for example, food, candles, soap, or clothing made for direct consumption and use—are conceived, not as private, but as a *shared* family property. These items are not incidentally but *essentially* communal. Indeed, I shall argue, that it is of the essence of such daily "reproductive" activity that its fruits cannot be privately owned (5.5). For, the proper *telos* of such laboring activities is nothing more than the simple reproduction of flourishing human relations for their own sake—in the best case, relations of *philia*, or friendship (2.5). For the moment, it is enough to note that this form of ethical, reproductive labor and activity is nowhere explicitly referred to by Locke; it is simply not acknowledged as a distinctive form of activity, nor recognized as a genuine type of labor to begin with.

Not surprisingly, it emerges that the paradigmatic "individual" presupposed in Locke's famous mixing metaphor is a politically free household head with a set of God-given rights, necessarily already a private property owner (at least with respect to his own life, limbs, and actions) and almost certainly male.[27] Moreover, Locke's primary concern in the *Second Treatise* is to determine the grounds and limits of legitimate state authority over *this* individual. Further, the introduction of the mixing metaphor not only sets the parameters of an urgent new problem—the limits of political authority over a now free, white, male property owner—but simultaneously indicates the terms of a solution. Legitimate political authority must now be based on this individual's *consent*. Henceforth, a reasonable sphere of this individual's private activity must be protected at all costs from governmental interference.

Over the ensuing centuries, the tradition of political liberalism works and reworks this territory originally charted by Locke in the *Second Treatise*. Where precisely the line falls between private person and public state is debated over and again. Just as Locke remains the quintessential liberal, the centrality of the mixing metaphor (as well as its implication-complex) may well be one of the common threads uniting all thinkers with claims to the liberal tradition. Or, at least, so I shall argue in the following chapters.

1.3 THE NEED FOR A NEW METAPHOR

If we turn to the problem of community, however, and to the question of how to conceive a fair and just social union, Locke's metaphor of the individual productive laborer with his surrounding sphere of privacy offers little material for elaboration. Worse, the metaphor actually suggests that any inroads into the sphere of this person's private activity and labor are identical to an invasion of his individual rights. Indeed, as already mentioned, many Marxists, communitarians, and feminists, in attempting to reestablish stronger bonds of community, believe that the true culprit of social disintegration is the notion of individual rights.

I believe this line of argument for greater community is dangerously mistaken, and I shall try to show how its proponents themselves remain trapped within the narrow confines of Locke's mixing metaphor. Just as the stories that need to be told about troublesome situations—about what is wrong and what needs fixing—have changed radically since the seventeenth century, so too the frame by which we set the parameters for problem-solving must alter. Locke's mixing metaphor must once and for all be dethroned from the power it has held over our thought for the last three hundred years.

I say "dethroned" and not "discarded," for the valid insights in Locke's theory obviously run deep. By dethroning the metaphor, I mean diminishing its importance, displacing it as the primary frame by which we view most problems, which in turn allows us to move on and address other issues. And thus there is no better way of achieving this than by seeing the metaphor through to its end—by exhausting its implication-complex, as it were—until a new metaphor is born from within: the image of traditional *woman* "mixing her labor." This new metaphor, as we shall see, is the tip of an entirely new model of activity whose submerged "associated commonplaces" are radically different. By thus switching metaphors and by elaborating the new metaphor's implication-complex, we will be well on our way toward viewing the world on what I am calling an "ethical reproductive" (rather than a "productive") model. Looking at the world in this way offers great advantages for the problem of social unity.

The tradition that views metaphor as a perspective or epistemological frame, as a way of interpreting and making sense of the world, harkens back to ancient times. Aristotle clearly recognized the cognitive importance of metaphor, particularly metaphor grounded on analogy. In the *Poetics* he writes, "But the greatest thing by far is to be master of metaphor. It is the one thing that cannot be learnt from others; and it is also a sign of genius, since a good metaphor implies an intuitive perception of the similarity in dissimilars" (*Poe* 1459a5–7). Through resemblance, metaphor not only "makes things clearer," it can actually render visible a hitherto unnoticed and "nameless act" (*Poe* 1457b28). It does this, according to Aristotle, by an analogical transfer of meaning that "consists in giving the thing a name that belongs to something else" (*Poe* 1457b7–8). The example Aristotle himself discusses is that of the poet's metaphorical depiction of the sun as "sowing around a god-created light" (*Poe* 1457b25–30).[28] Typically, the casting forth of seed-corn is called "sowing," but the act of the sun casting forth its flame "has no special name." Still, by way of the poet's metaphor, one can actually identify a something here, which the sun does, for sunlight stands in a similar relation to the sun's casting forth its rays as the seed-corn does to sowing. Thus, by way of an intuitive perception of the similarity of dissimilars, a hitherto "nameless" activity—one that was not even distinguished *as* an activity until the perception was so formulated by the metaphor—is brought to the center of our attention.

In a similar vein, the historical activity of women has never been perceived *as labor*, nor as a distinctive category of activity in our long philosophical tradition (at least until recently). By an intuitive perception of the similarity of dissimilars, however, and by way of an analogical transfer of meaning, we can give this activity "a name which belongs to something else": we can give it the name of "action" or of "labor." Not only will the proposed new metaphor thereby render this form of activity clearer, but it will actually be making visible a "hitherto nameless act."

The present study undertakes this task of making visible the category of reproductive action in its ethical (and non-biological) sense (chapters 2–4). From the start, however, we must be certain to avoid various possible misunderstandings. In elaborating the alternative model (and metaphor) of action, I am well aware that I am performing a selective "abstraction."[29] Moreover, the proposed model is "ahistorical" to the extent that it pertains in particular to the division of gendered labor emergent in modern Western society (no culture appears altogether free from some variation or transformation of it, however). The introduction of this alternative model is thus no more than a mode of representing to ourselves structural features of the social world, which I believe have theoretically long been neglected. To quote Goodman once again, presenting a new model or metaphor is a way of "casting our nets" in order to capture what may be significant likenesses and differences in the world. In the present instance, I aim to capture something important about human motivation in general.

Finally, I hope to draw important implications from this new model of labor—unacknowledged and undertheorized—for the study of the political state (chapters 5–7) and even for plausible motivation in the international domain (chapter 8). The vast literature regarding these various spheres contains implicit assumptions that are only just beginning to be challenged. In elaborating the new metaphor, moreover, we will not only have succeeded in fixing the terms of a new and different problem—namely, that of social unity—but we will simultaneously be developing the tools for its solution. For one thing I aim to impress upon my audience about all else. Switching to an ethical reproductive model of action—theoretically articulating the capacities, motivations, perceptions, and reasoning required, and directing our political practice in this direction—does *not* presuppose a utopian view of the person. The vast majority of the world's women, after all, have been trained for and operating on this model for centuries.

1.4 REMARKS ON PHILOSOPHICAL METHOD

This project leads me of necessity to certain remarks on philosophical method. My work has been much influenced by John Rawls's method of "reflective equilibrium"—though by no means uncritically.[30] Recall that, when applied to the moral realm, the method of reflective equilibrium is that method of philosophical reflection whereby sincere moral agents seek a mutual adjustment or "equilibrium" between their particular, considered moral judgments (formed through concrete observation and practice) and a set of general principles that purports to generate them. Such "back and forth" reflection between particular judgments and general principle operates first between the individual's own set of moral convictions (narrow reflective equilibrium) and then between his or her unified convictions and an ever-widening circle of others (wide reflective equilibrium). For Rawls, of course, there exists the possibility of not just a moral, but a political (as well as legal) reflective equilibrium whereby theorists elaborate "the basic intuitive ideas" and the "implicitly recognized principles" embedded in the "public political culture" of a particular society and seek to resolve specific historical conflicts.[31] The aim is always to generate a set of fundamental moral or political principles on which all (or at least most) can agree. Theorists now even aim for a unified set of equilibrium principles on the international level.[32] The distinctiveness of this method of reflective equilibrium is perhaps best understood by first grasping what it is *not*.

In general, the method rejects the view that morality is a matter of divine commandment, or that moral principles can be directly "intuited" by reason, or that they can be derived straight from "nature" or from some natural function (*ergon*) of man; such methodologies generally presuppose what they are meant to justify.[33] The method of reflective equilibrium thus not only explicitly rejects any form of Cartesian justification (which purports to deduce a sufficient set of moral standards accounting for our considered judgments from self-evident first principles), but refuses as well all naturalist attempts to reduce or express moral or value statements in a purely "empiricist" language (affording confirmation by the methods of empirical science only). In contrast both to the classical rationalist (formalist) and empiricist (utilitarian) approaches, the search for reflective equilibrium is viewed as the search for a *moral-practical consensus*: one addressed in the first instance to other human beings with whom we disagree, to whom we need to justify ourselves, and in terms that all can accept.[34] The aim of theory, in this view, is not to mirror some independent ethical order, but to extend the range of an already existing moral consensus. John Rawls calls the form his theory takes "constructivist."[35] By first making explicit what we minimally (morally speaking) hold in common, such a theory attempts to illuminate, but also if necessary to forge, further common ground of agreement on moral and political issues where discord now reigns. Such a "reconciliatory" view of the nature of moral and political theory is particularly appropriate for the workings of a democracy.

In its employment in Rawls's theory, the method of reflective equilibrium thus has a specific normative-practical goal; the theory is directed at a particular "impasse" reached in at least the modern, Western tradition. That is, justice as fairness aims to "reconcile by reason" our political tradition's conflicting intuitions regarding the relative values of freedom and of equality as these values are embodied in our society's basic structure (*PL*, 4–6). As mentioned, the construction begins by drawing upon the "basic intuitive ideas" and "implicitly recognized principles" embodied in the political and legal institutions of modern democratic society, as well as in the public traditions of their interpretation (ideas such as that society is a system of cooperation and not of exploitation, that citizens are conceived as free and equal, that government is to serve all and not just a few, and so forth). This Rawls calls the "public, political culture." In his view, the best conception of political justice will be the one judged superior (always relative to its competitors) in terms of the coherence, order, and unity it discovers—or forges—among our most deeply held ethical intuitions. Moral and political justification necessarily remains "holistic" on such a view.[36]

If we are convinced of the appropriateness of something like the method of reflective equilibrium in general—at least as an approach to moral and political issues—numerous problems nonetheless remain in our attempt to apply this method to the issue of social unity or to that of civic friendship. For one, as we have just seen, questions of community and a civic friendship have been neglected in our "public culture" for much of the last four hundred years; both our economic and governmental practice, as well as the dominant political theory of liberalism, have instead focused on other issues. It is thus unlikely that our official theory and practice contain many (or at least many forceful) shared intuitions regarding the issue of friendship from which to begin theory construction. Again, if we start only from the data presented by our own "public culture" or from the Western tradition of modern moral and political philosophy, a conception of civic friendship relevant to our times would appear impossible to construct due to the lack of an initial database. For this reason I intend not to limit our initial fund of particular moral and political intuitions to representatives of the modern period, but will include the considered judgments of much older thinkers—in particular the judgments of Aristotle, for whom the topic of a civic friendship was of great import (chapter 2).

Even more important, if a political reflective equilibrium begins with the garnered insights and basic intuitive ideas of "our public political culture" (even if we now include those of the ancient world), it is difficult not to notice that this public political culture (again, until very recently) was composed entirely of males. Women were long denied the right to vote, to go to university, to hold public office, to sit on juries, to own private property on their own, to speak, or even to appear at many public gatherings, and this often remained true well into the twentieth century.[37] It is highly likely that many of the particular, considered moral convictions shared by women—one-half the population, traditionally confined to the private and familial sphere, and who performed the preponderance of ethical reproductive labor—were all too easily excluded from the start in the balancing act of a political reflective equilibrium. Indeed, in a now burgeoning literature, feminists are revealing the degree to which this is the case; a deep bias toward examining our shared male experience—and our shared male public experience at that—pervades not only Rawls's theory, but the tradition of political liberalism as a whole.[38] But to what sort of distortions in our conception of the nature of the political state—as well as of its central functions and institutions—does such an absence lead?

To take one example of this modern bias against reflection in the personal sphere, let us briefly again consider the question of ownership. John Rawls has argued (persuasively, in my view) that any adequate theory of rightful possession will entail a weighting or balancing of what he calls the various traditional "common sense precepts" regarding ownership (*TJ*, 304). That is, different property theories will be distinguished (beyond the form their justifications take) by the relative *weight* they give to certain of our familiar criteria of rightful possession at the expense of others. Marxists tend to stress the familiar "to each according to his need," libertarians and followers of Nozick "to each according to his ability," and so forth. Rawls's own theory of distributive shares, rather than reducing the various notions to one "true" criterion of rightful possession, claims subtly to acknowledge them all: "justice as fairness" argues for a specific weighting, not only of need and ability, but of the familiar "effort," "contribution," and "risk" as well.[39] This move of Rawls's—from seeking *the* single concept of property to analyzing various conceptions—contributes substantially to clarifying traditional property disputes. We must note, however, that among the traditional common-sense precepts regarding ownership, the criterion of "care" is noticeably absent. The common-sense precept that "things belong to those who *care* for them," however, appears to me at least as much a part of our common-sense intuitions as, if not more so than, any of the other precepts (for instance, that things should belong to those who run "risks" for them). Yet this criterion of care (unlike risk or ability) is not even allowed entrance into the philosophical balancing act; the whole tradition of moral philosophy (other than a scattered remark by Aristotle or Hegel) remains silent in regard to it.

My aim here is not merely to help right this historical bias or prejudice against reflection in the private spheres, but to do so with the specific aim of developing a notion of public or civic friendship applicable to our times. My general methodological working hypothesis may be stated thus: for the construction of a plausible modern conception of a civic friendship between citizens, the vast repertoire of particular moral convictions hitherto relegated to the "private," the "personal," and the prepolitical "merely social" realm can no longer be excluded from the original data pool from which a political, reflective equilibrium begins. On the contrary, it is precisely from this sphere of close personal and social relations—the traditional home of women—that one of the most powerful resources for a renewed conception of civic friendship is to be found. And this is the case because this personal social realm is not only presupposed by life in the public political spheres, but also is pervaded by a host of implicitly shared common standards and intuitions just waiting to be thematized: common intuitions regarding personal responsibility and obligation, trust or care between persons as equals or as dependents, reflections on the alleviation of suffering or of pain and hunger, particular intuitions regarding friendship and the successful long-term reproduction of human social and communal relations, and so forth. Systematic reflection on these fundamental moral intuitions regarding the personal and social sphere—gathering them together, attempting to order them, and making them cohere—can no longer today be excluded as a first step in a political reflective equilibrium, and this for at least two further reasons.

The first is that any new account of civic friendship must clarify its relation to personal friendship—to those particular relations we enter into in our most private lives—as well as to the principles upon which we do so. Only if we have an adequate understanding of personal friendship and the particular judgments it engenders can we competently begin to grasp the further—and clearly derivative—issue of what friendship could mean as a requirement between citizens.[40] The second reason that we must draw on particular moral judgments from the so-called private realm is that only in this way will our conception of the new state be free from its current partiality and bias; only so will the political state be cognizant and truly representative of, give justice to, and include among its fundamental components those forms of practice and activity which have characteristically (particularly in the modern period, as we shall see) fallen to women's historical lot.

At this point, it becomes important still to distinguish two different senses of the term *state*. The first I will call the political state in the narrow sense, by which I mean the state *qua* its "internal organization": whether it is a democracy, monarchy, or something else, as determined by its political constitution and explicit laws. (As part of this narrower notion of the state, one might subsume the organization of the judiciary and the police, including the concrete physical manifestations of government, such as the courthouse and jails, and the positions of authority within such organizations.) If we look only to this narrower notion of the state, women for the most part have been historically absent. Although the laws applied to them either directly or indirectly, women (with but a few exceptions) played a negligible role in holding positions of political authority, in directly determining the nature of the laws, or in executing them. According to this narrower notion of the political state, women have traditionally been excluded from it.

There is a second, important sense of the term *state*, however, which I shall call (with Hegel) the "state proper."[41] This notion encompasses the previous sense, but it includes something more as well. The state proper includes the principles underlying the customs, manners, and the moral consciousness of a particular people historically united in a tradition. In the view presented here, moreover, the narrowly political state will be conceived as the legal articulation or explicit expression (*Entausserung*) of a people's prior and informal ethical practices. Granted, this is a rather "broad" notion of the state. Nonetheless, the conception of the political state as the formal expression of a people's prior ethical practices is part of a long tradition leading from Aristotle to Hegel, and recently again championed by Rawls and Ronald Dworkin. For these thinkers, the domain of "the state," of "government," or of "the law" includes the underlying moral principles implicit in the tradition's everyday practices.[42] And in this wider sense of the term *state*, no one denies that women have always been included.

The gulf or gaping hole that one finds when one compares these narrower and broader senses of the term *state* is, at least in part, surely due to the fact that the everyday practices of women—practices of feeding mouths and washing bodies; of caring for children, animals, and the local environment; of tending to the sick and elderly, and generally to the healthy maintenance and even joyful reproduction of daily life—have not properly been reflected, articulated, or expressed in the laws and institutions of the modern nation-state in the narrower, political sense. Quite to the contrary, the modern Western nation-state has remained largely the domain of the male and is quite naturally conceived in his image: in accordance with *his* historical activities and concerns. These concerns characteristically ranged from military security and defense (including war) to production and trade, with discussion and argument prized (if there was time left over) in a democracy. It is hardly coincidental, I believe, that the "proper" functions of the modern state—and particularly of our American one—are still primarily conceived as the maintenance of public law and order, a military prepared for war, and the productive regulation of economic competition.

If, by contrast, we thematize the many implicit principles common to the thinking and activity of those who have spent much of their lives absorbed in the local relations of personal and social reproduction, we might accomplish at least two things. First, we will be better able to grasp and to evaluate those social background conditions upon which the modern political state in the narrow sense has (until now) rested: those background practices and ways of thinking which enable and support the present political state to continue in its existence. Second, and even more important, that women are entering our public economic and political institutions for the first time in history en masse opens up the possibility that their distinctive forms of traditional activity and accompanying modes of thought may well provide a reservoir of new moral principles with which to confront—as well as help transform—the modern state in the narrower political sense.

Rawls himself stresses that moral philosophy (in contrast, say, to the study of physics) is "Socratic"; it is necessarily shaped by self-examination (*TJ*, 49). The methodological departure here from the received method of reflective equilibrium will be to rely on and to stress—far more rigorously than a Rawls, Dworkin, or Pogge—this Socratic aspect of reflective equilibrium. I plan to stress that aspect which apprehends our considered moral judgments, but now also in their most self-reflective, private, and *personal* form. By this, of course, I do not refer merely to reflection on my own individual views of various matters or to those of other feminists. I refer to the further step of reflection on society-wide, often common and shared fundamental principles regarding the ethical reproduction of persons. Such a reflective equilibrium on the "personal" (and on personal relations) thus not only illuminates the social background conditions on which the political state in the narrow sense rests, but it also prepares and facilitates the inclusion and incorporation of the views of all those who have traditionally performed ethical reproductive work, but been excluded from this powerful state. Moreover, I believe this process of reflection—all along guided by the new metaphor proposed here—must inevitably begin to transform (at least in thought) the artifice of the modern political entity. The reconception of the state I shall be arguing for lies in the direction of now conceiving the modern political state, no longer as an instrument concerned primarily with military might and war, with maintaining law and order, or with the policing of citizenry and productive competition, but as a new entity that above all seeks to maintain and further the conditions of the possibility for a civic friendship among all its citizens.

In sum, it can no longer suffice for the method of reflective equilibrium to be a consideration of the shared principles underlying our considered convictions when confronted with political concepts (such as freedom, property, or the person) known to us by way of "the tradition of moral philosophy" or of those "implicit in our public political culture." For precisely this whole tradition, as well as our official public culture, has systematically overlooked precepts and considered judgments that many of us, in our everyday lives, *share.*

In initially focusing on a reflective equilibrium of the personal—by investigating those principles underlying our most personal convictions concerning work, friendship, trust, ownership, or the reproduction of relations—our project (together with those of many other feminists) not only promises to shed light on the background theory of the person, but if allowed adequate development, may even offer a new standpoint (or original position) from which to evaluate our traditional moral conceptions and public state practices. In other words, we might consciously begin to construct a new and more adequate moral and political theory of the state, tailored to the specific needs of our time, and in light of concrete social developments. And who can say whether such a construction—clearly an act of the moral imagination—may not tap a deeply felt public need and ignite the fire of its imagination?

One final word on method. In what precise way, one may ask, will proposing and elaborating a new metaphor help us with the problem of constructing a new notion of civic friendship, much less with a strengthened appreciation and experience of the phenomenon itself? Clearly tracing the contours of the metaphor of traditional woman "mixing her labor" in different contexts will not solve all problems. For one thing, many men also do such labor (and some women don't do much of it) but precisely who does it, when, and where will only emerge after closer study. So, too, the oppressive, repetitive nature of much of women's traditional work, or the conflicts *within* and among women's roles (the very real conflicts, say, between the Catholic nun, an Islamic fundamentalist mother, or an impoverished lesbian Marxist of the third world), must not be minimized. But how large this conflict in reality is, how oppressive, as well as its true nature (the just-mentioned women at some point presumably still experienced society's expectations that they become mothers or that they care for dependents) can only be known if we first focus our attention in their direction.

My answer is thus that if metaphor indeed frames our vision of things, if it may be seen as a "window" on the world, then the birth of a new metaphor that questions at the same time as it preserves valuable insights of the old, cannot help but affect our vision of ourselves—and thus characteristically also our practice. How we see ourselves, our various self-conceptions, in large part determines what we take to be our duties, our rights, and our responsibilities. In this way a new metaphor may well lead to an alteration in practice—that is, if the metaphor is "fruitful."

The pregnancy of metaphor is well known as another of its outstanding characteristics. A profound metaphor elicits a web of near inexhaustible implications. From the explosion of work in the last few decades in feminist ethical and political theory, one thing seems certain: alternative conceptions of the person derived from reflection on the realm of women's historical experiences (including novel conceptions of action, autonomy, and care) are finally entering the official ballgame of social and political philosophy. A profound change is taking place in how we view ourselves, and by extension, in how we see our social and political roles. Introduced into the older realm of social and political philosophy, a new and fertile metaphor regarding labor, friendship, and genuine ownership may thus help generate further research programs, and elicit new ways of systematically approaching many of the problems that plague contemporary society. It is this hope, and not some final claim to truth, which inspires the present work. In the end I believe (with Kant) that the practical social task remains primary. If this book helps in the least to reaffirm the ideal of philosophy as a critical guide to the development of practice, it will have served its purpose.

PART I

THE PAST

2 THE FORGOTTEN CATEGORY OF ETHICAL REPRODUCTION

And why all this longing for propagation (genesis)*? Because this is the one deathless and eternal element in our mortality.*

PLATO

2.1 THE PRESUMED NONRATIONALITY OF THE REPRODUCTIVE SOUL

The term *reproduction* today elicits thoughts of either the biological or the strictly mechanical. Human beings biologically "reproduce" themselves via their children. Photographs or compact discs are mass-produced in the age of mechanical reproduction. The idea that there could be a reproductive *action* that is neither biological nor mechanical seems to elude us altogether, and yet such is the focus of this chapter.

My aim is to elaborate this forgotten category of ethical reproduction and to begin reflection upon its implications for the political realm. I begin with an analysis of Aristotle's account of the nutritive and reproductive soul (the *threptikon*) in his *De Anima,* and for several reasons. First, despite much twentieth-century feminist criticism of his thought, Aristotle's reflections on the basic faculties of the soul (*psuche*) remain among the most careful and elaborate ever written.[1] As such, they have carried tremendous weight for thousands of years, not only in medieval Christendom, but in the Judaic and Islamic worlds as well. Variations on the Aristotelian basic faculties of the soul, moreover, re-emerge in the modern period in such diverse but crucial political thinkers as James Madison, G. W. F. Hegel, John Stuart Mill, John Rawls, and even (as we shall see) in the early thought of Karl Marx (4.2). Finally, and most important, I believe we today (and many feminists are here included) have hardly begun to appreciate some of Aristotle's most valuable insights regarding the reproductive soul—nor have we freed ourselves entirely from some of his most insidious assumptions with respect to it. It is thus time to reacquaint ourselves with his studies.

In particular, my concern is with Aristotle's assumption, explicit in Book 1 of the *Nicomachean Ethics,* that reproduction is an essentially *biological* category. According to him, the reproductive soul lacks distinctively human and intelligent qualities, and hence an investigation of it has no rightful place in the study of ethics (*NE* 1102b2–12). My aim here is to reveal the misleading—even contradictory—nature of this claim. Although such is apparently Aristotle's official position on the reproductive soul, I aim to show that this claim cannot be correct *even on Aristotle's own view.* Finally, it is important to expose this incoherence in Aristotle's official doctrine of the first soul, because on this particular point the ensuing tradition of Western philosophy largely follows suit; the notion of reproduction has been, for the most part, reduced to its biological meaning. Plato, recall, in the *Republic* clearly recognized the ethical and political nature of how human beings reproduce themselves, their offspring as well as their relationships. It is Aristotle's official word on reproduction, however—and not that of Plato—which has held sway for over two thousand years.

In Book 1 of the *Nicomachean Ethics* Aristotle writes that the soul consists of two parts: one irrational (*alogon*) and the other capable of having reason or a rational principle (*logon echein*) (*NE* 1102a26).[2] The irrational part he divides further into a nutritive, reproductive faculty (*threptikon*), on the one hand, and a sensitive, desiring capacity (*aisthetikon*) on the other. The nutritive faculty—also called the "first" or "vegetable soul"—is that part of the soul that causes nutrition, reproduction, and growth, and its excellence, Aristotle stresses, is hardly peculiar to the human. In fact, that part of the soul is possessed by all living creatures (things that nourish and maintain themselves), animals and plants included. With respect to this first soul in the human, Aristotle writes, "For the vegetative element in no way shares in reason, but the appetitive and in general the desiring element (*orektikon*) in a sense shares in it (*logon echein*), in so far as it listens to and obeys it; this is the sense in which we speak of paying heed to one's father or one's friends, not that in which we speak of 'the rational' in mathematics" (*NE* 1102b29–33). Thus, for Aristotle the "second" or "sensitive soul" *in the human* is not fully nonrational after all; it too "shares in reason," but only in the restricted sense of being capable of listening to it or of being persuaded by it. Aristotle goes on to suggest that it is more accurate to classify the sensitive soul (*aisthetikon*) in the human being as part of the rational soul after all (*NE* 1103a1–3).

With regard to the human first soul, however (the *threptike dunamis tes psuches*), Aristotle persists in dismissing it as irrelevant to the study of ethics or politics. For, he argues, digestion goes on during sleep, but ethical distinctions are not applied to what goes on during sleep (*NE* 1102b2–12). The first soul remains nonrational (*alogon*) and so has "by its nature no share in human excellence" (*NE* 1102b10–12; *EE* 1219b20–25). This brief and dismissive argument, however, hardly bears the weight Aristotle appears to give it. The very same reasoning can apply to both the sensitive faculties of the soul and even to the rational part; both sensations (dreaming, rapid eye movement) go on during sleep, as do thought processes (in dreams). But these latter faculties are not *for this reason* considered nonrational (one might conclude that they remain so *in part*). Is it possible that with this faulty argument Aristotle dismisses the importance of the nutritive and reproductive soul for the study of ethical and political theory, as do by and large two millennia of commentators following him?

Since the *Nicomachean Ethics* explicitly dismisses the study of *threptikon* as irrelevant for the pursuit of ethics and politics, we must turn elsewhere in Aristotle's works for a fuller understanding of this aspect of the soul. It is in the *De Anima*, of course, where Aristotle attempts to answer the question "What is soul?"; the work is Aristotle's theory of soul in general. In Aristotle's day, the Greek term *psuche* lacked many of the eschatological connotations of our English "soul" (or even the Latin *anima*). Originally the term *psuche* meant little more than "breath" or "air"; those things that had breath were "alive," "animate," "ensouled."[3]

In general, Aristotle's *De Anima* may be viewed as the attempt to draw the line between the living and the nonliving—as the attempt to explain the "aliveness" of things. And, as a first, rough approximation, the work states that those things have *psuche* which have a capacity to nourish, grow, and maintain themselves (*De An* 410b18); which display flexible, adaptive behavior (*De An* 412a13); and which take from the environment that which they need, although this first approximation at a definition is not without its difficulties.[4] Still, much agreement existed in Aristotle's time that to be "alive" entails nourishment, growth, movement, and, in the better cases, perception, desire, and thought.

Aristotle, of course, proffers his own specific theory of the soul, one that not only attempts to identify the "inner principle" in virtue of which things have life, but that is a genuine alternative to the crude materialism of his day as well as to Platonic dualism. Aristotle defines the soul as the "form" (*eidos*) or "first actuality (*entelechy*) of a natural body having life potentially within it" (*De An* 2.412a26). *Psuche* is identified with the "substantial form" (*ousia*) of living things. In somewhat less technical language, the soul of a thing for Aristotle is that thing's characteristic "organization-to-function"; the soul is the "inner principle," or the distinctive way in which a particular thing goes about living. And he stresses that a thing's *psuche* is necessarily realized in a "suitable matter" (*De An* 412b12). In sum, Aristotle's position on the soul is hylomorphic; the soul simply *is* the potential form or activity—the principle of organization and of self-motion—whereby a creature exists as an organized material whole (*holon*), or as an organic living body, in the first place.

What is important for our purposes here is that differences in "modes of being" or "ways of living"—differences in soul—are reflected for Aristotle in the different material bodies and their potentialities, in the different organic structures and teleological functionings, of different types of living creatures. These different potentialities of bodies constitute the various basic capacities or faculties (*dunameis*) of the organic material beings. Plants, for instance, which possess only the nutritive and reproductive faculty (*threptikon*), are marked by its proper kind of self-motion; plants take from the environment, ingest, eliminate, and reproduce (*De An* 2.2). By contrast, the animal characteristically possesses, in addition to the nutritive soul, internal sensory (appetitive) and imaginative abilities, as well as external sensory (perceptive) and locomotive organs, which are foreign to plant life. This "sensitive soul" or capacity (*aisthetikon*) affords to the former the perceptions, desires, and increased spatial mobility typical of animal life (*De An* 2.3).

Of course, in the human being we find, in addition to the nutritive and sensitive mode of existence, the "intellectual soul" (*noetikon*) as well (*De An* 2.4). Unlike the simple perceptions and awareness of animal life—fundamentally an awareness of sensuous particulars—this part of the soul "apprehends universals" as well; it is with the rational soul that the human knows and understands, reasons, and contemplates (*De An* 417b25). The ability to apprehend universals signifies minimally that in going about its function of living, the human being—alone of all the animals—can do so according to a rational plan or principle (*logos*). At one point Aristotle speaks of the possibility that one part of *noetikon*, the so-called "active intellect" (*nous poietikos*), may survive the death of the body (*De An* 413b25–29).

Whatever the ultimate mysteries surrounding Aristotle's doctrine of the active intellect, however, it is clear that he believes that the three souls or potentialities in the human being form a hierarchy such that the higher functions "include" the lower. As one famous commentator of the *De Anima* puts it, "man has thus three natures united in himself."[5] The critical difficulty, of course, is to specify the proper relationship in which these three natures stand to one another.

2.2 ARISTOTLE'S HUMAN FUNCTION ARGUMENT

It is in the context of attempting to determine, in rough outline, the distinctively human "function" (*ergon*), and hence the good and happy life for the human being, that Aristotle ostensibly dismisses the relevance of the *threptikon* for the study of ethics in Book 1 of the *Nicomachean Ethics*. As a general principle, Aristotle assumes that if anything has a function or "characteristic activity," then its good (and happiness) will consist in doing that activity well (*NE* 1098b25–28). (An anteater will not be truly happy if she does not regularly eat ants.) In trying to determine the characteristic function of the human, Aristotle writes: "Life seems to be common even to plants, but we are seeking what is peculiar to man [*to idion*]. Let us exclude, therefore, the life of nutrition and growth [*ten te threptiken kai ten auxetiken zoen*]. Next there would be a life of perception, but it also seems to be common even to the horse, the ox, and every animal. There remains, then, an active life of the element that has a rational principle [*praktike tis tou logon echontos*]" (*NE* 1097b33–1098a6).

As is well known, interpretations of this famous "human function argument" tend to fall into two camps: an "intellectualist" or a "comprehensive" (or inclusive) reading.[6] On the intellectualist reading, Aristotle's remark "Let us exclude, therefore, the life of nutrition and growth" is interpreted to mean that nutrition, reproduction, and growth form no part of what is distinctive about human life. Since nutrition, reproduction, and growth are functions shared by plants and animals, these functions of the "vegetable soul" are not actual constituents of the specifically human good, or *eudaimonia*, at all. On this reading, a life will be distinctively human only to the degree that it maximizes the exercise of intellectual faculties, while minimizing or "escaping" from the nutritive and sensitive functionings as much as possible. The intellectualist interpretation of Aristotle claims that for him nutrition, reproduction, and sensation possess no intrinsic value; they are of value only instrumentally, insofar as they serve, as efficiently as possible, the activity of contemplation. Man's "true" nature is being identified with his intellect alone, rather than with his composite whole.[7]

I believe it is fair to say that the intellectualist reading of Aristotle's human function argument is the historically dominant one. A position popular in the medieval period, it is found, for instance, in the writings of St. Thomas Aquinas,[8] and it pervades as well Hegel's account of the three souls.[9] So, too, it is an interpretation defended by numerous contemporary Aristotle scholars. As one such thinker writes, the good for man is to concentrate on subjects "more elevated" than himself.[10]

The "inclusive" reading of Aristotle's human function argument, although historically held by the minority of scholars and philosophers, is nonetheless gaining adherents.[11] This reading holds that when Aristotle excludes nutrition, reproduction, perception, and sensation from the distinctive human life, he means only that these functions cannot be the aim or sole organizing principle of such a life. The human does not live in order to eat, or in order simply to see or hear. Nonetheless, a life "in accordance with rational principle" does not mean that the sole purpose of human existence consists in theoretical contemplation. It argues only for a life that is guided and organized by (at least) *practical* reason (*phronesis*), while also exhibiting theoretical *nous*. On this reading, the proper functioning of the intellectual soul is not to escape from or minimize the activity of the lower souls, but to "penetrate" downward: to infuse and rationally restructure the organization of those lower souls. To be part of a human life, such sensuous activities must be done according to some reasoned plan or principle, however poor or haphazard; to be done well, such activities must be performed in accordance with practical wisdom. Finally, insofar as reason pervades the functions of nutrition, reproduction, and perception, these functions take on intrinsic value; they remain constitutive of the specifically human (in contrast to the divine) good.[12]

Although both interpretations appear to find confirmation in the Aristotelian texts themselves (one might even conclude that Aristotle remains of "two minds" on the issue), there are compelling reasons for preferring the comprehensive reading of the human function argument. For one, as Nussbaum points out, it is what the conclusion of Aristotle's argument actually states. Aristotle does not write that the *ergon* of the human being *is* the activity of reason, but rather that it is the activity of soul *according to* reason or not without reason (*psuches energeia kata logon e me aneu logou*, NE 1098a7–8). This more inclusive formulation is better captured by the second interpretation. So, too, this second reading fits best with what Aristotle goes on to do throughout the rest of the *Nicomachean Ethics* (and in the *Politics*). Aristotle quite clearly does concern himself with the good and proper ways of desiring, nourishing oneself, and reproducing (activities that we share with the other animals). In discussing the virtue of temperance, or *sophrosune*, for instance, Aristotle writes "*Sophrosune* and *akolasia* (self-indulgence) are concerned with those pleasures in which the other animals also partake," in particular with touch and taste (*NE* 1118a23–25; see also 1104b34–35). Nor is there any indication that such reason-imbued, sensuous activities should be "minimized" or performed as rarely as possible. To the contrary, Aristotle explicitly states that a creature that does not find pleasure in such activities or that does them too little would be "far from being a human being" (*NE* 1119a9–10).

Not only does recent scholarship present mounting evidence that the intellectualist interpretation cannot be the final reading of Aristotle, but such a reading in general is characterized by a devaluation and distrust of the sensuous realm, by a deprecation of the physical body, of the role of the senses and of sensuous pleasure, as well as of the practical, political life—positions not typical of Aristotle. Nor is it a particularly plausible account of the human good standing on its own. A life where all practical activity exists merely in order to maximize "contemplation" speaks to the visions and ideals of the medieval monk or to certain philosophers (those whom Nietzsche termed "ascetic priests"), but hardly to the rest of us who hold a more "friendly attitude toward the human" (Freud).

What is important for our purposes here, however, is that even if we accept the comprehensive interpretation of *eudaimonia* as generally superior, and even if we can show that for Aristotle not only *epithumetikon* (appetite) and *aisthetikon* (perception and sensation) are pervaded by reason in the human, we are left with two problems. For one, we need a clearer account of what is meant by the claim that human reason is capable of "penetrating" downward, of pervading and restructuring the sensitive and nutritive souls—by no means a small achievement. If the organization is not simply to be in the name of "maximizing contemplation," what are its further ends? Second, we must still confront Aristotle's explicit claim in the *Nicomachean Ethics* that the *threptikon* remains nonrational and that this soul is of little concern for ethics (also *EE* 1249b17–24). What are we to make of this? At least in the case of the nutritive and reproductive soul, it appears that the intellectualist reading of Aristotle remains the right one after all. In what follows, I argue that even this cannot be the case. Part of the difficulty here is that we have not yet clarified all that is entailed under Aristotle's notion of the *threptikon*. Indeed, I shall show that a number of distinct activities are being run together under the rubric of this first soul. Again, this ambiguity in Aristotle's treatment of reproduction would not be of such interest today, if two thousand years of philosophy had not persisted in the tendency to dismiss the relevance of this first soul for the study of ethics and politics.

2.3 AN ETHICAL READING OF REPRODUCTION (THE *THREPTIKON*)

At first sight it appears odd that Aristotle, without further explanation, classifies the functions of nutrition (the assimilation of food, or *trophe xreisthai*) and the reproduction of one's kind (*gennesai* or *to poiesai eteron oion auto*) together under the *threptikon*, for these would appear to be two altogether distinct activities (*De An* 415a26–29). Raising one's young, after all, and eating one's dinner hardly appear the same activity (unless one happens to be Cronos). So too, we need look no further than the instance of a mule in order to find a living creature that can nourish itself, but lacks the capacity for reproduction. Aristotle surely groups these two activities together under the first soul because all living creatures—whether plant, animal, or human—*normally* have the capacity to do both. The normal conjunction of two activities, however, hardly proves the two activities are the same. And yet it is this stronger claim that Aristotle apparently wishes to make. In his *On Generation and Corruption*, for instance, Aristotle gives an argument whereby the faculties of nutrition and reproduction turn out to be aspects of the same process: that process whereby all things "return upon themselves" (*On Gen* 338b15). That is, in nourishing ourselves, we perishable things "reproduce ourselves numerically"; we reproduce ourselves as the same numerical individual. In reproduction, by contrast, we "reproduce ourselves specifically"; that is, we reproduce an individual who is not numerically the same to us but "the same only in species" (*On Gen* 338b13–15). It thus emerges that for Aristotle, nutrition is a "moment" or subset of the far larger process of cyclical reproduction. We eat in order to reproduce ourselves daily in existence; nutrition is but one aspect.

Of course, this way of looking at things tends to neglect the important differences between the activities of feeding oneself (reproducing oneself numerically), on the one hand, and all those which go into the bearing and rearing of children (reproducing oneself "in species"), on the other. (I return to this point.) Thus, I wish to distinguish clearly within Aristotle's work two very different interpretations of the nutritive and reproductive soul: the one interpretation is strictly biological, the other I shall call normative or ethical. My claim is that the Aristotelian texts themselves waver between treating human nutrition and reproduction as purely unconscious, nonrational biological processes (often shared with other animals) and treating these functions as highly intelligent activities involving rational choice, a proper emotional response, and moral *arete* (virtue or excellence). These latter activities at least *ought* to be performed in a reasonable and distinctively human fashion. Similarly, one may distinguish between the biological, nonmoral excellence of the *threptikon*—for example, efficient digestion, fertility, proper growth—and the moral virtues or excellences pertaining to human nutrition and species reproduction. In discussing the plant's production of a new plant, for instance, or the animal's of a new animal, Aristotle writes that both reproduce "in order that they may have a share in the immortal and divine in the only way they can; for every creature strives for this" (*De An* 415b3–6). Yet surely only in the human—in one who possesses the intellectual faculty—is this striving for the immortal and divine capable of becoming truly conscious. Similarly, in his biological works Aristotle characteristically treats nutrition, reproduction, and care of offspring as forms of instinctive biological processes, while in the ethical and political writings they are frequently the object, not only of the moral virtue of temperance, but even of the science of state legislation (e.g., *NE* 1180a). It is this normative and ethical reading of the functions of the reproductive soul in Aristotle that this study seeks to reveal.

Let us note the important differences between the biological reproductive process (Aristotle's works are filled with discussions of semen, menstrual fluid, pregnancy, and so forth) and reproduction as a normative and ethical category. By the latter, I intend not only the intelligent nurturing, care, and education of the young, but specifically all those rational and moral activities which aim at "reproducing" a concrete set of human relationships—in the best case, relationships as pure ends in themselves. That is, the category of ethical reproduction here includes all those human activities that consciously aim at establishing and reestablishing the best of human relationships among species members over time (including the relationship with oneself). Although Aristotle in the biological works largely concerns himself with the narrower sense of reproduction, throughout his two *Ethics*, the *Rhetoric*, and the *Politics*, we find myriad remarks on reproduction in this ethical and ultimately political sense.[13]

2.4 PRODUCTION VERSUS REPRODUCTION

Leaving a strictly biological reading of nutrition and reproduction to one side, I shall hereafter focus on what distinguishes these activities when specifically performed by the human. Beyond the capacity to live life in accordance with a rational principle, what further descriptions distinguish human life and activity? In general, Aristotle mentions three respects in which the human differs from other creatures, and all three contribute to making him or her the most "political" of animals (the *zoon politikon*). That is, all three contribute to making the human a creature that can only realize its fullest potential within the *polis* or in moral and political community with others.

The first, as Aristotle writes in the *History of Animals*, is that like bees, ants, wasps, and cranes, among men "something one and common becomes the work of all" (*HA* 488a8–9). Unlike ants and cranes, however, whose common work is for the sake of "mere life," in the case of humans the good life (leisured activities worthwhile for their own sake) becomes the focus of the community's life. Aristotle virtually defines the *polis* as that form of human association in which the good life is the *koinon ergon*, or common work (*Pol* 1252b28–31).

Second, on Aristotle's view, humans distinguish themselves from other animals insofar as human couples do not abandon their young and the unions between male and female last longer (*HA* 589a1–2). Such "permanent coupling" (*synduastikon*) leads to heightened social cooperation and role division, as well as to the natural expansion of kinship groups first into villages (formed by "milk peers" [*homogalaktas*] or the children of children), then into clans and nations (*Pol* 1252b16–19). The human is naturally inclined to form couples;

"he desires to live together [*sudzen*] even when he has no need of the help of others" (*Pol* 1278b17–21). Permanent coupling, for Aristotle, is an ineliminable condition of the *polis*, for without it there would be no stable long-term economic and political relationships.[14]

Finally, of course, humans distinguish themselves because they have speech or reason, which reveals to them not only the useful and the harmful, but also the right and the just (*Pol* 1253a8–9). In possession of practical reason, man has the potentiality for justice and civic virtue that can be realized fully only in the *polis*: in a life lived in moral and political relationships with others. Moreover, only because the human has this reasoning ability does he distinguish himself in the former two respects. Aristotle explicitly links the human's heightened "intelligence" and "memory" not only with the human capacity for a high degree of social cooperativeness (and hence for the intensification of functional differentiation necessary for the *polis*), but also with the human capacity for permanent coupling and for living with their offspring "for a longer period" (*HA* 589a2–3). In Aristotle's view, it is *reason* that furnishes the human with the distinctive ability for long-term care of others (4.6)

For the moment, it suffices to note that for Aristotle humans distinguish themselves from other animals insofar as they have speech and reason, are capable of sustained coupling and just relationships, and have the good life as the aim of their common work or function. All three aspects are necessary conditions for the distinctively human good life that is self-sufficient and complete (*NE* 1097b8–12). Aristotle here uses the term *autarkia* (sufficient unto oneself), which, he hastens to add, does not mean a solitary life (*bion monoten*) but a life lived together with "parents and children and women and generally with friends and fellow citizens" (*NE* 1169b17–19). Self-sufficiency, in Aristotle's view, is achieved not alone but in the midst of supportive relationships.

Much has been written on Aristotle's notion of reason (both practical and theoretical), and at least one aspect of Aristotle's idea of a common work is developed in the modern period by both Hegel and Marx. As we will see, particularly the Marxist idea that man distinguishes himself from other species by common and universal "production" (the way the human goes about nourishing himself and producing food is capable of choice and "free conscious activity") owes much to Aristotle (4.2). For the moment, I wish to focus on the third distinguishing aspect of the human: the capacity for "permanent coupling" (*synduastikon*) and what Aristotle at one point calls "common care" (*koinon epimeleian, NE* 1180a34–b1). The *way* the human goes about reproducing him- or herself specifically is also subject to choice, free conscious activity, and the determination by reason.

This important capacity for *synduastikon,* or the tendency to couple, not merely for a brief time (as in the sexual act), but permanently over a complete life and even over generations, will include "intelligent care" as well as all those activities that go into sustaining relationships; it is clearly a part of what we are calling "reproduction" in the normative ethical sense. Not surprisingly, however, an analysis of this capacity to sustain relationships has been largely neglected in Aristotelian secondary literature (a direct consequence, I believe, of the biological reductionist reading of the *threptikon*). To make matters worse, although Aristotle explicitly in the *History of Animals* distinguishes "common work and production" from "permanent coupling and reproduction," it is important to note that at other times and places he himself frequently runs these two conceptions together. For example, in referring to the reproduction of offspring, Aristotle sometimes employs, not merely the Greek *gennisis* (generation) but also *poiesis,* as in the expression "production of one's kind" (*to poiesai eteron oiov auto, De An* 415a29). But surely *gennisis* (which connotes not only "generation" but the idea of propagation, development, and the whole process of natural formation) is not the same activity as *poiesis*. Given the looseness of Aristotle's language here, let us be particularly sensitive to the differences between the two forms of activity.

The Greek *poiein* is a broad term that generally means "action" or "to act"; action is one of the Aristotelian *kategoriai* listed in the *Categories* (1b–2a). In an ethical context, however, Aristotle clearly distinguishes between *poiein* in the sense of "to produce" (hence *poietike episteme,* or productive science), from *prattein,* "to act" (hence *praktike episteme,* or practical science) (*NE* 6.1140a). How does he conceive the difference? In production or making (*poiesis*), Aristotle repeatedly emphasizes, the product (not necessarily a physical object) is the *telos* or end of the activity; *poiesis* aims at an end other than itself (*NE* 1140b6). At one point, Aristotle virtually identifies the activity of *poiesis* with *techne* (art, craft, skill); *techne* is a state of capacity (*hexis*) geared toward making or production rather than action (*NE* 1140a). And with respect to *techne,* he writes that the active principle of movement or of becoming is "external" to the thing; namely, it rests in an external agent (sculptor, architect) who is the primary source of change (*NE* 1140). Finally, *techne* is contrasted with *phusis* (nature) whereby the thing's coming into being has the principle of movement within itself (*Phy* 2.199a).

Praxis, or action, by contrast, differs from production precisely because it is its own end or *telos; praxis* is done for its own sake (*NE* 1140b6; *EE* 1219a). In mentioning this point often, Aristotle seems to think the distinction between action and production is an obvious one.[15] Although hardly obvious, the distinction is of critical importance; there is a significant difference between the class of what we today would call "moral actions" and other types of acts or productions. Most important perhaps, *poiesis*, or making (which includes artistic productions), can be done from a variety of different motives; I can dance or make shoes for myself, for my loved ones, or for money on the market (in each case I am still dancing or making shoes). The type of activity is here logically distinguishable from its aim or motive. In the case of genuinely moral action, by contrast, the aim becomes constitutive of the action-type. Let us take, as an example, the act of giving a gift to my beloved or to my boss. If the action is done from love or "overflow," it is normally considered an act of love or "generosity." If, however, the same physical action is done with the aim of advancing my career, it can no longer be considered an act of generosity at all, but edges closer to a "bribe." Moral action (*praxis*) necessarily expresses virtue and conveys moral character.

The question now becomes: Into which category do all those activities fall that aim at the simple reproduction of flourishing relations between persons over time? I here include such activities as feeding, playing with, or caring for infants and children, but also the more general and iterative encouragement and attention to the development of their emotional, moral, and intellectual capacities—surely many of these activities may be considered "ends in themselves," or *praxis* (in contrast to reproductive *labor*).[16] Nor may one simply equate such ethical reproductive activity with *paideia* (rearing) or education; many activities of care and giving have no didactic purpose at all, but aim at "fun and games." Finally, I see no reason to limit the object of this form of reproductive *praxis* to mothers, on the one hand, and to infants and children, on the other. *All* persons, including the aged and those in their prime, need to give and receive such repeated acts of unique attention and care if their lives are to flourish.[17] Once again, I am only here stressing the difference between the process that "reproduces" a human offspring, biologically speaking (a process that can take place in a coma, as it were), from that highly conscious, reasoned activity that aims at reproducing *persons* and their relationships.

In contrast to the notion of a human being, the notion of a "person" is an entity that plays a recognizable, public role.[18] It is an agent accorded rights and obligations, one held responsible for its actions, and one toward whom we should act with a certain respect. The concept of a person is primarily normative, not descriptive.[19] Thus, the activity of bringing a *person* (including its new set of relationships) into being by way of "reproductive activity" is a process that falls neither under Aristotle's category of *techne* or *poeisis* (production) nor under his notion of *phusis* (nature).

On the one hand, Aristotle's category of *techne* is inappropriate for referring to the developmental processes of persons, because the child's (other person's) life principle develops "internally" on its own; it cannot be imposed from without as in a *techne* (or *poiesis*). The generation of persons is thus some form of "natural" process. On the other hand, the development of a person does not fall unambiguously under a pure process of *phusis* either (say, as with the growth of an oak tree), because an inordinate amount of externally derived attention, care, and intelligence (*logos*) go into its proper development. Indeed, I wish to argue that reproductive activity, in the ideal case, falls under Aristotle's category of *praxis*—that form of rational, moral activity done for its own sake. For the moment, however, it suffices to note that the problem we are confronting is that of the role of intentional agency in things that, according to Aristotle, develop "naturally," such as a person or a *polis* (*Pol* 1252b30).[20]

It has often been claimed that there is a fundamental contradiction in Aristotle's position that the *polis* comes into being "by nature," given the undeniable role of human agency, design, and purpose in the development of any city or state.[21] And yet, as one author has argued, Aristotle never denies the necessary role of intentional agency in the development of a city or state, but is making a further point: the entire developmental scope of the *polis*, emerging through many generations, could never be the object of any one person's (or one group's) intentions or *techne* (even that of its original founders).[22] The *polis*, which comes into being for the good life, comes into being "behind the backs," as it were, of its citizens.

If this is correct, a similar line of reasoning surely holds for the "natural" genesis of the person. Aristotle is not saying that intentional actions, foresight, care, and rational principle are not essential to the process of normal development. To the contrary, he claims only that the end result—a person—cannot be reducible to the sum of original intentional actions of any or of all the caretakers; the child has its active principle of movement within itself. (No matter how hard the parent wishes and encourages their child to become a great pianist, say, the result is never guaranteed.) This fundamental difference between generation by nature and generation by art allows us to grasp further differences between the activity of production, or *techne,* on the one hand, and what I am calling ethical reproductive activity—a form of *praxis*—on the other.

2.5 ETHICAL REPRODUCTIVE *PRAXIS*

In contrast to most *technai,* ethical reproductive action necessarily entails a proper emotional response (*pathos*). The emotions, for Aristotle, involve a cognitive element (*Rhet* 1385b10–1386b7). In the context of his discussion of reproduction, moreover, Aristotle repeatedly uses the Greek term *epimeleia,* whose primary meaning is "care" or "concern."[23] In his *Generation of Animals,* for example, Aristotle claims that nature implants in animals "a caring sense" for their young (*e ton texnon aisthesis epimeletike, GA* 753a8). A few lines farther he writes that in those animals "which have a greater portion of intelligence we find familiarity and love shown also towards the young when perfected, as with men" (*GA* 753a10–13). Aristotle here explicitly links the capacity for long-term care of particular others with the human capacity for higher intelligence. As holds true for the Aristotelian virtues in general, such natural impulses to give (or to care) do not yet amount to generosity (or to friendship or love) without practical wisdom (*phronesis*), which tells us what to give, when, to whom, and in what amount.[24] Thus imbued with reason, however, these natural impulses also become the most noble.

Similarly, in contrast to production or making, the Aristotelian four "causes" of (*aitia,* or ways of explaining) the activity of bringing a person into being (or maintaining him) are radically different. The material cause (or "that out of which") a statue arises, for instance, consists of passive inorganic matter (wood, bronze, or marble) to be imposed upon with form from without, while in the case of a child the material cause is an organic material body already informed with *logos* and a human soul. (The activity of husbandry or of gardening—where the material cause is an organic body but one lacking *logos*—will stand somewhere midway between these other two forms.) Further, as in all natural processes, *tuche*, or chance, will play a far larger role in the development of a child than in the production of artifacts (*NE* 1140b).

Similarly, the formal causes of the two processes greatly differ in kind: one imposes form and shape on a relatively passive matter, while the other nurtures and elicits emotional responses and *logos* from a highly active and changing youth. Let us also note that the process of caring even for an infant (in contrast to that of producing a statue, say) is characteristically mediated through and through by explicit *logos*. Not only does the activity typically involve speech or song (from the very beginning, as in singing a lullaby), but it is also one that from the start repeatedly encourages dialogue and speech in the object of attention. Good childcare is fundamentally a process that listens and "coaxes forth *logos*," as it were, as well as a whole range of other appropriate physical, emotional, and moral responses in the other. Again, this process of caring and nurturing another cannot simply be identified with *paideia*, or education, for many actions here performed have no didactic purpose at all, but aim at fun and simple pleasure.

This last point leads us to the important question: What *is* the final cause or "that for the sake of which" ethical reproductive activity takes place? In the case of producing a statue, the final cause will be the "why" or reason the sculptor undertakes to sculpt in the first place, whether for money, to bestow a gift, or to satisfy himself. Some of these ends, however, are more "proper" to the activity than others; producing shoes (as Socrates notes in the *Republic*) is the proper end of shoemaking, while making money is "external" and common to many forms. The question now becomes: What is the proper end, or *telos*, of reproducing (or helping maintain) another person?

In the *De Anima*, Aristotle writes (echoing Diotima of Plato's *Symposium*) that in producing another member of their kind, all things fulfill their yearning for immortality: "Since then no living thing is able to partake in what is eternal and divine by uninterrupted continuance (for nothing perishable can for ever remain one and the same), it tries to achieve that end in the only way possible to it, and success is possible in varying degrees; so it remains not indeed as the self-same individual but continues its existence in something like itself—not numerically but specifically one" (*De An* 415b3–8). Mere yearning for the eternal and divine, however, does not distinguish human reproduction from that of other living creatures, since even the plant and animal (dimly aware as they are) aim at this, according to Aristotle. Clearly, reproduction of one's kind in the human entails the capacity for consciousness of one's relation to the eternal and the divine, and hence the capacity for *logos* and its actualization. If I am correct, moreover, this *logos* is characteristically first coaxed forth by the direct speech of ethical reproductive labor and *praxis*.

If the ultimate aim of reproduction, for Aristotle, is participation in the eternal and divine, I now put forth the hypothesis that the proper earthly, let us say practical, *telos* of reproductive activity (always taken in its normative sense) is the reproduction of "another self": what Aristotle calls a friend (*philos*) (*NE* 1166a31). This other self is numerically different from me; he or she need not be my biological offspring, but a friend is—in an important sense—the moral continuance in existence of another like my self. Interestingly enough, this hypothesis accords with much of what Aristotle says elsewhere. The existence of some form of friend, for instance, is a necessary condition for the actualization of *logos*, and hence also for the human's awareness of the good and divine (*NE* 9.9). So too, the human cannot exercise his or her highest moral and intellectual capacities except in friendships, and only a friend can bring us knowledge of our most intimate and best self (which the divine aspect surely is). A friend is thus not only a necessary condition for the awareness of our selves, but also for their further illumination. I shall next show that the creation and maintenance of a friend or "other self" is indeed a necessary part of the proper end of reproductive *praxis*, and that this truth—having been forgotten in the modern period—was fully recognized by Aristotle.

2.6 PERSONAL FRIENDSHIP (*PHILIA*)

Aristotle's notion of *philia* is far broader than the English *friendship* (or the German *Freundshaft*); *philia* includes the good relations between marriage partners, parents and children, siblings, lovers, and even fellow citizens. In the *Rhetoric*, Aristotle indicates the common core of all these relationships. He defines *to philein* toward someone as the reciprocal "wishing for him what you believe to be good things, not for your own sake but for his, and being inclined, so far as you can, to bring these things about" (*Rhet* 1380b36–1381a2). Indeed, mutual awareness and liking, a reciprocal wishing of the other well for that other's sake and a practical "doing" for the other, may be considered the common denominators of all friendships throughout Aristotle's works.[25] Finally, at the center of Aristotle's analysis of *philia* stands his theory that there are three basic kinds or species (*eide, NE* 1156a7), depending upon what it is that attracts and binds the two friends to each other: whether it is primarily pleasure, advantage, or the good character of the other.

Aristotle is explicit that character-friendship—a love of the other for the goodness of that other's character—is the most perfect (*teleia*) and enduring kind of friendship (*NE* 11567b7–9). Nonetheless, pleasure and advantage friendships for Aristotle also retain the aspect of wishing the other well for that other's own sake. That is, in the less perfect types of friendships (say, between mere sexual partners or between business associates), neither friend can be said merely to use the other as a means to their own pleasure or advantage. Such purely self-interested relations Aristotle would not consider instances of friendship at all.[26]

What distinguishes character friendship from the other two kinds is, rather, that the description under which one loves the other is a description of that other's whole (or near whole) character. In the case of pleasure or advantage friendships, by contrast, one loves the other friend under some limited description only—for example, as someone who generally brings advantage to me or who is typically fun to be around. Thus, although advantage and pleasure friendships are indeed instances of real friendship for Aristotle, such relationships are restricted and unstable; they tend to fall apart as soon as the specific description under which one loves the other alters (e.g., "Peter has become a bore"). Character friendship, by contrast—since it entails a greater reciprocal knowledge and love of the other's good character—is far more stable, long lasting, and rare. Only this kind Aristotle calls friendship "without qualification" (*NE* 1156b13).

If this much is granted—if mutual awareness and liking and reciprocal wishing the other well for that other's own sake are considered necessary aspects of all species of friendship—I now wish to concentrate on what Aristotle means by the third necessary ingredient of *philia*: the tendency of friends to "do things" for the friend's good, or the tendency of "being inclined, so far as you can, to bring these [good for the other] things about" (*Rhet* 1380b37–1381a1). This practical and active element in friendship has generally also received far less attention in the secondary literature. Indeed, one might here too distinguish a "comprehensive" from an "intellectualist" reading of Aristotle's notion of *philia.* In the latter, the emotional bond, as well as the practical doing of things with and for the friend, are ignored as fundamental components of the friendship relationship. Two men who have nothing in common other than their shared philosophical thoughts might be considered the paradigm of human "friends" for the intellectualist (and again this seems the traditional interpretation of Aristotle's *philia*).

Aristotle himself, however, repeatedly stresses that friends do not just wish each other well (this mere acquaintances can do), but they characteristically "live together"; they spend time together (at least their days), and share practical things such as meals, plans, and common activities (*Rhet* 1381a30–31; *NE* 1157b7, 17–22, 1158a9, 1170b11). Significantly, human friends also "share in discussion and thought . . . for this is what living together would seem to mean in the case of man, and not as in the case of cattle, feeding in the same place" (*NE* 1170b10–14). Aristotle here stresses that mere physical closeness or shared activity (simply sleeping in the same bed) does not suffice for distinctively human friendship; such friends must necessarily share their thoughts, aims, and plans.[27] But although sharing in discussion and thought is a necessary component of distinctively human friendship in Aristotle's view, it cannot be a sufficient one—as the intellectualist reading would lead us to believe.

For one, among the "shared activities" central to Aristotle's account of friendship is the activity of sharing in the friend's pleasures and pains, and for the friend's sake and "no other reason" (*Rhet* 1381a4–6); such is clearly a sensuous, emotional activity and not an intellectual one. So, too, in light of the earlier analysis of character friendship, the friends love each other for their *whole* character, and thus necessarily for their natural as well as cultivated desires and emotions, as much as for their intellect (*Rhet* 138a5–1381b34). Finally, in Aristotle's discussions of the love character-friends feel for each other, he repeatedly uses the Greek term *stergein* (love, affection); the word ordinarily applies to a mother's love for her children and to other close family attachments. An emotional bond is essential to Aristotle's account of all genuine *philia.* Even sheer physical separation, if it is lasting, tends to make men "forget their friendship" (*NE* 1157b11–13).

There is, however, another important type of practical activity upon which friendship depends for Aristotle: this is activity done not so much *with* the friend but *for* the friend. Again, many modern accounts of friendship overlook this further practical aspect.[28] Nonetheless, Aristotle writes: "Things that cause friendship are: doing kindnesses; doing them unasked; and not proclaiming the fact when they are done, which shows that they were done for our [the friend's] own sake and not for some other reason" (*Rhet* 1381b35–37). Such kindnesses include, not just "treating us [the friend] well", but also treating well those others the friend cares about, such as his family or other friends (*Rhet* 1381a16). Similarly, "treating us well" typically involves instances "where money or our personal safety is concerned," and therefore we value those who are "liberal and brave" (*Rhet* 1381a20–22). Doing things for the friend's good and for that friend's own sake (and not for ours) is an essential originating (and, we may assume, sustaining) cause of all friendship for Aristotle. He stresses that the virtue of friendship is "activity," and it depends more on loving than on being loved; hence "loving seems to be the characteristic excellence of friends" (*NE* 1159a32–35).

If this practical and emotional element is acknowledged as crucial to all genuine friendship, it now becomes clear why Aristotle repeatedly mentions mothers in his discussion of friendship; simply put, virtuous mothers exhibit all the characteristics of a friend. Mothers and children characteristically "delight" in each other's company, they "live together" and share in discussion and thought (*NE* 115927–28). So too (good) mothers wish their children well for the child's sake, which can be seen, Aristotle writes, by the fact that mothers "seem to be satisfied if they see [their children] prospering" even if the children are brought up by another and (due to ignorance in the child) "receive nothing of a mother's due" (*NE* 1159a28–32). In fact, mothers exhibit par excellence the many other attributes Aristotle mentions as characteristic of a friend. They "share in your pleasure and pains" and "for your sake and for no other reason" (*NE* 1381a5); they "treat us well" where our material well-being and safety are concerned (*Rhet* 1381a21); they "desire the same things as we desire, if it is possible for us both to share them together" (*Rhet* 1381a17–19); they have "serious feelings towards us, such as admiration for us, or belief in our goodness, or pleasure in our company" (*Rhet* 1381a11–12); and they "do" an endless amount of things for us.[29]

Although the mother–child relationship is evidently a case of genuine *philia* for Aristotle (as are most kinship relations, *NE* 1162a4), three aspects of this relationship appear to bar it from being an instance of the "best" type or of perfect character friendship.

First, in Aristotle's view women are generally of a morally and intellectually inferior sort; they are not capable of the highest sort of friendship, the paradigm of which is two men, each of high moral and intellectual virtue. This particular premise of Aristotle's account, however, may confidently be rejected today; women have shown themselves eminently capable, not only of the highest intellectual and moral accomplishment, but of long-term binding friendships with either men or other women. Far from revealing anything essential about the nature of genuine friendship, this assumption only points to Aristotle's well-known sexism.[30]

A second difficulty is more serious. Aristotle claims that perfect friendship requires "equality"; there cannot be a great interval "in respect of excellence" (*arete*) or in respect of those things which affect excellence, such as (in Aristotle's view) status, wealth, power, moral and intellectual abilities and age (*NE* 1158b34–35). The idea seems to be that it is difficult for a very rich man, say, to cultivate a long-term friendship with a poor one, since the former would tend to express his love in ways that the latter could not reciprocate. Such "inequality" strains the relationship, conflicts arise over discrepant goals, and thoughts cannot be unreservedly shared. For the same reason, I believe, many infer that equal character friendship between parents and children is impossible due to the discrepancies with respect to age, power, status, and developed abilities. On the issue of the extent to which the age or wealth of two parties can diverge before equal character friendship becomes impossible, Aristotle notes only that the answer cannot be determined "exactly" (*NE* 1159a4).

Is Aristotle correct in assuming, as he appears to, that there cannot be an equal character friendship between parent and child? What of the case of a virtuous father and son, both in mid-life? Or the case of two good women, say fifteen or twenty years apart, one being the mother of the other? In both cases, one may find mutual wishing the other well, a reciprocal delight in and a practical doing for the other, intellectual and moral equality, a "living together," as well as shared activities and thoughts. Such may be rare, but all true character friendship is rare on Aristotle's view. More important, a reciprocal (moral) equality appears to be a critical *ideal* or *goal* in the best parent–child relationships, whatever the ages and circumstances, at least today. The mother who wishes continued dependency and subordination for her child is hardly worthy of the name. So, too, good children characteristically reciprocate; they often gratefully aid the parent in old age, many care for them themselves, and they frequently seek the parent's comfort and independence for as long as possible. Thus, we might say that, when the parent–child relationship is conceived over the course of a complete life, a flexible give and take may well be achieved in the best case, despite all the differences in age, temperament, or circumstances.

This notion of a flexible "give and take" among differently situated selves is fully *under*-appreciated by Aristotle (who holds that children, say, are eternally indebted to their parents), and it is so, I believe, because he has not yet attained to the clear idea of "moral equality" in the midst of social and other differences. Aristotle is well aware that if material or other inequalities are too great (e.g., in age, wealth, intellect, social status, and so forth), a great strain may be placed on the relationship. But does such difference *necessarily* make character friendship impossible? Aristotle appears to remain of two minds on this point. While his materialist tendencies (stressing physical differences) and hierarchical commitments (stressing higher and lower worth of humans) might indicate yes, at other times Aristotle appears fully cognizant that the relevant "equality" in question is one of excellence, virtue, or moral *arete*. The good mother, for instance, is one who seeks the independence and maturity of which her child is capable as an adult—she will aim for an equality of material circumstances, and of those things which affect virtue or excellence, at least equal to her own. What thus emerges as critical for genuine friendship is not so much the presupposition of equality, as a reciprocal equality as *aim or goal*.[31] I return to this point below.

Here we must still note Aristotle's claim that the best types of friendship are freely "chosen" (*NE* 1157b30), while the particular relationship between a parent and child cannot be said to be the result of choice in any normal sense (at least from the child's perspective). This, of course, is true, but it also remains true that each member (at least when grown) can *choose* to continue the relationship. The best mother, we might say, is one we "would have chosen" had we originally been given the option. Considering this degree of choice, it emerges that parents and children—despite vast differences in age, circumstance, and realized abilities—may reciprocally seek to establish and maintain the moral equality and autonomy of the other (to whatever degree possible) *when the relationship is conceived over a complete life*. In the best case, parents and children may clearly become and remain genuine friends.

My point is only to show that even the relationship between parents and children—with or without blood ties and always taking the long-term view—need not fall outside Aristotle's conception of equal character friendship. More important, the best parent–child relationship actually seems to aim at this moral equilibrium—as I believe all genuine friendship does. If this is indeed the case, the requirement of a strict equality and sameness as a presupposition of the friendship relationship (similarity in age, wealth, gender, status, and so on) has been made far too much of in discussions of personal friendship, not only in Aristotle's account, but generally.[32] It is true that the best type of friendship will aim for, exhibit, and attempt to maintain an equality of virtue and of those things that effect virtue. But where there is de facto material or strict equality (say, between business associates with respect to intellect, money, status, and so forth) there need not be character friendship, and where there is character friendship (say, between virtuous parent and child) there need not be strict equality. Yet character friendship is always superior in Aristotle's view.

In sum, Aristotle recognized that the important "equality" referred to in his discussions of friendship is the equality of virtue (*arete*) and of those things that contribute to it (not the other way around). What he did *not* recognize was that an essential aspect of friendship is *the reciprocal goal or desire* to establish and maintain this moral equality as well, including the autonomy of the other. This necessary aim or goal can continue to be the case despite vast differences in actual abilities and without much similarity of external circumstances. One might even claim that such *philia* in difference is the mark of many of the traditional friendships *women* possessed: with their children, with their husbands, but also with the old and the sick whom they primarily have tended. These others are hardly "identical" to themselves. Similarly, what other goal than the aim (or maintenance) of moral equality can explain how genuine friends fear that the physical, intellectual, or other differences between them may grow too wide, or the belief that certain inequalities must be diminished (as when my friend grows arrogant or presumptuous and I must put them "back in their place")?

If I am correct, moral equality between friends (as well as all that affects it) is not so much a necessary presupposition of virtuous friendship, as it is a crucial *goal*. And this good will becomes all the more important once the real, concrete differences and the diverse circumstances between the particular friends are acknowledged and brought into the foreground and the illuminating and educative role these material differences can play is revealed. In stressing this last point, my position clearly begins its departure from Aristotle's official doctrine. Central to true friendship, I am claiming, is the *reciprocal desire to maintain equality*—in virtue and in all things that affect it—over the long run. Nothing is so painful as when a beloved friend lapses into ignoble thoughts or actions, or when they are hurt or unjustly treated by others; one wishes immediately, somehow, to mitigate the wrong. This altered conception of *philia* will now entail, first, stressing the many concrete inequalities and material differences involved in actual long-term friendship relations (whether of age, skin color, education, background culture, gender, and so forth). Today—clearly a consequence of the modern fact of pluralism—people may and *do* become close, lifelong friends with others from distant countries, with those from different religions, classes, cultural origins, age groups, and so forth, or even with others possessing stark differences from the self in all these areas at once (such as the lifelong relationship between a young American boy, say, and an old African woman). Something other than similarity here—something deeply personal—sparks and maintains the relationship. Second, this new conception of *philia* emphasizes the concrete activity of supporting the other—of lifting them up, as it were, when they are down—as well as the responsibility of reining them in when they grow arrogant. In fact, this transformed notion of personal friendship—of a moral equilibrium of aim or good will in the midst of shifting material and other differences, and always backed by concrete, practical actions with and for the other—exposes various persistent prejudices we still have today concerning personal friendships. It also has important consequences when we turn to the modern political realm (chapter 5). I will argue that a political version of *this* conception alone supports true democracy.

Aristotle's ideal or paradigm of friendship, by contrast, is that of two mature, independent and autonomous, similar and similarly situated males: an ideal I will henceforth call "fraternity." Here the friend is similar to myself in abilities, status, and age; he is fully autonomous (and thus I, another male, needn't do many things for him); he stands by my side (we rarely look into each other's eyes), but I trust him and thus we may cooperate. Indeed, we are like brothers. This paradigm of fraternity is obvious in Aristotle as well as in much of our philosophical tradition generally.[33] Far less obvious is the degree to which many contemporary conceptions of friendship continue to track this male experience originally charted by Aristotle. Modern conceptions of friendship, that is, tend to persist in their requirement of equality as presupposition (rather than goal), in the foundation of physical sameness (race, age, and so forth) to self (instead of in variety and difference), and in stressing a practical doing *with* (in contrast to a doing *for*). At the same time such conceptions exclude many of those highly significant and complex personal relations of *philia* that women historically possessed. Modern friendship for the most part continues to be conceived (whether consciously or not) on the equal fraternal model.[34]

Thus far, I have stressed the important and neglected role "mothers" play in Aristotle's account of *philia*. I shall conclude this section by noting one further consequence of Aristotle's position: the virtue *philia* must play in the life of mothers. That is, those many "endless kindnesses" mothers perform daily for their children and extended family can, in the ideal case, be conceived as done for no other sake than for *philia*: for no reason beyond reproducing a set of shared, flourishing human relationships as ends in the themselves (*NE* 1159a27). As Aristotle notes, "[A] friend is one who lives with and has the same tastes as another, or one who grieves and rejoices with his friend; and this too is found in mothers most of all" (*NE* 1159a27). Earlier I argued that *philia* is the proper (legitimate) practical *telos* of "bringing another person into being" or of having children in the first place; the intended contrast is always with having (and using) children as a mere *means* (as work hands, old-age insurance, status symbols, and so forth). Now I would like to refine this claim somewhat. Since, surely, once one has a child, the proper end of raising it should remain the good of the child, I would like to reformulate my claim such that *philia* becomes the *legitimate, self-related interest* of ethical reproduction or of bringing another person into being. That is, such an interest may be a proper satisfaction sought by the reproducer, which is a satisfaction *of* the self but not necessarily "selfish." This "unselfish satisfaction" appears a part of the goal of successful childrearing; it would be lost in those cases—detrimental to both parties—where the child grows up, say, to hate the parent.

In any event, considering that Aristotle assumes that the whole of woman's characteristic function (*ergon*) is the reproduction of children and nurturing (*threpsai*) (*Eco* 1344a7), we reach the interesting conclusion that on his view woman's distinctive activity, virtue, and function (far more so than man's) is simultaneously to further relations of *philia*. If we take Aristotle at his word and view *philia* as a practice not only of intrinsic value to the good life, but one that actually "holds states together"(*NE* 115a22), we are led to the suggestion that women play a critical role in the *polis* even if they have not officially been recognized as a part of it.[35] We reach a similar conclusion if we drop Aristotle's anachronistic assumptions that women have a natural "function," that they are by nature intellectually and morally inferior to men, as well as that their particular biology somehow "determines" their traditional behavior. Insofar as women have—for thousands of years now—been trained socially and de facto for the primary role of reproductive *praxis*, they have been educated to further the ethical virtue of *philia* in the ideal case. Perhaps they have even acquired a special disposition (*hexis*) for it by way of repeated habit and educated choice.

2.7 POLITICAL FRIENDSHIP

Let us turn, finally, to the political domain in order to see how for Aristotle personal friendship compares with political friendship (*politike philia*): that type of friendship in which citizens of the best *polis* stand to one another. Aristotle is careful from the start to distinguish the community of the *polis* from all other communities. Generally, the Greek word for "community" (*koinonia*) is derived from the verb "to share" (*koinoneo*); a community is literally "a sharing." Depending upon the nature of the things being shared, the nature of the community will alter. For Aristotle, political community has two specific characteristics. First, the *koinonia* of the city entails a shared system of courts and officials (including a common set of laws and a shared conception of justice), which will distinguish the community of a city-state from a set of mere contractual or commercial relations, say, between two cities (*Pol* 1280). Such a shared scheme of cooperation or "mode of life" Aristotle calls "the constitution," which assigns the allotment of goods, services, and duties, as well as the many offices and honors that distinguish one political community from another (*Pol* 1295b). But so too, citizens of the best *polis* care "what kind of persons" their fellow citizens are, a concern business partners normally do not possess (*Pol* 1280a–b5). Aristotle here points to a general concern that lawmakers and citizens of the best cities have for the character of their fellow citizens: that no one taking part in civic life be unjust or vicious in any way according to their shared sense of justice (*Pol* 1280b2–4). Indeed, such general and mutual concern of fellow citizens for one another's "good character" is a central aspect of what Aristotle means by *politike philia* (*Pol* 1295b23). Such "political friendship" must not be confused with the very different phenomenon known as "political patronage."

By "political patronage" (or what might also be termed a "friendship politics"), I intend the position of one such as Polemarchus in Plato's *Republic*: that justice and politics are essentially nothing other than "helping one's friends and harming one's enemies" (*Rep* 332d)—a modern proponent might be Carl Schmidt.[36] That Aristotle does not hold such a view is certain. For one thing, although such a highly partial friendship politics may have been closer to the actual practice of the ancient Greek *polis*, Aristotle's notion is clearly also normative; as is well known, he defends impartiality and the rule of law (*Pol* 1287a15–33; *Rhet* 1354a30–b15) even if he has not yet arrived at the idea of universal individual rights.

More important, however, although Aristotle at numerous points classifies political friendship between citizens as a form akin to "advantage friendship" (*EE* 1242b22, 1243b4; *NE* 1161b13), we have seen that civic friends nonetheless retain the three necessary aspects of all friendship noted earlier (2.6). That is, although this form of friendship is based upon the general experience or expectation of "mutual benefit," it is still a *real* friendship. Like all relationships deserving the name, political friendship must involve mutual good will and trust (including the interest citizens have in one another's character), a reciprocal wishing fellow citizens well for their own sake, as well as a practical doing of things for them. The term never applies to the case of simply using fellow citizens as a mere means to one's own ends; such is not an instance of friendship for Aristotle at all. Political friendship makes fellow citizens' well-being matter to one another *as such*, and in this respect it distinguishes itself from all simple commercial transactions. Finally, unlike in the case of commercial or private contractual arrangements, the virtue of civic friendship necessarily becomes a communal good shared in by all: the good fortune and character of particular members is experienced by fellow citizens as part of their personal good as well.

The central difference between personal character friendship and the mutual advantage of political friendship has more to do with the latter's far more limited or narrow description of the friend. Among civic friends, for instance, an intimate knowledge of the friend and a close emotional bond are characteristically absent. In a city-state animated by political friendship, therefore, it can never be required that citizens have a personal knowledge of (or intimacy with) all or even most of their fellow citizens. Nonetheless, the traits of mutual awareness, good will, and practical doing must be retained in order for a genuine friendship to exist at all.

Aristotle's position appears to be that such traits are evidenced now in a general concern expressed in society's public and political norms—in recognized standards concerning the treatment of persons, say, in a knowledge of the nature of the constitution, of its general level of support among different elements of the population, in what is publicly expected of persons, what is due them, and so on.[37] Such public norms of regard and habitual civic behavior are the normal way citizens now "know" of each other's reciprocal good will. Civic friendship—in contrast to personal friendship—works through the public processes of the state's social and political, legal, and educative institutions.

This crucial difference between personal and political friendship leads to another important contrast: in personal friendship, the intimate knowledge of, and the close emotional bond between, friends allows for far greater temporary "inequalities" to be maintained over time without destroying the friendship itself (as in the case of the flexible "give and take" of family relationships). Precisely the reverse, however, appears to be the case with civic friends. Here there are normally no ties of intimacy, of individual knowledge, or of personal affection. Because the friendship is based from the outset on a more limited conception of the other (and on reciprocal advantage), it is all the more crucial that political equality be maintained if the civic relation is to endure. In this case *perceived* injustices or inequalities between the citizens (i.e., the perception by some that others are gaining "more than their due") will far more swiftly bring an end to the friendship relation. It is for this reason, apparently, that Aristotle considers the cultivation of unanimity and friendship in a population by the legislator to be more important than cultivating even justice itself. In a well-known passage he writes: "Friendship seems to hold states together, and lawgivers to care more for it than for justice. For . . . when men are friends they have no need of justice, while when they are just they need friendship as well, and the truest form of justice is thought to be a friendly quality" (*NE* 1155a22–28).

Why does the truest form of justice need political friendship in addition? The critical point, I believe, is that in a general atmosphere of distrust and mutual ill will, citizens may still perceive themselves to be unjustly treated *even if they in fact are not so*—even if justice in some narrower sense (e.g., "proportionate equality") is strictly being adhered to. In aiming for unanimity and friendship between his citizens, therefore, the task of the legislator is to manage *perceived* as well as real injustices; his goal is to strengthen the civic bond. This is not to say that there are never justifiable grounds for breaking the civic union; it is only to claim that, without a general reciprocal awareness, a basic trust and good will between citizens, as well as a practical doing for one another—in short, without a civic friendship not only evidenced in custom, but reinforced in the constitution, society's basic institutions and laws—genuine justice becomes impossible. A minimal civic friendship emerges as a *necessary condition* for true justice in any state. Without such a flexible "give and take," citizens will simply be unable to recognize as well as accept in practice the burdens of justice in any particular case. They will be unable to entrust their interests to hostile others even if required, or to forgo their special and unfair privileges when called upon to do so. In such cases "justice" becomes nothing more than the imposition of the interests of the stronger.

Another way of stating this crucial point is that justice by means of force (a fair distribution, but imposed on parties unwillingly) is an inferior sort of justice to an arrangement willingly acknowledged; the former breeds resentment, misunderstanding, distrust, and ill will; is unstable over time, and so on. Given our natural and often unreasonable propensities to favor ourselves, true justice can result *only if* a friendly quality (background) exists to make us yield. The requirement of a trusted and friendly background in order for parties voluntarily to yield ground in the name of fairness, not only is recognized by Aristotle, but it must be among the most elementary facts of our human psychology. Humiliated hearts and minds are the deadliest weapons of mass destruction.[38] We can now see the critical role *politike philia* plays for Aristotle; a society not animated by a civic friendship can never be a truly just (or genuinely peaceful) one. Friendly civic relations are a necessary component and constitutive element of any good society.

We have not yet discussed, of course, the issues of what *degree* and *kind* of civic friendship are necessary for justice (and peace), nor how this may be determined or implemented. Such topics will concern us in the following chapters. One last word of caution is still in order here, however. To claim that friendly civic relations are *constitutive of* true justice is *not* to claim that such relations are a simple *means to* or merely *instrumental for* justice. We need to recognize a class of actions that are simultaneously *both* ends in themselves *and* constituents (not a "mere means to") some wider end: a class of actions that will include genuine moral actions or *praxis*. To enable this, consider the individual steps of a dance; each step is not a mere means to the dance as a whole, but each is ideally performed for its own sake *and* for the sake of the whole. My thesis is that a similar relationship obtains between friendship and justice. Friendly civic relations are valuable for their own sake *and* they are necessary constituents of genuine justice. One might just as well argue the reverse: that justice helps sustain and establish friendship—a flourishing human relationship as end in itself—which remains an independent value.

2.8 CONCLUSION

If the above is correct, it emerges on Aristotle's view that the political legislator's task is more properly conceived on an ethical *reproductive* model rather than on a technical productive one.[39] The primary job of the legislator's *praxis* is to cultivate unanimity, friendship, and a rough equality between citizens (rather than producing more goods or effecting a mere coordination of behavior). This hardly entails that the goal is unanimity for its own sake or a "thick brotherhood" where friends "possess all things in common" as advocated by some. Aristotle's critique of Plato's ideal state and its neglect of diversity and difference is well known. Rather, the goal appears to be a necessary unanimity and friendly regard concerning at least "large scale, practical matters" (*NE* 1167a28–29) or "constitutional essentials." In the view of Aristotle, political science is an extension of household management that "attends more to men than to the acquisition of inanimate things, and to human excellence more than to the excellence of property which we call wealth, and to the excellence of freemen more than to the excellence of slaves" (*Pol* 1259b18–21).

So too, in the *Eudemian Ethics*, Aristotle writes that it is in the "household that one finds the first origins and sources of friendship, of constitutional government, and of justice" (*EE* 1242a). Thus, the primary concern of the political legislator in general (similar to that of the mother or friend in particular) is a concern with the moral, emotional, and intellectual habits of their object of focus. Again, without firm and friendly dispositions in place among citizens of the *polis*, no amount of just distribution of burdens and benefits will be experienced *as such*. The good legislator must seek above all else to bring about the reproduction of a flourishing set of political relations over time and (to whatever degree possible) as ends in themselves.

A structural similarity between fostering personal and political friendships emerges. Both contrast, in the first instance, with what we have called productive activity (chapter 3). Neither aims ultimately at the production of things or services, but in both the labor or activity is performed for its own sake or for the ultimate good of its direct beneficiaries (whether one's children or fellow citizens), and such is typically accompanied by the "unselfish satisfaction" noted earlier. In production, by contrast, the ulterior motive of a good to the private self (or to the family conceived as extension of self) may remain primary.

The *differences* between personal reproductive *praxis* or labor and the legislator's public and political reproductive one now also come to light. The differences follow roughly the same lines as those distinguishing personal from political friendship. That is, in the case of personal reproductive *praxis*, close emotional ties are furthered and maintained, one shares and does particular things for the friend in the concrete, while in the case of political *praxis* such "liking" and "doing" works through the political process, the constitution, and the public standards of acceptable civic behavior. Thus, I may not know or may even personally dislike a fellow citizen of mine, and yet I can remain her civic friend; I will uphold certain public standards and procedures by which she must be treated in any concrete situation.

Aristotle writes in Book 10 of the *Nicomachean Ethics* that it is imperative that the legislator ensure that the youth obtain, by way of good laws in the state, "right education in virtue [*aretes*] from youth up," and indeed citizens must receive "right nurture and care [*trophes kai epimeleias tuxein orthos*]" not only in youth, but "throughout their lives" (*NE* 1180a2). He speaks further of a common or "collective care" (*koinon epimeleian*), which is plainly affected by laws and "good care by good laws."[40] As I have tried to show, these "reproductive" concerns all distinguish the practical wisdom (*phronesis*) of the legislator or good citizen from *poiesis* or *techne* strictly speaking. In the latter, neither the active principle of movement, nor *logos* resides within the subject matter itself (2.4).

Finally, if, as I have claimed, the legislator's activity is a form of reproductive *praxis*, then the last lines of Aristotle's *Nicomachean*

Ethics contradict some of the first. In Book 1.13, Aristotle claims that the nutritive and reproductive soul contains no "specifically human excellence" and is of no consequence for a treatise on ethics or politics (*NE* 1102b2–12). Book 10.9, by contrast, proclaims that a critical (if not the overriding) concern of the political legislator is the lifelong "right nurture and care" (*trophes kai epimeleias tuchein orthos*) of his citizens and the reproduction of relations of civic friendship among them. Moreover, this apparent contradiction in the *Nicomachean Ethics* can only be resolved, I have argued, if we keep distinct a biological from an ethical reading of the reproductive soul in the larger corpus of Aristotle's works.

In sum, after all our excursions and excavations into the texts of one of the great foundational pillars of Western thought, we have hopefully established at least one thing: despite all the ambiguities residing there, the category of what I am calling ethical reproductive *praxis* emerges as of critical importance for Aristotle's ethical and political thought. In the chapters that follow, I aim to establish the category's abiding and critical importance for us today in the modern world as well.

3

THE LIBERAL PRODUCTION MODEL

The labour of his body, and the work of his hands,
we may say, are properly his.
JOHN LOCKE

3.1 DEVELOPMENTS OF THE MODERN PERIOD

What accounts for the near absence of all talk of political friendship when we turn to the modern period? We have just seen that for Aristotle such friendship actually "holds states together": without the reciprocal flexibility, general good will, and a willingness of citizens practically to do things for one another—without the virtues, social practices, and institutions of a political friendship—genuine fairness and justice between citizens becomes impossible. In this chapter I argue that this insight of Aristotle's remains valid even for the modern period. Despite endless claims to the contrary and despite the many major transformations the political state has undergone in the past centuries, a form of political friendship remains a necessary condition for justice, and for the same reasons already noted: institutional friendship is a critical background condition for the "give and take" that is required to surmount the burdens of justice in any particular case (2.7). Still today—perhaps especially again today—civic friendship remains a central criterion distinguishing just regimes from unjust ones. It must only once again be recognized as such.

As also already noted, when we turn to the modern period, we find a multitude of views on the problem of social and political unity, which either omit mention of the friendship between citizens altogether or else explicitly reject it as a serious contender (1.1). Hegel's claim from the *Philosophy of Right* that talk of love and *philia* in a political context is fine and well for the ancient republics, but hardly feasible once we turn to the far larger and more complex modern state, appears to be axiomatic of the modern view.[1] Indeed, no major liberal theorist of the modern period argues that furthering friendship between citizens is a primary function of the modern nation-state.[2] Instead, shared interests in security and a commodious life, the protection of property and individual freedom, or the establishment of law, order, and justice are normally invoked. As a consequence, the idea that social union might require conscious ethical reproductive *praxis* or activity—and an appropriate training of its citizens—is rarely acknowledged or elaborated.

The assorted reasons for this disappearance of the language of friendship in the modern era are not easy to determine. Such reasons (and causes) are surely multiple, but I will argue that many remained linked in a significant way to the growing dominance of a production model of labor and action, which model continues to reign up until the present day. In the modern Western tradition, that is—alongside the development of the new mechanical physics, a burgeoning marketplace, and the emerging nation-state—a production model of activity gains such ascendancy, both theoretically and practically, that the category of "reproduction" is reduced to the thoughtless and biological (a process already begun, as we have just seen, by Aristotle). More, a practical *doing things for others* begins to be equated with mere dependence and even servility. An "ideology of production" holds sway for the next four hundred years, one from which we (I here include many feminists still [compare 7.2]) are far from liberating ourselves. But I am getting ahead of myself. Let us start our analysis of the disappearance of the political language of friendship in the modern period, for the analysis of what needs fixing depends upon what we take to be broken in the first place.

At first glance, the far greater size of the modern state would appear to be the main culprit for the modern dismissal of the importance of political friendship. While the idea of friendship between citizens might conceivably still apply to a population the size of an ancient Greek *polis* (roughly forty or fifty thousand), the term tends to lose all determinate sense when applied to 4 million inhabitants, say, or to 270 million as in many modern states. On further scrutiny, however, the rejection of Aristotle's conception of political friendship by the moderns has little to do with the mere size of the newly emerging nation-state.

Significantly, as we have stressed, the Aristotelian position (outlined in chapter 2) does not confuse personal with political friendship. Aristotle did not claim that in the just *polis* all members know each other, are emotionally close, or personally like each other. Such a situation was as impossible given the forty thousand citizens (not including their families and slaves, foreigners, and so forth) that made up his ideal *polis* as it is today with close to 300 million. In

Aristotle's view, political friendship is evidenced by a *general concern* and attitude in the everyday lives of one's fellow citizens, and operates through the political constitution and laws, public institutions, and social practices. It is recognized in legal and social norms regarding the treatment of persons in the society—Aristotle was a clear advocate of the rule of law—as well as in the willingness of fellow citizens to uphold them. But if this is the case, then such public norms of concern for each citizen—the normal way citizens experience each other's good will—can apply equally well to any modern state as to the ancient *polis*. Indeed, one might even argue that many of today's public norms (institutions and citizen behavior) are of a higher moral standard than in the ancient world. We no longer officially condone slavery, for instance, as did the ancient world. Elevated moral and public norms of citizen concern are fully compatible with a state of millions.

But are such norms *realistic*, one might justifiably ask? In what specific sense can citizens reciprocally feel affinity for, as well as practically do things for, fellow citizens whom they do not know personally and whose very existences are often unknown to them? A society animated by civic friendship is clearly an *ideal*. It is not satisfied if each citizen likes some citizen (which is far too minimal), nor can every citizen know every other one personally (which is impossible). Again, such liking and doing does not operate personally, but through the intelligent and orderly construction of political institutions, rights, and social practices. The three necessary traits of all friendship—reciprocal awareness and liking, good will, and practical doing—become embodied in public institutions and laws, which in turn educate and encourage others to similar behavior; they are willingly upheld in the everyday habits of the citizenry.

Thus, a reasonable ideal of my "liking" each citizen in another part of the city or country, say, would characteristically entail that I consciously aim to root out any and all prejudice I may have concerning them. The ideal demands that I consider it *a civic duty* to cultivate good will toward them, am concerned about their welfare, at the same time as I become aware of the true nature of that people or city's population, become informed about their history, customs, general standard of living, and so on. Such willingness and concern I can feel for other citizens whom I have never met, and surely the state here plays a critical role in regulating our awareness of the facts of other citizens' lives, as well as in stipulating what are to be considered our minimal responsibilities toward them. Thus, such reciprocal good will must simultaneously be encouraged "from above," as it were, at the public, state level: through the system of education (7.4) and the citizens' general knowledge of history and their constitution; through the careful guidance and regulation of institutions of civil society (as in the fair dispersal of information in the media, or of property [compare 5.5 and 5.6]); through the diligent construction of social and political programs; as well as through the reduction of those institutions that set people or groups at odds (for example, by refusing to allow vast accumulations of unequal wealth or power, by working to maintain fair background rules, and so on [chapters 5–8]).

Finally, the *practical doing* of citizens for one another may be seen in their willingness to aid fellow citizens in need—whether in terms of direct public service, disaster relief, the fight for and upholding of fair institutions and their fellow citizen's rights, or (most minimally) in terms of lack of opposition to the higher taxes one pays for the support of their general welfare (7.4 and 8.3). It is thus a mistake to believe that civic friendship must entail a small ancient *polis*, personal knowledge or liking, or what has come to be known as democratic "face-to-face assembly" among all citizens.[3] Such beliefs persist in confusing personal friendship with the political or civic form.

Other modern critics fear, however, that reviving an account of political friendship today may be not so much impossible or implausible as unnecessary or even undesirable; some consider it downright dangerous. According to this last set of critics, reviving a notion of political friendship will only further partiality, faction, and the (pre-Socratic) "friend versus foe" mentality so often found in the ancient republics (and defended by Carl Schmidt, leading theo rist of the Third Reich). As one critic writes of granting friendship a political role: "In a world in which Serbs and Croats or Hutus and Tutsis seek to 'ethnically cleanse' themselves of one another, the last thing we need to do is champion the idea of political responsibilities as contingent on anything like our affection for others."[4] Friendship is inherently exclusive; it sets "us" against "them." It is thus the wrong foundation for viewing our political obligations to others. Alternatively, an Aristotelian stress on political friendship might lead to a totalitarian state apparatus imposing a uniform "solidarity and comradeship" on all, as in the former Soviet Union.[5] And, indeed, although Aristotle himself stresses the objective rule of law, his theory lacks any place for the concept of minority protection or of universal individual rights. It must be granted as well that in the modern era certain well-known structural changes—one might call them momentous developments of the modern period—appear to justify the rejection of all political friendship talk. So this second class of critics has a genuine basis for concern. Let us turn to each of these modern developments in succession.

1. The Reformation. One such distinctively modern development is surely the Reformation, which led to the acceptance of the principle of liberty of conscience and eventually to religious toleration more generally.[6] Politically speaking, the liberal argument goes, we can no longer demand of all persons one and the same comprehensive view of the good life (or of God); happiness is not something that can be imposed on the individual from above or without. Further, just as the state can no longer dictate one conception of the good life to all—it must remain neutral with regard to many conceptions—so, too, it can hardly dictate to a man who his friends are to be. Citizens are now proclaimed to have diverse conceptions of the good—as well as of friendship—which they are free to pursue in private associations. The heterogeneity of the modern state (in contrast to the ancient *polis*) is surely one reason why friendship between citizens today is often considered an unrealistic means or goal of state unity. The modern liberal state consists of peoples of different religions, and increasingly of peoples of diverse races, cultural origins, and languages, who nonetheless must all make do with one territory and live in accord with one set of social, political, and economic laws—which laws now guarantee a sphere of individual privacy for all.

2. The doctrine of individual rights. A second critical development of the modern period was that of the centralized nation-state, accomplished first under the direction of the crown. This gave rise in turn to attempts to limit the sovereign powers of the monarchy: to subject monarchs to the rule of law and often to the constraints of a bill of rights. Such modern rule of law stipulated a set of individual rights and liberties applicable now (in principle at least) to all men. The antagonistic origins of the modern doctrine of individual rights—its emergence in the struggle against royal absolutism—as well as its universal and legalistic language protecting a sphere of privacy, again appear to fly in the face of ancient and feudal concerns with loyalty, trust, and the local commonalities of friendship. As noted in chapter 1, Marxists have long stressed the essentially antagonistic and exploitative nature of individual rights (particularly the right to private property in means of production), whereas more recent communitarian accounts locate a major source of community breakdown in their fundamentally "individualistic" character.[7] So, too, some feminists have proclaimed the apparent incompatibility of a feminist perspective of care and concern with that of a more self-directed orientation toward individual rights and justice in general.[8]

3. *The modern market.* A third crucial development of the modern period was the rise of the free market economy. Not only does the realm of market relations expand exponentially, but a new glorification of economic instrumental activity emerges that is altogether foreign to the ancient world: a celebration of "free labor" and its "productivity." Indeed, conceptions of value, of the citizen, and even of the state (in direct contrast to the Aristotelian view) now generally become tied to a production model of activity.[9] Such veneration of production takes place, moreover, at the expense and devaluation of what we are calling reproductive *praxis.*

Kant, for example (but also Locke, Hegel, and many others), now makes it an explicit requirement for active citizenship not only that the individual be independent and "master of himself" (as Aristotle had already argued), but that he now also be "productive." The active citizen must depend for his support "on his own industry" and not on the "arrangements of others." Kant even proceeds to equate the notion of "industry" with the producing of an independent—often physically independent—*product.* In the *Metaphysik der Sitten,* for example, he distinguishes between the "wig-maker" and the "barber," and goes so far as to attribute to the wig-maker (who produces an independent physical object, namely, the wig) full-fledged active citizenry, while he denies full citizenship to the barber who merely "serves" another and cuts his hair![10] Kant's view may appear extreme, yet Adam Smith also classifies all occupations that approach ethical reproductive activity—those of churchmen, physicians, men of letters, dancers, and opera singers—in the same category with the "menial servant" and the "buffoon," which Smith considers the lowest form of "unproductive labor."[11] In all these cases, the activity "perishes in the very instance of its performance" and seldom leaves any trace behind it.

While Aristotle had glorified political reproductive activity, or *praxis,* the moderns tend to associate any "nonproductive" activity with the past unfreedoms and dependencies of serfdom or slavery. Shaving another's hair remains a form of "servitude" for Kant—

presumably one takes orders, is directed here and there by another; the movements are dull and repetitive, and so forth—while forming and finishing the product of a wig reveals a greater independence of thought, complexity of skill, choice, and "autonomy." That both types of activity ultimately remain dependent on "the arrangements of others" is now overlooked in the face of subtle differences in the various types of the newly emerging free labor.

Even the political state itself comes to be viewed according to a production model. When Thomas Hobbes writes at the beginning of *Leviathan,* for instance, "For by art is created that great Leviathan called a Common-wealth or State," he is not merely claiming that the state is the result of "artifice"—the work of human reason and foresight (as we saw, this is a claim Aristotle would never have denied [2.4]). On the contrary, Hobbes is claiming something more: that the state ultimately comes into being for other ends (glory, acquisition, security, and a commodious life) beyond the simple reproduction of flourishing human relations for their own sake. Similarly, according to Locke, man enters the civil state for the mutual preservation of property (in Locke's extended sense of "Lives, Liberties and Estates"), while in Kant, the state is considered a necessary means (at least on standard interpretations) for the purposes of making the freedom of one compatible with the freedom of all.[12] In all these cases, the activity of bringing the political state into being is viewed as purely *instrumental*; it is desirable not for its own sake, or because it is in the nature of human beings to live together in political communities, but for a set of further specified reasons. By now it should be clear that the ideal of ethical reproductive *praxis* (activity that aims at friendship between humans for its own sake) has generally receded into the background of modern political analysis—if it has not altogether disappeared from view.

In the face of such powerful modern developments, one can thus well understand how political *philia,* as a mandatory relationship between citizens, begins to fall by the wayside. Nonetheless, although such historical developments clearly help explain, they hardly *justify* the jettisoning of Aristotle's general thesis regarding political friendship.

Need it be the case, for instance, that with the Reformation and the establishment of the principle of tolerance, citizens no longer view themselves as political friends? Recall that Aristotle never stipulated that civic friends must be of the same religion or race, or that they must hold *all* values in common. He says only that such friends must, first, share a system of courts and a sense of justice, and second, possess a general good will and concern for the moral character of their fellow citizens (2.7). The first characteristic—a shared conception of justice—citizens in the liberal state presumably also possess (or at least strive to possess, as John Rawls has argued). The second criterion is more problematic. Can good will and a general interest in the moral character of fellow citizens be considered an essential component of the modern liberal state? Is not the assumption of antagonistic aims, mutual indifference (as posited in Rawls's original position), or at least independent goals, not only far more realistic, but also more desirable?

Although the concept of moral virtue becomes problematic with the Reformation, and a sphere of privacy is politically instituted for all, it does not follow that the *political* or *civic* virtue of fellow citizens—how citizens behave in the public domain—is not or should not be of crucial concern. At this point I begin my (liberal) departure from Aristotle. Civic friendship in the modern state—owing to the heterogeneity of the population, multiplicity of religions, and so forth—can no longer reasonably entail that citizens concern themselves with the comprehensive moral character of their fellow citizens, but only now with their public, *political* character. Nonetheless, Aristotle's general point still holds; the truest form of justice can only be realized in a public context of good will and mutual concern, not in one of enmity or indifference.

If this is the case, the Reformation has indeed caused a transformation in our ideal of the civic relation, but the change is not necessarily best conceived as one from good will and friendship to neutrality or indifference. The change might just as well (I believe better) be conceived as a change from *one kind* of good will to another: from a more stringent, Aristotelian concern with the moral virtue of one's fellow citizens (*politike philia*), to a more tolerant, enlightened concern primarily now with their political character (the English *civic* friendship). This latter type of political regard is fully cognizant that there exists an individual private sphere which is "off limits," as it were, to its good will. Just as there are different conceptions of personal friendship—some of which stress tolerance and individual autonomy of the friends more than others—so there will be different conceptions of civic friendship (see, especially, chapters 5–7). As various thinkers have by now noted, it is simply not true that all or even most citizens of a modern liberal state (despite the sphere of institutional privacy), possess no de facto concern that their fellow citizens be fair and law-abiding, committed to the constitution, as well as to its underlying spirit.[13] Rather than abandoning the notion of political or civic friendship, therefore, perhaps we should acknowledge that the phenomenon to which it refers has not so much been extinguished as subtly altered its form.

A civic friendship between citizens today can no longer refer to a state (if there ever was such a state) where citizens all share the same "thick" values (belief in one God, one way of life, and so forth), or to one where all possess the same skin color, background culture, or even the same language (think of Switzerland with its four official languages). A feasible modern political friendship, therefore, will be evidenced rather by a certain degree of concern, good will, and practical agreement between citizens regarding primarily *constitutional essentials* (and the quality of that friendship will be given by the substance of that same constitution [chapter 6]). It is true that in Aristotle's time citizens de facto shared various religious beliefs and possessed racial or cultural commonalities that can no longer be taken for granted today. But, again, this is not to say that citizens of a modern pluralist nation-state hold no fundamental values in common.[14] On the contrary, one can argue that the shared values modern citizens possess have merely altered, grown more abstract and "second order." My fellow citizens are expected to be tolerant (tolerance was not an ancient virtue); they must acknowledge universal principles of respect for individual persons; have the ability to acknowledge the rights of others (and their sphere of privacy); and they should explicitly recognize a universal value of friendship as well (chapter 7). The Reformation hardly makes a civic friendship between citizens impossible, nor is it clear that such is undesirable.

Two further objections may here be raised. The first concerns the retention of the word *friendship*. Numerous writers have argued that traditional liberalism indeed needs to be supplemented by an account of modern "civic virtue"; it is clearly better (and necessary for justice) to have good-willed citizens rather than bad, but this means only that citizens must be "virtuous," *not* that they must be civic friends.[15] My response to this objection is quite simple. Far from being opposed, the ideal of civic friendship proffered here actually gives content to the notion of "civic virtue"—particularly in a democracy. Which political virtues are we trying to encourage, after all: those of high birth, unquestioning loyalty, and submission to authority? No. In a liberal *democratic* society, the political virtues must include those of law-abidingness, reciprocal recognition of the political equality of all, individual freedom, tolerance of differences, and (I am now arguing) a necessary awareness, good will, and willingness to do practical things for fellow citizens. Recall that the point of stressing similarities between the personal and civic forms of friendship is not to identify the two, but to reveal how in a just society they possess far more traits in common than traditional liberals (and certainly libertarians and neo-conservatives) acknowledge; the friendship between equals may be used as a political *guiding ideal* (6.4 and 7.3). Again, Aristotle already recognized that such a model is central to the notion of democracy; we must only take care today not to fall back on the old fraternal (male) conception (preface and 2.7).

A second concern with my account arises from the communitarian direction (including from some feminists) and concerns the doctrine of individual rights itself. Is not this critical development of the modern period necessarily antithetical to a political conception of friendship between citizens?[16] Here I would like to stress that the modern institution of individual rights—although perhaps antagonistic in its historical point of origin and at certain junctures—need not be so in its *aim*. On the contrary, the modern doctrine of individual rights, recently extended to include ever larger portions of the population, such as men of color and all women (and now being applied by many to animals and even to natural objects [8.4]), might be considered one of the highest expressions of a civic friendship ever. For, by guaranteeing to each individual—simply on the basis of his or her humanity—a basic set of rights (including rights to freedom of thought, due process of law, and so on), and further, by upholding these rights and seeing them realized in practice, citizens acknowledge and express their general concern and good will toward the interests of each particular individual in the concrete. A doctrine of individual rights, far from necessarily revealing conflict or indifference between citizens, may be seen to embody a fundamental regard—if not love—for the special interests of every human being.[17]

In the language of Kant, individual civil rights (and even more so human rights) rest on a general recognition of the dignity of intelligent sensuous nature to set its own ends, and thus on the awareness that it is wrong to impose on any such creature a conception of happiness "from without." A lesser known theme of Kant's work, however, is that the recognition of the universal rights of the human, as well as the realization of them in practice, rests on a deep and abiding concern for humans in general—on what Kant calls philanthropic love (*Menschenliebe*).[18] Indeed, Kant lists the sensitive capacity for such love among the *necessary subjective conditions* for the possibility of an agent's responding to moral notions in the first place. In a similar vein, and far from grounding individual rights on personal feeling (Wellman's concern voiced earlier about the Hutus and Tutsis), our moral capacity for *philia*—and the human emotional capacity generally—can be viewed as the necessary, subjective condition for the universal recognition of individual rights in practice.

In contrast, thus, to many Marxist, communitarian, various feminist (and even postmodern) critiques, a doctrine of universal individual rights (and the general regard for them) emerges on the view presented here as a necessary aspect of any adequate modern conception of civic friendship. Only by embodying some such public and impartial standards of concern for each individual and her interests in the concrete can a civic friendship between citizens be kept from degenerating into a mere "friendship politics": into a partial and destructive "us versus them" mentality (2.6). The doctrine and fair practice of universal individual rights are properly seen as a concerted collective and social (institutional) effort to overcome the *problem of partiality*—the natural tendency of citizens to favor and unfairly advantage those "near and dear" to them—in the circumstances of modern pluralism. It is important still to note that ours is an institutional view of individual human rights. The institutional view conceives individual rights as primarily *claims on coercive social institutions* (and only secondarily as claims against those who uphold those institutions).[19] This contrasts with the common view that conceives individual right as a form of meta-right: a moral right to effective legislation. In the view presented here, however, an individual's right to nutrition (say) may be fulfilled by traditional or secure access to healthful food, without there being a juridical right to food in the society's constitution (if it even has one). Individual rights may thus be protected in social practice, even without an explicit legal right to the good in question in the society's constitution. Conversely, a society can list and showcase important rights (much as the 1946 Universal Declaration of Human Rights does), but they may be widely ignored in general social and governmental practice.

It is precisely this *gap* between possessing explicit legal rights (the narrow conception of justice) and experiencing genuine justice (as true fulfillment of basic rights in practice) that the notion of a civic friendship aims to fill. I shall reserve the term *civic friendship* for that kind of more general political friendship, which—in direct contrast to Aristotle's view—necessarily honors universal individual human and civil rights in practice, whether or not those rights are juridically explicit. This is not to say, of course, that the particular *content* of the basic set of universal rights granted individual citizens is not of critical importance. Indeed, I believe the true nature of the general concern (or lack of it) that citizens feel for one another in any given state is revealed in the specific content of the rights granted to each individual, whether in practice or as reflected in the substantive principles of the constitution (6.1). Socialists may still be correct, for instance, that the right to private property in the major means of production creates a rift running throughout society, which is essentially antagonistic (5.2). Similarly, we must ask ourselves why (at least in the U.S. tradition) there is so much emphasis on *liberty* rights (to own private property, to buy and sell, to dismiss employees, to own guns, to alter the environment, and so on), at the same time as there is so little concern with other forms of right (to a secure job and home, to free quality medical care and higher education, to a safe, healthful, and beautiful environment). We are granted the right formally to vote, but without necessarily the right to participate. We possess the right to choose our occupation, but with no freely available childcare or adequate family leave plans, and so on.

The working hypothesis put forth here is that to the degree we distance ourselves from a production model of activity and move to an ethical reproductive one, to that degree the rights people consider most important *will alter* (chapters 5–8). In response to the Marxists, communitarians, and sundry feminists, therefore, it is not a doctrine of universal individual rights per se which is problematic for community or a modern civic friendship; some such doctrine is essential to the minimal fair treatment and public evenhandedness toward all citizens. The specific content of the actual rights we moderns possess, however, remains a major cause for concern, because it continues to track not only the ancient, elite fraternal model, but now the activity of production as well (3.5, 6.1, and 6.2). Finally, let us consider the rise of the free-market economy and the instrumental action it encourages. It is often overlooked that on any classical liberal view—from the work of John Locke and Adam Smith to that of Rawls—certain measures were always specified to assure that citizens have adequate means in order effectively to use their basic liberties and opportunities. Such proposed measures (some more successful than others) have ranged anywhere from free-market distributive mechanisms, to laws of inheritance and bequest, to the direct provision of public goods and services. Thus, even the market (once duly regulated and directed toward the common good, at least in classical liberal doctrine) is considered an efficient means of expressing citizens' newfound respect for each other. It is thus mandated neither by the size, nor by the new complexity of the modern nation-state, nor even by the presence of a market, that all forms of a political friendship between citizens become impossible.

It has certainly not been shown that the reciprocal awareness, good will, and practical doing is undesirable. Rather, it appears that the notion of *philia* has faded into the background of modern political analysis, where it may still be found to operate, but in a subtle and near invisible form. One central reason for this we have also begun to understand: an overwhelming new practical concern with, and a theoretical concentration on, production. In concentrating on production, however, one does not in the first instance concentrate on the relations between persons as valuable in themselves. Rescuing the notion of *philia*—both theoretically and practically—can thus be of critical import in altering the present direction of things.

3.2 LOCKE AND THE PRODUCTION MODEL

It is now time to look more closely at some of the further assumptions accompanying the modern productive model of activity. Nowhere are these assumptions clearer than in the thought of that paradigmatic liberal theorist John Locke. Locke's *Second Treatise of Government* has exerted tremendous historical influence (much of it being carved into the grooves of the U.S. Constitution [chapter 6]), and his theory is also a vivid illustration of how an older, essentially still Aristotelian conception of activity and self succumbs to the modern conception. So, too, Locke, in introducing his new labor theory of value and property, gives perhaps the most important grounding to the institution of private property, as well as to what I am calling the modern productive conception of citizenship.

Locke introduces his famous labor theory of property—and the claim that man owns that with which he has originally "mixed his labor"—in order to answer the question of how the earth, originally given to all men in common, comes to be unequally divided among them. His answer, as we have seen (1.2), is that "different degrees of industry and ability" were apt to give men possessions in different proportions. But which type of industry and what forms of ability does Locke have in mind? At the heart of his famous mixing metaphor is clearly the paradigm of labor as agricultural activity; the verb *to mix* in the seventeenth century still primarily meant "to manure or fertilize" (*OED*). Locke was an early theorist of the agrarian capitalism then beginning to dominate and transform parts of rural England.[20] Finally, all the examples of work that Locke cites in the *Second Treatise* relate to agricultural activity: the gathering of acorns, the tilling of the soil, the processing of grapes and water into wine or leaves into bread. Locke's metaphor, of course, easily extends to other forms of laboring activity also. It covers hunting and gathering, at least small craft production or artisan labor (such as Aristotle's paradigm of carving a statue), independent manufacture, and even day or wage-labor, where the ownership reward now takes the form of a wage. In all these cases, a common feature is that the reward of labor can essentially be conceived as *private property*.

According to one thinker, the central intuitive idea behind Locke's mixing metaphor is that value-creating labor grants a private right in and over its products.[21] Locke considers the responsibility for an effect of which the agent is the cause to be a self-evident law of reason. And, indeed, the first instance of this more general truth in the *Second Treatise* lies in the notion of God himself who has dominion over the earth and its creatures, not because He is omnipotent (as in Hobbes), nor because He is their father (as in Filmer), but because He is their "Maker" (*ST*, para. 6). The human in turn is the "workmanship" of this infinitely wise Maker and because man is continually "dependent" upon God for his existence, the latter has an absolute and legitimate authority over him.[22] The human is God's rightful "property" and as such he has a duty, usually pleasurable, to self-preservation (*ST*, para. 6). A limited and clearly derivative right of "making" will apply to man and his productive works, again for the reason that these works are in part—but now only in part—causally dependent on a now human activity.

It is thus from the duty of self-preservation that each person owes to the one all-creating and all-preserving God that Locke derives the sovereignty of each individual with regard to his own life and limb. *Relative to other men*, "each has a Property in his own Person" (*ST*, para. 27), and "each is absolute Lord over his own Person and Possessions" (*ST*, para. 123). At the same time, however, Locke proclaims that each remains God's "servant" and "property" (*ST*, para. 6). From these apparently contradictory claims—the political person is simultaneously "absolute lord" and "servant"—it emerges that Locke in the *Second Treatise* in fact operates with two quite different conceptions of ownership. Elsewhere I have called these two conceptions "stewardship" and "private property," respectively.[23]

3.3 STEWARDSHIP VERSUS PRIVATE PROPERTY

The idea of ownership as *stewardship* is intimately connected with the notion of possessing something obtained as a gift. By the idea of an (authentic) gift, I have in mind, first, some unearned value that is intentionally bestowed upon us by another (a donor) for our benefit.[24] In Locke, primary examples of such gift-property are our life, limb, natural freedom, and the equal political jurisdiction granted us all by God in the original state of nature. We did not "earn" such values; they were freely and generously given. Second, an authentic gift is something that may be rejected, but only at the cost of offending the donor. I reject gifts from those persons with whom I no longer wish to have relations. (If the donor should be God, of course, such rejection is far more serious; in the Christian view it amounts specifically to sin.) Third, "owning" such gift-property is essentially a form of *guardianship*; gift-giving and acceptance here are far more than a simple transfer of value between agents (as in a market exchange). The genuine gift is a moral reality laden with subtle but very real "oughts"; it brings into being a new (or further solidifies an old) relationship. Implicit in the acceptance of an authentic gift, therefore, are appropriate and inappropriate uses of it, and these are determined (at least in part) by the original intentions of the donor.

Consider the case that an old philosophy professor of mine has given me a rare edition of Kant's works. Do I not violate the "spirit" of the gift (and the intentions of the giver) if I turn the books over to a paper recycling plant? The authentic gift (unlike the commodity) remains far more closely tied to a specific set of concrete social relations. If the object as gift is removed from these concrete relations, it tends to change its "value." Such is the case in many a fairy-tale, for instance, where the wicked child sells (or is stingy with) the loaf of bread given it to forge its way in the world; the "spirit of the gift" flees and the bread turns to stone. Again, this may be accounted for by viewing the spirit of the true gift (and the reward of giving) as *the establishment of a particular relationship*. In accepting a gift I become a participant, as it were, in the way of life of the giver.

In Locke, although property in our life and person is exclusive relative to other men, we are yet always morally responsible and grateful to God our benefactor. We are in his "service," we are his stewards, and this awareness imposes strict limits on our conduct. The most visible expression in Locke of such inherent limitations over our actions imposed by our stewardship roles are the two *provisos* he cites on our natural right to appropriate things in the state of nature. Both what is often called the "spoilage clause" (that we appropriate only so much as we can use before it spoils), as well as the "sharing clause" (that there be "enough and as good" left in common for others), follow directly from our most primary duty to God of preserving mankind in general (*ST*, paras. 31 and 27); the preservation of mankind is proclaimed by the First Fundamental Law of Nature (*ST*, para. 6).

We thus find in Locke a form of activity and "owning" very different from the modern conception of private property: first, various items are unearned givens obtained as gifts (our life, limb, equal juridical freedom); second, we relate to these (normally inalienable) items as stewards or guardians; and third, our particular relations to others (to, or by way of, the donor) remain in the foreground. Our moral relations and our duties to other humans *directly condition and circumscribe* our legitimate private use and enjoyment of our property. In sum, authentic gift-property and the activity of stewardship are distinguished by the continuing moral obligation the recipient has to the original will of the donor "in whose service" he remains. And unlike the strict obligations set forth in contract (obligations that are explicit, precisely defined, and narrowly limited), the moral "pull" of gifts is far more flexible and open; there remains an *indeterminateness* in the content of the obligation at the heart of gift. One sees this in Locke's thought insofar as the individual is left a certain latitude in determining what specific forms his grateful response to God's gifts should take. In the state of nature, the individual himself interprets natural law, decides when the food is about to spoil, how much is "enough and as good" for others, and so on. Indeed, in the practice of gift-exchange, not only is there an opportunity for interpretation and creativity, but creativity appears a must.[25]

We might here add (and as scholars have long pointed out) that in the high medieval period what one "properly considered one's own" included one's relations to others—to kinship and inheritance groups.[26] The term *property* was not confined to physical objects or land; it referred as well to the quality of "belonging" to a specific clan or family. Such inclusive membership was considered a natural (given) presupposition of a free and propertied being. Further, we need to recall that for much of the medieval period there were no abstract and absolute standards of land measurement. The measurements of size of plots were not uniform but varied from place to place; area measurements such as the "journal" or "morgen" were based, for instance, on a "morning's work." Standards of ownership were thus linked to a particular area, to a type of land and to its specific cultivator. This well-known medieval "contempt for calculation" illustrates further how *qualitative* considerations—and our ascribed duties and responsibilities to particular others—predominate in ownership as stewardship. Such considerations remain primary, even with possession of physical objects or land, and they heavily restrict and condition our private enjoyment.

It is also the case, of course, that Locke's *Second Treatise* gives one of the first and perhaps the most important justifications for the modern conception of "private property." In this conception, ownership includes—beyond the various rights of use management and enjoyment—the right to exclude all others, as well as the right to capital and the power to alienate (1.2). Ownership as private property is typically viewed, first, as something I have earned by my own efforts and will (e.g., by way of my labor or by my voluntary contract). Hence, second, it is also something I can freely alienate or dispose of at will. This new conception of ownership, moreover, is progressively modeled—not on the relationship between two moral agents as symbolized by a physical, material thing, but on an individual human being's exclusive relation to a single material object.[27]

Elsewhere I have argued that Locke's labor theory of value and ownership can only properly be understood as the result of the tension between both these conceptions.[28] Here, I hope to show at what point the older category of stewardship indeed begins to succumb (whatever Locke's original intentions) to the modern notion. Although the concept of a stewardship of God's property remains the background normative standard of Locke's theory—continuously regulating the modern form of property in civil society—it becomes increasingly imperceptible in the thought of later thinkers and ultimately vanishes in the thought of a contemporary libertarian such as Nozick.

Having distinguished the two conceptions, we can see that for Locke each person owns his own life and limbs primarily in the sense of an exclusive inalienable stewardship before God, and it is from such a form that Locke derives the claim that "the Labour of his body, and the Work of his hands," are properly the individual's as well (*ST*, para. 27). This Locke believes to be "unquestionably so," assuming, as he does, that labor is a necessary means to our positive duty of preserving life and limb. Locke then goes on to formulate the more controversial claim that that with which man has "mixed" his labor becomes his exclusive property, too. In this famous pronouncement at least two different strands of argument may be found.

Let us call the first the argument simply for "taking"; it is based on the principle of need and on the common inclusive right of all in the state of nature to make use of things necessary for their preservation (*ST*, para. 25). Because without individual appropriation the common is of no use and man would have starved (*ST*, paras. 326 and 28), the privacy of the means of appropriation (individual hands, labor, mouth) necessarily extends a privacy to the object appropriated (*ST*, para. 26). Locke cites the case of gathering acorns and apples, the direct appropriation and consumption of which is necessarily individual and exclusive. One strand of Locke's argument thus rests on the conceptual model of individual *biological incorporation*, on "mixing one's labor" in the sense of taking from the environment for the sustenance of life.

The second, quite different, and more complex argument that Locke gives for the exclusive right to the object appropriated (and which applies to more extensive cases, such as land) refers to mixing one's labor in the sense of "adding" or "making." Locke writes that individual labor "adds something" to the thing—namely, "value," which both distinguishes the thing from and removes it out of, the common state of nature (*ST*, para. 27). Human labor not only puts "nine-tenths of the value on things" (*ST*, paras. 39 and 40)—in contrast to the earth and nature, which are now seen to furnish "only the almost worthless materials" (*ST*, para. 43)—but in an important sense it even "constitutes" them.[29] Man's labor transforms wheat into bread, plant fiber into cloth, grapes into wine (*ST*, para. 42). Moreover, in acknowledging this power of "making"— this God-like bringing into existence of new useful things—Locke assigns it in his theory of property an appropriate return: the newly constituted thing. Ownership in accordance with productive labor is most just because God commanded men to subdue the earth and "improve it for the benefit of Life" (*ST*, para. 32).

It is important to note that any purely "naturalistic" interpretation of Locke's theory misses his central point. The physical act of laboring does *not* grant a right to the product labored upon for Locke, at least not as physical (causal) laboring, nor does the object become some sort of physical (or metaphysical) extension of "me."[30] I obtain a right *only* because my producing or causing such things to be furthers God's underlying intentions for the preservation of mankind. Only insofar as my labor is "productive"—turns barren land into lucrative fertility and furthers the "conveniences of life" (*ST*, para. 41)—does it obtain its *title*. This normative dimension of labor as a positive duty to God is explicit in the two provisos Locke places on labor and accumulation. Both the spoilage clause and the sharing clause mean that Locke fully recognizes the conditional nature of—and the direct communal restrictions surrounding—ownership in the original natural state. Moreover, it is only to the extent that our fundamental duty of preserving mankind can be satisfied in alternative ways that the two limitations on accumulation in the state of nature cease to impose serious restrictions once man enters civil (or political) society.

According to Locke, the inconveniences of the state of nature, where each is his own interpreter and executor of natural law, as well as the inadequate protection and regulation of property in its extended sense ("Lives, Liberties and Estates"), drove men to set up an "Authority to determine all Controversies" (*ST*, para. 89). Men set up government, and henceforth civil laws were to regulate the right of property (*ST*, para. 50). Already in the last stage of the natural state, however, the spoilage clause aimed at uneconomical waste (which restricts appropriation to what a man can make use of) is largely rendered inoperative by the introduction of barter and money. Especially money, which may be hoarded without injury to anyone, allows each to hold more than he can immediately enjoy (*ST*, paras. 36 and 50). It is important to note as well that the direct communal dictates of the sharing clause are weakened with the introduction of money. This may be accounted for because the institution of money, to use modern economists' parlance, is considered "Pareto efficient"; it allows each in the end, even those with minimal possessions or no land, the expectation of a larger absolute share of the nation's wealth (*ST*, paras. 41 and 50).

Locke's belief that a money economy can better satisfy the sharing clause is attested to by his claim that an American Indian king of a large and fruitful territory (in the state of nature) "feeds, lodges and is clad worse than a day Labourer in England" (*ST*, para. 41). Men have "tacitly consented" to unequal portions of wealth (even before the social compact) due to the efficiency of a money economy (*ST*, paras. 45 and 50). But thereby we must note that it is not the case (as C. B. Macpherson has claimed) that Locke seeks to remove the natural law limitations on property in civil society.[31] Locke's aim is precisely the reverse. His aim is to show that the natural law restrictions are more surely to be satisfied within civil society. Once man enters the state (men having left the insecurities of the last stage of their natural condition), the job of interpreting the provisos is given over to government representatives who henceforth, in accordance with them, regulate property in the public interest (*ST*, paras. 50 and 222).

This final and critical argument for private property in Locke may be called the argument for "initiative"; it essentially has to do with the incentive of money and the market economy. It is true that this argument remains rather sketchy in Locke's writings; it is not, in fact, fully developed until nearly two hundred years later in the second book of John Stuart Mill's *Principles of Political Economy*.[32] Nonetheless, the argument's basic contours are clear; its first premise continues to be the proclaimed preservation and welfare of mankind (the law of nature continues to operate in the midst of civil society). So, too, productive labor continues to be regarded as the chief means to this end because it is at least ten times more efficient than nature. Furthermore, labor is assumed to be something unpleasant, enough so that people do it only in the expectation of a return. Without money, Locke asks, "what reason could any one have there [on an Island separated from all possible Commerce] to enlarge his Possession beyond the use of his Family" and his own consumption?" (*ST*, para. 48). In this paragraph, Locke justifies the more extensive acquisition of nonperishable goods and money, *in the name of the initiative* this new form of property excites in the individual to produce beyond his needs (see also *ST*, para. 37). Further, since he has already equated common land with "uncultivated" land (Locke lacks any notion of productive common or social labor [5.4]), the private "inclosing of land" is now worth the bother, that is, in the event that the cultivator can "draw Money to him by the Sale of the Product" (*ST*, paras. 48 and 37).

Locke's main point, finally, is that such private enclosure of land (contrary to what one might think) "does not lessen but increase the common stock of mankind" (*ST*, para. 37). The provisions yielded by one acre of enclosed and cultivated land are roughly ten times that "yielded by an acre of Land, of an equal richnesse, lyeing wast in common" (*ST*, para. 37). And given the assumption of trade and commerce (as well as of a just government in civil society regulating property rights), this heightened productivity will actually benefit all. Thus, the man who encloses and works ten acres of land "may truly be said, to give ninety acres to Mankind" (*ST*, para. 37). The consequence of the institution of private ownership of land (including its concomitant rights to interest and capital)[33] is a productive efficiency and general increase in wealth, which not only now causes "no loss" to those who own no land (it having at some point become scarce), but even "betters" their lot relative to the absence of the institution in the original state of nature (*ST*, paras. 37, 38, and 41).

The clearly superior position, in Locke's eyes, of the English day laborer (who possesses no land) relative to the American Indian king (who rules over a large territory) in terms of the conveniences of life drives this point home (*ST*, para. 41). Men have "by common Consent, given up their Pretences to their natural common Right" to land and "by *positive agreement, settled* a Property amongst themselves, in distinct Parts and parcels of the Earth" (*ST*, para. 45, emphasis mine). And they have done this in the name of a greater security and material wealth: better food, clothing, and housing (*ST*, para. 41). Thus, the modern institution of private property fulfills what may be called Locke's "social contract criterion for legitimacy"; it is rational from everyone's point of view.[34] Of course, for Locke to argue that this institution is the "surest way" to increase the common stock (and not merely one possibility among others), a tacit assumption, not only about land or value, but about the self's motivation must be accepted. Locke must maintain that *laboring under the incentive of exclusive, private ownership is the most intense value creator.*

This study questions this reigning assumption of Locke's, together with his views on nature and value. Before turning to such issues, however, it is important still to stress that for Locke himself, the natural law restrictions on private property are never transcended (as Macpherson argues). The human community is still perceived in the service of one God who dictates (via natural law) that differences in ownership are legitimate *if and only if* they work to the advantage of others (or at least do not work to their disadvantage relative to the original state of nature); this background condition continues to justify, as well as guide, the regulation of all property in political society.[35] The new twist in Locke's theory is that the role of *interpreting* the natural law provisos—at the time of the social compact—is taken from the hands of the average individual and given over to the new government officials, who now alone retain the role of stewards. The upshot of the social contract is that property as stewardship—requiring a direct awareness of social duties and responsibilities to others—is a form that disappears from the everyday life of the average citizen. Henceforth, each is free to go forth in public primarily (even exclusively) on the private property model. There is no longer the requirement to interpret (or even to consider) the needs of others, but only to remain within the boundaries of the new civil law. In Locke's social contract, one form of property has been exchanged for another.

3.4 TWO MODELS OF POLITICAL AUTONOMY

Just as there are two distinct conceptions of property and ownership operating in Locke's theory, so one may distinguish two respective underlying conceptions of the political person, autonomy, and primary motivation. Let us call the first model of political autonomy (accompanying the notion of stewardship) an Aristotelian "communal" self. This conception of the political person is in an important sense an "older" self and reflects the medieval natural law tradition. Such personhood has two distinctive characteristics. First, a definite hierarchy exists among the various capacities of the individual. The individual's substantive political personality—for example, reason, freedom, and equal political jurisdiction—consists of inalienable personality characteristics that set man above the beasts and determine his essentially "dignified" nature. Second, the exercise of these higher capacities not only can motivate the individual to action, but is even perceived as a fulfillment of his distinctively human nature. Such a conception of the person is clearly presupposed still in Locke when he assumes that the individual is capable of following the dictates of natural law (= reason) against his own immediate sensuous inclinations and self-interest. Law, writes Locke, does not restrain man's freedom, but ultimately preserves and enlarges it (*ST*, para. 57).

Of course, there is a second and better known conception of the political person in Locke, which I will call the "private acquisitive self." This conception accords with the newly emerging model of private property. By the private, acquisitive self, I intend, first, that the passion for material appropriation is viewed as fundamental—

even primary—in motivating the creative, productive acts of the individual. Second, and importantly, the person's very growth and fulfillment is perceived on the model of private acquisition; the individual's fulfillment consists in enlarging and preserving his property in its extended sense (*ST*, para. 123). In the extreme case, even the "higher pursuits," such as freedom, the life of the mind, science, and so forth, are viewed as exclusive, private possessions of the individual.

Once again, elements of both conceptions are operative in Locke's thought; his ultimate position is not to be found by ignoring the first or by overlooking the latter. The issue, rather, is to assess the relative weight and respective scope of these two conceptions in Locke's theory—and elsewhere. Here I shall show, in yet another way, how the model of stewardship and its respective, socially aware self in Locke succumbs to the private property model. It seems clear that, at least as regards the average citizen (I am thus not concerned with contrary claims Locke makes elsewhere concerning education, civil servants, and so forth), the acquisitive self not only surfaces in his thought, but ultimately "wins out." It triumphs, as it were, just as the paradigm of private alienable property will historically.

Let us focus one last time on Locke's comparison between the American Indian king and the English day laborer. My claim here is that *only* by presupposing a private acquisitive person at the time of the social compact—a self that considers a vast range of human experiences and characteristics on a par and as attributes to be individually acquired or alienated—can we resolve a longstanding difficulty in Locke's property theory. This difficulty may be formulated as follows: at first sight it appears highly irrational that individuals in Locke's state of nature, which is a state of equal political jurisdiction, should agree in the social contract to inequalities of property ownership. For, it turns out, these inequalities inevitably lead in civil society—on Locke's own account—to an inequality of the vote (and hence to an inequality in political representation). That is, the "true proportion" of legislative representation that any part of the people can pretend to, according to Locke, proceeds "in proportion to the assistance, which it affords to the publick" (*ST*, para. 158). And considering that Locke had earlier stated that appropriate levels of assistance are a function of amounts of taxable estate (*ST*, para. 140), any agreement to property differences in the social contract is in effect an automatic agreement to *unequal political jurisdiction* in civil society. The social compact results in an arrangement whereby rational individuals—originally juridically equal—exchange their position for "the worse" relative to the state of nature. The move violates Locke's social contract criterion for a legitimate social institution.

It is important to recognize, however, that for individuals to exchange equal political jurisdiction for unequal political representation remains irrational *only* if the self continues to be viewed on the older Aristotelian model, according to which equal political jurisdiction remains an *inalienable* characteristic of a free and rational being. If the person is conceived on the private appropriative model, by contrast, the inconsistency in Locke's view suddenly disappears. In this case, equal political jurisdiction becomes the object of but one more private exchange among many. What at first sight appears to be its inalienable, dignified, and essentially public character makes no difference; equal political jurisdiction is treated as an object of personal exchange and is being traded for secure protection of property, greater material wealth, as well as what is often called freedom from the necessity of active jurisdiction (ancient citizenship). *Only* if such a private, acquisitive individual in the extreme is presupposed by Locke's social contract, moreover, is it no longer surprising that a self could rationally prefer the material advantages of the English day laborer—without land or the vote—to the political autonomy of an Indian king ruling over a vast and fruitful territory in America.

3.5 THE MODERN CITIZEN AS PRODUCER AND THE TWO MORAL POWERS

A number of characteristics of this soon-to-be-dominant modern conception of the citizen, his surroundings, and characteristic activity have now come to light. In contrast to Aristotle's view, this new individual must be "productive," creating value not only for himself, but in principle also indirectly for others. So, too, the individual is now conceived as creating value against a conception of the natural world, which is 99 percent unfruitful or barren. In the early classical thinkers (as we have seen) such productive "mixing" was conceived largely as the production of an independent physical object (Locke's agricultural crop or Kant's wig). Historically, of course, the focus on an independent physical object gives way to production of a discernible product (whether physical or not) for the market and soon includes the modern category of "services" (over the centuries, that is, *both* the wig-maker *and* the barber become eligible for active citizenship). Ethical reproductive labor and *praxis*, however, the work of directly satisfying human needs and the provision of use-value in the family (e.g., cooking and feeding its members) are now relegated to mere servile and "unproductive" activities. Finally, we have seen that true productive labor presupposes not only that nature itself is of almost worthless value, that the individual must already be private owner of his life, limbs, and labor (1.3), but that the aim of private property is the primary means of motivating the individual to labor for more than he (and his family) needs (3.3). Stated somewhat differently, underlying the modern Lockean conception is the deeply ingrained, paradoxical belief that the incentive of exclusive private ownership is the most intense value creator; it is the "surest means" for getting the individual *to produce for others* as well.

The productive model of citizenry contrasts clearly with that of the ancient citizen as warrior. In the ancient world, recall, not only could the production of food and nourishment often be left to the abundance of a rich and fertile nature or to the work of slaves, but sharing in military defense of the homeland was historically the citizen's first obligation. In the early Greek city-states, full citizenship was often granted simply to those individuals who possessed the heavy armor or a horse. So, too, the modern liberal productive model contrasts with Aristotle's more refined (legislative) citizen's practical wisdom, leisure, and *praxis*, among whose primary functions it was to create and maintain relationships of political friendship and justice (2.7). And just as the citizen as warrior must be versed in the reasoning and skills of war, and the man of *schole* must possess practical wisdom and political friendship toward all, the modern productive citizen will characteristically possess a new set of technical skills and capacities distinguishing him or her. If I am correct and Locke's metaphor of mixing one's labor with the material world is as central as I claim, this will be reflected in dominant modern conceptions of the citizen's basic capacities. And, indeed, this may be shown to be the case.

Since Aristotle, the leading criterion of the active citizen—defined as he who has the capacity to take part in the deliberative and judicial functioning of the state (*Pol* 1275b)—has been that the individual possess full-fledged *practical reason*. However, not only *who* is said to possess such reason (the modern period increasingly grants it to all adult, mentally competent individuals), but also *how* such practical reason is modeled and conceived has changed dramatically over the millennia. This becomes clearer if one compares

Aristotle's model of practical reason as *phronesis* (practical wisdom) with that of the two dominant modern conceptions: moral utilitarianism and moral deductivism. I shall not undertake such a full comparison here, for this has been carefully performed by others.[36] I will, however, briefly note central differences, because once again Aristotle's model of practical reason emerges as far more appropriate to that form of reasoning required in ethical reproductive *praxis* (with the goal of *philia*), while the two modern forms track the requirements of modern productive activity.

At least in its classical form, moral utilitarianism identifies some end or goal (result or product) posited by our desires as the good (public utility as pleasure, happiness, contemplation, profit, etc.) and views practical reason as the foremost *means or instrument* for obtaining that end. Typically, utilitarian reason is conceived as either a simple calculation (Bentham's Hedonistic Calculus) or as a more complex process of inductive inference to the pregiven desirous end (as in Hume). In either case, it contrasts with the model of ethical reasoning championed by the moral deductivist. In the latter case, reasoning about practice begins from a set of self-evident moral rules (obtained from the Bible, rational intuition, or from the self-evident facts of nature), and practical reason's task is to apply the universal rules to particular cases, deducing, if possible, necessary moral consequences. St. Thomas Aquinas (and in the view of many, Kant) exemplifies this latter position. In both instances, the form of reasoning differs significantly from Aristotle's notion of *phronesis,* or practical wisdom.

First, and most important, while both utilitarianism and deductivism strive for a precise "scientific" account of reasoning in practice and in accordance with strict universal rules (of either calculation or deduction) Aristotle stresses that practical wisdom cannot be an *episteme* or a form of "scientific knowledge" at all (*NE* 6.5). This is the case because the subject matter of an *episteme,* or science, is eternal and unchanging objects (including the laws of nature), while practical wisdom has as its subject matter variable human actions and the specifically human good (*NE.* 6.3–5). As we shall see (4.5), the reasoning entailed in ethical reproductive *praxis* (action that aims at the reproducing of the best of human particular relationships) clearly has such "variable objects" as its center of focus: other particular human beings, their needs, and relationships.

Similarly, Aristotle does not classify *phronesis* (practical wisdom) as a *techne,* or skill (*NE* 6.4–5). Not only are the basic rules of such reasoning "flexible" guidelines, garnered from the (often contradictory) sayings of the many and wise, and holding only "for the most part," but so too—unlike the various *technai*—practical wisdom requires its practitioner to possess the moral virtues (*NE* 6.5). Aristotle stresses over and again that the proper functioning of practical reason (its aim being to usher in right action) must rest on an "educated perception" of concrete particulars, which perception in turn must be grounded on a prior training and habituation of the emotions (*pathe*) (*NE* 2.9). For Aristotle, the emotions are "ways of seeing"; they create salience in the environment and thus have cognitive power and content (we return to this important point in 4.5). For all these reasons, Aristotle classifies *phronesis* not as a science, skill, or production, but as a moral virtue or excellence (*arete*) (*NE* 6.5).

None of these characteristics need be the case in production, however; in productive activity (*poiesis*), the *type* of activity is logically distinguishable from its aim or motive (2.4). A skilled shoemaker, or a brilliant dancer, clearly need not be a morally virtuous person. Similarly, in the two modern forms of practical reasoning (utilitarianism and moral deductivism) reason is characteristically viewed on the model of a *techne*. The concern in both cases is with the *right result* in either deduction or calculation (and not in the first instance with the character or state of the agent or other person). So, too, rules tend in both cases to be considered inflexible, scientific guidelines and, the emotions—so long as they do not disrupt—are typically viewed as cognitively irrelevant. That is, in contrast to Aristotle, who depicts the positive and necessary role certain emotions play in the proper functioning of practical wisdom, the modern tendency has been to identify moral judgments with those rational judgments unblemished by any sensuous or emotional content (as in Kant's theory) or (as for utilitarians such as Hume) to elevate the emotions such as sympathy to moral status, but to view them as *lacking all cognitive content* (3.6 and 4.5). And this modern deprecation of the cognitive role of the emotions has been reflected in our notions of the citizen as well. Thus James Madison expresses the new standpoint well when he writes, "it is the reason, alone, of the public that ought to control and regulate government," the passions ought only to be controlled.[37]

One way of summing up the central difference is to note that, unlike for Aristotle, in the modern period the (abstract) capacity for friendship is never *explicitly* listed among the citizen's fundamental "moral powers of personality," to use a phrase made famous by

Rawls (*TJ*, 505). Rawls identifies two moral capacities that modern conceptions of liberal citizenship tend to presuppose. These are, first, the "capacity for an effective sense of justice" (the capacity to understand, apply, and act from and not just in accordance with universal principles of justice); and second, "the ability to form a plan of life" (the post-Reformation capacity to form, revise, and rationally pursue a conception of the good). However, if genuine justice requires a prior political friendship between citizens (2.7), then a further "power" of personality must also be presupposed in the average citizen if justice is to be possible. I will call this "third moral power" the abstract capacity for *philia* (friendship). And by this I intend nothing more than the minimal moral capacity to note and interpret the particular needs of fellow citizens (conceived as moral equals) and to respond appropriately with good will and practical care in the concrete.[38] One might here think of such simple cases as the activity of helping a fellow citizen across the street, helping a lost visitor find his way, or coming to the aid of someone who is being rudely treated. That such simple, everyday activities point to a third "competence"—not to be subsumed under either of the other two—follows, I believe, from various considerations.

Such an abstract capacity for *philia* has to do with abstracting from one's own needs (as in Rawls's first moral power), but here not in order to follow an abstract rule or principle (at the least an ambiguity lurks under Rawls's first moral power). On the contrary, the "looking away" from one's own needs takes place, but now in order better to perceive and interpret another human in the concrete: to interpret him or her in the here and now, not as a faceless fellow citizen, but as someone in a particular dilemma, with a certain age and set of abilities, and so forth. The abstracting from one's own needs and desires thus takes place in order to interpret and respond to another's concrete needs and desires.

I am not saying that cognitive capacities do not come into play; indeed, interpreting the needs of other humans—particularly of strangers and especially in hard cases such as that of conflict resolution—and setting about to satisfy those needs entails the exercise of elaborate rational faculties. It involves, for instance, the careful discernment of beliefs, intentions, and feelings, or what might be called the "art of perceiving the person" (*TJ*, 465). My point is only that such a complex art cannot be captured on the simple model of following a universal rule or principle. Quite to the contrary, in addition to knowing general facts about humans and their psychology, the art of perceiving the person and responding appropriately to him or her presupposes a prior *open* emotional stance and emphasizes the very different capacity of imaginatively and empathetically elaborating upon the particular (4.5).

If this much is granted, it is clear that the capacity to interpret and respond to concrete need cannot be subsumed under Rawls's second moral power of personality, either: the ability to form, revise, and execute a plan of life. One may clearly pursue one's own conception of the good while only minimally—and purely instrumentally—noting the needs of others. So either there is a third capacity for friendship here, or the perception and interpretation of concrete need and the ability to respond appropriately to it are not any part of political personality and remain a purely private one. Again, by a different route, we arrive at what I believe to be the modern position; we tend to assume that the detection of particular need and our response to it are either "supererogatory" (beyond the call of citizen duty) or better left to the "private domain." It is something women do in the home, for instance, when they take care of the needs of their particular children or husband, or it is the job of the doctor and nurse in their private practice, or of the firefighter and the legislator in their particular job. But it is not a concern of the modern citizen *as citizen*. I believe this is indeed the reigning modern conception, but I also believe it is wrong.

For one thing, the law already does de facto recognize this capacity to a certain extent. It does so in laws that forbid, say, leaving the scene of an accident (with a victim lying bleeding in the street) or in cases where the principle of "due care" is invoked in the ordinary course of events. That modern citizenship presupposes some such capacity is clearest in the formulation of Good Samaritan laws or in those countries that impose mandatory civil service. Granted, in the United States, civil service is never routinely required (only as punishment for a crime) and Good Samaritan laws are rare and rather weak, but this appears to be a contingent feature of *our* (American) legal system. In various European countries, by contrast, if I do not help a drowning person when there is little risk to myself, I can go to jail (certainly this is the case if I do not lift a finger to call 911 when a woman such as Kitty Genovese is being brutally raped and murdered in the parking lot outside my apartment window). And, indeed, there seems to be something seriously wrong with both the theory and practice of a modern state, which can demand that citizens abstract from their own needs to the point where—in times of war—they may be required to kill others or themselves be killed, but which does not have the power to demand of its citizens the abstraction from their own desires long enough to care for other particular citizens in times of genuine need.[39]

My point is only that there exists another "moral power" here, vaguely intuited by the law, but largely submerged or forgotten by political theorists in the modern period, in explicit contrast to the ancient view. And my claim is that for someone to be a citizen—and not a monster—entails having this capacity. At this point, however, my critic will find his voice and exclaim: "But it is precisely the modern, liberal state that has *freed* the individual from such constant care and concern for his fellows! In arranging social institutions that will watch over those who fall through the cracks (institutions such as hospitals, public education, social welfare, day care, etc.), the state today liberates the average individual (including women) to pursue *other* concerns. Are you not merely trying to return us to old tribal restrictions and attachments?"

It is true that the modern period has witnessed the construction of such important social institutions as those just mentioned, and in my view many of these public institutions that contend with individual need are a great step forward. However, not only the construction, but the maintenance, reproduction, and improvement of such institutions presuppose a fundamental *responsibility* on the part of each citizen to care for and (ethically) befriend fellow citizens even if he cannot do a fraction of the work himself. In other words, the unacknowledged and perhaps best political justification for such public social institutions may just rest on what I am calling the fundamental moral capacity for *philia* in each of us. If this third moral power is not explicitly recognized, encouraged, and publicly reinforced, moreover, then the social institutions grounded on it will likewise begin to lose their viability. Indeed, in the present atmosphere of individual license, hectic production, and "privatization," the important public institutions mentioned here are increasingly being called into question.

3.6 A BRIEF NOTE ON UTILITARIANISM

Others will object that the criticism regarding the omission of an explicit emotional power of the citizen may apply to the Kantian conception of the political person, as well as to the moral deductivist or social contract traditions, but it hardly does justice to the utilitarian one. The utilitarian principle of "sympathy" in a Hume, Bentham, or Mill, after all, is clearly intended to operate in the public and political sphere. And this is true. If we turn our attention to an analysis of Hume's "principle of sympathy," however, the critical *differences* between the utilitarian stress on the passions and sympathy, and what I am calling the capacity for *friendship* (personal or political), only come to the fore (see also 4.5).

First, and as already mentioned, for Hume (and many utilitarians) the passions and emotions are conceived as noncognitive; they are neither imbued with nor structured by reason, which for Hume remains "impotent."[40] On such an interpretation, the only thing that can arrest or change the direction of one passion from its original course is another, even stronger passion (for example, my desire to smoke may be halted or supplanted by an even stronger desire to be healthy). Practical reasoning is only a *means* toward this new goal. If this is the case, however, then one reaches the rather odd position that, since reason cannot directly influence the passions and only other desires or passions can, our desires (in their search for greater utility) will inevitably be pulled hither and thither by many different *types* of impulses: by brute desires, passions of greed, instinctive responses to natural disasters, persuasion by emotional and political rhetoric, terror, and so on. It is difficult to see how such *causal* interactions are different in principle from simple *manipulation* of desire—whether this manipulation be by a different set of my own passions, or by those of other people, or even by a political regime with all its sound bites and imagery (a state that Kant calls "heteronomy").

In slightly different terms, whatever "expansion of citizens' sympathies" utilitarian doctrine advocates as necessary for a just political regime, such expansion might well rest on highly questionable foundations: on whether the particular regime simply manages causally to control (or manipulate) the sentiments of its citizens in one way rather than in another. There is no requirement here (at least in classical utilitarianism) that such "enlarged sympathies" come about through the critical intellect of the individual or directly through a reflective, educative *praxis*. Thus one finds such claims as that of Adam Smith repeated *ad nauseam*: that much collective good can emerge "behind the backs" of the actors and be socially useful products of individual motives of greed, self-interest, and fear. Utilitarian good, at least in its noncognitive mode, is particularly susceptible to *ideology*.

Related to this point is the further one that all utilitarian doctrine remains *consequentialist*. The principle of utility directs us to strive for certain products or effects, either directly or indirectly, and it is from the value of this *ultimate product* (overall utility conceived as the public good, the happiness of the greatest number, the general pleasure or interests of mankind in the long run) that the moral value or rightness of particular actions *derives*.[41] But thereby, we must note, the very notion of *praxis*—of virtuous activity valued and performed *for its own sake* (and under which we have argued the motive of true *philia* falls)—is left by the wayside in this tradition. Genuine *philia*, enacted for its own sake, becomes suspect.

Recently, there have been numerous attempts to claim that these two approaches—being a genuine and loyal friend to someone and remaining a consequentialist—need not be opposed.[42] It remains doubtful in my view, however, that such "sophisticated" or "indirect" utilitarian attempts can fully succeed when it comes to accounting for the phenomenon of genuine character friendship. I am not here of the opinion that it is "logically impossible" (as Badhwar Kapur claims) that the motivational structure of friendship (where the friend is valued for her own sake) and the motivational structure of consequentialism (where cultivation of a friendship is *conditional* on its contribution to the overall good) are compatible; this claim appears too strong.[43] The logical compatibility (or lack of it) between friendship and consequentialism will depend on one's particular conception of a friend, as well as on how sophisticated and refined one's particular conception of utility or the overall good is. (If the ultimate good, to take an extreme example, were conceived as furthering personal friendship itself, there need be no conflict.) Far more important, in my view, is the issue, not *whether praxis* and consequentialism can be made logically consistent under some interpretation of utility and friendship (which I'm sure they can), but *how easy* it is for these two motivational structures in everyday life to come apart. That is, there are far too many instances of furthering a conception of the general good (say, for the sake of the community, for overall profit, or for the *Führer*) that will require that I betray my friend.

Even if there can be consequentialist justification for having nonconsequentialist motivations, moreover (as in the more recent views of a J. J. C. Smart or Peter Railton)—and possessing dispositions to genuine friendship generally are viewed as the best means, all things considered, to the end of overall utility maximization—one is still left with the ultimate *point* of these friendly dispositions. They remain instrumental to the overall good. But, again, what stops even these more sophisticated, indirect versions of consequentialism from collapsing into a manipulation of others—unless the very stricture "no manipulation allowed of friends" is now built into the conception of the general good to be maximized? In this latter case, however, consequentialist doctrine simply moves closer and closer to a nonconsequentialist (deontological) position. The problem of not regarding others as ends in themselves and for their own sake is only being pushed back one level. If my friendship (or my disposition to friendship) with you is conditional on furthering what I take to be the project of objective overall good, little room for our friendship is allowed in cases of serious conflict; I ought to end the friendship. I am not saying that this ought never to be the case. I am saying that, in any characteristically consequentialist doctrine, it is all too easily the case. (I believe this is the more important lesson behind Kapur's article.)

There is a further difficulty in being a thorough consequentialist and being a genuine friend to another. Let us call it the *problem of arrogance* regarding knowledge of the ultimate good. The idea that I might actually learn something about the objective good by means of my friendship to you does not fit naturally within this model. If you might be a part of my source of knowledge of the ultimate good, I would have to suspend my seeking this good at least temporarily and simply listen to your words and observe your actions. In this case, your actions and words *themselves* (and not their consequences for any as yet unspecified good) will be the source of their own value.

In a consequentialist doctrine, our first concern is with causal knowledge of bringing about certain desired products or events (as in a *techne*), and not with our own or another's motives or immediate actions (again, except indirectly). Similarly, the activity and labor of production also prejudices the product and characteristically may presuppose a host of different (and even contradictory) kinds of motives and human relations sustaining it (2.4). The practice of genuine friendship, by contrast, necessarily focuses on a specific relationship (or set of relationships) between concrete individuals, and the friendship motive becomes constitutive of the relationship itself. But thereby objects and products—as in all true *praxis*—

become of secondary, background concern. If particular persons are our immediate and true concern, the "ultimate good" and calculating toward it begins to look distant and unreal—even superficial.

To say that the "consequences" in *praxis* are of secondary concern is not, of course, to say they are of no importance—certainly not that they should be ignored (this would be to commit a category mistake). As one scholar has noted, our response to the consequences of our actions (we failed despite our intentions or we by mistake brought about hurt) just sets up a further round for revealing our good will or lack of it, our care or its absence, in the relationship.[44] The critical point is that the value of the activity is not derived from the end state of affairs that is actually brought about; the product is hardly—among human beings—the end of the story. In sum, utilitarianism is essentially consequentialist and as such, no matter how indirect, it has the structure of an *ethics of production.* But this means that, like the classical *poiesis,* it cannot easily accommodate the moral value of a range of activities performed purely for their own sake.

3.7 CONCLUSION

We have seen that it is neither mandated by the size of the modern state, nor by its various new dimensions of complexity (such as the doctrine of universal individual rights) that all forms of political friendship between citizens become impossible. Certainly, there has yet to be an argued defense that civic friendship—operating through law, political institutions, and a doctrine of universal individual rights—is *undesirable.* To the contrary, Aristotle's basic insight still holds, and this despite the changing circumstances and the new developments of the modern era: a civic friendship—a reciprocal awareness and good will among citizens, as well as a practical doing, embodied in the basic social and political institutions of a society—remains a prerequisite for "the give and take" of genuine justice.

So, too, we have seen that the notion of *philia* as a *political* capacity has not so much been discarded as it has de facto faded into the background of modern political analysis (operating still as a vague natural law requirement or as a principle of sympathy), but subtly altered and near invisible. A central reason for this we have also discovered: a new practical concern with, and a theoretical concentration on, production. In focusing on production, however, one does not, in the first instance, concentrate on the relations between persons as valuable in themselves. These important relations are increasingly left to look after themselves.

Finally, we have also seen that at one critical juncture, the position argued here begins to distinguish itself, not only from Aristotle's view, but from liberal theory as well. Unlike political liberalism, I reject granting the category of production the weight it almost everywhere still holds (3.1 and 5.3). Like Aristotle, I seek to focus attention once again on the importance and value of ethical *praxis*. Unlike him, however, my project now entails—in common with liberalism and the modern period generally—a necessary emphasis on universal individual rights as well. The break with liberalism begins with the belief that these universal rights need now be reconceived by keeping ethical reproductive *praxis* and its aim firmly in mind. For, although ethical reproductive *praxis* is strictly speaking not "productive," it retains the utmost value.

4 THE SOCIALIST TURN
Missing Faculties

But life is action [praxis] not production.
ARISTOTLE

4.1 THE ARISTOTELIAN INFLUENCE

If the Aristotelian worldview in general, and Aristotle's political theory in particular, was largely ridiculed by early modern thinkers such as Hobbes, Locke, and Kant, numerous Aristotelian doctrines soon had their defenders. In particular, various German idealists and socialist thinkers attempted to reintroduce the Aristotelian notion of *praxis* (and even a version of *philia*) within the context of modern developments. In this chapter I argue that perhaps the most important of these theoretical attempts to reawaken a political version of friendship—that of Karl Marx—ultimately fails. It fails, however, *not* for the reasons that are normally cited—not because a form of free democratic socialism is "unrealistic," "utopian," or somehow "against" human nature. On the contrary, I will argue that Marx's theory does not succeed because it is *all too human*—or perhaps we should say, all too *male*. For, like so many of his brothers in the modern period, and despite all his attempts to overcome the ills of capitalism, Marx remains mesmerized by the production model of activity. His thought remains captive to the existing scheme of things.

I shall argue that Marx's theory does not succeed, first, because it possesses no adequate conception of *social labor* (nor does the work of the vast majority of his socialist followers). As a consequence, second, the theory lacks an account of those actions, emotional dispositions, and capabilities which would support a more egalitarian, free, and democratic socialist society; that is, there is no account of friendship, civic or otherwise. Finally, I aim to show that the "mystery of socialist property"—how, in an advanced capitalist world, one might yet realistically motivate persons to labor *without* the assumption of a Lockean acquisitive self (with its dominant motive of exclusive, private gain)—will never be solved on a production model of activity, even if *collective*. At the very least, the problem of how to imagine an adequately free and socialist form of property is never solved by Marx himself. For those sympathetic to a more egalitarian and just society, therefore—one animated not just by the institutions but by the habits of a genuine civic friendship—this chapter provides one further reason to take the category of ethical reproductive *praxis* seriously.

4.2 MARX'S *1844 MANUSCRIPTS*

As has oft been argued and yet still not widely known, Karl Marx's work may naturally and quite profitably be viewed as the culmination of a "left-wing Aristotelian" tradition of thought. Marx's naturalistic anthropology and his hylomorphism may be considered a variant of Aristotle's.[1] Similarly, Aristotle's *Politics* was a major influence on the development of Marx's own theory of class struggle.[2] Even more important for our purposes, Marx was producing a German translation of Aristotle's *De Anima* at the time he was writing the *Economic and Philosophical Manuscripts of 1844*.[3] As one author argues, while Hegel's interpretation of the *De Anima* in the *Lectures on the History of Philosophy* stresses an "intellectualist reading" of the three Aristotelian souls (2.2), Marx's *Economic and Philosophical Manuscripts of 1844* is perhaps the most sustained attempt in the modern period to give an "inclusive" or "comprehensive" reading of them.[4] Let us thus turn briefly to these famous manuscripts of the early Marx. I do so not only in order to illustrate one sustained modern attempt to give an inclusive reading of the Aristotelian souls, but also to reveal where Marx's project essentially still remains incomplete.

The *1844 Manuscripts* are Marx's first attempt to give a "critique of political economy," a task that constitutes his life work from this time forward. Under "political economy" Marx has in mind that body of economic and political writings (from Hobbes and Locke, to Adam Smith and onward) that purport to give a justificatory blueprint of the emerging modern state and capitalist economic system. As is well known, Marx's aim is to reveal, in the face of the modern period's new proclamation of the universal freedom and equality of all men, the limitations and misery this new social system imposes on the worker: on the person who must sell his labor-power. To reveal its crippling effects on a large portion of the population, however, Marx must first give an account of minimally correct human functioning. For this purpose, apparently, he turns to Aristotle's *De Anima*, although other philosophical predecessors (such as Hegel or Feuerbach) also directly influenced this work.

Like the *De Anima*, Marx's *1844 Manuscripts* stress early on that the human is a "living, natural being" (a paradigmatic substance in Aristotelian language) and that humans share the need and the capacity to nourish, maintain, and reproduce themselves with both animals and plants (*EP*, 336). Further, as is the case with the animal and even plants, a discrepancy exists in humans from the start between the power (*Kraft*) to satisfy a need and the realization (*Verwirklichung*) of this power as actualized ability. Such realized ability, Marx never tires of telling us, entails a dependence on "material objects" outside the individual (*EP*, 336–37). Not only do human powers necessarily inhabit a sensuous object—namely, the individual's body—but they are also realizable only in other objects; "man can only *express* his life in real, *sensuous* objects" (*EP*, 336). The dependence of human beings on material objects and on a sensuous natural world outside themselves, in the pursuit of their most basic metabolic and other activities, is apparently all Marx means by "materialism" in the early works.[5] A necessary link has been established between human capabilities and the material support required for the realization and expression of their capacities, abilities, or actions. Marx's emphasis on the close link between human life and material support appears to originate in the Aristotelian dictum that a living, ensouled creature is a certain self-organization of form or activity necessarily realized in a properly suitable matter (*De An* 412b12) (2.1).

Of course, the human is a specific natural being with needs, powers, and dispositions peculiar to itself (*EP*, 337). If animals, in the Aristotelian view, are distinguished from plants by their new capacities grouped around sensation (such as appetite, desire, and locomotion), the human is distinguished by its new capacities grouped around intellect—in Marxian terms, "self consciousness and will." That is, the sensory-motor capacities of animals (in contrast to plant life) allow animals a far greater freedom in pursuing their metabolic activity, which in turn minimizes their dependency on the immediate environment (*De An* 413b2). Animal life is witness to a greater range and quality of activities, although this entails the possibility of a greater suffering and passivity (*Leiden*) as well, if the object of desire is withheld. As Marx notes, "to be sensuous is to suffer" (*EP*, 337).

In the case of the human, who possesses intellect and whose species-character is, for Marx, "his free conscious activity" (*EP*, 276), the ability to control the environment, as well as the capacity to suffer, is intensified. True to the Aristotelian tradition, Marx views human consciousness as including not only the capacity for deliberation and choice but the ability to subsume particulars under a universal. The human is that distinctive creature who can grasp himself both theoretically and practically as "an instance of a kind"; "man alone can treat himself as a *universal* and therefore as a free being" (*EP*, 275). It is for this reason that Marx labels the human being the "species-being" (*Gattungswesen*).[6]

My claim here is that while deliberative choice and the employment of the kind-member schema have already consistently been applied to the Aristotelian intellectual and sensitive souls (by Hegel and Feuerbach, respectively), Marx's distinctive move in the *1844 Manuscripts* is to extend these insights to the Aristotelian nutritive soul as well.[7] It is only thus that one can explain his famous claim that, in contrast to the animals, the human alone can produce and reproduce "universally" as a conscious instance of a kind even when (or especially when) he is free from immediate need (*EP*, 329). Marx's attempt in the *1844 Manuscripts* stands in explicit contrast to the tradition's dominant depiction of the nutritive soul as essentially "crude and blind," encountering particulars only as particulars (Hegel's depiction, in the *Enzyklopaedie*). For Marx, only in the human can the higher psychic functions—free exercise of choice, universal intelligence, foresight, imagination, awareness of sociability, and the laws of beauty (*EP*, 276)—self-consciously *restructure* the manner in which his or her most elementary life-functions are carried out. To act and labor as a species-being is for the human to form and produce objects (himself included) according to the "laws of beauty" and intelligence, and in the horizon of a concern with the entire species.

If my interpretation is correct, Marx's theory of alienated labor is largely a description of deprivations that deny people a good life on Aristotle's view.[8] In these early writings, Marx's primary condemnation of capitalism concerns the system's relegation of the wage-worker to a mere "animal-like" existence. Not only is the worker's mind "ruined" by engaging in monotonous, repetitive activity controlled and directed by others, but he "mortifies his body," too (*EP*, 274). His senses (like those of an animal) are caught up in crude practical need and have "only a *restricted* sense"; they become dull and focused on the private and immediate (*EP*, 276). Significantly, Marx's criticism is extended to the functions of the nutritive soul. Under capitalism, the alienated worker all too often goes home exhausted in order to nourish and reproduce himself "one-sidedly," focused only on his own immediate needs. For Marx "it would be impossible to say wherein this feeding activity differs from that of animals" (*EP*, 276, 301).

Marx thus stresses the *privation* this form of laboring activity entails. The self is preoccupied with itself and its most elementary and exclusive functions; in the extreme case, the individual is aware only of its own immediate states of pleasure and pain. For the ancient Greeks, as is well known, the life spent in the privacy of what is "one's own" (*to idion*)—such as the life of a slave or woman denied access to public life—was considered "idiotic" by definition. Moreover, it is quite certain that for Marx, not just wage-labor but the capitalist, too, in his private compulsion to accumulate money, profit, and capital, does not escape the charge of a crippled and essentially solipsistic inner life (*EP*, 300). Far from being a "natural" state of the individual, such a solipsistic self bent on pleasure and the avoidance of pain (essentially the private consumer self of much utilitarian doctrine) is an artificially induced state that—under modern market conditions—has been elevated to a cultural norm.

"Alienated appropriation" thus refers in the *1844 Manuscripts* to that form of human appropriation reducible to an animal, even biological, model. Particularly in the domain of wage-labor, one sees the destruction of what Aristotle considered "distinctively human" capacities—including now also Rawls's "two moral powers" of modern political personality (3.5). Both the capacity to abstract and distance oneself from particulars (presupposed in the ability to act from and be bound by universal principles) and the ability to posit one's own goals in existence (given to oneself by oneself) are in the case of wage-labor systematically crippled. The former, because the worker's most basic capacities for movement, sensation, and intellect are repeatedly denied enjoyment and expansion outward to a public world of common activity and shared objects; the latter, because the tools, aim, and product of the labor process are owned and controlled by others. "Free conscious activity" thus stops at the threshold of the realm of production (and reproduction). The two fundamental moral powers underlying modern political personality itself—not to mention our third moral capacity for friendship—are systematically being undermined from "within" the competitive system itself.

The alienated, animal-like world of the modern factory worker Marx contrasts with what he calls "real appropriation" (*wirkliche Aneignung*). Genuine appropriation is the "appropriation of human reality" or, alternatively, the making one's own of the "world of culture" (*Bildung*) (*EP*, 299, 295).

> *It is obvious that the human eye enjoys things in a way different from the crude, non-human eye; the human ear different from the crude ear, etc. . . . [In real appropriation] the senses and enjoyment of other men have become my own appropriation. Out of these immediate organs develop social organs in the form of society; thus for instance, an activity in direct association with others, etc. has become an organ for expressing my own life, and a mode of appropriating human life.* (EP, *300–301)*

When Marx speaks of appropriating the "world of culture," therefore, he does not merely refer to the fact that all appropriation (perception, linguistic acquisition, science, and so forth) takes place within the horizons of a specific human culture or a particular set of social practices. This is surely the case, but it is only part of the story, for on this minimal interpretation of true human appropriation, the institution of private ownership of productive means (as well as the activity of private, selfish acquisition) is still equally and necessarily "cultural." Marx's claim is stronger. Nonalienated appropriation involves that form of appropriation between humans that "makes one's own" distinctively human capacities: reason, foresight, and imagination, together with beauty and sociability. Such human sociability does not negate the "personality of man," but must grant each individual "human status and dignity" (*EP*, 280). In short, genuine appropriation, for the early Marx, is a universal "making one's own," not of physical objects but of species-specific abilities, including the three moral powers of personality; it is an appropriation of human species capacities compatible with a like appropriation by all others. Although Marx's discussions of "truly human" perceiving, sensing, and thinking are mostly absent from the later writings (he never develops a theory of perception or consciousness), the extended use of what I am calling truly human or cultural appropriation remains.[9]

In a similar manner, when Marx speaks of "unalienated production" in the *1844 Manuscripts*, he primarily has in mind the production, again, *not* of physical objects but of human species capacities.[10] Marx here clearly operates with Hegel's more elaborate paradigm of productive labor as self-determination and the confirmation of individual powers.[11] Not only can laboring activity—conceived, say, on a free artisan model—develop the individual's capacities of rationality, discipline, memory, foresight, deliberative choice, imagination, and sense of beauty, but the products of such activity allow the human being self-consciously to confirm his or her individual powers in an objective, public world. Laboring activity can be self-confirming and *emancipatory*. The worker is able, by way of his physical creations, to "contemplate himself in a world that he has created" (*EP*, 277). It is precisely such valuable attributes of productive work on the direct formation of individual species-capacities, moreover, that in Marx's view the ancients in general and Aristotle in particular had failed properly to appreciate.[12]

The all-round development of "human capabilities" thus contrasts with a work process that stunts and cripples these same abilities. In referring to the capitalist production process, Marx writes, "Production does not simply produce man as a *commodity*, the *human commodity*, man in the role of *commodity*; it produces him in keeping with this role as a *mentally* and physically *dehumanised* being. —Immorality, deformity, and dulling of the workers and the capitalists—its product is . . . to be *indifferent*" (*EP*, 284). Particularly in the early works (and contrary to the many strictly economic or technological interpretations of his view),[13] Marx's concern with the economic production process (production in the narrow sense) is with its wider influence on human physical, sensitive, and mental capabilities. In this respect he again edges closer to Aristotle. As in the latter's ethical and political writings, Marx's concern is with a delineation of those concrete human institutions and arrangements that impede or further proper human functioning. In both cases, the standard of a flourishing life will entail *minimally* that human species powers *pervade and restructure the lower souls*—pervade the way individuals go about their most everyday practical activities of production and reproduction.

This is, of course, not to overlook the many differences between the two thinkers. Most important, for Aristotle the activity of making or production (*poiesis*) is explicitly distinguished from action or *praxis* by the fact that the latter (but not the former) is done for its own sake (2.4 and 2.5). So, too, we should stress that Aristotle continues to view *poiesis* as essentially "unfree" activity; it is performed primarily out of necessity, and thus artisans and craftsmen, who have little leisure time, are denied the status of active (participatory) citizens in the *polis* (2.7).

For Marx, by contrast, in uncoerced and "truly human" production the individual can be seen to exercise his or her physical, intellectual, moral, and aesthetic capacities *for their own sake*. While Aristotle viewed all production (*poiesis*) as fundamentally different from *praxis* or action, Marx now claims a *subcategory* where they emerge as identical. Unalienated production simply *is* a form of free *praxis* for Marx. The general, modern elevation of the work process as something fundamental to the constitution of a positive human self-conception is confirmed in the thought of Marx.

One important consequence of this differing valuation of the production process by these two thinkers will be a difference of opinion regarding *which* human capacities (as well as their relative worth) are distinctive of the human in the first place. If the type of valued activity differs for the two (both stressing that capacities are grounded and developed in different activities), then those human capabilities minimally required for a human good life will surely differ for the two as well. The question of what constitutes an adequate list of proper human functionings—even whether there can be such a list—continues to be a significant issue in contemporary debates.[14] Before turning to this topic, however, it is important to note that this interpretation of the *1844 Manuscripts*—reconceived in light of Aristotle's *De Anima*—continues to escape the notice of most contemporary scholars.

4.3. RAWLS'S MISREADING OF MARX

We have argued that for Marx unalienated production and appropriation refers, in the final analysis, to the production and appropriation of species-specific human capabilities: to the free exercise of choice, universal intelligence, foresight, imagination, awareness of sociability (friendliness), and the laws of beauty. All these capacities are capable of penetrating and restructuring the lower sensitive and nutritive souls. Recall Marx's words: "[T]he senses and enjoyment of other men have become my *own* appropriation . . . an activity in direct association with others, etc. has become an organ for expressing my own life, and a mode of appropriating human life" (*EP*, 300–301).

Interestingly enough, John Rawls in *A Theory of Justice* also claims that activities in direct association with others "develop man's distinctively human powers" (*TJ*, 523n.4). Rawls argues this by way of elaboration of his notion of a "social union" (*TJ*, sec. 79). Considering the tremendous influence Rawls's work exerts on contemporary thought, not to mention the relative clarity of his exposition, a brief comparison between his idea of social union and that of true human appropriation in Marx becomes of interest.

Rawls's idea of social union is drawn up in explicit contrast to what he terms "private society" (*TJ*, 522). Private society is a form of social organization distinguished by two chief features: first, the individuals who compose it have their own exclusive ends, which are either competing or independent, but in no case complimentary; and second, social relations and institutions are assessed primarily as *means* to these private ends (*TJ*, 521–22). Rawls notes, moreover, that "the natural habitat" of the idea of private society is "economic theory," and he equates the idea with Hegel's notion of civil society (*TJ*, 521n.3).

Relations of social union, by contrast, are marked by three characteristics:

1. Members of the union have shared final ends.
2. They value their common activities or institutions as ends in themselves.
3. There is an agreed upon scheme of conduct leading to a complementary good for all. (*TJ*, 522–25)

In explicating this notion, Rawls acknowledges his debt to the German idealist tradition; the vision of social union is one in which the needs and the capacities of the individual can reach fruition only by participating in the realized natural assets of others (*TJ*, 523). In his view, social union is decidedly *not* a zero-sum game; one person's gain is not another's loss. On the contrary, social union exemplifies a win-win situation where "the successes and enjoyments of others are necessary for and complimentary to our own good" (*TJ*, 523). To illustrate his idea, Rawls relies on an example that also pervades the German idealist tradition: that of a group of musicians (of roughly equal ability) playing together in an orchestra. In this instance, the musicians play various instruments, and each has a different realized musical capacity. Nonetheless, none develops his individual skill, or perfects his musical ability, other than by way of the collective achievement of all—in the actual performance of the musical score. Men here enjoy and participate in one another's excellences for their own sake. Rawls writes, "It is only in active cooperation with others that one's powers reach fruition. Only in a social union is the individual complete" (*TJ*, 525n.4).

At first sight, this realization of individual powers only in social union appears to approach Marx's notion of truly human appropriation, whereby the senses and enjoyment of other men become "an organ for expressing my own life." My direct awareness and response to others, as well as their affirmative recognition of my unique powers, are critical moments not only for the development of my own powers, but for my participation in the realized species capacities of others. Surprisingly enough, however, Rawls does not find the idea of social union expressly stated in Marx (*TJ*, 523n.4), and he explicitly distinguishes his view from what he takes to be the Marxist position.

According to Rawls, when Marx speaks of the individual becoming a species-being and "complete in himself," Marx means that the future communist society is one in which each person "completely realizes his nature, in which he expresses all of his powers" (*TJ*, 524). But this is a perfectionist, utopian vision:

> *It is tempting to suppose that everyone might fully realize his powers and that some at least can become complete exemplars of humanity. But this is impossible. It is a feature of human sociability that we are by ourselves but parts of what we might be. We must look to others to attain the excellences that we must leave aside, or lack altogether. . . . The division of labor is overcome not by each becoming complete in himself, but by willing and meaningful work within a just social union of social unions in which all can freely participate as they so incline.* (TJ, 529)

According to my reading of the *1844 Manuscripts*, however, Rawls's criticism here rests upon a critical misunderstanding. If Marx means by realizing one's species-nature that each individual, under socialism, will develop and realize each of his native endowments—competently play all the instruments of the orchestra, say, while simultaneously painting with the talent approaching that of Michelangelo or composing poetry like Shakespeare—the charge of utopianism is clearly well founded. On the Aristotelian interpretation proffered above, however, "to realize one's species-powers" means nothing more or less than that *each* of the three Aristotelian souls—the individual's powers of intellect, of sense/perception, and of nutritive reproduction—operates in an intelligent and distinctively human fashion. For a *fully* human life, each of these spheres of activity must be marked by free reason (at least practical reason) to a substantial degree, as well as by some awareness of a universal kind-member schema—whatever the particular concrete forms these activities take, and whatever the specific and limited native endowments possessed by the individual.

The mistake in Rawls's reading (a mistake hardly peculiar to him) is that he takes Marx's famous claim that communism will overcome "the division of labor" to mean that it will overcome all specialization and "dependence on others" (*TJ*, 529), but this is *not* the Marxian meaning. Strictly speaking, the phrase *division of labor* refers to the "division between material and mental labor" (*GI*, 44, 45). Socialism is not meant to overcome all division of labor in Adam Smith's sense of simple specialization (which is impossible), but it just might overcome that distinction between a whole class of lives devoted purely to intellectual matters (and on which all major decisions devolve), on the one hand, and a class reduced largely to menial and physical tasks, on the other.

This is merely another way of stating Marx's main thesis regarding an adequate anthropology. The ideal of a flourishing society is one where, within each individual and to a significant degree, the intellectual capacities (to abstract, universalize, choose, plan, and so forth) pervade and restructure the way the most elementary functions of the sensitive as well as the nutritive soul (the *threptikon)* are carried out. In the left-wing Aristotelian tradition, no one capable of it should be denied the opportunity for this distinctively human way of functioning, whatever their concrete endowments and whatever specific activities they in fact take up.

If my reading is correct, the real difference between the idea of a species-being in Rawls and Marx rests on the question of whether the former would agree with the latter that an adequate human life necessarily requires a conscious and universal restructuring of the Aristotelian nutritive and reproductive soul. Does Rawls believe that attributes of intellect, affirmative cooperative relations, and activity performed for its own sake—in short, social union—should extend into the domain of economic productive labor? As we shall see, on this issue Rawls's theory remains at best ambiguous, while at worst it proclaims "no" or "not very much" (5.2 and 5.3). And this is the case because Rawls defines the very notion of a social union in explicit contrast to that of a private society whose "proper home" is the economic sphere (*TJ*, 522). Similarly, among his list of social unions—Rawls mentions art, science, religion, sexual relationships, families, school, friendships, games, and the well-ordered society itself—all mention of labor, the workplace, firm, or productive relation is conspicuously absent (*TJ*, 525–27). When it comes to the possibility of social union in the economic sphere, Karl Marx and John Rawls part ways.

For the moment, it is enough to note that even if one is sympathetic to my "inclusive" reading of Marx's notion of a species-being (that distinctive human capacities must be allowed to penetrate and restructure the realm of economic labor), one is still left with the problem of defending or delineating more carefully a specific set of species-capacities attributable to the human. This adequate set must—to a substantial degree—be exercised and developed for a truly human form of life to be possible. On this point, however, not only do Marx and Aristotle differ in important ways, but the issue itself opens up a whole new can of worms.

4.4 THE ABSENCE OF THE CATEGORY OF REPRODUCTIVE *PRAXIS*

There probably are more ways to divide and categorize the basic faculties of the human being than there are ways to organize a library or map progress. Whichever ways one in the end fixes upon, however, the capacity for friendship, or *philia*, must be among them. No one can sincerely conceive of a decent human life (versus that of a monster) that lacks this capacity. Earlier we saw, however, that acknowledgment of this fundamental human capacity (emphasized by Aristotle in the ethical writings) tends to get lost in modern political theory. Surprisingly enough, Marx—the socialist—is here no exception.

Marx clearly believes, in contrast to capitalism's production of the man of "indifference," that socialism will be marked by the recognition of other individual humans as the "greatest wealth" (*EP*, 91). He everywhere hints that such affirmative relations between humans will be the achievement of socialism, and such indications have led at least one thinker to claim that communist society will be held together by relations of *philia* and mutual caring.[15] The difficulty is that such hints in Marx remain largely that—mere intimations. In contrast to Aristotle's elaborately developed moral psychology, Marx barely has one. Further, as we will see, it remains altogether obscure how new affirmative relationships of socialist man are to emerge out of the exploitative and competitive conditions of advanced capitalism *on Marx's own account* (4.8). This leads me to the following hypothesis: although the early Marx partly rests his analysis of human functioning on the *De Anima,* there is little or no evidence that he was equally influenced by Aristotle's *Ethics* or *Rhetoric*—including the latter's involved discussions of the moral virtues, of friendship and the emotions. If this is the case, a critical aspect of Marx's anthropology—and of the feasibility of socialism—remains at best imprecise and underdeveloped, at worst downright misleading.

Again, I am not here repeating the standard criticism of Marx that his socialist future remains impracticable or utopian. On the contrary, I am pointing to a theoretical weakness in Marx's background account of minimally adequate human functioning. In unison with nearly the whole of the modern tradition, Marx nowhere gives an explicit analysis of friendship (civic or otherwise), or of the conditions for its possibility and development. This gives rise to a central difficulty of his theory: How are social relations of solidarity to come about in the midst of modern competitive conditions if the basic capacity for political friendship (sociability, solidarity, comradeship) is assumed, but not clarified, nor its political feasibility accounted for? It would appear that friendship (personal or civic) cannot be imposed "from above." We have reached not just a practical, but a theoretical impasse in Marx's thought.[16]

If this argument is correct, it should come as no surprise that Marx also has no conception of "reproduction" in our established ethical sense: that intelligent, sensuous activity manifested in the material world, which consciously and directly aims at reproducing relations of *philia.* Marx's notion of "social labor," as we shall see, is ill equipped to perform the job (4.8). Similarly, if one studies predominant uses of the term *reproduction* in Marx's writings, the ethical and political categories we have identified fall by the wayside; *ethical reproduction of human relationships* is fully subordinate to an analysis of the production process as a whole. This may be seen in various ways.

For one, there is the simple fact that both Marx and Engels regularly refer to the biological or ethical reproduction of human beings as a form of "production"; reproduction for the most part is not even acknowledged as a separate category.[17] Where reproduction is mentioned as a separate category—as in a number of statements by Marx and Engels on the "materialist conception of history"—there indeed exists the important acknowledgment that such activities might be of a *different order* than production. This is an insight, however, which is immediately forgotten. For example, Engels writes in *Origins of the Family* that the determining factor in history is of "a twofold character," and he lists the "reproduction of human beings" themselves alongside the production of the means of existence, such as food, clothing, shelter. And yet, despite this apparent promise to accord human reproduction an equally important and independent place in historical and social development, neither Marx nor Engels delivers an analysis of the former type of relations; they concentrate exclusively on the latter.

In Marx's later writings, the term *reproduction* becomes narrower and progressively confined in its meaning to the reproduction of *whole social systems.* In a typical passage from *Capital* Marx writes: "The maintenance and reproduction of the working class remains a necessary condition for the reproduction of capital. But the capitalist may safely leave this to the worker's drives for self-preservation and propagation" (*C* 1:718). Working-class "reproduction" is here viewed from the point of view of the reproduction of the *system* of capitalist production relations, and not from that of the reproduction of particular humans, or of their concrete relationships. Worse, in this passage Marx, in referring to human propagation, operates with a purely naturalistic, biological conception. Reproduction remains something that will "take care of itself" by way of natural drives, despite much lip service to the existence of alternative ways of organizing families and social life, on the part of both Marx and Engels.[18]

We have already noted that the term *production* (*poiesis*) refers in Marx, not just to the production of exchange or use values, but to that of human powers and faculties themselves (4.2). So, too, we have seen that unalienated production is considered an end in itself—a characteristic that Aristotle reserves for action (*praxis*) and the exemplification of virtue (4.2). We now find that under the category of production, Marx subsumes relations of ethical *reproduction* as well. That conscious activity which aims, not at the production of things or services, but at the simple reproducing of concrete human relationships, is either subordinated to the social, technical production process, on the one hand, or is reduced to its "merely biological" sense, on the other. In neither case is it acknowledged as distinctively human in the first place.

This suggests that Marx's use of the term *production* is far too wide; a number of critical distinctions are being lost. While his theory may be the most radical attempt in the modern period to give a consistently "inclusive" reading of the Aristotelian nutritive and reproductive soul, we now see that he fails to acknowledge numerous distinctions and capacities within this soul: distinctions that were the focus of Aristotle's ethical writings. Specifically, Marx gives no account of those ways in which humans directly and consciously reproduce particular relations as ends in themselves; such tend to be considered mere "reflexes" of the productive mode. Simultaneously, he fails to give an account of those background subjective capacities and emotional dispositions of persons—as well as of the social and material conditions for their education and development—necessary to the establishment and maintenance of generalized *philia* between citizens over time. In sum, Marx's is an inadequate account of the subjective conditions for the possibility of any form of free and genuinely democratic socialism.

Before turning to a more careful examination of these subjective conditions, I shall add that in accordance with our hypothesis regarding historical influence (4.2), this inadequacy in Marx's theory may be traced back to his near exclusive reliance on the theoretical account of human functioning discussed in the *De Anima*, at the cost of the practical lessons of Aristotle's ethical writings. For, unlike the tripartite psychology of the *De Anima* (where the primary distinction is between intellectual, sensitive, and nutritive souls), in the bipartite, practical moral psychology of Aristotle's *Ethics* (and *Rhetoric*), the crucial division is between reasoned deliberation and *emotional response* (2.2 and 2.3). This latter distinction, moreover, emerges as central to an understanding of *phronesis* (practical wisdom), as well as for the activities of friendship and *praxis* in general. In thus revealing Marx's neglect of important practical ethical distinctions, my aim has been to reveal that his thought—as Aristotelian as it is—remains captive to many of our modern prejudices. Another prejudice, which goes hand in hand with the ideology of production (2.4), is the tendency in modern practical philosophy to devalue the emotions: to neglect them altogether or to deny their central and critical role in the proper exercise of practical reason.

4.5 THE EMOTIONS AND THEIR ROLE IN PRACTICAL REASON

There is a marked tendency in philosophical circles, particularly visible in the modern period, to view the emotions as natural antagonists of reason. Indeed, the emotions do appear to be the most "biological" or "somatic" of our mental faculties; rage, love, and sadness are intimately tied to bodily response. But the emotions have further been interpreted as essentially noncognitive, irrational entities, whether reducible to certain kinds of "felt experiences" (like itches and sensations), to patterns of behavior, or to sheer bodily physiological states (as in the thought of B. F. Skinner, say, or in that of William James). Fortunately, this reductionist tendency appears to be nearing its end as ever more sophisticated studies of the emotions appear.[19] And these recent studies all stress—as Aristotle originally did—that cognition is an essential part of emotional response, thus clearly distinguishing the emotions from pure bodily states, drives, or brute appetites. The necessary involvement of cognition in emotion entails, moreover, that many emotions can be *reasonable* or *unreasonable* (not a mere matter of charm or enchantment), and as such they will form, not only a necessary part of any adequate moral psychology, but of an adequate ethical and political theory as well.

But what are the emotions, and why are they of critical importance not only to ethical but to political theory? Aristotle originally defines the emotions (*ta pathe*) in the *Rhetoric* as "all those feelings that so change men as to affect their judgements, and that are also attended by pain or pleasure. Such are anger, pity, fear and the like, with their opposites" (*Rhet* 1378a21–23). This initial definition of the emotions emerges as too broad, however, for it would include physiological disturbances, such as headaches and stomachaches. Indeed, Aristotle immediately goes on to qualify his earlier claim. It is necessary, he tells us, to analyze each particular emotion in three ways. Using the example of anger, he says we must distinguish how men prone to anger are typically disposed, at whom (*tisin*) they are accustomed to be angry, and on what grounds (*eppi poiois*) (*Rhet* 1378a24–26). The mention of "objects" and "grounds" with respect to emotions reveals that Aristotle is aware of their cognitive nature and intentional structure (at least in a vast number of cases); the identification of an emotion, he argues, is determined by its (formal) object. One cannot (normally speaking) be angry without an appropriate cognition that one has been slighted or unjustly injured (*Rhet* 1378a30–32), nor does one fear without imagining or having a belief in some imminent danger (*Rhet* 1382a23, 33). Such beliefs or cognitions are essential conditions for having the emotion to begin with.

The cognitive element in what we characteristically call emotions reveals that they are far more than simple blind impulses, such as a mental or bodily feeling or sensation. Emotions are intentional states directed at articulated features of an agent's environment. This cognitive element entails further that emotions can be correct or "mistaken," as well; if the perceived object of fear or of anger is without any basis in reality, the corresponding emotion is without foundation or "unwarranted." Finally, as Aristotle repeatedly stresses, if the emotional response is unwarranted, the ensuing practical moral judgment of how one should act in a given situation is sure to be thrown off as well.

In trying to understand the nature of practical ethical judgment, therefore, it is not sufficient to study how one goes about making good moral decisions. Preliminary to deciding how to act morally in a particular situation is the acknowledgment that the situation is one requiring moral action to begin with (which not all situations do). One must first read the situation in such a way that ethical considerations become relevant and are brought into the limelight. According to Aristotle, our perception of the situation as a moral one is necessarily informed by the moral virtues. The state (*hexis*) of the agent's passions and emotions is thus critical in appraising the situation correctly from the beginning: for acknowledging that the situation is one that requires moral deliberation in the first place.

A critical function of the emotions thus emerges: they create *salience* in the environment. We actually *see* (or omit to see) things by way of them. If an agent is angry or flustered, she may well overlook important details critical to her situation. A person in love will focus on minor perfections in the lover, such as his "rosy cheeks" (as Socrates already noted), and overlook major flaws. This is not to claim, of course, that the most adequate emotional response is necessarily some form of "neutral" detached response that observes from a cool distance. It is often only *because* we care for X that we notice X's repeated thoughtfulness (or lack of it); a neutral, third party might well miss this real virtue (or flaw) in X's character. In general, emotions are critical "frames" for our perceiving real things out there in the world; they are ways of seeing even before we consciously begin to deliberate and judge. They are much like compasses that set our personal horizons.

Numerous recent studies have again stressed the critical role the emotions play for the very possibility of the proper functioning of our reason. It has been argued by de Sousa, for instance, that the emotions are one way of solving an important epistemological problem: the problem of how we as finite organisms, continuously confronted with a vast store of potential factual information, select what is relevant and ignore what is not (*Rat*, 193). No logic can determine salience or the choice of a significance level: what to notice, attend to, weigh or investigate further, and so on. For a variable, but always bounded time period, an emotion (like the act of perception itself) limits the range of information that the organism will take into account. But it thereby also limits the inferences actually drawn from a potential infinity, as it does the set of live options among which the agent must choose. Given this "strategic insufficiency" of our reason acting on its own, the emotions are one source of necessary supplemental principles.

Emphasizing the role emotions play as a required frame to an otherwise endless source of information is not to view them necessarily as an obstacle to reason and objectivity, any more than my wearing glasses necessarily "distorts" my vision. Proper eyeglasses—like mature and well-educated emotions—allow us to focus all the more clearly on what is objectively out there before us. The emotions may be a barrier to completeness, but completeness and objectivity are not one and the same. My two eyes do not allow me to see "everything," but I have good reason to say they allow me to see (when healthy, under good lighting conditions, and so forth) many things that are objectively there before me. Given the seriousness of what de Sousa calls "the epistemological framing problem," the existence of emotions, far from being an obstacle to the proper functioning of reason, appears to ground the very possibility of human practical reason itself (*Rat*, 193).

But what are mature and well-educated emotions? Clearly, they will not be ones that project onto the target something that is not there, such as when a husband suddenly exhibits jealous behavior toward his wife because *he* is the one engaged in an extramarital affair. (It is due to such projections, apparently, that the emotions have gained their nasty reputation.) Similarly, mature and well-educated emotions cannot be mere habituated responses to what one has been taught—in the original "paradigm scenarios," as it were—in which the responses were learned. If, for instance, Maximilian repeatedly learned from his parents to respond to all foreigners with disdain, and then he, in a new situation, responds with disdain to foreigners, his emotions have a certain "minimal rationality"; they extend in a consistent and coherent way the language of emotions taught to him. This does not mean, however, that we must fix the rationality of emotion irretrievably to its origins. The original paradigm may always be challenged in the light of new and competing paradigms (in the case of Max, say, by his getting to know his best friend's foreign girlfriend). Emotional maturity, I want to say, is a maturity arrived at through long testing of one's own responses against an ever widening range of potentially applicable scenarios; it is to obtain a form of reflective and ever widening *emotional equilibrium,* as it were (1.4 and 6.3). Not only do healthy and mature emotions thus help us focus on real traits out in the world, they also are critical for focusing on ourselves and our own reactions; they even become a central means for revealing to us our normative commitments.[20] Further, since on this view the emotions are conceived as imbued with reason and cognition, they also become susceptible to reasonable *persuasion* (which is not the same as saying they are fully cognitive or rational). That is, no reflective equilibrium of pure thought will ever get to the heart of morality if the person performing it lacks the courage, say, or the generosity of spirit or even the friendliness, that first *impels* thought and reflection into disquieting and even painful domains. A reflective equilibrium of thought grounded on, for example, stingy, fearful, or hostile attitudes will avoid certain critical moral issues from the start; it will dismiss them as trivial or refuse to recognize them as important moral and ethical considerations in the first place.

There is an important final point regarding the emotions that should still be mentioned. If emotions can play the role of arbitrators among different reasons (principles of reason alone remaining insufficient), surely reason has an effect on the quality and fabric of our specifically human emotions. In particular, I am here interested in the fabric and quality of the human capacity for *philia* and its accompanying emotion of care (*epimeleia*). What characterizes their distinctively human form? In suggesting that human friendship and care are transformed by our possessing the faculty of reason (*logos*), I should note that my position stands opposed to one strand of contemporary feminism that stresses the naturalness and the noncognitive and even "nonrational" nature of much human care.[21] As we noted earlier, what distinguishes human friendships for Aristotle from those between animals is the exercise of speech, or *logos,* and thus *logos* must distinguish human care, or *epimeleia,* from the mere animal version as well (2.4). But how can this be so?

For one, care in humans (unlike in most animals) is shown toward offspring not only when young but even when the children are grown and live far away. So what constitutes care, or *epimeleia,* as fully human is its capacity to be imbued with the structures of reason, again, in the sense of exhibiting foresight, memory, an awareness of the laws of beauty, universality, and so on. For example, I can care about my daughter in a way that our family dog—even though he loves her madly—cannot. I think about her past and worry about her distant future, I am aware of her relation to others in her generation, concerned with what is happening generally on the globe as she grows older, and so on. My having reason thus affords me the capacity *to care over the long term* and deeply for my daughter and (as Marx says) in the horizon of a universal concern for the whole species. There is also something more, however. My being in the possession of reason avails me of a capacity for genuine *singular* reference in the first place (as de Sousa has argued). That is, granting the cognitive and intentional structure of most emotions—that they are goal-oriented or *about* something—it now emerges that such intentionality admits of degrees. We can have a vague feeling of anxiety in regard to nothing we can pin down specifically, but we can also focus all our attention on, identify with, and love one or more *unique individuals*. Animals, by contrast, seem easily fooled by relatively coarse decoys. After one year, my dog may still recognize "me," but this is because he has picked out a sensible bundle of characteristic qualities (he remembers my smell, the sound of my voice, and so on). There is no evidence, however, that Fido has the linguistic apparatus that is necessary to distinguish logically between me and my *Doppelgänger* (*Rat*, 195).

The minimal condition for singular reference—for nonfungible identification—thus appears to be the capacity to intend a logical distinction between qualitatively indiscriminable individuals. This is not to say that, although we assume we refer to unique individuals, we can ever guarantee that our references succeed. It is only to say that such intended unique reference is peculiar to those of us with reason, as well as something we generally care *about*. I am in love with and care about the particular identity and character of X, not that of his identical twin brother, even if I cannot always tell them apart. Moreover, such unique and specific reference—let us call it "intelligent care"—may be learned second- and third-hand from other members of a human community, an ability apparently beyond any denizens of the animal kingdom. With time, that is, my child may come to refer to and even love her great-grandmother who died a heroic death long before the child's birth.

4.6 THE WORK OF CARE (VERSUS SYMPATHY)

If my argument thus far is correct, what follows for the study of politics and of the state? That is, if indeed our emotions "frame" our perception and cognition of the world; if, further, they have a cognitive and intentional structure; and, finally, if given our distinctive linguistic abilities, our emotions (unlike those of other creatures) can fix not only on the universal but also on the unique and nonfungible nature of individuals, what follows for the study of politics? It follows, I will try to show, that the emotional states of the citizen as citizen once again become of critical political importance for the well-ordered society. Once the view of emotions as noncognitive entities is rejected, it can no longer suffice to view the resentment between citizens or between classes of citizens, or the violence or indifference, apathy, and so on, as mere blind impulses or brute "natural" feelings that must be manipulated or causally controlled (as on a production model). If these emotions are essentially imbued with structures of reason and reveal a minimal rationality, they must be granted respect and must emerge as fundamentally *capable of education*—a prime reproductive task.

I thus sidestep the debate of whether it will always be in the "nature" of humans to be greedy, say (as in much capitalist theory), or to express *ressentiment* toward those who have more or who are perceived as superior (as in Nietzsche); I don't know how such claims could ever be proven definitively. What does follow, by stressing the ability to educate the emotions, is the importance of constructing social and political institutions that emphasize and encourage collectively reasonable feelings (friendship, security, trust, and so forth) and that minimize irrational and destructive ones (humiliation, fear, hatred). The virtue and emotion of civic friendliness, as we have seen, is not only necessary for genuine justice, but it is also collectively rational; it is beneficial from everyone's point of view. (*Ressentiment,* by contrast, is the reverse; widespread or collective resentment—bringing others down even if it means you yourself are brought lower—makes everyone worse off.)

That the political state cannot help but educate its citizens one way or the other—that whatever stand it takes, it is "always already" implicated in the emotional and intellectual states of its citizens (even if it tries a hands-off, *laissez-faire* approach)—also follows from the above conception of emotion embodied in everyday action and set within a framework of social practices and political institutions.

Thus, the real issue is not whether the state should be in the business of education—for it cannot help but set the framework—but how and to what degree and purpose the modern state should educate its citizens. Specifically, I will next undertake an analysis of the emotion of "care"—reciprocal care being a necessary and distinctive element of friendship properly construed. I will argue that care—like friendship itself—has an important political dimension.

As we have just seen, the disposition to care in the human is necessarily imbued with structures of reason; it includes the capacity not only for universal awareness (memory, foresight, awareness of others outside the relationship, and so forth) but also for unique reference (4.5). It is also clear that this disposition or emotion—like others—is developed early; it is strengthened by repeated exercise and habit. Just as I become courageous by first imitating the courageous actions of those around me, so I develop the disposition (*hexis*) to care by imitating the caring actions of others. If someone soothes or quiets me, I learn to quiet others in similar circumstances.

With the development of the modern market and the newly emerging nation-state, moreover, the historical division of labor between the sexes grows more defined and rigid. For Aristotle, a central feature of active citizenship was the virtue of friendliness—including the capacity to perform practical acts of care for fellow citizens (2.7). So, too, Aristotle urged his statesman to establish a "common care" (*koinon epimeleia)* for all citizens (not only in their youth but throughout their lives) and such "right care" (*ortho epimeleia*) becomes for him a political imperative in the framing of just laws (2.7). Similarly, the German notion of duty (*Pflicht*) still means simply "to care" (*zu pflegen*) in both Old and Middle High German—that is, well into the seventeenth century.[22]

The modern gendered division of labor between productive (male) and reproductive (female) work is thus of relatively recent origin. It emerges clearly with the developing nation-state, the rise of a complex capitalist market, and the newly institutionalized sphere of privacy. Caring activity, for the most part, recedes to the private sphere, while production takes on "public" features—in many ways the reverse of the situation in the ancient world. While women in the seventeenth century (at the time of Locke) were still widely employed in small cottage industries (it was mainly women, for instance, who ran the breweries), with the rise of the nation-state, the new civil society, and the realignment of the private sphere, women are increasingly identified with the latter. As care becomes private and nonpolitical, that is, it increasingly becomes stamped as purely *women's work*.

But what exactly is "care"? Elsewhere I have defined care as that competent, reasoned activity which not only seeks to perceive the general and concrete good of a person (or an animal or thing), but which also actively seeks to bring that good about.[23] Admittedly, this is an idealized notion, for what people actually call "care" is a many-sided concept; care can be paternalistic, hierarchical, smothering, or tender. Even as an idealized normative standard, however, care need not be reciprocal, and here the concept distinguishes itself from genuine friendship (7.3). I can truly care for X even though she returns neither my labors nor my affection (while I cannot truly be X's friend unless the caring is mutual [7.3]). It is due to this one-sidedness, I believe, that the English term *care* is connected etymologically with the notion of burden, worry, or woe (as in the expression "being burdened with cares"). At the same time, nothing in our definition requires that the activity of care be all self-sacrifice, burden, or altruism. On the contrary, caring activity may be highly rewarding personally, done for its own sake, as well as reciprocal. Indeed, the emotion and activity of care seem particularly rewarding when they are reciprocal. The German language, for instance (unlike English), possesses two distinct terms for "care": *Sorge* and *Pflege*. While *Sorge* connotes the burdens of "worried concern" and even "anxiety" (as in the writings of Martin Heidegger), *Pflege* typically connotes a calm ordering and nurturing. The latter also refers more to the actual hands-on, material process or practice of delivering care and of responding to particular need, whether it is a tending to one's garden, to one's own body (*Körperpflege*), or to the various activities performed by a nurse or "care sister" (*Pflegeschwesterin*). All these activities may be experienced as joyful or not. Thus, caring may refer to the *manner* in which one executes one's duty, or "to care" may even be seen as a prime duty itself. Again, not only is *Pflege* related in its meaning (as just noted) to the German *Pflicht*, or "duty"; but as we argued earlier there is no necessary opposition between care and duty as many seem to think (3.1).[24]

Consider even the deontological theory of Kant himself. Many argue that at least in his thought there exists a necessary opposition between care and duty (presumably because of Kant's technical notion of "duty"),[25] but I believe there is more to the story. Kant clearly distinguishes the practical "duties of love" (*Liebespflichten*) for one's fellow humans, for instance, from the *emotion* or *disposition* of love itself.[26] The practical duties toward fellow citizens (for example, helping them when in need) may be done reluctantly (especially at first), but Kant also states that if they are practiced or performed often enough, one may develop love for the person one helps. "You ought to love your neighbor" according to Kant means "do good to your fellow man and the love will follow." The emotion of care and love may thus emerge from within—or follows upon—the actual practice, proving that the "duty of care" not only need *not* be in opposition to the emotion, but that it can actually bring about the latter by repeated practice. Finally, much caring behavior is explicitly conceived as a legal duty—for instance, the important duty of parents to tend and care for their children. We must, thus, distinguish care as a disposition or emotion from care as an activity or practice. Duty does not preclude putting oneself into what one does and caring about it, in contrast to doing it reluctantly. Similarly (with Kant) I argue that we have not only the legal duty practically to care for our children (one hopes the emotion will follow if it is not there from the start), but also various duties of minimal care for our fellow citizens—again, practically speaking.

Feminists have begun to analyze the various phases or stages of the activity of care, and at least four such stages have been distinguished by Joan Tronto; these four should be seen as part of an ideal of an integrated and well-accomplished process or practice of care.[27] I might add that while the first two stages appear to correspond more closely to the German *Sorge* (concern, worrying about), the second two tend to track the hands-on nurturing *Pflege*.

1. Caring about. The first stage of caring entails noticing the existence of a need, and as such it presupposes an appropriate state of emotional readiness (4.5); let us call it a receiving mode. The one who notices another's need is characteristically not absorbed in something else, or preoccupied with his or her own needs, enraged, and so forth. At the same time, such "noticing" already embodies a judgment—a description of the need—and this will be culturally and individually shaped. Women trained in the activity of caring, for instance, will hear the cry of an infant at night when others hear nothing but the wind. Significantly, noticing can also take place at the political level; the federal government might officially recognize the existence of the problem of homelessness, the new hepatitis C epidemic, or the need for compensation for longstanding wrongs. Although it is a necessary condition for actual care, noticing by itself is hardly sufficient, for in merely noting the existence of a need, no action is necessarily taken and hence the need for care can go unmet.

2. *Taking care of.* The next stage is reached when the agent assumes a certain responsibility. The caring individual recognizes that he or she can and ought to address the unmet needs of another (to whatever degree) and takes the first steps toward doing so. At the political level, the government might accept responsibility for its role in the problem (or at least in the solution) and take steps towards rectifying it, for example, by commissioning studies of the identified problem, its causes and consequences, as well as possible remedies, ways of raising funds, and so forth.

3. *Care giving.* This stage refers to the direct and concrete meeting of the perceived need for care in the other. Actual care giving involves the concrete work of ethical reproductive labor. This stage of the practice of care requires not only a form of practical reason, but typically also "hands on" physical contact with the objects of care, with their bodies and their needs. As Tronto notes, "giving money" is not properly a part of this stage of care giving (it belongs more appropriately to stage 2), for giving money merely provides a way for someone else to do the actual hands-on work.[28] Money does not directly fulfill human needs (it has no use value) but must be translated into such fulfillment by work or other forms of action. On the political level, the actual building of low-income housing for the homeless (with a concern for its quality, combined perhaps with job, drug or mental counseling centers, etc.) would be a political correlate of individual care giving.

4. *Care receiving.* The last phase of caring is being cognizant of whether or not the object of care is responding positively to the care given—that is, whether the patient is better or the flowers in the garden are reviving or the previously homeless successfully managing in their new homes. Here it is important not simply to project or "put ourselves in another's shoes"; we must consider the other's position *as they see and express it.* A heightened responsiveness to the receiver of care is critical to a well-integrated action of care, for only thus can one know whether their needs have been met, the original description of their plight accurate, and the means of care appropriate. All too frequently the best intentioned giving of care emerges as blind, eliciting resentment or humiliation on the part of the receiver.

In considering these four different phases of care, it is clear that the phases can and often do involve conflict. Actual hands-on physical care might not entail caring about (although it usually seems to); taking care of and assuming responsibility (stage 2) might conflict with the awareness of the receiver's actual needs (stage 4). So, too, the different phases can devolve on different persons. As Tronto also argues, it is typically women or men of color in our society who perform the hands-on, care-giving activity (stage 3)—whether nursing, babysitting, house cleaning, or gardening—while white males in the public domain still tend to dominate the more "abstract" intellectual work of phases 1 and 2.[29] The traditional doctor, for instance, describes (diagnoses) the existence of a need and takes some responsibility for its cure, although the practical work of testing, curing, checking on, and caring for the patient is often done by a nurse or lab technician. Finally, the last two stages of the process of care (what I am equating with the German *Pflege)* appear definitively to distinguish the idea of "care" from that older and more traditional notion of moral theory, *sympathy*.

Care and sympathy are not the same; the notion of care, as emphasized by many feminists, and considered here as part of a larger civic friendship, cannot simply be subsumed under older notions of sympathy (or compassion), but is something genuinely novel. At first sight, given our stress on the cognitive side of the emotions generally and of care in particular, sympathy might appear to be a "natural moral sentiment" and essentially noncognitive. This was indeed the view of Hutcheson and of the early Hume in *A Treatise of Human Nature*, where Hume famously claims that reason is nothing but a "slave of the passions."[30] On further reflection, however, the difference between the two notions must lie elsewhere. For the fact remains that numerous members of the Scottish Enlightenment, and Hume himself when read more carefully, clearly recognized that sympathy (and the communication of passions) is not automatic but rests on rational inference.[31] Both Adam Smith's and Hume's notions of the "ideal spectator" and the "artificial virtues," after all, acknowledge the important role reason plays in tempering, broadening, and extending, as well as in rendering impartial, the emotion of sympathy.

The difference between care and sympathy lies elsewhere. The real difference, I now suggest, is that sympathy (and compassion, too)—unlike care—are primarily dispositions (psychological or emotional notions); neither can properly be conceived as a sensuous material practice. By a "sensuous material practice," I here mean a coherent and complex form of cooperative human, embodied material activity that can persist over time and is often institutionalized with an explicit set of social rules, accompanying virtues, and character states. For instance, I can care for someone for weeks on end (feed them, cloth them, and so on) but it seems odd to say I sympathize with them for weeks on end. Sympathy does not have the temporal, physical staying power of care, as it were, not for the reason that reason is not involved, but because sympathy is not viewed as an embodied physical activity.

By contrast, full-fledged care taking, in addition to being an emotional or psychological state, is also a concrete, sensuous activity, traditionally performed by women (or servants), and it necessarily involves hands-on reproductive work (which sympathy does not). There is no such thing as the physical practice of sympathy or compassion. Similarly, I can truly (psychologically) sympathize with someone but do nothing, while I cannot truly care for someone and do nothing (if it is within my powers to act). It is thus little wonder that the disposition of sympathy has often been touted by male moral theorists (such as for those of the Scottish Enlightenment), while an ethic of care—and a full awareness of the material sensuous practice and its significance—needed to await the modern women's movement.

That care should be conceived as a practice, and not merely a disposition, has numerous important consequences. For one, treating care (like sympathy) as primarily a disposition or emotion tends toward treating it as a mere property of the individual. Such a trait may then be romanticized or sentimentalized (as in the expression "some just care more than others"). Viewing it as a practice, by contrast, entails the recognition that certain traits, competences, and ways of perceiving may be socially encouraged by, and dependent upon, larger social and political institutions. Viewing care as a practice, that is, shifts it from being a matter of mere private concern and thrusts it out into the contested political domain.

4.7 MARX'S "COPERNICAN REVOLUTION"

I now return to Marx's position in order to reveal how—despite his penetrating critique of capitalism—the omission of any serious discussion of ethical reproductive *praxis* (whether of friendship or care, or of the emotions) throws Marx's account of the transition to socialism into question. Marx's project, we have argued, can be read as a version of Aristotle's political one (4.1 and 4.2), only now firmly placed within the context of modern developments. Marx exhibits a newfound respect for individual productive labor, and he does so within the horizon of a concern for universal personhood and dignity. The aim of his theory is to bring about a society no longer riddled by class conflict, but animated by a "solidarity" that affords all persons the minimal development of their distinctive human powers. Due to Marx's continued reliance on a production model of activity and labor, I will now argue, his socialist theory (and not just much socialist practice) is doomed to founder. I believe this point is best made by an analysis of how Marx himself envisions a socialist society emerging out of the "historical conditions" created by advanced capitalism. I will argue next that—after a promising start in the *Grundrisse,* Marx's final account of the transition to socialism in *Capital* emerges as mere fantasy (4.8).

A central Marxist claim is that from the conditions created by advanced capitalist production, where the dominant form of property is private property in the major means of production, a new form of socialist ownership (and a new socialist individual) is in the making. Generally speaking, by the term *property* Marx has in mind the relations of (and between) individuals to the major conditions of production (to raw material, instrument, and fruit all in one (*GI,* 492). Now, the notion of "conditions" in German philosophy is both difficult and complex. From the start we must be careful to distinguish Marx's use of the term *condition* (*Bedingung*) from at least two other dominant senses. The first of these may be called the term's *logical* sense as "rational necessity," whereby, say, the two premises of a syllogism are said to be the logical conditions for its conclusion. Marx's term has repeatedly been so interpreted. Particularly, proponents of so-called "dialectical materialism" (those who, like Engels or Lenin, interpret Marx's materialism as an ontological doctrine) tend to read his theory of history as a theory of rational (or iron) necessity, presumably capable of deducing one stage of history from the next. I reject such a reading of Marx's term *Bedingungen* for the simple reason that it has inadequate foundation in Marx's texts themselves, as numerous others have by now shown.[32]

Similarly, we can distinguish an empirical *mechanical* sense of the term *conditions,* whereby we say, for example, that one billiard ball "conditions" the movement of another, as in Hume's paradigm of efficient causality or in the behaviorist's model of stimulus-response. Again, many of the empirical and technological interpretations of Marx's theory of history (e.g., Plekhanov, Bucharin, but also more recently G. A. Cohen) tend to interpret the Marxian term *Bedingungen* in this way.[33] And yet, that Marx cannot be employing the notion in this empirical sense, either, follows from his general critique (inherited from Hegel) of what may be called a "conceptless empiricism."[34] Marx everywhere attempts to resist a strict dichotomy between facts and events, on the one hand, and our ideas or concepts, on the other. In his thought, the concrete fact is already a form of *synthetic* knowledge: it entails "a concentration of many determinations, hence unity of the diverse" (*Gr*, 101). Rather than employing either of the two senses of the term already identified, Marx's use of the German *Bedingungen* harkens back in important respects, I believe, once again to Kant.

In the *Critique of Pure Reason*, Kant announces his famous "Copernican Revolution," which attempts to reverse the traditional and common-sense view of the relation between knowing subject and object known. In the preface, Kant puts forth the "hypothesis" that instead of mind conforming to its object, as had hitherto been claimed, the object of cognition, in order to be known, must conform in crucial respects to the conditions imposed by the nature of our mind.[35] But for Kant, ultimately, the conditions of the possibility of experience (including the forms of sensibility and the categories of the understanding) refer not to static rules or categories, but to the *Leistungen* (the contributions, activities or performances) that the subject of experience must bring forth in order to experience anything at all.[36] We ourselves, writes Kant, prescribe the laws to nature a priori (*CPR*, B165).

Elsewhere I have argued that a similar "Copernican Revolution" is central to Marx's thought, only now in relation, not to the object of knowledge, but to the object of labor and ownership.[37] That is, one finds in Marx (from the *Grundrisse* onward) a similar "hypothesis" also directed against the traditional and common-sense view, only now in regard to the "object of labor." Marx claims that the labor object—in order to be "owned"—must conform in crucial respects to the nature and form of our producing activity. The claim is that the underlying structure of the capitalist production mode (who owns the initial resources, who is defined as free laborer, who labors, and so forth) will essentially "constitute" the property relations and those types of things that can, in turn, become the objects of private ownership.[38]

Kant, of course, considered the "conditioning" activity of the mind to be the a priori product of a formal, timeless, transcendental consciousness. Beginning with the "conditioned" or object of knowledge (the present state of modern science), he inquired into the a priori, formal and subjective "conditions" that make this knowledge of nature possible. As is well known, Kant was not interested in restoring knowledge (under attack by Hume, among others) ex nihilo; rather, he wished to draw limits to a certain misguided exercise of our cognitive faculties. In a parallel vein, Marx's project begins with the "conditioned"—the present state of political economy (in *Capital* with the analysis of the commodity)—and proceeds to ask what the *conditions* are that make this modern form of ownership possible. Of course, unlike Kant, Marx explicitly by the time of the *Grundrisse* considers his method to be "historical" as well as "materialist." The practical productive activity, which structures or conditions the world of human activity, is no longer considered the result of an ahistorical consciousness, but refers instead to the historically evolving, social and economic productive interaction of the human species taken as a whole.

As one author has stressed, the English term *condition* (derived from the Latin "a talking with") indicates that which is public and objective; it points to the nature and limits of social agreement.[39] Although the German *Bedingung* is without the strong linguistic connotations of its English counterpart, it too indicates that which is commonly dealt with and generally agreed upon. *Bedingen* originally meant *verhandlen, vereinbaren.*[40] When Marx speaks of the conditions of capitalist production, therefore, he refers not to some rationally deducible iron laws of history, nor to some mechanical cause of capitalism, but to the generally accepted limitations, agreements, or stipulations on productive economic activity (whether theoretical-linguistic or material-practical) that result from the historical cooperation between individuals, against the background of man's raw biological inheritance and the material potentialities of nature. In sum, with the term *Bedingungen,* Marx refers to those generally accepted (but not necessarily formalized) background *social rules* embodied in material laboring activity in a particular time and place.

If this much is granted, we may now ask: What is it about the developing forms of property (as well as newly emerging social rules) of advanced capitalism that set the stage for and eventually will bring about the transition to socialism? This new society will be marked primarily by cooperative relationships, the major means of production will be democratically controlled, and every individual will be encouraged to develop his or her distinctively human capacities. On the Marxist view, the tremendous productive power of capitalism that sets the stage for socialism is *not* due to the "increased initiative" capitalism excites in the individual (the usual explanation). For Marx, on the contrary, capitalism demoralizes the mass of propertyless workers. Marx attributes capitalism's tremendous historical productive power, rather, to the fact that this system has, for the first time, united on a large scale labor that had previously been scattered and isolated (*Gr*, 586). Such "concentration of many living labor capacities for one purpose," now no longer compelled by direct physical force, has produced a surplus hitherto unknown in history.[41]

In regard to ownership, one of Marx's central claims is that the capitalist concentration of scattered labor under one roof will eventually collectivize property itself (*TSV*, 426). By slowly eliminating the self-earned property of the producer (of the individual artisan, the small farmer, and so forth), industrial capital compels the association of workers through "objective association"—the concentration of material conditions and social rules—whether in the modern factory or the scientific research center (*Gr*, 590). Unlike the inherited image of individual labor we receive from Locke, these productive means cannot in essence be privately worked, nor the result of any one individual's effort. The "awareness" that such collective means should rightfully be their "own" will presumably dawn upon the working class in much the same way as the slave historically awoke to his freedom (*Gr*, 463).

By the "collectivization of labor," Marx does not simply mean the bringing together of different laborers under one roof. This no doubt, as Adam Smith already noted, leads to a heightened efficiency, discipline, and regularity being imposed upon the working masses. By "collectivization" Marx intends something more: the linking of individual labor to the collective and accumulated knowledge of mankind, to the point where "laboring society relates scientifically to the process of its progressive reproduction" (*Gr*, 325). With the development of modern industry, the accumulated scientific knowledge of mankind is implemented in the collective labor process (*Gr*, 705).

It remains unclear, however, why this new link between scientific knowledge and the economic production process should lead to a more socialist or democratic ownership of the means of production, and not merely to some form of continuation of the present system. And, indeed, a tension does appear in Marx's discussion of the superseding of capitalist property by socialism: at least two dominant but conflicting models have been pointed out in the literature.

Let us call the first model that of the "glorified proletariat," for it emphasizes the "historical mission" of the working class on the basis of its indispensable role in the economic production process. For Marx, industrial labor is here considered critical to the education of the worker. In accordance with Hegel's master–slave dialectic, the worker with time will acquire not only the techniques of mastery over external nature (he runs the machines, etc.), but over his own internal nature as well (he learns forbearance, discipline, new forms of association) (*Gr*, 325). Moreover, the inevitable "crises" of industrial capitalism make the recognition of labor variation, and hence fitness of the worker for numerous different kinds of tasks, a necessity. Developed capitalism itself already replaces the "partially developed individual, who is merely the bearer of one specialized social function . . . by the totally developed individual, for whom the different social functions are different modes of activity he takes up in turn" (*Gr*, 325). On this model of transformation, socialist revolution would appear nearly automatic. With time the parasitic upper crust, having progressively distanced itself from the critical economic production process and the new abilities developed therein, will be shrugged off, and the worker will emerge as the all-round "developed individual" and rightful owner of that which he in practice already operates and controls. That revolution in this manner has historically not come to pass speaks against such a theory, nor is the view very convincing when one considers another strand in Marx's writings.

This second strand, which I will call the model of the "wretched proletariat," is far subtler. It emphasizes the fact, repeatedly noted in both the *Grundrisse* and *Capital*, that in capitalist production it is not the worker who controls and directs the immediate appropriation process (unlike, say, the peasant or medieval craftsman). Rather, wage-labor is alienated not only from the product of labor, but also from the *capacity* to run the production process (*C* 1:60). Marx repeatedly speaks of the "de-skilling" that occurs with regard to the worker: "The accumulation of knowledge and of skill, of the general productive forces of the social brain, is thus absorbed into capital, as opposed to labor" (*Gr*, 684). The capitalist's *machine* now absorbs the discoveries of technology and science, while such knowledge and skill become alien to the worker. Capitalism's various methods for raising productivity in the end only "distort the worker into a fragment of a man, they degrade him. . . . [T]hey alienate from him the intellectual potentialities of the labor process in the same proportion as science is incorporated in it as independent power" (*C* 1:799). On this second reading, successful revolution appears impossible. The working class has been so degraded (which may lead it to revolt) that it has lost all knowledge and skill of the production process itself. There is here the possibility (to use a phrase from Habermas) that "men would make history with a will, but without consciousness," which was not in Marx's intentions either.[42]

The impasse reached in Marx's thought is irresolvable, however, *only* if he in fact reduces the notion of "appropriation" of productive means and forces to the strictly technical and economic: to a mastery over external, material nature, as on the production model. If this is the case, considering that this technical know-how is progressively being transferred to capital as machine, conscious and intelligent revolution on the part of the proletariat becomes impossible. A different result is reached, if we read Marx's theory of appropriation in the extended sense established earlier, whereby it refers to an appropriation of distinctive human "powers" or true "cultural appropriation" (4.2). Various rarely noted passages of the *Grundrisse* support the contention that for Marx, the proletariat will triumph not because it has superior technical knowledge (which it does not), but because it has developed of long necessity a form of nontechnical understanding in regard to the "combination of human activities" (*Gr*, 705). Marx writes, "The principle of developed capitalism is precisely to make special skill superfluous, and to make manual work, directly physical labor, generally superfluous both as skill and as muscular exertion: to transfer skill, rather, into the dead forces of nature" (*Gr*, 587).

Such passages point to the well-known Marxian thesis that with industrial capitalism the possibility of a general reduction of socially necessary labor time is given for the first time, allowing in turn the "free scientific and artistic development of the individuals in the time set free" (*Gr*, 706). But they also indicate something more. They point to a new set of capacities demanded of the modern individual, which are replacing older technical skills. With the growth of industry, direct physical labor and skill play an ever decreasing role; the human now "steps to the side of the production process rather than being its chief actor." Instead of inserting a "modified natural thing" as tool between himself and nature, he increasingly inserts simply his knowledge of the social process itself: "In this transformation, it is neither the direct human labor he performs, nor the time during which he works, but rather the appropriation of his own general productive power, his understanding of [internal and external] nature and his mastery over it by virtue of his presence as a social body [*sein Dasein als Gesellschaftskörper*] it is, in a word, the development of the social individual which appears as the great foundation-stone of production and wealth" (*Gr*, 705).

With the advance of industrial production, the nature of the capacities society requires of the individual changes. Rather than directly participating in the physical labor process, the human increasingly becomes "watchman" over it. Rather than aiming only to appropriate the external physical world, the need becomes one of appropriating the human's own powers—including the "combination of human activities and the development of human intercourse" (*Gr*, 705). The new capacities to which Marx points are decidedly *intersubjective* ones. And, we might add, the conception of "knowledge" based on the natural sciences begins to give way to that of "a science of man" (*Wissenschaft*).

My claim is that, particularly in the *Grundrisse*, Marx points to a form of labor that will become increasingly important in the future: what he refers to as "social labor." In contrast to the model of a technical appropriation of the physical world (progressively performed by machines), this new form of activity will be directed toward an understanding and appropriation of the social world and the "combination of human activities." (Rawls, we might note, expresses a similar position when he writes that, with the improvement of conditions of civilization [material and otherwise], a point is reached when the marginal significance of further technical and economic advantage diminish relative to man's interest in autonomy and "purposeful action" [*TJ*, 543].) In both cases, the material conditions of purposeful action are given, such that men can now begin not merely to live but to "live well": to perform actions for their own sake.

If the model of social labor for Marx is a form of *praxis* and has the end of the development of distinctive human capacities in all, then "progress" on this model will mean something quite different from what it means in present-day economics (whereby "economic progress" or "efficiency" means number of goods or services produced per hour). The idea of progress, when directed toward an understanding and furthering of human capabilities, will require the progressive ability to make "inner nature" transparent—human needs, desires, and capacities—as well as the ability to help realize human species-powers. In short, such activity develops the art of perceiving and respecting the person, referred to earlier (4.2). And on this alternative model of social labor—unlike on the technical-instrumental one—the very *aim* of exclusive, private acquisition becomes a counter-productive one.

If I am correct, Marx's important argument in the *Grundrisse* for both the need and the possibility of worker ownership and control of production means does not revolve (any more than in the early works) around the greater production of material things; the possibility of such greater material production is *already given* with modern industrial conditions. Rather, the argument centers on the possibility that this fact opens up for the first time: the possibility of using such productive means and economic organization as gauges of need and in the name of furthering universal values, such as autonomy and self-realization. For the first time, that is, productive means may now be *withdrawn* from society's incentive system and come to be employed instead as collective instruments for the development of distinctively human capacities in all. The conditions are given whereby Marx's "Copernican Revolution"—the awareness that we ourselves prescribe not only the laws of nature, but also (by prescribing the laws governing our social, political, and economic institutions) the formation of our own fundamental desires and capacities—becomes a realistic challenge of practice.

4.8 SOCIAL LABOR: MISSING FACULTIES

It is thus not some automatic economic or technical development that is to initiate socialism out of the death throes of capitalism, but the emergence of a required new form of "social labor" and activity. This collective and other-directed activity (to whatever degree) marks the new social individual, one who can regard other human beings as "the greatest wealth." And to the extent that this new form of social labor aims at autonomy and purposeful action *in others* (even if not personal friends), Marx begins to operate on a model of what we have been calling civic friendship. At the same time, however, Marx's conception of "social labor" is marked by sketchiness and ambiguity. Is his notion similar to our notions of ethical reproductive labor and *praxis* that aim in the best case at *philia*? And if it is, how is the new sense of solidarity (and the disposition of *philia* and care) to be developed and furthered, considering the solipsistic, self-directed individual that characterizes both employers and workers under developed capitalism in Marx's view?

We have struck a major weakness in Marxian theory. Marx's view is utopian not because he believes that an "other-directed" individual is possible, even on a wide scale (I shall argue that he or she is), but because it gives a wholly unrealistic and faulty account of how this transformation from capitalist to socialist individual is to come about. Nowhere is this clearer than in his magnum opus *Capital*. In *Capital*—in contrast to the novel notion of social labor hinted at in the *Grundrisse*—Marx falls back on an acquisitive, production model. The original Lockean metaphor of productively "mixing" one's efforts with a thing (whether working with bronze or soil, or laboring in the modern factory) as a paradigm of laboring activity retains a firm hold over Marx's thought, just as it continues to plague the thinking of most twentieth-century scholars' attempts to argue for economic democracy.[43]

Marx's account of the transition from capitalist to socialist ownership in *Capital* proceeds in very different terms from those in our sketch based on the *Grundrisse*. In *Capital*, the transition is described once again in "narrowly economic" terms. There the modern "joint-stock company" is seen as representative of a "transitional phrase" in the establishment of socialist "people's property" (*C* 2:103). People's property (explicitly distinguished from "state property" or a form drawing rent from, and offering wages to, the people) is one whereby productive means will be managed democratically by the "associated producers" themselves. The transition in *Capital* may be summarized roughly as follows.

In the joint-stock company (in contrast to earlier capitalist forms) the newly pooled capital and developing credit system afford the possibility of an enormous expansion in production (*C* 3:436). Further, such shared property entails the divorce of ownership from the direct management and control of the production process. In contrast to earlier family-run businesses, that is, modern shareholders emerge as simple "rentiers"; ownership is reduced to a portion of the surplus value produced, while management is relegated to a group of paid workers. Marx predicts that this tendency of divorcing ownership from control will lead in the future to greater worker-management; it will entail the "reconversion of capital into the property of producers, although no longer as the private property of the individual producers, but rather as the property of associated producers, as outright social property" (*C* 3:438).

Two questions must be raised in regard to this hopeful picture of the "reconversion" of capital and property into the self-managed association of producers. First, this process has (arguably) failed historically to come about. As numerous authors have noted, the modern corporation, far from being in any sense transitional, may even be considered the dominant form of capitalism itself.[44] Marx consistently confuses capital as a social relation with individual rights of private property; the latter may be near obsolete, but this tendency only indicates that the primary unit of possession of capital (and of productive means) is now no longer a private individual but a corporation. This shift in the "unit of possession," moreover, has by no means secured a return of worker control over production. On the contrary, most large companies today employ a self-replacing managerial elite. Similarly, Marx's identification of the joint-stock shareholder with the rentier owner of capital (a presumably ever more marginal class) directly counters the actual tendency of shares to be held increasingly, not by a declining group of individuals, but by a growing number of other major corporations and financial institutions (banks, insurance companies, pension funds, and so on). The transition from joint-stock company to a reconversion of capital into the self-managed association of producers is not only far from automatic, but appears to be the precise *reverse* of the actual historical tendency.[45]

So, too, the story may be questioned, not simply because its empirical predictions have failed to come about, but, more important, because of the absence of any adequate account of *how* the new "social labor" is to usher in a new "social property." In describing the future cooperative factory, for instance, Marx claims the "antithesis between labor and capital" will finally be overcome even if at first only "negatively"—that is, "only by way of making the associated labourers into their own capitalist, i.e., by enabling them to use the means of production for the employment of their own labour" (*C* 3:440). In contrast to the argument of the *Grundrisse*—where the growing recognition of the need for a new form of other-directed motivation or social labor initiates the first stage of socialist ownership—in *Capital* such ownership arises at first only "negatively": through a more universal realization by all of the acquisitive form. These two processes are hardly one and the same, however.

In the first, there exists a growing awareness that *praxis* and relations of collective purposeful action with others (and *their* autonomy, as well as my own) become my primary concern, at the same time as the private acquisitive motive in production is recognized as actually thwarting such concern. In the second, by contrast, the motive of private acquisition is developed and realized by all—to the point where all have been made into "their own capitalist." In his later writings, Marx simply assumes that once each has become his own capitalist—and shared physical control of the economic production process can be secured for all members of society—a concern with the questions of the autonomy of others, and the corresponding motivation, will follow automatically. But why? The questions is *how* such an altered, other-directed *caring* motivation toward others is meant to emerge once the private capitalist self is granted universal primacy in the realm of labor. To my knowledge, Marx nowhere deals with this question adequately; he simply assumes it will happen. At precisely the critical point in his thought, the question is obscured by the necessity of "violent revolution." The Marxist theory of the transition to socialism, however, thereby takes on the form of a mystical leap.

Clearly, insufficient consideration has been given to the origins and nature of this "social labor"; an ambiguity adheres to the very notion. For, even if in the future labor *with* and directed *toward* other human beings grows in importance—as with, say, the expanding service sector—such labor may well *continue to operate on an acquisitive production model.* My services for another, increasingly and of necessity demanding of me an "understanding of human associations," may still be performed primarily for the sake of the *product*: for no other motive than my own exclusive, private gain. (This has happened with many other-directed forms of labor, such as that of the doctor, lawyer or surrogate mother.) If this is the case, there is no reason to believe that—even with greater collective control over the means of production brought about by revolution plus a growing service economy—a free and other-directed "socialist individual" is in the making. If anything, the various experiments with socialism prove the opposite; all of them have been cursed by the notion of a *forced* social labor.

Once again, this is not to claim that a free democratic socialism is impossible, only that Marx (and much of the ensuing tradition) operates with an inadequate conception of social labor, especially considering the important role the notion plays in the argument for the future society. In *Capital,* social labor and production remain tied to the model of a now collective "mixing of one's labor" with external physical nature (as in a factory, say) and in the first instance still for individual gain. Marx is unable to break with Locke's original metaphor. In falling back on the production model (though now a collective one), the Marxian theory of the transition to socialism takes on aspects of the fantastic.

I believe we can now see that this fateful ambiguity in Marx's concept of "social labor" is tied to the fact that he also has no adequate account of *philia,* or friendship (personal or otherwise), nor of the emotional capacity for friendliness or care (*epimelia*), nor even of *praxis* separate from a model of production. Nowhere is there an account of how one might educate (or how new labor conditions might necessitate) emotional capacities of friendliness, much less transform them into stable dispositions under modern conditions. Stated somewhat differently, Marx lacks an awareness of our category of ethical reproductive labor or *praxis.* Finally, all these inadequacies are compounded by the fact that Marx and Engels (to a degree that even Aristotle did not) simply disregard both the quality and quantity of the truly "social labor" that women continue to perform in reproducing relations of *philia* outside the market and throughout the capitalist period. In sum, unlike Aristotle, Karl Marx did not recognize the extent to which life is not production, but also ethical *reproduction*—still today in the heart of advanced capitalism.

PART II

THE PRESENT

5 THE POSSIBILITY OF A MODERN CIVIC FRIENDSHIP

The delight of friendship does not consist in the discovery that there is a shilling for me in a stranger's money box.

IMMANUEL KANT

5.1 CONCEPTIONS OF STATE AND ECONOMY

How might it be possible to bring about today a far greater civic friendship between citizens, after nearly four hundred years of the dominance in both theory and practice of the production model of activity? This question will occupy us for the remainder of this book as we trace the problem through economic, legal, social and political, as well as international domains. In Part 1 we argued (*pace* Aristotle) that a minimal civic friendship remains a necessary precondition of genuine justice in any state, including in the large, complex modern nation-state, and despite its various historical transformations. So, too, we found nothing in the "nature" of the modern nation-state that necessarily blocks the possibility of such friendship, other than a strong focus on the activity of economic production (chapters 2 and 3). Finally, in chapter 4 we saw that Marx's socialist critique of liberal capitalism hardly displaces such a model of activity; in many ways it may even be said to strengthen it (4.8). Classical Marxist theory remains captivated by the ideology of production, and hence its vision of a future socialist society with a free democratic property takes on mythical proportions.

Nor do leading theorists of the twentieth century fare much better. Despite recognizing what we have been calling "the problem of community"—the problem of what it is that ultimately binds a just society together—the vast majority of leading political liberals, socialists, communitarians, conservatives, republicans, and even postmodernists have neglected to focus on ethical reproductive *praxis* or the political capacity for friendship. Even many twentieth-century feminists must here be included; for very different reasons, they continue to skirt the issue (7.2).

This chapter begins to flesh out what it might mean for friendship to "go public," as it were: for this value to be embedded—to a far greater extent—in contemporary society's basic institutional and social structure. We have argued that, contrary to many Marxists on the left and communitarians on the right, a doctrine of universal human rights is a necessary condition for the recognition of an impartial civic friendship in the diverse and pluralistic modern world (3.1). The *particular set* of individual economic, social, and political rights we have at present, however—primarily privileging male productive activity, according to my hypothesis—is clearly compatible with the grossest social and economic inequalities, as well as with a general neglect and even hostility between citizens themselves. Although a doctrine of individual rights is thus a *necessary* condition for an impartial civic friendship, clearly not just any doctrine will do. The moment of a *concrete practical concern*, of a reciprocal good will and duty embedded in our basic institutions and practices—as well as in the particular hearts and minds of citizens—must be present.

The central question thus becomes: How do we begin to reconceive our essential rights and duties in order now to include—even temporarily favor, considering its abandonment and neglect—ethical reproductive labor and *praxis*? This is no small undertaking, for it will entail also reconceiving the modern state from its foundations upward. How do we do this without simultaneously violating anyone's legitimate rights, without foisting our worldview unto others and restricting their rightful liberties? Once we acknowledge the fundamental importance of ethical reproductive activity—as well as more fully understand its nature—I believe half the battle is won. Taking care of people and their needs, and producing objects in order to satisfy those needs, are of equally critical value. Indeed, producing objects and services is presumably done for the satisfaction of those needs and not vice versa; the former, properly understood, are of only derivative value.

Once this is genuinely acknowledged, moreover, the various reasons given why the political state should protect and further the activity of production—and ignore that of ethical reproduction—begin to lose their validity. Despite all the advances of modern technology and of what many perceive as capitalism's historic role in the production of plenty, the continuation of this dominant model—of the citizen as producer in times of peace, backed by the soldier in less fortunate times—is leading us to little more than war and environmental destruction.

At the start of this book, we argued for the critical importance of the means by which we conceive of ourselves—of the reigning models and metaphors we use in self-reflection—for they not only frame the type of questions we ask, but also limit the possibilities of the kind of actions we undertake (1.3). Surely, one difficulty in conceiving of a viable modern civic friendship lies simply in the manner in which we continue to view the modern person and "his" characteristic activity, but the modern political state and its economy as well. This modern liberal state (whatever else it is) is still centrally organized around production. It is characteristically conceived as the legitimate use of the monopoly of force (Weber) with penalties of death (at least in the United States) for the purposes of maintaining law and order, a military prepared for war, and with the central goal of policing citizens' productive competition. This same liberal model, until recently at least, not only labeled women's historical activities in the home and neighborhood as "unproductive," but is now, I believe, nearing the end of its rope.

Recall the two different senses of the term *state* distinguished earlier (1.4). On the one hand, the political state in the narrow sense (from which women were traditionally excluded) refers to the legitimate monopoly of organized force qua its formal organization—whether the state is a democracy, monarchy, or oligarchy, as determined by its political constitution and explicit laws. What we called (with Hegel) the "state proper," on the other hand, encompasses the previous sense but includes as well the everyday customs, manners, and moral consciousness of a people historically united in a tradition. From this second and larger perspective, the narrowly political state is viewed as the legal articulation or the formal expression of a people's prior ethical practices. We noted as well that this Hegelian idea has again come into prominence in the writings of various contemporary political philosophers (such as Rawls and Dworkin), for it allows thinkers to plumb anew the genuine moral principles underlying our political tradition. So too, it allows us here to investigate those background moral principles and values embodied in ethical reproductive *praxis,* which have as yet found little reflection in modern conceptions of the political state. The idea of the state proper affords us the theoretical opportunity to rectify the lacuna of women and their traditional activities in our conceptions of the political state narrowly conceived. For, the fact remains that women are finally entering our public state and economic institutions *en masse* (and not merely one by one in isolated fashion), and this opens up the practical possibility that their traditional forms of laboring activity and accompanying modes of thought can provide a reservoir of alternative moral principles with which to confront—as well as help to transform—the modern political state in the narrow sense. In this manner, the modern women's movement (the movement beginning at least with the mid-twentieth century) affords the possibility of a major transformation of state and economy in both theory and practice.

Stated somewhat differently, if women's historical activities of attending to others are actually a form of Aristotelian *praxis* (2.5), and if such activity in the ideal case aims at *philia* for its own sake, then we have before us the unique opportunity of explicitly reintroducing the issue of friendship into political life. Indeed, I believe we now have the elements of an alternative model not only of the state, but of the citizen's characteristic practical activity, one that may compete successfully with both the ancient warrior type and the liberal economic production model that has dominated in recent centuries. Women, after all, make up over half the population, and the vast majority of women share a thorough training in ethical reproductive labor and *praxis* (1.3). In sum, by reflection on the mass movement of women into the public spheres, we may glean elements of a genuinely new conception of both state and the economy—including citizenship.

As one illustration, let us consider further the notion of care that is central to traditional women's work, pivotal to all friendship, and that is much under discussion at the moment. We defined *care* as that intelligent and emotionally competent activity which not only aims at the concrete and general good of a person (or object or thing), but actively seeks to bring that good about (4.6). I also argued that nothing in this definition requires that the activity of care be pure altruism or self-sacrifice; on the contrary, such activity may be highly rewarding personally, done for its own sake as well as reciprocally. In fact, care is often highly rewarding at times when it is reciprocal. The claim that a fundamental aim of the modern state might be to secure and to encourage a "greater care among citizens," however, strikes most thinkers as alien, if not repugnant. I believe the claim unnerves us still today for at least three reasons.

First, all talk of the state "caring" for its citizens, or protecting and encouraging practices of care among them, smacks of a feudal-like *paternalism*. The king was said to *care* for his subjects, the lord for his serfs, the slave owner for his slaves. Historically, relationships of *carer* and *cared for* have all too often played themselves out between *unequals*. The principle of care that I wish to introduce as part of a larger conception of civic friendship, however, is to be conceived as a *political* principle. It will be applied to universally free and equal democratic citizens, and its basis rests in the acknowledgment of the fundamental common interest all persons have in friendship: in minimally caring and being cared for. There is nothing in the nature of such caring, after all, that necessarily subordinates the giver or receiver, whatever historically may have been the case. Thus, much like freedom or equality, the value of care might become part of a political construct developed within the context of a modern participatory democracy. So, too, as we have seen, the care of *philia*, or friendship, is not just any caring for another, and it is certainly not a smothering, oppressive paternalistic (or maternalistic) one. Conceived as a political principle in the modern period, it will be a form of *philia*, which fundamentally aims at the equality and greater autonomy of the other (2.5; see also 7.2).

Second, critics often object that care is a principle derived from certain everyday practices between intimate family members or between close personal friends; it is inappropriate to extrapolate what is suitable for such private contexts to the public, state level. But, again, we must ask why. Here it is critical to stress that probably all our economic or political principles can be shown to derive originally from some private or particular concrete context. The principle of "efficiency," for instance, surely first applied to specific practices (e.g., the making of a particular pair of shoes) and then was generalized and applied to larger institutional domains (where it even comes to mean "Pareto Optimality"). Why should the term *care* or *friendship* not be allowed this more developed and generalized extension also?

Because care is first and foremost a private feeling, many will say. Its generalization to many instances or to institutions will dilute and destroy it (much like adding water to wine) or simply transform the emotion beyond recognition into something else. I find this common response to be fully mistaken. First of all, care is not a mere "subjective feeling." As we have seen, it is also an "objective activity" or practice; one may actively care for someone for months, for example (4.6). Emphasizing this point distinguishes our position from all those who would advocate a greater citizen sympathy or compassion or fellow-feeling, but one not grounded in particular forms of labor or anchored in specific social institutions. Of course, care is *also* a feeling, but so too are hate, distrust, and fear, and yet Hobbes meaningfully spoke of a generalized state of fear and mistrust: he called it a "state of war." Surely, it cannot be the case that only negative, hostile feelings and actions may legitimately "go public."

Again, my critic will respond that it is a question not of legitimacy, but of *possibility*. Hate quite easily and naturally generalizes, while love does not. The latter's natural home is in relations of personal intimacy. But is this true? My suspicion is that it is false. Not only do most murders (and batterings, and so on) occur among "intimates," but so, too, persisting activities of hate, prejudice, or indifference appear to need reinforcement and habituation (even institutionalization), as much as care or love. I recall a veterinarian once telling me of her observations regarding new slaughterhouse workers on their first day of the job. The young men were horrified, paralyzed at first and tears came to their eyes at witnessing the treatment and death of the animals. Of course, the older workers laughed at the neophytes, cajoled them, and whipped them into shape by words, and it was not long before the general house practice became acceptable to those who remained. What if such pointed training were exercised in the opposite direction, say, *against* the killing of cows or pigs? We already know the answer; in India the cow has long been revered as sacred, and in many areas could wander the streets untouched despite a starving populace.

I believe the central mistake here of critics is to confuse the necessary concreteness of care with its necessarily being *personal*. In order adequately to care for someone (or something), one must take that other's concrete attributes and situation into account; but one need not thereby have a *personal* relationship with them. The example of the professional nurse comes to mind (say, treating a patient in a coma), as well as all those activities we perform for perfect strangers (from giving them the correct time or proper directions, to fighting for their rights and liberties), or those institutions through which we respect others, help them in troubled times, etc. The critical point is that to persist in seeing others in this "friendly" way requires training, repetition, and above all, public reinforcement.

It is true that the principle of care, or *philia*, originating in the household and sphere of close personal relations, will need (much like concepts of trust, equality, liberty, and so forth) adjustment and refinement as it is broadened to the democratic political domain and embodied in institutions (compare 7.2–5). Nonetheless, we are still speaking of *care*: of a political form, as it were, which now applies to the basic institutions of our society. At issue is the creation of a background general concern and good will between citizens, which works through a society's constitution, a doctrine of individual right, and public standards of acceptable civic behavior. Such general activity may well express the essential characteristics of all care: heightened awareness of fellow citizens, a competence in understanding their good, and a willingness to bring that good about. Although interpretations of an adequate "public care" will undoubtedly be controversial (7.4), this counts for little as an objection; conceptions of political efficiency, freedom, equality or justice are also topics of endless political debate.

I believe the real reason we still today feel so uncomfortable in speaking of care or *philia* in public contexts is that both have been indelibly stamped in the modern period (given its division of productive and reproductive labor) with private *female* activity, contrasting too sharply with the traditional masculine sphere of the public state. And yet, recall, this rigid, gendered division between productive (male) and reproductive (female) labor has only rather recently been the case. Aristotle uses the term *care* (*epimeleia*) in a political context throughout his ethical and political works, and the German notion of duty (*pflicht*) originally meant simply "to care" (2.7 and 4.6).

The claim that a political care or friendship is too much to demand of the modern citizen must await, I believe, details of a particular political conception of care; an outright rejection hardly does the work that libertarians and other advocates of extreme liberty maintain (we return to this point in 7.5). For the moment, it is enough to note that the prevalence of care, benevolence, and friendship talk in ancient and medieval thinkers (not to mention in other cultures) speaks against one recent criticism of care ethics made by some feminist thinkers themselves: that feminist appeals to care are nothing but the desperate expressions of the continued subordinate position of women under patriarchy. That so many ancient philosophers, including Aristotle—white, male, and from the upper classes—actually acknowledge the central political importance of care surely suggests to the contrary that *all* persons, even those in their prime and in prime social positions, need to give and receive such care if their lives are to flourish. This being the case, the real feminist concern should be not to deny the importance of all caring activity (or women's historical role in it), but to analyze and elaborate the notion further, to rectify the vast injustices in the distribution of its benefits and burdens, as well as to recognize the limits of the concept itself (chapter 7).

It thus emerges as a deep prejudice of our modern culture that we are so embarrassed by all talk of care and friendship in political contexts. Finally, it is simply high time for women to demand that the modern political state, including the type of economic labor it officially acknowledges, be as much a reflection of *their* historical activities as of any traditional male pursuit (such as production or war). For what is government itself in the end—as James Madison wrote—but the greatest of all reflections on human nature? The question now becomes how to elaborate this public political conception of friendship, together with its subcategory care.

5.2 RAWLS'S PRINCIPLE OF FRATERNITY

One good starting point for understanding what we shall call the modern historical turn toward the recognition of the political value of friendship is to take another look at undoubtedly one of the greatest political theories of the twentieth century: that of John Rawls. Significantly enough, in *A Theory of Justice* Rawls considers his famous difference principle as providing a political "interpretation of the principle of fraternity" (*TJ*, 105). Although I will argue that Rawls's theory ultimately remains tied to an acquisitive conception of productive labor—and hence the criticisms that his other-directed difference principle is "unrealistic" and "unworkable" have a certain truth to them—the mistakes of Rawls's project are illuminating. So too, the hard-won insights of his theory should not be forgotten—least of all by feminists.

According to Rawls, the value of fraternity (in contrast to that of liberty or equality) has generally held a "lesser place in democratic theory." Fraternity has either been conceived as a mere attitude of mind (one that in general respects rights, say) or as a vague sense of social solidarity and friendship; on either reading it expresses "no definite requirement" politically (*TJ*, 105). To make up for this failing, Rawls argues for his difference principle, a political principle he feels corresponds to "a natural meaning" of fraternity, that is, "to the idea of not wanting to have greater advantages unless this is to the benefit of others who are less well off. The family, in its ideal conception and often in practice, is one place where the principle of maximizing the sum of advantages is rejected. Members of a family commonly do not wish to gain unless they can do so in ways that further the interests of the rest" (*TJ*, 105).

Let us contemplate this thought for a moment. Rawls's idea embodies an important aspect of family, but also of friendship: that of wanting "to bring the other along," as it were, to raise them up, and *for their sake* and not one's own (2.6). Translated into a political principle, this insight has a number of corollaries: I do not want special or unfair advantages in society at the expense of others whom I consider my moral and political equals; I wish these others well (I not only do *not* want to exploit them, but I actually wish for them to flourish); I must in any event be aware of them and to a certain extent of their particular needs, and so on. Finally—at least once this political principle becomes embodied in institutions (and the collective action problem solved)—I can expect the same from my fellow citizens as well.

In Rawls's theory, this principle of everyday life translates into the political injunction that government must see to it that differences in the basic structure (the distribution of benefits and burdens and the social primary goods) generally work to the benefit of the whole group (including the worst off): no one may be left behind. For Rawls, that is, there is no natural (contextless) notion of individual "desert"—the latter is defined in the final analysis by the reasonable democratic community at large. One group of citizens deserves more than others, politically speaking, if that group serves and benefits the community as a whole (including the worst off), and not for any other reason. Implementing the difference principle becomes the duty of democratic government, and it imposes a "definite requirement" on the basic structure of society; any gains or differences in social primary goods are conditional on (and must systematically work toward) bettering the position of the worst off. No representative individual may be left behind. Together with his first principle of liberty and the idea of fair equality of opportunity, the difference principle completes Rawls's political interpretation of the democratic ideals of "liberty, equality and fraternity" (*TJ*, 106).

Significantly, Rawls gives only cursory attention to *why* this principle of fraternity is of such prime importance for his theory. Rather than friendship being a condition for genuine justice—as in our view—Rawls presents his principle as a solution to the modern conflict between the values of freedom and of equality (*TJ*, 106). That is, methodologically, the difference principle is derived via the construction of an original position where the primary motive of the parties (beyond that of wishing to secure justice in the first place) is the maximization of their self-interest behind the veil of ignorance (that is, without recourse to knowledge of particulars such as class, race, gender, and so on) (*TJ*, 175–82). I believe this indirect grounding of the principle of fraternity in "justice as fairness"—that is, rather than directly positing a capacity for friendship in the parties or a "third" moral power in all of us (3.5)—is one reason why critics have found the motivation for Rawls's difference principle to be rather weak and "unrealistic"; the difference principle at least appears to emerge from the motive of self-interest plus the veil of ignorance, and as one result only. Again, if one begins from the assumption of rational self-interest (even adding the veil of ignorance and a desire for justice), it is difficult to arrive at any notion of friendship that is not instrumental—much less at a widespread political or civic friendship as we have defined it. Helping others for their own sake, in this case, strikes many as supererogatory and hardly as a necessary requirement of justice.

To make matters worse, in Rawls's later works, rather than clarifying and elaborating his position in *A Theory of Justice* (say, by showing that a realistic desire for justice and entry into the original position already presupposes a third moral power for friendship), discussions of the difference principle rarely make an appearance. Rawls neither develops this principle of fraternity further, nor does he ground it or defend it more fully, and he even claims that the difference principle (as an economic principle) should not be written into a society's constitution.[1] Nonetheless, despite all these theoretical inadequacies, America's leading liberal theorist has made the turn toward a modern conception of political friendship, and therein surely lies a part of the greatness of Rawls's theory.

Beyond assuming (but never explicitly acknowledging) a capacity for friendship in the political person, Rawls's difference principle suffers from two further problems. First, an indeterminacy or fundamental ambiguity lies at its heart. Second, the principle continues to presuppose a productive model of labor and thus (as for Marx, see 4.4–8) the *other-directed motivation* required to realize the principle remains mysterious. I believe these two problems have contributed to the widespread belief that Rawls's difference principle is unworkable, impractical, and unrealistic. However, the criticism that the difference principle ultimately goes "against human nature" is not one that I am upholding here. Quite to the contrary, if one begins (as we have done) from a model of ethical reproductive labor and *praxis* (routinely performed by at least half of the population), the other-directed motivation for the difference principle appears to follow naturally.

Let us imagine for a moment that we place only traditional *women* in Rawls's original position (leaving aside all those who perform the productive labor, much as Rawls de facto leaves aside all those performing reproductive work). I believe the likelihood that the difference principle would be chosen is now high indeed—a version of it may even be chosen prior to the principle of liberty. That is, if parties to the original position were first thoroughly trained in ethical reproductive activity and care, and if such parties were to choose basic principles of justice from behind the veil of ignorance, these parties would likely make certain that all persons were minimally and equally cared for (including the caretakers themselves) before all else. Why? Because this is the goal and aim of their traditional activity (much as the production and accumulation of goods is the aim of productive labor). In such an alternative hypothetical case, always behind the veil of ignorance, the greater liberties granted some representative persons may even be viewed as conditional on the prior and more important satisfaction of the basic needs of the group as a whole (including of the worst off). In this manner, not only would it be highly *likely* that a form of the difference principle—which allows some to possess more only on condition that they benefit the group as a whole—be chosen, but the priority of Rawls's two principles might well be reversed. I will not pursue this line of thought here, however. It is enough, for the moment, to take a closer look at Rawls's principle itself.

5.3 THE INDETERMINACY OF THE DIFFERENCE PRINCIPLE

Rawls's difference principle is fundamentally a social and economic principle, which is meant to operate as a directive of government; it is to be implemented by the various "branches" or functions of government (*TJ*, sec. 43). A central problem, however, is that it is not always clear what the difference principle is meant to be a directive *to*. The difference principle explicitly states that once the principles of liberty and fair equality of opportunity are satisfied, any institutional social and economic inequalities in society must be so arranged as to be "to the greatest benefit of the least advantaged members of society" (*TJ*, 75–80). The index of benefit is made in terms of a list of primary social goods: those all-purpose, institutional means (or features of social institutions) necessary for rationally pursuing a conception of the good.[2] As is well known, this list includes a rather diverse set of goods: basic liberties, free choice of occupation, powers and prerogatives of office, wealth and income, and finally, the social basis of self-respect.

Elsewhere, I have argued that, depending on which social primary good one focuses upon, both the quality and the degree of inequalities that the difference principle allows will differ. Indeed, the principle appears to allow incompatible directives.[3] That is, beneath the surface of the difference principle, two quite different conceptions of the self and ownership operate. (This ambiguity also accounts for widely opposed evaluations of Rawls's theory.) For instance, if one focuses primarily on the social primary good of income and wealth (as many Marxists are wont to do), Rawls's difference principle appears unduly concerned with private material benefit to the exclusion of such values as community, self-realization, meaningful work, and so forth. For those such as A. Esheté or G. A. Cohen, Rawls's talk of fraternity remains "ideological."[4] It assuages the consciences of the capitalist rich insofar as it proclaims that differences in income and wealth (including hierarchical control and private ownership of the major means of production) are justified to the extent that the poor are "better off" in monetary terms (although they may be "worse off" by any other measure).

Such a reading also emphasizes in Rawls's thought a Lockean acquisitive conception of the self (3.4). On this model, the urge for material appropriation is viewed as fundamental in motivating productive acts of the individual (and in the extreme case, the self's growth and fulfillment is viewed as a private acquisition). Social institutions and relations, in turn, are little more than a means to the individual's private (competing or at least independent) ends. This reading of Rawls's difference principle, which stresses the acquisitive self and the most minimal moral duties required by fraternity, I call the "weak interpretation." Political fraternity might here be satisfied, say, by some "trickle down" effect of Reagan economics.

Now, it is true that the acquisitive self operates in Rawls's theory to the extent that the proper distribution of shares is viewed, significantly, as an *incentive* system (*TJ*, 126). We find, for instance, to the shock and dismay of many (e.g., Sandel), that in a just distribution individuals are rewarded by income and the good things in life not according to their "moral worth" (which for Rawls is an impractical notion for political purposes and would be rejected in the original position), but in order to direct abilities to where they are needed most: to encourage learning, cover costs of training, and so on (*TJ*, 315). From the standpoint of distributive justice, the individual receives only "his due" or entitlement; his legitimate expectations—those thrown up and encouraged by the existing social arrangements—must be satisfied. Thus, Rawls does view the just distribution of shares as a scheme of private incentives, taxes, and burdens, guiding men's actions hither and thither to the mutual advantage of all. And, notably, among the constituents of exchangeable wealth, he includes scarce natural resources, means of production, and the rights to control them.[5]

Rawls's difference principle, however, has also been interpreted—and rightly so, I believe—as drawing attention to the responsible aspects of ownership to a degree rarely seen in the liberal tradition. According to the principle, after all, unequal ownership of property is conditional on benefiting the group as a whole—and not only as my having more helps "preserve" others in minimal material existence (as in Locke, say), but to the extent that my greater share actually raises the social basis of their self-respect in the long run (SU, 363–64). Rawls explicitly claims that the social basis of self-respect is the "most important" of the social primary goods (*TJ*, 440). This "strong" reading of the difference principle, moreover, pushes Rawls toward the socialist camp. It proclaims a far weightier civic duty toward others insofar as it points to our role and responsibilities in the social basis of their self-respect. Of course, this emphasis on responsibility—what I am calling the responsible aspect of ownership—many find oppressive in Rawls's thought. It is perceived as a threat to our legitimate individual freedom.[6]

The strong reading of Rawls's difference principle clearly presupposes what we earlier called a "moral, purposeful" conception of the self (3.4): a conception of the self going back at least to Aristotle and more fully elaborated in the modern period by the German Idealist tradition.[7] In contrast to the acquisitive self's simple motivation of private gain, the moral purposeful conception includes the importance of a self-conception or "plan of life" embodied in a recognizably public realm. The individual's nature is here viewed as a function of the aspirations and goals it adopts and seeks to actualize, and its freedom and satisfaction are seen to lie in bringing its distinctively human capacities to fruition and its goals into harmony with those of others. This second model of the person stresses not private consumption, but shared final ends and our responsibilities—our abilities to respond—to others. Unlike the acquisitive model, this model views the self as dependent not merely on coordinated, minimally cooperative activity of others, but on the good of reciprocity and the necessity of positive social ties—what Rawls calls "social union"—both in the bolstering of its self-respect and in the development and exercise of its highest capacities.

Indeed, as we noted earlier, Rawls is well aware that an individual's "due" or "entitlement" is not something given once and for all, but a derivative product of the prior form of social, political, and economic cooperation. To this extent, Rawls's theory has incorporated the socialist insight that the rightful "fruit of labor" will be determined and circumscribed by the background conditions (the economic and social rules) of the type of labor to begin with (4.7). Rawls fully recognizes the influence of the basic structure (a common achievement) on human wants and aspirations, and the influence of the economic system on the "kind of persons" men will be (*TJ*, 259). Hence, to the degree these background conditions become the subject of deliberate activity and construction (which they must, if the principles of justice are to be realized), the difference principle necessarily presupposes a purposeful conception of the self. Rather than emphasizing private acquisition (and the primary good of income and wealth), this conception stresses *action ascribed to us* in a social context, as well as the social basis of individual self-respect. Finally, ownership or property on this conception is not viewed so much as a private incentive to labor but rather, more appropriately, as a necessary background condition (typically shared) for the exercise of highest order interests.[8]

The crucial point for us here is that depending on the extent to which one invokes one primary social good over another (and the underlying acquisitive or purposeful model of the person), both the nature and the degree of social and economic inequality Rawls's difference principle allows will vary. The acquisitive model affords a far greater *qualitative* (practical or functional) inequality in society, for example, because only the most rudimentary needs of the least advantaged have to be provided for. The difference principle (on the weak interpretation) is satisfied when the worst off gain the greatest feasible measure of income and wealth. On the purposeful model, by contrast, the imperative to such equality is far more urgent. Since "benefit" is interpreted ultimately in terms of the social basis of self-respect, the worst off must participate in the major social and political institutions for the development of their capacities. The strong interpretation demands, at the very least, that a growing portion of tax revenues be devoted to job training and self-management of the disadvantaged, in contrast to simple welfare payments.

Similarly, on the acquisitive model income differentials serve as major incentives for individuals to achieve certain skills and accept responsibilities (*TJ*, 151). It can thus justify significant degrees of quantitative income inequality in the name of motivating economic progress. On the purposeful model, however, the added incentive of higher income diminishes in importance relative to the satisfaction of the Aristotelian Principle as a principle of motivation; human beings can be powerfully motivated by the exercise of their innate or trained abilities purely "for their own sake."[9] Economic "progress" may here proceed with a far lower degree of income inequality.

Thus, two different conceptions of self and ownership operate beneath the surface of Rawls's difference principle, and they lead to incompatible interpretations of permissible inequalities. This is not to claim that Rawls's theory is simply confused or hopeless, however. In the tension between the two conceptions one perceives the movement or direction of his thought itself. Of the two conceptions, that is, the latter, or purposeful self, is clearly superior *from Rawls's own perspective*. This is obvious not only from his critique of the utilitarian "consumer person," while emphasizing his own view as "Kantian," but also from his repeated proclamations that as conditions of civilization improve, the marginal significance of further economic advantages diminishes relative to our interests in autonomy and purposeful action. Men at some point "come to aspire to some control over the laws and rules that regulate their association" (*TJ*, 543). The general thrust of Rawls's famous principle of fraternity is to encourage the political transformation of a society from private acquisitive individuals into moral purposeful ones, not through fear and punishment but through a carefully constructed system of positive incentives.

If this is the case, however, we return to our earlier question (4.3) of why Rawls does not think we can assume the moral purposeful self *in the realm of labor*. One would think that at least the long-term tendency of Rawls's difference principle would be to extend social union into the economic sphere. Why does Rawls not want to encourage the moral purposeful self in the laboring realm also, and extend shared ends and participatory control over the laws regulating the workplace and economy?

Of course, Rawls does not feel that all socialist arrangements are necessarily incompatible with his own theory, and he does consider the possibility of a free form of socialist ownership. In *A Theory of Justice* he distinguishes between the "allocative" and "distributive" function of market prices (*TJ*, 273). The former (allocative function) is connected with the use of competitive markets and prices to achieve economic efficiency, while the latter (distributive function) relates to their employment for the purposes of determining wealth, income, or power received by individuals. It is perfectly consistent, Rawls argues, for a democratic socialist regime (where the major means of production and natural resources are publicly owned) to make use of the allocative function of prices, as indicators for an efficient schedule of economic activities, while restricting their distributive role. Democratically reached decisions, for instance, could set the optimal scale of production, establish an interest rate allocating resources among different investment projects, and determine rental charges to various associations for the use of capital and scarce natural assets, such as land and forests.

In such an event, there need be no private persons to whom, as owners of these assets, the monetary equivalents for these evaluations accrue (and hence private capitalist profit making no longer functions as a motivational force in production). Rather, the net rental income imputed to natural and collective assets accrues to the larger enterprise, community, or state, while that which pertains to particular individuals is determined by decision on other grounds: for instance, by the demand price of labor consistent with social expectations (of health care, welfare or ecological considerations, and so forth). Prices here have a restricted distributive function, and the extent of the market is clearly limited. The distinction between allocative and distributive price functions allows us to conceive of restricted competition as a good *between associations,* without viewing it as necessarily detrimental to what J. S. Mill called the "noble idea of co-operation" between individual workers and citizens themselves. The concern of many that the positive effects of competition will inevitably be lost in a socialist society might thus be overcome by a form of "market socialism," of which, as Rawls notes, there are a wide range of intermediate forms.[10]

But, again, although Rawls notes the compatibility of market socialist arrangements with his own theory, he does not require a form of economic democracy for the realization of his two principles of justice. Why? His official view is that the historic question of private property versus socialist democracy cannot be determined "in advance"; the issue depends ultimately "on the traditions, institutions, and social forces of each country, and its particular historical circumstances" (*TJ*, 274). That is, for Rawls, the question of the superiority of private property to socialist property remains an *empirical* question.

As I shall show, the property question for Rawls hardly remains only an empirical question, but emerges as a conceptual one as well. Rawls remains captive to one of the most pervasive dogmas of liberal economics: the private production model of labor. As noted earlier, among his list of social unions all mention of the work relation or firm is conspicuously absent (4.3). Even more important, Rawls draws up the very idea of social union in explicit contrast to private society, whose "natural home" is the economic sphere; in private society human relations remain instrumental. Although the moral purposeful self is clearly viewed as morally superior in Rawls's view, when it comes to the realm of economic labor, the acquisitive self seems to retain primacy. Apparently, Rawls is unable to conceive of a realistic form of free and uncoerced laboring activity where the primary motivation does not remain private personal gain.

That the acquisitive, productive model of labor remains central to Rawls's theory can also be seen by the fact that he views part 3 of *A Theory of Justice* as an attempt to demonstrate that the principles chosen in the original position are "compatible with our human nature" (*TJ*, 580). Nothing can be demanded as a matter of justice if it is in general beyond our capacities as human beings. That social union and self-government in the economic sphere are not a *requirement* of justice must mean that Rawls remains uncertain as to whether they could ever be achieved without too great a sacrifice—for instance, sacrifice of freedom or efficiency in production (*TJ*, 272). Again, although the purposeful self is clearly morally superior, Rawls remains skeptical that a majority of members in a modern industrial society—when it comes to questions of labor motivation—could ever accurately be so described. And, on the surface at least, Rawls has reason to be skeptical. The nineteenth-century predictions of a Marx or Mill in regard to a free and uncoerced social union in the economic sphere have hardly come to pass, whether in capitalist or state socialist societies. On the contrary, capitalist private property systems appear to be triumphing everywhere.

5.4 AN ALTERNATIVE MODEL OF SOCIAL LABOR

Rawls's skepticism remains reasonable to the degree that there exists at present at least one major "tradition, institution and social force" that his theory has not taken into account. This "social force" is the large-scale movement of women into the labor market over the last one hundred years or so. A careful analysis of women's traditional ethical reproductive labor as, among other things, caretakers, friends, and reproducers of children, family life, and neighborhood presents us, I argue, with a *third* model of labor and ownership. Moreover, when the implications of this third model of genuinely "social labor" are taken into account, the strong reading of Rawls's difference principle, which requires social union in the economic sphere, emerges as fully "compatible with our nature." It could now even be demanded as a matter of justice (5.6). Simultaneously, the issue of a realistic motivation in transitions from late capitalist to democratic and socialist ownership forms begins to gain plausibility (4.7)

Ethical reproductive labor, recall, is to be distinguished, not only from (individual or collective) productive labor, but also from ethical reproductive *praxis,* as elaborated earlier (2.5). *Praxis* is that form of action done purely for its own sake. Reproductive *labor,* by contrast, will be that form where the laborer is concerned with the other's good, takes care of them, furthers their abilities, and so on, but the burdens for the self in such caretaking may be great. Ethical reproductive *labor* (unlike *praxis*) requires outside reinforcement, whether by way of a wage (as in paid day care, nursing, etc.) or through the traditionally praised and valued status of wife and mother (as in the case of much unpaid child and family care).

I am not claiming that this reproductive model of social labor should displace all other forms of laboring activity. My claim is rather that this form must be recognized *as labor,* its nature better understood and its importance and value acknowledged at the level of the political state. So too, this activity offers a *third* critical model of individual citizen motivation and activity, to be contrasted with the two reigning liberal conceptions of political personhood discussed earlier: the acquisitive model, on the one hand, and the moral purposeful conception, on the other (3.4 and 5.3). In revealing how many persons de facto still operate on an ethical reproductive model—not only most women, but many people in nonmarket societies of the Third World—a *motivational antipode* to the acquisitive self is established. This third motivational model not only throws greater weight behind Rawls's purposeful conception of the person—even now in the realm of labor (5.6)—but also exposes the primacy of the acquisitive *Homo economicus* for what it is: a largely ideological, longstanding (powerful) myth. "Economic man" is not only a creation and fixation of our capitalist ideologies (of our economic departments, business schools and financial institutions), but as various studies have shown, the myth tends to bring about precisely what it projects; it justifies much greed and private plunder. Many other types of laboring activity continue to operate in the background of both local and global economies; it is time these are brought to the fore.

Earlier we noted that the paradigm of the production model (Locke's mixing metaphor) presupposes an individual subject who confronts and labors upon a physical thing (1.2). We saw that the metaphor easily accommodates artisan work, individual farm labor, and industrial labor (as in a factory): all these types of labor share the form of being an appropriation (a making one's own) of the material, physical world. In the modern period, further, where commodity production is viewed as the norm, such individual labor ushers in a legitimate private right to the object produced (or at least to some presumed private equivalent). In Locke, such private possession is justified by the natural law proclamation that the individual's own need be satisfied. The individual is justified in accumulating more than he needs if (1) his greater share improves the lot of others (or at least does not worsen it) or (2) in a variation such as Nozick's theory, if the greater accumulation is the result of a series of legitimate contracts (3.2). Critical to this making and taking model, moreover, is the assumption that the primary motive of labor is exclusive ownership, and it thus presupposes an acquisitive conception of the self. In turn, private property rights are viewed as a major incentive to labor, an assumption that remains crucial still to Rawls's theory, as we have just seen (5.3). Finally, even Marx continues to conceive labor on this production model in the first stages of the transition to socialism, although it is now conceived as a "collective mixing" of the joint labor of workers in a factory (4.8).

A major theme of this work is that this dominant model of labor as an appropriation of the physical world has blinded us to a form of activity that is at least as fundamental. Socialists have long argued that the Lockean model abstracts from the "social nature" of the labor process. All labor, even that performed in isolation, presupposes a prior cultural formation—an exchange of language, abilities, and patterns of interaction—as a backdrop against which the individual develops his aims and realizes his intentions in the first place.[11] The conception of labor I develop here, however, goes one step further. Ethical reproductive labor is not only indirectly but *directly* social and interactive. Its aim is the direct fulfillment of human need and the furtherance of another's abilities.

In elaborating this category, I focus on the realm in which women have for centuries been "mixing their labor" and effort: the realm of childcare. I do so because childcare is a particularly "thick" instance of ethical reproductive labor. At the same time I recognize that men have always, to varying degrees, performed such labor, and that women of differing classes and ethnicities have also been farmers and producers, tillers of the soil or artisans, and so forth. Here I am assuming only one anthropological "fact of difference" between women and men: that in the known societies both past and present, and with only rare exceptions, *men as a group* have not been the primary caretakers of young children.[12] This form of ethical reproductive labor has traditionally been women's lot, and (we may assume) it has surely had a formative influence on her distinctive social role and public personality. Even those women who never had (or wanted) children are characteristically prepared for this role in early life.

So, too, I emphasize that while childcare may be a particularly "thick" instance of reproductive activity, it is hardly the only form. Tending to other family members, to the old or sick or wounded, even caring for those in their prime (as in love, teaching, artistic performances, and so forth) are all forms of ethical reproductive labor. (For this reason I reject the term *dependency labor,* used by some feminists, as unnecessarily restrictive.)[13] I even include tending to the feathered and wild—whether farm animals or birds and beasts of the woods, including the care of streams and forests themselves (8.4). In short, I include all those reproductive activities which aim at the good of the other *for that other's own sake,* whether the "other" is animal, vegetable, or mineral.[14] Thus, tending and ministering activities, the fight against poverty and injustice, good teaching, many artistic endeavors, the work for animal welfare and environmental concerns, all are properly considered instances of ethical "reproductive" (rather than productive) labor. To the extent that such activities become ends in themselves, ethical reproductive labor gives way to *praxis* (2.4).

Finally, as noted already in chapter 1, in elaborating this new metaphor of traditional woman "mixing her labor," I am well aware that

I am performing a selective "abstraction" (1.3). The metaphor is the tip of a submerged model and it is "ahistorical" to the degree that it pertains in particular to the strict division of gendered labor emergent in modern Western society. (Again, no culture or class appears to be free from some variation or transformation of this division.) The introduction of this alternative model is thus to be considered no more than a mode of representing to ourselves structural features of our modern social world theoretically long neglected. I am also not proposing the paradigm of childcare as the norm for all citizen relations—as some feminists have done (7.2 and 7.3). Rather, the presentation of this new metaphor is a way of "casting our nets" in order to capture what may be significant likenesses and differences out there in the world. I aim to reveal and expose something important about human motivation generally.

Thus, while Locke's older mixing metaphor (the model of craft, farm, or technological labor) involves a working subject confronting a given material object, the model of ethical reproductive labor involves a subject essentially confronting another subject: the child, the elderly person, the beloved, or an animal. In Aristotelian language, the "material" as well as "formal" cause is, in the first case, raw matter to be imposed by form, in the latter, matter already informed by a human (or animal) soul. Regardless of how young the child, the woman as caretaker is in the presence of another living being with elaborate needs, desires, and developing capacities to which she is expected to respond. Her labor is essentially other-directed or socially "interactive"; it pertains from the start to direct need-interpretation.

This fundamental difference between the two models indicates in turn a distinction in the "final cause" of the respective activities. While the immediate aim or purpose of the craft, say, of shoemaking (as Socrates argued) is to produce good shoes (whether or not this is done for money), it is clear that the aim of childcare is to encourage the healthy development of the child. The ultimate goal, "for the sake of which" the activity is performed is to bring about (as far as possible) a mature, healthy adult. Thus, while the best craft labor may be said to aim indirectly at the satisfaction of human needs (good shoes, after all, are those which produce "happy feet"), reproductive labor aims directly at it. Its goal is not, in the first instance, a transformation of the external physical world, but is "communicative" for it aims at a transformation of human relations.[15] In the best case, on our analysis, it aims at helping bring about, not only a mature independent adult, but relations marked by *philia* (2.6). Such is the underlying ethical reproductive ideal.

Another possible misunderstanding must still be avoided. In pointing to the "other-directed" nature of traditional female labor, I am not claiming that women are inherently less greedy, self-seeking, etc. than men. My point is structural, not psychological. Unless the mother (biological or otherwise) in fact looks after the child and responds to its needs (whatever her individual psychological motives), the latter will not flourish. Moreover, it is clear that the mother often receives some personal "reward" for her efforts; her work is not pure self-sacrifice. In noting the moment of self-interest involved in child rearing, however, we must be careful not to assimilate reproductive labor to the modern category of "human services," from which it differs in one important respect. The public labor of the doctor, lawyer, or nurse (to the degree that their services are sold on the market) is generally felt to require some tangible reimbursement for efforts expended (usually a wage).[16] In the case of rearing one's own child, by contrast, the reward is often perceived as "internal" to the activity; it is performed for no reason beyond the establishment and furtherance of a good relationship.

In our real day-to-day existence, however, we all know that caring even for one's own child, or one's sick and elderly in-laws can be a tremendous burden and entails a good deal of work. Moreover, the ideal of friendship hardly seems to have played a significant role in the reason why women traditionally bore and raised children. The actual historical goals of "mixing one's labor" with children (and other family members) are surely complicated and diverse. Women bore and raised children because children just came along (there was no birth control); being a mother was expected of them, by custom and/or law; children were a source of status and wealth, or an extra pair of farm hands; children represented old-age insurance for parents; there were no alternative roles for women; and so on. With the advance of contraceptive means and education, however, women in large numbers are now capable of having far fewer children. Many women today—especially many younger ones in industrial countries—want none at all. The "burdens" of childcare both economically and personally (and as institutions are arranged at present) are becoming all too visible. Children in today's complex world are frequently viewed as little more than financial *liabilities*. Nor is this new attitude altogether a bad thing, considering the earth's exploding population (8.4).

I still maintain, however, that the rewards of ethical reproductive labor partake in friendly relations valued for their own sake (and such distinguishes this activity from productive labor). Most people enjoy other humans, they do not wish to be alone, nor do they desire to be surrounded only by strangers, much less enemies, and they are willing to expend significant effort in this direction if necessary. The preponderance of this friendship ideal thus continues to distinguish ethical reproductive labor. Thus, even though by definition such is not done solely for the sake of friendship (and hence is not *praxis*), as a general rule it still partakes of the friendship ideal. Paid nurses or governesses, for instance, often become fast friends of the charges they cared for so extensively. And it is this structure or relation to *philia* that separates this form of laboring activity from the received notion of productive labor, strictly speaking.

At the same time, the category of reproductive labor is still *labor*; it simultaneously partakes in the main characteristics traditionally assigned to this category. For one, reproductive labor distinguishes itself from *praxis*, because it is characteristically *also* performed for reasons beyond the activity itself. This is to say, historically, such labor was simply expected of women; they had little or no choice with regard to performing it. The characteristic of being largely a means to other, clearly specified ends—a stable home, support by and protection of a man, insurance for old age, and so on—thus qualifies it as labor in the first instance. So, too, like all other labor, it is necessarily intentional and rational—not merely haphazard or serendipitous. Taking regular note and care of others requires the systematic application of reason and foresight, the disciplining of one's own desires, the frequent deferral of immediate satisfaction, and so forth. Further, again typical of labor, reproductive work sustains, reproduces, and creates *use value* (the sewing of clothes, the cooking of meals, or calming of a fever). And like all forms of labor that are reiterative over time, ethical reproductive activity develops certain capacities in the workers themselves (as well as it neglects others). In the best case, ethical reproductive skills entail developing the emotional and intellectual capacities of what we called the art of perceiving (and encouraging) the person (4.6).

Finally, like all forms of laboring activity, this direct social labor may be more or less "freely chosen." With the advent of relatively safe contraceptives (and despite continuing historical and social pressures), modern woman may be said to "choose" motherhood today (or its opposite) a bit more freely than could her historical sisters. All demographic studies reveal the declining birthrates of advanced industrial societies when women are given alternatives—particularly education.[17] For the first time in history women are forgoing in large numbers some of the heaviest forms of reproductive labor that accompany the bearing and rearing of their own children. It even seems that humans on a large scale are awakening to the fact that they are the only species on the planet that can freely choose *not* to reproduce biologically. Choosing not to perform the labor accompanying biological reproduction, however, hardly excludes one from the joys and sorrows of close personal (or civic) relationships. Similarly, forgoing biological reproduction hardly exempts one from the duty of ethical and social reproductive labor in general. On the contrary, finally acknowledging reproductive labor *as labor*—as fundamentally a form of rational, ethical, and necessary social activity—simultaneously reveals to us that it is at least as much a duty of every human to perform such labor as it is to be "productive."

5.5 TOWARD A NEW CONCEPTION OF OWNERSHIP

The feminist critique of *Homo economicus* is well under way. Surprisingly enough, however, despite much criticism of "economic man" and the private acquisitive motive, the capitalist institution of private property emerges relatively unscathed.[18] Many recent (American) feminist accounts, for example, argue for adjustments in the market for mothering practices, or for state subsidies for dependency work in the private sphere, or for a new "culture of care," but they do so without casting any suspicion on the capitalist institution of private property directly. Perhaps this is not so surprising, considering how deeply lodged this institution is in the collective consciousness of most Americans. Nonetheless, the implications for ownership of the model of social labor sketched above leads in a different direction.

Beginning from this model, for example, there is little difficulty in conceiving of "social union" in the sphere of labor: of a relatively free activity where ends are shared (or at least not antagonistic or indifferent to one another) and where background property is treated as a commonly held asset (4.3 and 5.2). So, too, there is little difficulty in conceiving of a form of activity performed by vast numbers of people where much of it is done *for the sake of others*. If such social and ethical reproductive labor is not *praxis* (done purely for its own sake), the motivation to perform such labor (and to work hard and for long hours) hardly requires extensive private ownership in the means of production with all its power and control over the lives of hundreds of workers, nor does it require the incentive of exorbitant salaries and the vast inequalities in wealth that the extreme acquisitive model naturally supports (and encourages) under present conditions (3.4 and 5.3). Consequently, the implications for "ownership" of this alternative model of social laboring activity emerge as revolutionary. The sacred cow of Western capitalism—the primacy as well as the superiority of the institution of capitalist private property—is called into question, only this time from a feminist and not a classical Marxist point of view.

In chapter 3 we saw that Locke's labor theory gives one of the first important groundings to the modern conception of private property: of what A. M. Honoré calls the "full, liberal conception of ownership" (3.3). This modern conception includes, beyond the various rights of use, management, and enjoyment, the right to exclude others, as well as the right to capital, the power to alienate, consume, and even to destroy the thing. Historically, private property has included such objects as land as well as the major means of production: not just small family-run shops and businesses, but vast empires of industry. The primary constraint on this form of property is that the owner must not violate the rights of others.

Honoré insists, moreover, that Locke's "making and taking" model of ownership is still the "most morally satisfactory" as a model of original acquisition, when taken together with "consent and debt" as derivative forms. He writes that exclusive physical control of a thing is "the foundation on which the whole superstructure of ownership rests," for "to exclude others from what one holds is an instinct found in babies and even . . . in animals."[19] Honoré here assumes two fundamentals of what I am calling the ideology of production: first, that the form of private property is *morally* superior because it produces more for all (an assumption, as we have seen, going back at least to Locke); and second, that private, exclusive ownership is somehow a "natural instinct" of humans and thus the proper foundation of property (a fallacy that Locke himself did not commit). In light of the new model of social labor presented here, however, both assumptions must now be questioned. For instance, pointing to an "instinct in babies and animals" to grasp and hold things proves little; one can with equal certainty point to an instinct in babies and animals *to include others* in what they hold. Why should this inclusion not be considered equally fundamental to ownership, to the conception of "making something one's own"?

So, too, women have been "mixing their labor" for centuries with their children and other family members, *not* with the aim of exclusive private appropriation and to "dispose of the product as they please," but even with the goal ultimately of "giving" the child away as it reaches maturity. This is one reason why women's labor has been called "gift labor."[20] At the same time, and despite many legal appearances to the contrary, traditional woman (but for the legal slave) could still say "mine," and the children (as well as household, husband, and so on) were typically still "hers" in some sense. It is apparent that here we are operating with an alternative paradigm of "making something one's own," a number of whose features are as follows:

1. Nonexclusive ownership. What a woman traditionally called "hers"—the children, husband, general household, utensils, and so on—were possessions essentially already *shared*. Ownership for her, whether legal or customary, was never (in the Western tradition) equated with an absolute and exclusive control over them, although periodically (as at one point in Roman law) she was herself subject to such absolute control. The right of private property in land and goods was not granted most women in Europe and America until the latter half of the nineteenth century (and even today women own exclusively only a small fraction of the world's property). My first claim is thus that women's traditional situation points to important aspects of shared, communal property maintained in the modern period. What has been considered "hers" is the result of (and constituted by) numerous intentions and collective agreements, never by her individual will alone.

2. Noneconomic ownership. To the degree that women have not been the major, but only the supplementary breadwinners, their traditional realm (children, household, utensils, clothing, food, and so on) remains an interpenetration of the economic (the useful) with interpersonal and qualitative considerations (such as religious, moral, or aesthetic ones). Such "possession" contrasts with the modern tradition's progressive reduction of the term *property* (that which is "properly one's own") to purely economic, physical—ultimately quantitative—terms. I stress the narrowness of this modern conception of property. It is not only *not* prior in any historical sense, but it also emerges as conceptually far less fundamental. It presupposes, both historically and conceptually, a far broader conception of "owning."

3. *Stewardship.* Unlike the paradigm of property as commodity, which may be acquired and disposed of at will, the children and home of the woman are clearly hers in an *ascriptive* and not an acquisitive sense; they are first and foremost her responsibility. Traditional "owning" in the case of women is thus a form accountable for the environment, prior to any need or claim exclusively to appropriate that environment. The form emerges as fully consistent with the traditional legal sense of the term *possession*, whereby things are considered highly "restricted objects" of the will. I wish to suggest, moreover, that a central criterion of rightful possession in this case is the criterion of care, or *Pflege* (4.6). The woman who does not care for her children usually loses them in one way or another. Again, we note the German *Pflege* because the German term (unlike the English *care*) maintains a close etymological connection with the concept of *Pflicht,* or "duty." At least for women, to care (in our sense of practical love) has always been the first duty.

With the emphasis on responsibility and *Pflege,* traditional (female) patterns of ownership invite comparison with older, precapitalist property forms. The reigning conception of property in medieval times, for instance, was that of a stewardship of another's (God's or the lord's) property (3.3). Such ownership excluded both alienability and the rights of disposal. The advantage of introducing the category of ethical reproductive labor and activity here—and the form of ownership appropriate to them—begins to emerge. The category allows us to recapture not only aspects of presumably long-lost worlds (aspects such as *Pflege,* stewardship, communal or shared property), but it affords a fully modern and realistic interpretation of them without committing ourselves in the least to a medieval (or any particular religious) metaphysics.

4. *Gift.* Finally, if the dominant form of property tied to the production model in modern times is the commodity, the ideal form tied to ethical reproductive activity more closely resembles the "gift"—inviting further comparison with ownership patterns in what have come to be called "gift cultures."[21] As noted earlier, a gift is something "bestowed" upon us by another; strictly speaking, it cannot be obtained by one's own efforts or an act of will (3.3). Far more than the commodity, the gift remains tied to a specific set of relations such that if the object as gift is removed from these concrete relations, it tends to change its "value." (We noted how in many fairy tales, when the wicked child tries to exploit the bread given it, the "spirit of the gift" flees and the bread turns to stone.) The "spirit" of the genuine gift (and the reward of giving or of generosity, sharing, etc.) is the establishment of a new (or maintenance of an older) relationship. The exchange of gifts stands in stark contrast to that of commodities, in which the two parties have motives beyond the relationship itself and are left relatively indifferent by the exchange.

My claim here is that traditional woman—to an astonishing degree—is surrounded by such gift-property. In most cultures her own child is considered a "gift" (and we still speak of "the gift of life"). More important, gift-exchange and the social labor of women even in our own capitalist society—the female passage of food, clothing, and presents within the extended family and neighborhood—leave a series of interconnected relationships in their wake. This casts important light on the problem of social unity or community in society (1.1). It has led one thinker to speak of women's work as essentially "ligational": an "activity of binding."[22] Finally, such exchange reverses the mythology of the marketplace where private acquisition is the mark of a substantial person. In gift-exchange or in gift-labor, "to possess" is "to give."

The alternative model of "making something one's own" presented here is one that *by definition* cannot be exclusive and private. Such "owning" may be considered an appropriation, not of the natural physical world, but of the human social one. It implies that in an important sense we do make other people our own, although this form of possession must clearly be distinguished from traditional ownership as a control or domination of them. To the contrary, this form entails "responsiveness" to concrete need, as well as the encouragement of another's autonomous capacities. It thus emphasizes that long-neglected aspect of ownership as an *inclusion in* (participation, belonging to, *zu Hause sein*) the specifically human community. The model clearly presupposes, moreover, an altered conception of personality: one that now emphasizes the "the fact of continuity" with others over that of separateness.[23]

An obvious objection arises at this point. Why not claim that the type of ownership pertaining to women over the last few hundred years (and which retains aspects of precapitalist, stewardship forms) only indicates the "primitiveness" and inadequacy of this form? Such ownership, after all, has essentially been bound to the historical lack of independence and separateness of choice characterizing women's subordinate position. My response is that, although historically this has undoubtedly been the case, there exists no *necessary* connection between such dependence and the form of ownership under investigation. There is nothing incoherent about the notion of a joint stewardship on equal terms. Any society, after all, must consist of and maintain certain forms of social labor and concrete bonding activities—that is, if it is going to reproduce itself and flourish into the next generations. If this is the case, moreover, there will have to be a certain amount of shared and common property, as the precondition of such necessary social labor. The real question thus becomes not *whether* such a joint stewardship is natural to the human (it clearly also *is*), but what precise *form* such communal property should take and how extensive its scope should be (5.6 and chapter 7). Until now, I have tried to show only that far from the "making and taking" conception of ownership being the "most natural" and "morally satisfactory" one, stewardship is equally "instinctive," foundational, and "in accordance with our nature." Indeed, once we take an ethical reproductive perspective, this alternative form becomes far more primary, necessary, and important.

While I may share voluntarily with my wife and children or with my personal friends, some may object, why should I share with others whom I don't even know, much less with members of other nations? Here a return to Rawls's theory may help reveal how this question again presupposes the extreme acquisitive conception of the laboring self. Continuing to assume such a self in economic and political theory now begins to emerge as a bit too strong: many individuals think along these lines in our society, but we can now see it as a case of being blinded by our reigning egoistic self-conceptions (1.3). In the midst of the most advanced capitalist society on earth, it turns out that there exists a vast quantity of alternative laboring forms and incentives.

Before turning back to Rawls's theory, however, one final point should still be made. It is not only the liberal-capitalist tradition that has overlooked the category of direct social labor (ethical reproduction)—and thus also the notion of a joint stewardship—but the Marxist one as well. As we have seen, Marx's conception of common property, at least in the first instance, is conceived as the end result of a now "collective mixing" of productive labor, where each finally becomes his "own capitalist" (4.8). In predicting capitalism's inevitable downfall, moreover—in arguing that capitalist commodity production ultimately "tears" a society apart and will be replaced by a socialist form—Marx apparently failed to recognize the large portion of noncommodity labor that behind the scenes, as it were, and outside the market goes to binding relations together again. Marx, that is, not only underestimated the "resiliency" of capitalism (as is often claimed), but also failed to recognize the importance of ethical reproductive labor. Part of our present system's adaptability can surely be explained, however, by showing to what degree capitalist productive activity actually rests upon other forms of noncommodity labor. Of course, if ethical reproductive labor is progressively pulled into the market and subjected willy-nilly to its laws, then who knows—Marx's predictions may yet come to pass.

5.6 CIVIC FRIENDSHIP IN THE ECONOMIC DOMAIN

The present (neo-liberal) blind faith in the fundamental superiority of any type of private property and "the market"—as well as disdain for all forms of limitation and common ownership—will surely one day give way before the onslaught of feminist (and other) criticism, although how far in the future no one can know. In this final section, I hope to indicate the powerful *theoretical* potential that displacing Locke's original metaphor has for reconceiving certain fundamentals of our economic system. Specifically, I aim to show that by focusing on the category of ethical reproductive labor and its accompanying forms of possession, a viable conception of a free and socialist property opens up in liberal democratic terms, that is, as one reconstruction of John Rawls's theory. Since I can hardly give a comprehensive account or defense of market socialism here, I consider my discussion as only adding force to arguments already in existence (5.3).[24]

Let us return finally to Rawls's theory. We noted how his difference principle incorporates both acquisitive and ascriptive (responsible) forms of ownership (5.3). We noted as well his "skepticism"—given what appears to him to be our human nature—that the moral purposeful self today could ever become primary (collectively speaking) in the realm of economic labor without too great a sacrifice (in terms of either liberty or efficiency). Thus, the strong reading of the difference principle, which requires social union in the economic sphere, cannot be demanded as a matter of justice. In Rawls's view, the property question in the end remains dependent "on the traditions, institutions, and social forces of each country, and its particular historical circumstances" (*TJ*, 274).

In having turned to the sphere of women's traditional activity, however, we now have presented an alternative model of self, labor, and ownership in which responsible ownership is primary (and private property secondary), and yet which is undeniably central to our modern capitalist institutions and traditions. We thus have a new way of conceiving of the viable realization in practice of the strong reading of Rawls's difference principle: with the present era's "social force" or mass movement of women into the economic sphere. The strong reading of the difference principle emerges as fully compatible with "our" human nature. Further, we have a viable way of conceiving of a modern civic friendship in the economic sphere, which can bring an end to the vast material inequalities of wealth presently existing between persons and as a precondition of genuine justice (2.7).

Let us next distinguish between a thinner and thicker sense of responsible or ascriptive ownership: that form of "owning" which considers responsibilities to others first, before going on to acquire for the private self. Earlier, we noted four different stages of the ability to respond and care for others: initial noticing; accepting minimal responsibility (*Sorge*); hands-on caregiving; and seeing the care reception through to its end (*Pflege* [4.6]). Corresponding to these four stages we can now distinguish at least two ideals of responsible autonomy as well. The first ideal is quite explicitly incorporated into Rawls's difference principle; the latter, I believe, is not.

The first ideal of responsible autonomy (essentially Kantian) may be described as assuming the standpoint of the "generalized other."[25] It is crucial to what I call "responsible ownership." This form of autonomous activity recognizes that a necessary condition for owning anything (as well as developing my talents, and so on) is that there is a set of established social rules and legal institutions that afford others the opportunity to do likewise. Responsible ownership rests on the increasing capacity of the self to act on universalistic principles of right, and it requires us to recognize other humans as reasonable beings entitled to the same rights and duties we ascribe to ourselves. In pursuing my own goals, I am thus minimally required to respect the dignity of others, as well as to recognize their legitimate property holdings. Rawls's original position is clearly constructed in order to highlight this relationship to others governed by the institutional norm of symmetrical reciprocity. (As noted earlier, he derives his principle of fraternity through this construction [5.2].) Here the reigning moral categories are legal right, obligation, and entitlement, grounded on the values of equal respect of persons, dignity, and worthiness: traditional values of liberalism.

The last two stages of caring for others, however—what we have termed *Pflege,* or the actual helping of others in practice—rests on the increasing capacity of the self to render *inner* nature transparent: human needs, desires, drives, and so on. From this perspective, we not only seek to comprehend the needs of others as they comprehend themselves, but we also act to bring about the satisfaction of those needs. The governing norms in this case are closer to care and friendship, accompanied by moral categories of bonding, greater responsibility, and sharing. I can expect *more* in this instance than the simple assertion of my rights and duties in the face of your needs, and vice versa. Let us call this second ideal of autonomy and its accompanying forms of possession, "responsive ownership." Responsive ownership is a form that not only guards the social conditions for the development of another's autonomy, but in the pursuit of individual ends simultaneously maintains the shared conditions for the possibility of genuine *philia.* Here, *philia* (personal and civic) becomes—at least ideally speaking—among my personal ends as well. This second ideal of autonomy and responsive ownership—really, shared possession—has been little recognized in modern social and political theory, and Rawls's theory is here no exception. As women progressively move from the private arena and enter the public labor markets en masse, however, it is clear that a crossroads is being reached that may lead in one of at least two directions.

At one extreme, the large-scale movement of women entering the marketplace will effect a transformation of the capitalist economy in the direction of greater economic democracy. In this case, women could demand the retention of certain positive aspects of their traditional reproductive roles, foremost among which are common activities valued for their own sake and shared final ends—social union—in laboring activity (a responsive workplace). If this increasingly becomes the case, classical capitalist assumptions, such as that workers inevitably seek ever higher wages and ever greater instrumental power over others (the Lockean acquisitive ideal), might actually repel rather than entice many workers. For those schooled in ethical reproductive labor, there is often a more important goal: to transform the competitive rules of the productive workplace itself and incorporate within it reproductive concerns. As numerous feminists have argued, being the "ideal worker" today conflicts with being an ideal mother or parent, and therefore change is mandatory.[26] I would go one step further. Particularly in the high-paying competitive firms, being the ideal worker conflicts not only with being a good mother or parent, but with being a good child or helper (to your elderly parents, say), with being a genuine neighbor or friend (and not merely an instrumental one), and with being a responsive citizen generally (capable of genuine public concern). The immense effort and self-focus required by success in high-status "jobs" often leaves little time for anything—or anyone—else.

Simultaneously, of course, the feminist movement could press onward and (despite backlashes) demand that men participate equally in the raising of small children.[27] There could be a growing demand that the whole sphere of market labor change: hours of paid work, for instance, must be shortened (to allow greater time for ethical reproductive work), become more flexible, and open to discussion and exchange. The private life and concerns of the individual (including the importance of relationships) must be acknowledged to a greater degree in the public realm of labor. Further, such novel participation in shop-floor decisions (concerning hours, job rotation, vacations, and so forth) could encourage a growing interest and understanding on the part of the individual worker for the ends and requirements of the business association itself. Surely, such increased participation would lead to a growing capacity on the part of each laborer to participate in progressively more complex and significant decisions.

Many have by now argued for the superiority of a participatory economic democracy (in comparison to our present privatized system) in terms of fairness and values such as individual dignity and freedom; benefit to the local community (worker-owned firms are more committed to the towns in which the worker-owners themselves live); and in terms of important schooling for the larger political democracy.[28] The counter-charge has always been that this presupposes an unrealistic and utopian view of human labor motivation—a doubt that, as we saw, Rawls himself continues to harbor (5.3). However, once we consider the structure of the "ethical reproductive self" elaborated here, this counter-charge begins to lose much of its force. Since the reproductive self stands as the antipode of the acquisitive one—and actually still exists en masse—the private acquisitive self can no longer blindly be posited as primary, even in the realm of labor. It is a false elaboration (moreover, it tends to promote the very self it projects outward). This being the case, the weight of a renewed realism is thrown behind Rawls's moral purposeful self, and now in the laboring sphere; similarly, his "Aristotelian principle" as a principle of motivation (developing abilities for their own sake, the goal of *philia* for its own sake, etc.) can clearly play a far greater role. Labor motivation and effort on this alternative model may proceed with far less qualitative and quantitative (income) differentials (5.2). Finally, recent empirical developments in the United States lend credence and support to this direction and particular trend. There are now an estimated 11,500 companies in the United States totally or substantially owned by the people who work in them—up from a mere handful thirty-five years ago.[29]

Let me be very clear. My claim is not that other forms of private incentives (lesser differences in incomes, positions of authority, social acclaim, and so on) cannot or should not continue to operate; the restriction of responsive ownership in no way assumes human beings are all altruists or angels. Rather, the scope of the exercise of acquisitive motivation will clearly be limited to a degree unknown in traditional liberal theories, but this means only that other forms of nonacquisitive motivation (e.g., better family relations, friendships, community service) may be given their due. This proposal would entail, for instance, that the present differentials of our new "gilded age"—where in 2003 executive officers of major businesses earned roughly 472 times the pay of the average worker—would be a thing of the distant past.[30]

Indeed, the mass movement of women entering the workplace in the twenty-first century might just bring that needed push for a widespread democratic socialist ownership from the "bottom up," as it were (in contrast to a command economy where a social labor is imposed "top down"). Worker demands for democratic decision making in regard to the conditions of work might even come to include not only the aims and products of the production process, but control over decisions regarding society's major means of production. This need not mean that each worker co-decides each decision (which would be far too cumbersome), but that a process of democratic discussion and participation in the election of managers, boards of directors, and so on might commence to operate within the firm itself. By "socialist ownership," I thus intend nothing more than that shared final ends (social union) extend into the economic sphere and that differences in individual income and social positions of authority now become *conditional*, not merely on bettering the financial position of all concerned (including the worst off), but on furthering their conditions of autonomy, participation, and self-governance. I intend, that is, the strong reading of Rawls's difference principle (5.3).

More specifically, I intend the strong interpretation of Rawls's difference principle, which now increasingly operates *within the firm*. For Rawls, recall, the difference principle guides government in the regulation of the economy as a whole (implemented by government's various "branches"). On the strong reading presented here, by contrast, the difference principle would be implemented by demands from below—from within the firm or local community—as well as from above, or by government. Let us call this far stronger principle *the economic principle of civic friendship*. This newly required concern for others will surely appear "oppressive" to present-day owners of vast capital and to many executive officers (those still operating on the private, control model), but such concern emerges as a natural extension of the traditional goals of other-directed reproductive activity (7.5). Labor, after all, is not only production. Moreover, the demand that the strong reading of the difference principle should increasingly apply within individual firms (and even to local communities where the firms are anchored) entails that the business or firm begin to be perceived as a form of "joint property" with shared (or at least overlapping) ends whereby individual differences pertain, in turn, to the traditional realm of "possession." What is social and what is private has been reversed. Private differential rewards now emerge from and are conditional upon their social and ethical reproductive role. A legitimate institution of private property may thereby reveal itself as little more, on this reading, than a privately held, temporary stewardship (3.3). Considering the modern women's movement—as well as our analysis of an ascriptive self educated to respond to and develop the basic attributes of other persons—this scheme of laboring on a shared possession no longer appears as "unnatural" or utopian as it once may have.

The opposite tendency, of course, is that whereby women, as they progressively enter the labor force, take on the acquisitive personality marked by competition, production, and private appropriation. Indeed, we can identify a historical movement in this direction also. Not only has the women's movement of the last fifty years been unable to arrest the burgeoning new inequalities of economic wealth just mentioned—apparently acceptable to many Americans—but a number of recent feminist demands seem to argue only that women should claim a larger slice of the pie (positions criticized in 7.2). In this instance, the model of private exclusive appropriation—for the first time in history—would truly be generalized to *all* adult members of society, including now to women themselves.

In the extreme case, on such an exclusive private model even the higher pursuits of the mind, as well as our relations to others, take on the form of instrumental acquisitions. My claim here is that such a total transformation of traditional female ethical activities into the modern productive role will find its limit in societal reproduction itself. In such a case the children (as well as all relations of personal and civic *philia*) are truly left "unattended." These relations would be relegated entirely to wage-labor care (which would now include the labor itself of parents, friends, and fellow citizens). In such a world where there is no longer any gift-labor at all—no longer any activity of bonding and sharing for its own sake—the society will not long maintain itself, or at least not long maintain itself *as a democracy*. In such a Hobbesian society, necessary social compliance will require ever greater threats of physical force, and cooperation will be plagued by violent upheavals, as well as (finally) both internal and external wars. Such an alternative stands in stark contrast to the sketch of the move to a democratic socialism given earlier, whereby all labor would be considered as in part gift-labor, as labor done for no other reason than to maintain the social conditions for the possibility of genuine *philia*.

It is possible, of course, that a situation might emerge somewhere between the two alternatives identified here. As new forms of progressive ownership emerge, CEO salaries might continue their upward motion, at the same time as conservative forces try to lead women back into the kitchen, etc. So, too, much of society's response and accommodation of women in the labor force appears to be through relatively marginal adjustments such as flex-time, job-sharing, some guaranteed maternal leaves, and so on—adjustments that only minimally affect the basic structure of capitalist ownership and corporate decision making. My aim here is not to argue for any automatic and inevitable road toward social democracy, however. Rather, I have been concerned to reveal—from the standpoint of perhaps the greatest political theory of the twentieth century—the moral superiority of democratic socialism *once standard charges of motivational utopianism can be met.* And these charges can be met, I have argued, with the elaboration of an alternative to the production model, coupled with the mass movement of women into the market. In the end, the choice of which route is finally taken remains up to us.

At this point a number of objections must still be answered, even if briefly.[31] Will not this social form of ownership, where differences in property and in private incentives pertain to the sphere of possession, bring with it a reduction in economic efficiency? The motive of exclusive private ownership, after all, has long been considered a great "incentive" to laboring activity, and only by maintaining an abundant material base can modern society continue to support the individual freedoms and benefits we have all come to enjoy. To this I offer a number of counter-suggestions. First, not just Karl Marx but J. S. Mill also argued long ago that if everyone is considered a part-owner of an enterprise (as in a worker's cooperative), the incentive to do well is far greater than in the case of laboring for a mere wage, where the individual has "little personal interest in his work."[32] Further, few seem to have considered the possibility that women in particular (but also persons from other cultures) may actually perform less well when they are removed from a concrete set of responsive social relations and thrust into a competitive market scheme. Under present working conditions, their labor may be highly inefficient. Similarly, recent industry studies of publicly owned companies belie the general charge of inefficiency. Customers of various locally controlled electric utilities, for instance, typically pay 7 to 10 percent less for their electric service compared to investor-owned utilities, and studies show that most of the advantage is due to the fact of public ownership itself; locally controlled public utilities can be especially responsive to customers' needs and do not need to pay dividends to private shareholders.[33]

To claim that private ownership of major means of production—including the exclusive and hierarchical control over a vast labor force—is so strong an incentive as to outweigh these other considerations emerges by this point as simply *too strong*. The claim presupposes a private, acquisitive self to the extreme. Rawls's theory does not rest on such an extreme version of the acquisitive self (as we have seen, his view presupposes an individual capable of progressive motivation by the Aristotelian Principle), and given our previous account of women's traditional activity, this private acquisitive self—rather than reflecting some general norm of human motivation—begins to emerge as the anomalous case. Thus, even should there remain an irreconcilable conflict between material productive efficiency and the development of human capacities and relationships of friendship, why should this matter if the latter is considered of greater importance? Finally, for serious ecological reasons, we must free ourselves from the destructive goal of ever greater material production and wasteful consumption (8.4). The ideology of production must give way to a concern with relations of ethical reproduction.

A similar set of concerns arises regarding the value of liberty: Will not my proposal for social union in the economic sphere land us in a "command society"? The worry is not only that labor will end by being centrally directed, but that individual freedom of movement, of thought and creativity, will somehow be abolished or at least suffer unbearable pressures from "the many." In response, I believe that the form of democratic market socialism sketched above (inclusive of the economic principle of civic friendship) is less susceptible to this charge than perhaps any other economic form—including present conceptions of private property (capitalist) democracy. For one, the average "worker" (and the "worst off," i.e., those who have few or no skills) under the strong interpretation of the difference principle will be guaranteed encouragement of their autonomy and self-governing capacities, whether through government programs (for the unemployed) or as part-owners in a firm (allowed to take part in the decision-making process, and so on). The average worker can hardly be said to possess such options and conditions for the exercise of their liberties at present.

So, too, we must remember that in Rawls's theory, the application of the difference principle presupposes the prior satisfaction of the first principle of equal liberty (guaranteeing the liberties of free speech, personal property, integrity of the person, freedom of occupation, etc.). There is thus no question here of a centralized state commanding the direction of all labor. The worry that a socialist property necessarily leads to a command society (as in the former Soviet Union, say) derives, I believe, from continuing to conceive of ownership on the model of productive *control*. With our notion of "responsive ownership" as awareness and participation, however, a wedge is driven between the notions of "owning" and "controlling" in the first place. So, on the contrary, what I am calling the economic principle of civic friendship must work from *both* above and below. The demand to realize the difference principle "from above" through government would need to proceed through the legitimate and expanded democratic process; it would have to be voted in (chapter 7). At the same time, the requirement to realize it within the firm (and progressively to move toward a cooperative, economic democracy) will come through the demands of workers and other social movements (neighborhoods, environmental groups, and so on) "from below." Foremost among these various social movements, I would like to think, is the women's movement itself.

It is thus only the "liberty" of the private owner of major means of production (and of vast wealth) that must be reined in. Such liberty is really only license, however, for its legitimacy presupposes an extreme acquisitive conception of the self—a conception we have found good reason to reject. Once this notion of the self has been dethroned from power, the vision of a free democratic socialist property emerges where the holding of private property (at least in scarce natural resources, in extensive land, or means of production) would be the exception rather than the rule. Individuals would here have to earn by their actions the social right to exercise authority over others, and—critically—such authority would be heavily circumscribed by direct civic responsibilities.

I conclude this chapter by suggesting that with the introduction of the new model of direct social labor, a major difficulty in Rawls's theory is actually resolved. This difficulty may be called that of *practical realizability* of the difference principle (see also 8.3). That is, if Rawls does not reject outright the extreme acquisitive self in the realm of labor (i.e., one motivated by "m-c-m" and not merely by "m"), the problem emerges of how *any* reading of the difference principle could be implemented at the state level (much less our strong interpretation). Where, for instance, will the moral impetus arise in the average—private acquisitive and laboring—person to elect a government that decides to act for the common good and in accordance with the strong requirements of this principle? Nozick (quite rightly, I believe) faults Rawls for leaving this "caring role" to an arm of government for which "we the people" should, at least in part, feel responsible (which is not to conclude, as Nozick does, that the state should play no role).[34] Not only does the danger exist that government becomes too large and cumbersome, but more important, representatives in government are often furthest removed from those daily concerns in which concrete need can alone be identified.

As we saw earlier (4.3), Rawls believes that the schooling in communal values may proceed by way of association in the family, school, neighborhood, and short-term forms of cooperation (*TJ*, 467). If we consider the time people still today spend in economic laboring activity—as well as the consequent weight and influence this area holds over their lives and character formation—it is highly implausible that such extra-economic activities are sufficient to produce the "sense of fraternity" Rawls actually assumes (much less the civic friendship we are advocating). Again, already J. S. Mill pointed to the workplace as the natural home for the "schooling in social sympathies." My suggestion here is that we cannot realistically demand so much more *from our representatives* in government in terms of fairness, compassion, and public concern than we are capable of and willing to achieve in our everyday lives. Nor can we demand so much *from ourselves* that—given that extreme acquisition is encouraged at work—we yet emerge unscathed and other-directed in the voting booth.

If we consider that the strong interpretation of the difference principle (which naturally tends, we have argued, in the direction of a workplace democracy and a market socialism) necessitates no loss in terms of fundamental liberty or efficiency, we are left with the suggestion that *unless* this principle is also demanded from "below"—at the ground level—it will never come to be implemented by the state from "above." Rawls's difference principle will remain utopian and never be set into practice. Again, such a ground-level implementation is hardly unrealistic once the role of ethical reproductive labor, its alternatively structured motivation, and the significance of the women's movement are all granted their due importance.

In sum, if civic friendship is a necessary condition for genuine justice (2.7), then one way of making the turn to such friendship in the modern period is by revamping the fundamentals of our economic system and not only condemning, but actually reversing, the trend to material inequality. This is perhaps the most difficult goal of all to achieve, considering the vast and powerful nature of the vested interests at stake, but it must not therefore be lost from view. So, too, I have tried to show that Rawls's theory is a good place to begin, for his difference principle (unlike so much recent philosophical discussion) embodies a *substantive* economic duty of friendship, even if established "indirectly" (5.2). Rawls's difference principle genuinely embodies the first stages of caring for fellow citizens: those associated with the German *Sorge*, and which are often attributed to men (4.6). There is genuine *friendship* embodied in this principle: it expresses the attitude that I do not want systematic advantages at the expense of others (the worst off); that I am aware of and concerned about their plight; that my representatives must work to link any structural inequalities to the condition of the worst off benefiting also; and that I am willing to give a significant part (at least of my earnings) to see that this happens. What we called the latter stages of care, however—the concrete stages of *Pflege,* or the practical activity of caregiving itself—these stages are vaguely left to others in Rawls's theory.

Not surprisingly, that is, political friendship in Rawls takes the form of traditional "fraternity"; it is a relation that pertains between citizens essentially still conceived as independent and *male.* Rawls's political person possesses only two moral powers (the third power is hidden deep within); he is conceived as a free and functioning equal to his fellow citizens, and these others he sees as more or less similar to himself; they are his "brothers." Conceived thus, "justice as fairness" has no room for the possibility that I, as a citizen, might actually in practice have to *care for others myself*; that at some point in my life, I may have a *general civic duty* of hands-on ethical reproductive labor for fellow citizens who turn out to be very different from myself in terms of class, race, gender, ethnicity, and so forth (7.3). It is this seemingly incomprehensible civic duty—not only theoretically to befriend, but practically to care for fellow citizens who are no longer conceived as mirror images of oneself—that I continue to argue for in the following chapters. Such a direct civic duty is central to a *civic friendship* as here conceived—economic and otherwise.

6 WOMEN, DEMOCRACY, AND THE U.S. CONSTITUTION

For what is government itself but the greatest of all reflections on human nature?
JAMES MADISON

6.1 THE LACUNA IN THE REPRESENTATION OF WOMEN

If pressures "from below" are demanding changes in the world of work and even in the structure of ownership itself (5.6), and if (as we shall argue in 7.3) a greater portion of responsibility for the satisfaction of individual needs and developing capacities must in future be taken over by others outside the family narrowly conceived (e.g., in worker cooperatives or neighborhood associations), this is not to deny the important role the state must still play in the redirection of wealth "from above" and in implementing the strong reading of the difference principle (5.3). Many theorists have convincingly argued for the necessity of an effective state—some collective arrangement that proceeds by way of the democratic political process—in addressing the traditional free-rider problem as well as in countering the problem of "externalities" (the problem whereby isolated rational actions may yet lead to collectively irrational outcomes).[1]

Further, if the women's movement is a powerful impetus in bringing about a greater civic friendship between citizens, how can this impetus arrive at the highest reaches of the U.S. government? And why are we not today further along? Women in the United States, after all, have had the vote for almost ninety years (ever since 1920, and far longer than in most other countries). When one considers the statistics, however, the United States ranks among the worst of the advanced industrial democracies in terms of the self-representation of women. Out of the top twenty-six advanced democracies in 2002, for instance, and in terms of the percentage of legislative seats won by women, the United States and England ranked only eighteenth and seventeenth, respectively, just above Portugal and Ireland.[2] There is something about the structure of the U.S. government also, which keeps women from gaining their rightful due (6.5).

A part of the answer surely lies in the nature of our slow moving, eighteenth-century Constitution itself; recent scholarship has again emphasized its conservative, resistant-to-change nature, as well as its various "undemocratic" aspects.[3] So too, for the most part. feminist legal scholars have tended to approach the Constitution in a somewhat piecemeal fashion. With but a few exceptions they have focused on specific areas of constitutional doctrine—for example, on the First Amendment in their fight against pornography,[4] or on the due process and equal protection clauses of the Fourteenth Amendment in their attempts to defend abortion.[5] But they have rarely taken on the Constitution as a whole. That is, far less emphasis has been given to general constitutional interpretation: to the significance of the fact that this document was written over two hundred years ago and wholly by men, that it never refers to women explicitly (in fact, it uses the masculine pronoun thirty times) and that it all too often (especially when originally enumerating the rights of citizens) implicitly excluded them, and so forth.[6] So, too, under it, women for scores of years were denied the right to vote, could typically not hold property on their own, and were relegated to the domestic field, out of view of public life and subject to the whims of their fathers or husbands. What kind of document is this? How can women's allegiance to it and its history be maintained? What sort of obstacles does it present, not only to women's full participation in the legal and political institutions of the modern world, but to the theme of the present work: a greater civic friendship among citizens in general?

This chapter proffers one analysis of what our Constitution, as well as the ensuing history of its interpretation, may be lacking insofar as women were not only *not* among its original authors, but were rarely among any of its authors or interpreters in the intervening two hundred years. So too, I offer one suggestion as to how this lacuna of the self-representation of women might be mitigated within the present context—at least to some extent. Although my project builds upon the work of other feminist political and legal theorists, I also begin explicitly here to distinguish my view from their accounts. I hope to provide, as well as to legitimate, a promising new feminist interpretation by way of which we may approach the U.S. Constitution as a whole and evaluate the direction of its development.

6.2 THE ANALYSIS OF WHAT IS LACKING

Perhaps the central criticism feminists have proffered of the liberal political tradition in general and of our constitutional regime in particular, is that the conception of the individual presupposed in both is quintessentially "male" and does not match descriptions women give of their own selves and agency. The abstract legal person, bearer of universal rights against the state, is often presumed to be autonomous, separate, self-determining, and self-interested.[7] Feminists, by contrast, are surprisingly united in their characterization of women's experience as far more circumscribed. Historically women have tended to see themselves as largely defined by their concrete relationships, as more "connected" with or focused upon others, and—as Carol Gilligan has argued most famously—far from immediately resorting to the language of rights in moral dilemmas, they tend to stress their responsibility and duties to particular others first. This has led many feminists to claim that women possess a different perspective, even speak in a "different voice."

Two points may be made regarding this contrast. First, if some of these differences do hold (Gilligan's empirical results have been questioned), a sustained consensus on why they hold has still not been achieved. Various "materialist" feminists concentrate their attention on biological differences between men and women: either on the fact of pregnancy (e.g., Shulamith Firestone) or on the sexual act of intercourse (Catharine MacKinnon or Andrea Dworkin) or on both (Robin West).[8] MacKinnon and Dworkin, as is well known, view women's oppression as derived primarily from their subordinate role in sexual intercourse; women are passive ("the fucked") and men are active ("the fuckers"). Firestone, by contrast, views women's oppression as lying in their vulnerable and exploited role as pregnant mother. These radical feminists see in women's different biology not only the source of patriarchy, but an invasion of women's physical integrity, an intrusion into their existential condition, which will only be alleviated if biological reproduction is artificially managed (Firestone) or if women separate themselves from heterosexual intercourse altogether (Dworkin).

More recently feminists have tended to reject this negative and extreme vision; women's biological differences should be positively evaluated, a cause for celebration, and even stressed in the fight against patriarchy. Thus, Robin West puts forth her "Connection

Thesis," which holds that women are essentially more connected to other humans than men are, and that this may be traced to the biological-material fact of pregnancy, penetration during intercourse, menstruation, and breast-feeding. "Women are actually or potentially materially connected to other human life. Men aren't." (*CJ*, 500). West claims, moreover, that this female "lack of separation" carries over into the psychological and moral realm: "Women are therefore capable of a degree of physical as well as psychic intimacy with the other which greatly exceeds men's capacity" (*CJ*, 501). The American legal system, however, views men as the paradigm of legal personhood: as discrete, separate individuals, autonomous and self-determining. What is needed if women are ever to achieve equality, in West's view, is not the continued denial of woman's intimate, relational nature, but that "the fact of connection be recognized in law" (*CJ*, 523).

A sustained critique of the materialist position in general or its more attenuated version in West's thought is not in order here. Despite many valuable insights, however, these theories all commit a version of the naturalistic fallacy; they illegitimately move from material, biological fact to normative value. West's position surely overstates her case. From the material *fact* of physical connection, such as in pregnancy (or lack of it), one cannot derive the fact of psychical or moral connection. A careful study of individual and cultural differences underscores this point; many men (especially men of other times and cultures) may be more "other-directed" and embedded in their particular relations than are, say, certain individualistic American business women (even those who have had numerous biological children).[9] Biology alone is incapable of accounting for these individual and cultural differences. West, in seeking to account for the "different voice," has apparently confused a historical and social connection to the separate biology of women with an essentialist one.

A more promising approach is to stress that any difference between men and women is to a far greater extent "socially constructed" upon the original biological differences—but then an account of the nature and form of this social construction is required. The analyses of Nancy Chodorow and Sara Ruddick, both of whom claim that the construction has something to do with "mothering," may be seen as a step forward, to the degree that mothering is viewed as an *activity* in their theories. As an activity, mothering is performed primarily by women, though men can do it as well (i.e., parenting).[10] The category begins to move beyond the merely biological and can include wide variations in cultural form. But by the same token, these analyses reach their limits for much the same reason as West's Connection Thesis. They are bounded by the extent to which they acknowledge that much of the behavior and activity that is meant to be peculiar to "mothers" is in fact a part of the behavior of female nonmothers and of fathers—as well as of people of both genders and of all ages in many different contexts in all countries in the world. Men, after all, often "care" more than women or think in terms of duties to particular others (say, they have to drive little Joey to baseball practice), and women have certainly caught on to the self-interested language of rights at least in the industrialized world (as in divorce courts, business, and so forth). So what becomes of the presumed "mothering" difference between men and women? A more satisfying theoretical account of the "difference"—if there is a difference at all—remains outstanding.

The second point that I believe is worth making here is that due to the unclarity of (and the controversy surrounding) the difference between male and female standpoints, sweeping generalizations regarding the nature of the female or male "self," "autonomy," or "agency" appear premature. This fact becomes of particular importance when we enter the political and constitutional domains, where weighty decisions affecting many lives are being decided in the name of political reform. Is it, for instance, really "connection" (in the abstract) that women are seeking and that should be expressed in law, as West claims? This cannot be the case. The slave was legally "connected" to a particular master, the serf by custom to his lord, and the traditional and subservient wife to her husband. West is surely not advocating this type of connection, but then what type is she recommending? In a later work, West confesses that such "connections" should be caring and "life enhancing," but she never enters into the difficulties with such notions, apparently thinking they are more or less obvious.[11]

I do not mean to single out West's theory. Many feminist analyses of law have been caught in such simple abstractions. For example, at least one recent theorist has suggested that it might be helpful to think of women in legal contexts as "partial" or "incomplete agents."[12] Both Nancy Hirschmann and, following her, Tracy Higgins have argued that under a liberal constitutional, capitalist regime and in terms of liberty and equality, women can only act "incompletely" relative to men. Women are incomplete agents for the reason that much of their oppression lies not in the area of public law (where they are more or less granted equal rights), but in the familial realm (patriarchal control of wife, restricted role of mother, and so on). This private realm is typically considered beyond the legitimate purview of the liberal state.[13] This being the case, according to Higgins, there is tremendous need for greater *affirmative state intervention on behalf* of women: intervention that works positively to free them from the tyrannies of private power, and supports them until they reach full and equal agency.

Although on many (perhaps most) particular policy recommendations, I may well side with Higgins or Hirschmann, my concern here lies with the basic analytic tools of feminist analysis. If we are being asked to view women as "incomplete agents" under present conditions, this might facilitate change in the direction of state intervention in certain contexts on behalf of women's freedom and equality. But by the same token, something very like "incomplete agency" has been invoked historically in the name of paternalistic guidance and control of women. How could such a loaded concept as "incompleteness" avoid these paternalistic connotations in the future?

Similarly, Higgins's analysis implies that typical male action under today's circumstances is somehow closer to "complete agency" than female activity is. But should feminists grant this? Is the woman who responds to the call of her child at night any less "self-determined" than the Wall Street trader's knee-jerk reaction to the fall of the price index? Is her vote for president more socially circumscribed than his? It is not at all clear that this is the case. Higgins takes extant male political action as the standard of legal "complete agency"—the norm to be lived up to—but this is one traditional assumption other feminists are working hard to overthrow. Once again, we are left in a quandary as to how to view "the difference" between women and men (if there is a difference), as well as how to formulate its nature.

Before we speak of different "selves" and "freedoms," "complete autonomous action" and "connection," I believe we need to look far more carefully at the historical and cultural context, as well as at the underlying social roles men and women have traditionally played. This is why, in this work, I focus on the category of ethical reproductive labor and *praxis* (1.4). In this manner, we may avoid confusing a clearly historical, culture-bound self with some abstract, metaphysical one of "connection," "completeness," or "free agency." At the same time, we will be in a better position to look more closely at the U.S. Constitution and the context of its creation, in order to determine what this Constitution lacks, given that women had so little voice in its construction and development. What were some of the reasons, for instance, why women were originally excluded as full citizens? It was not for the simple reason that they were perceived as lacking active reason *simpliciter* (Aristotle's excuse): by this time in history women were largely recognized as having it. So, too, many men were denied full citizenship despite the assumption of their possessing reason (e.g. nonwhites, the propertyless, and so on). In the following sections, I argue that women (as well as certain categories of men) were excluded from full citizenship at least in part because of the *type of labor* they performed. In contrast to production, ethical reproduction continued to be viewed as subservient.

If I am correct, and a primary difference between the genders (at least politically speaking) is the type of labor they performed, many women indeed still today speak in "a different voice." They show a marked tendency to appeal to concrete responsibilities before abstract rights, to insist on the importance of relationships before personal autonomy, and to stress the value of care and *philia* over freedom and property. But this difference can be traced back, not to women's special biology or capacity for motherhood, nor to some psychological "nature" of theirs, but to the thought patterns, concerns, and aims appropriate to their traditional practice. This hypothesis appears to be confirmed to the extent that men and women of different cultures—cultures still operating on a reproduction model, in contrast to ours of advanced commodity production—show similar marked tendencies.[14] As we have seen, the category of ethical reproductive *praxis* has been neglected by modern philosophers. Similarly, the tendency of our political Founders was also to view it as either supererogatory or sub-political. In the face of an ever growing concern with production, ethical *praxis* was either identified with virtuous but rare civic behavior (no longer to be expected of the average citizen) or it collapsed into the category of a quasi-biological labor that took place in private (performed by women or slaves). In either case, it was not viewed as an integral duty of American citizenship. We should hardly be surprised, therefore, that there is so little appeal to a civic friendship in the American tradition—certainly none in the 1787 Constitution. In step with the whole of the modern period, our Founders' concerns lay elsewhere. Before turning to an analysis of this Constitution, however, a few words on the general issue of constitutional interpretation are in order.

6.3. REFLECTIVE EQUILIBRIUM AND CONSTITUTIONAL INTERPRETATION

Scholars have distinguished at least four interpretative approaches to the U.S. Constitution: what might be called the appeal to authoritative historical exemplars, appeal to convention, appeal to moral reality, and the "constructivist" approach.[15] The first two approaches (although not without their distinguished defenders) have been widely criticized as inadequate, and they hardly seem capable in addition of rectifying the lacuna of women's representation in our tradition. The first, which appeals in questions of constitutional interpretation to the Founders' "intentions" in drafting the Constitution, begs the very issue at question: Why should women listen to this group of white men (including slave owners) holding a convention well over two hundred years ago in which women had no participation? What *grounds* the moral authority of the "original intentions" of these men (even if one could make determinate sense of this notion)? Similarly, the appeal to a positivist conventionalism should strike women as suspect for similar reasons. The view that law is neutrally given to us by a conventional legal authority independently of any need for interpretation does nothing to justify the authority of these legal conventions—particularly when they all too frequently neither defended women's interests nor worked for their good. We are thus left with one of the latter two approaches: the direct appeal to moral reality or some form of legal constructivism.

The direct appeal to moral reality is tempting, for we all tend to think we have a good grasp of it. This school of constitutional interpretation advocates reading the text, its history, and tradition in light of the best moral theory available, revising and even excising the text where necessary.[16] Such an approach may also seem particularly appealing to women who have historically suffered so from exclusion within the legal tradition. Why not reject the U.S. Constitution altogether? Why should women not hold their own convention, write a new constitution, and now pledge their allegiance to this new constitution's more-friendly-to-women principles?

Beyond the practical difficulty of such a move, this approach suffers from two major problems. The first is that women have no unified moral and political theory they jointly endorse (and they likely never will). The danger in this instance is one of forsaking the somewhat uncomfortable "known" for the radically unknown, which could be far worse. The second reason for not attempting this move is even more important: such an approach eschews the lessons of history. It views moral insight not as something garnered from long experience and interaction with others—as something also embodied in custom and practice—but as the product of some individual's (or group of individuals') reflection alone. Where the first two approaches uncritically accept the historical given, this third way (in Hegel's words) tries to leap over its own shadow; it is neglectful of its own sociohistorical conditions.

So it appears we are left with a position midway between a simple deference to the Founders' words or a conventionalism, on the one hand, and direct individualistic appeals to moral reality, on the other. In short, we are left with the necessity of *interpreting* our Constitution and its history, and hence with some form of legal "constructivist" approach. This fourth way is best exemplified in the writings of such legal theorists as Ronald Dworkin, David Richards, and Cass Sunstein.[17] Moreover, whatever the particular differences in the legal constructivist positions, the general approach may be traced back to John Rawls's method of reflective equilibrium (adapted from Nelson Goodman), a method that is now being employed in the legal sphere. This method was briefly discussed in chapter 1 (1.4). What is its promise for a feminist constitutional theory?

The method of reflective equilibrium is that method of philosophical reflection whereby sincere moral agents seek a match, or "equilibrium," between their particular considered moral or political judgments (formed through concrete observation and practice) and a set of general principles that purports to generate them (1.4).[18] We saw that such "back and forth" reflection between particular judgments and general principle operates first between the individual's own set of moral convictions (narrow reflective equilibrium) and then between his or her unified convictions and an ever expanding circle of others (wide reflective equilibrium). Significantly, there exists the possibility of not merely a political but a *legal* reflective equilibrium, according to Rawls, whereby theorists elaborate "the basic intuitive ideas" and "implicitly recognized principles" embedded in "the public political culture" of a society, with the goal of resolving particular historical conflicts.[19] In the legal case, the aim is to arrive at the best interpretation of the U.S. Constitution, say, with the aim of forging common ground in areas where discord now reigns.

In this legal instance, the particular judgments appealed to will include not only those embodied in the text of the Constitution itself, but those found in the history of its construction and ratification, as well as in its interpretation over the past two centuries (e.g., in the Declaration of Independence, the *Federalist Papers*, the Court opinions, the thousands of statutes enacted, the various rules and principles appealed to, and so on). This legal database is then subjected to differing general interpretations, which aim not only to "fit" and organize the data but to present the Constitution in its best light—that is, make it a sounder and more just legal document. As one theorist notes, U.S. constitutional interpretation inevitably requires us to use principles external to that Constitution itself.[20] The "text" is not self-interpreting, but necessitates deep forays into moral and political theory for its best reading. This is necessary not only for the clarification of the historical texts (the original intentions, records, traditions, etc.) but also for the identification of the more general truths contained therein and of the more abstract background rights that the Constitution protects.[21] Moral and political theory, in conjunction with interpretive history, plays an essential role in U.S. constitutional interpretation and in understanding the American legal tradition.[22]

If we are convinced of something like the appropriateness of the constructivist method for U.S. constitutional interpretation, we are still left with numerous difficulties if our concern is the traditional lacuna of women's representation. As noted in chapter 1, if reflective equilibrium must begin with the particular judgments and "basic intuitive ideas" of our "public political culture," it is difficult not to notice that this culture was composed (until very recently) entirely of males (1.4). Women were typically denied rights to vote, to go to university, to hold public office, to own private property, or to speak or appear at public gatherings, and this often well into the twentieth century.[23] It is thus highly unlikely that many of the considered moral convictions *shared by women*—by those confined to the private familial sphere and who performed the preponderance of ethical reproductive labor—ever found their way into the original balancing act of a public and legal reflective equilibrium. This means, however, that traditional public reflection excluded from the start many collective insights of such labor: insights regarding the alleviation of emotional and physical need; the resolution of dilemmas of social trust and cooperation; concerning the social and material conditions of human communal existence, or regarding care, friendship, and the maintenance of long-term relationships. To what sort of distortion in our Constitution—and by extension in our public conception of our selves—does this absence lead?

Two points should here be stressed. First, regarding method, it is clear that if feminists are to overcome the male bias in even the best of legal constructivist thought, they cannot rest content with examining only the public texts and the history of their interpretation, for these public texts have largely ignored women's traditional concerns. Hence, for a more adequate political and legal reflective equilibrium (including a more adequate constitutional theory), the constructivist method must be radicalized and extended into new domains: the vast repertoire of particular, considered moral convictions hitherto relegated to the "private," nonpolitical, and noneconomic spheres—whether the diaries of the housewife, the manifestos of the slave, or the rantings of the abolitionist—must now be drawn into the original data pool from which a society-wide reflective equilibrium at least begins. Earlier I referred to this method as a reflective equilibrium that now stresses *the personal* (1.4). This is not to say that we must end with unmodified concepts of individual care and concern, friendship, and so on in the public realm, but it is to insist that they not be excluded from the start.

Second, the project of including a reflective equilibrium of the so-called private sphere promises to shed new light in a number of areas. Not only will it illuminate background conceptions of the legal person (the different assumptions regarding gendered social roles), not only will we be able better to understand those social conditions upon which our political state in the narrow sense—and our Constitution in particular—until now rests, but further, if allowed adequate development, such a project may offer a new standpoint from which to evaluate our traditional notions of "constitutional essentials" and even of the state itself. That is, we may consciously begin to construct a new and more adequate Original Position—this time from the perspective of *the ethical reproduction of persons*—from which to evaluate traditional legal theory, relative now to the specific needs of our time and in light of concrete social developments. Perhaps we might even make good the demand that a central function of the state of the future be, not merely the maintenance of law and order and a military prepared for war, nor simply a policing of citizenry and productive competition, but the furtherance of the conditions of the possibility of a genuine civic friendship as well.

6.4 THE FOUNDING PERIOD AND "FRIENDS OF MANKIND"

It is now time to proffer my feminist reading of the U.S. Constitution. My claim is that the best way of interpreting the history of the U.S. Constitution—from the Declaration of Independence, the

Federalist Papers, and ratification debates, through Reconstruction, the New Deal, and up to the civil rights and women's movements—is to view the (zigzag) evolution of the document, not simply as an elaboration of the basic concepts of freedom and equality between persons (as has often been claimed), but as an elaboration of the value of civic friendship as well. Further, I shall claim that *only* some such reading—one that finds central room for the independent and distinct value of *philia*—will afford the genuine and equal inclusion of half the population in the modern state, whether theoretically or practically.

It is generally recognized that there are at least three major "transformative" periods in the history of the U.S. Constitution, periods when crucial substantive change was brought about: the Founding, Reconstruction, and the New Deal.[24] These periods were times in which profound changes in popular opinion gained authoritative constitutional recognition; they were also times of growing inclusiveness and a diminished inequality. Indeed, I believe these periods may be described as ones in which it is increasingly (if begrudgingly) acknowledged that the political state is—or at least *ought to be*—an expression of a *civic friendship* between citizens. Aristotle's thesis is by no means dead. Here I will briefly discuss the Founding period, turning to Reconstruction in the following section (6.5). Issues surrounding the New Deal and the welfare state I leave to the next chapter.

The great eighteenth-century slogan, "*Liberté, Egalité, Fraternité*" rang out across Europe and surely (to some extent) inspired the American Revolutionaries. Oddly enough, however, unlike the first two terms of the famous triad, the notion of "fraternity" did not work its way into the Declaration of Independence or into the new U.S. Constitution (although it does appear in the Articles of Confederation).[25] Nor does the notion of friendship—at least at first sight—play any significant role in the *Federalist Papers*. Still, I wish to argue that the new American republic implicitly furthered the value of fraternity along with those of equality and liberty, and this to an extent the world had rarely known.

For one, the Declaration of Independence publicly proclaims that "all men are created equal," and the American Founders clearly sought (again, only to some extent) to embody this self-evident truth in the new republic. This claim is more than simply an appeal to the value of equality, however. For, when I deny that the aristocrat or any other man is better than I am (politically speaking), or when, in doing so, I further deny that any man has authority over me without good reason, I appeal to "equality." I can thus further the value of equality by *promoting only my own* (let us call this strategic or "Hobbesian" equality). The case is quite different, however, if I sincerely proclaim that "all are equal." For here I simultaneously grant that those *traditionally beneath me* are my equals as well. Here, ipso facto, I grant or extend my position of equality to others too—and *that* is furthering not just the value of equality but of friendship as well. One of the distinguishing marks of genuine friendship, as we have seen, is *wanting the other to be equal too* (2.6). Similarly, the most minimal friendship characteristically requires providing the other with good reasons and not appealing to force, fraud, or subterfuge.

If we consider the attempt to embody a doctrine of universal equality between persons in legal institutions of right (again attempted in the Constitution), we have a clear instance of what I am calling "civic friendship." Here, I do not personally know the vast majority of these other persons, nor am I ever going to; nonetheless, I wish them well. I seek a general system whereby any rights and privileges that I seek for myself are granted to them also (including even to my personal enemies). I seek a public order whereby I at once relinquish my superiority as well as refuse my subordination, which thus embodies a reciprocity of principle upon which I act.

The critical point is that modern proclamations of universal right (unknown to the hierarchical thinking of the ancient world) theoretically embody a high degree of public regard for the special interests of *every* human being—however limited this regard may be in practice. They proclaim a guarantee to each citizen of a basic set of rights—to life, liberty, the pursuit of happiness, and so forth—which in principle is meant to be an impartial standard of public concern (3.1). So, too, such public universal norms, if genuinely upheld in practice, can prevent the civic union from degenerating into a partial "friendship politics," into a power play of private sects and hostile, opposing factions (2.6). Finally, in the efforts to uphold and to realize these universal rights in practice, citizens may acknowledge and express their general concern and good will toward the interests of each particular individual in the concrete. Such norms, together with the effort to uphold them, may be considered an expression of a modern impartial civic friendship. Surely, the U.S. Constitution's enunciation of various rights—from the personal rights of freedom of thought and religion to the more political rights of free speech and the press, of assembly, due process, the denial of the legitimacy of ex post facto laws, and so on—publicly acknowledges and protects central concerns of each citizen and aims to establish new and higher standards of civic behavior.

Of course, in the Constitution of 1787 such expressions of civic friendship were quite limited: titles of nobility were explicitly prohibited, a basic set of rights and civic equality was proclaimed, but full citizenship was granted in practice to a relatively small group of propertied white males. Women, blacks, those without property, Native Americans, Asians, and others were characteristically excluded from the start from active citizenship.[26] Thus the scope of early American fraternity did not extend far and its content was relatively homogeneous (restricted to predominantly white, Protestant propertied males of northern European descent). Nonetheless, by the lights of the day, the new nation repudiated inherited privilege, attempted to establish a "republic of reasons" over arbitrary privilege and force, and allowed the extension of equality to a rare degree.[27]

So why is there so little appeal to "fraternity" by the Founders, whether in the *Federalist Papers,* the ratification debates, or in the U.S. Constitution itself? In accordance with my general thesis regarding political liberalism, much of the absence can be explained by noting once again the rise and pervasive influence of the production model of activity (3.2–5); the Founders are simply no exception. In the *Federalist Papers,* for example, the authoritative explanation and defense of the 1787 U.S. Constitution, the central arguments presented by Madison, Hamilton, and Jay (alias Publius)—regarding the advantages of a strong national government, the analysis of factions, the role of commerce, the necessary checks and balances of government—all assume that personal reproductive labor (childcare, household and local duties, and so forth) will continue to be performed primarily by women, servants, or slaves. Such activity is neither problematized in these papers, nor considered a form of rational labor at all. If one searches for any equivalent of what we have been calling civic reproductive *praxis*—the distinguishing mark of Aristotle's full citizen (2.5)—it does emerge, but the category remains sketchy and appears restricted in the new republic to a small group of elected representatives. That is, in Madison's theory of "enlightened" and indirect representation, such representatives have the job of deliberating about the interests of others and regarding the body politic as a whole. These enlightened men are chosen by the other citizens not so much to do the latter's bidding as to "deliberate the public good" by way of "refining and enlarging the public views."[28] It is clear that for Madison, these men should exhibit a "civic virtue" and a "love of justice" to a high degree (Fed, No. 10). Interestingly enough, he even makes appeal to such impartial, virtuous citizens as the "friends of mankind" (Fed, No. 40). It is one of the central benefits of a large republic, in Madison's view, that less worthy candidates will find it more difficult to gather widespread support and be elected to office; a large republic thus reduces the danger of unfit self-interested men or factious majorities ruling (Fed, No. 10).

Because such "friends of mankind" are so rare, however, while the "unfriendly passions" and "the propensity of mankind to fall into mutual animosities" are so great, a general strategy of dividing government against itself, of controlling the effects of the factious spirit by checks and balances, and of using "auxiliary precautions" such as restricting popular participation is the ultimate route advocated (Fed, Nos. 10 and 51). It is thus clear (at least for Madison) that the proposed Constitution is far more than a mere set of ground rules for interest-group struggles pursuing their private self-interest. The *Federalist Papers* reveals repeated appeals to civic virtue, to public service, and to "friends of popular government," as well as to "the friends of liberty," "of faith," and "of mankind" (Fed, Nos. 10 and 40). The great weakness of these famous papers is that they provide no institutional way of reproducing such friends; these virtuous men presumably spring up here and there like mushrooms. Again, while there is much institutional provision made by Publius (and by extension the tradition) for countering effects of public hostility, animosity, and faction, there is little or no provision made within the government for the institutional reproduction of friendly civic relations. These crucial relations will presumably "take care of themselves."

Indeed, if one seeks positive provisions, one is far more likely to find them in the American anti-Federalist writings that criticized the new 1787 Constitution: in Brutus's discussions of greater popular "participation" as a check against corruption and greed; in Cato's claim that political participation is an "education in virtue"; in Federal Farmer's call for more direct and "substantial representation" by the people and in his awareness of the "expense" and "time" needed for it; in DeWitt's insistence that the "means of education" should continue to be attended to and "the fountains of science brought within the reach of poverty" and "every child"; and in Cato's claim that public service is the only honor, "but the framers have departed from this democratic principle" by leaving men in office for so long (six years in the Senate).[29] These distinguished critics presumably "lost the debate," but it was central to their criticism that civic reproductive *praxis* be institutionally embodied in any political state genuinely calling itself "democratic." And their writings underscore this original lack.

If we take another look at arguably the most famous of all passages in the *Federalist Papers*—"The Federalist No. 10," in which Madison discusses "the causes of faction" among men and pronounces the solution to lie in the "checks and balances" of power—this original inadequacy is only driven home. Madison writes: "The diversity in the faculties of men, from which the rights of property originate, is not less an insuperable obstacle to a uniformity of interests. The protection of these faculties is the first object of government."

It is quite certain that Madison, in pointing to the sources of faction here, has in mind the diverse faculties of those who perform the productive labor. That is, the deliberative and emotional "faculties" of women—or of those primarily involved in ethical reproductive labor and *praxis*—are not being included for reasons that, if spelled out, are quite illuminating. It is obvious, first, that women's traditional activity is not being included because at this point in history women's reproductive labor (or any of her labor for that matter) ushered in no property rights at all. The fruits of whatever work women did in the home (or even outside it) typically belonged to their father or husband (under Blackstone's Community of Persons).

Second, it would be odd to draw attention to ethical reproductive labor as an "insuperable obstacle to a uniformity of interests," for (as we have argued) it is precisely that type of labor that characteristically seeks to forge or further a trust and unity of interests—in the best case, freely and autonomously. The proper *telos* of reproductive activity is not private property at all, recall, but a "shared appropriation of the human world" (2.5). The appropriate type of ownership such activity ushers in, therefore, is hardly the institution of private property, but something closer to a joint stewardship or common possession (3.3 and 5.5).

In the above passage Madison clearly has in mind different types of *male* productive laboring activities: individual farming or large-scale agriculture, small- or large-scale manufacture, different branches of commercial activity, banking, and so forth. The issue for him is how to protect these different branches of competitive productive industry without the civic body being rent by faction. The question for *us* now becomes: Why should it be in the nature of government to protect the different "productive" faculties of men and not those of ethical reproductive activity?

The answer more than two hundred years later can only be that it is *not*. Insofar as ethical reproductive labor and *praxis* are acknowledged as being of critical importance—not only for the ethical reproduction of persons, but for that of just civic relations (2.6)—it is impossible any longer to believe that such forms of labor lie "outside" the public's concern. Of course, the modern state has been implicated in this type of labor from the start by promoting, protecting, discouraging, or simply tolerating different forms: whether forced, slave, gendered, or private. What the state has not so far done is to perceive its involvement or role in the reproduction of citizen relations as an explicit—and specifically democratic—responsibility. The burning issue for us today is thus not *whether* the state should involve itself in the sphere of the reproduction of civic relations, but what *form* such involvement should take (7.3). And on *this* question, of course, the Founding Fathers have little or nothing to say.

At least two points may be gleaned from our brief survey of the founding period. First, while recognizing the necessity that other-directed "friends of mankind" must legislate in order to preserve peace and afford genuine justice, when it comes time to provide for the education or reproduction of such civic friends—and for positive civic relations generally—the Federalists (as well as much of the ensuing tradition) have little to say. There is no recognition of the affirmative political obligation or necessary cooperative *praxis* that goes into creating fair and equal background civic relations.

It is thus not particularly surprising that today, at the beginning of the twenty-first century, we have hardly avoided injurious "faction." On the contrary, the gap in the United States between the haves and the have-nots grows ever larger (it is already greater than at any point since the Great Depression), with corporate executives of the top companies earning over four hundred times the wage of the average manufacturing worker.[30] We have a ruling corporate culture that is hierarchical, secretive, and tyrannical—anything but open and democratic[31]—at the same time as the electorate is so apathetic that roughly half of eligible citizens do not even bother to vote.[32] We are perhaps the most violent of all advanced industrial nations, with gun ownership still enshrined in our Constitution and with one out of every thirty-two adults behind bars or on probation or parole.[33] U.S. military expenditure outstrips that of all the other military powers in the world *combined*. And yet, despite all our American wealth and power, we are among the most pusillanimous of modern democratic nations in terms of the public granting of welfare or benefits.[34] We are one of the few without universal health care (and with nearly 50 million uninsured); we have a system of inadequate family leave plans and of short-term, punitive welfare benefits; our public schools are failing; and our aid to foreign countries has fallen to as little as 0.10 percent of our rich economy.[35] Simply put, our level of awareness and positive concern for fellow citizens—and our practical or material doing for them—is shockingly low.

Secondly, once we view ethical reproductive labor as a distinct form of rational activity—and acknowledge its central importance—it becomes the duty of government to protect, promote, and distribute it fairly in the same manner as it protects and promotes manufacturing or farming or any other form of productive labor (7.3). Indeed, when we look to the history of the U.S. Constitution over the nineteenth and twentieth centuries, we can identify extraordinary periods where this awareness slowly dawns on future generations—although hardly without struggle and certainly not without strenuous opposition.

6.5 REVISITING RECONSTRUCTION

The second great transformation normally cited by scholars in American constitutional law is the change leading up to and culminating in the Thirteenth, Fourteenth, and Fifteenth (the so-called Reconstruction) Amendments to the Constitution. On the reading proffered here, this legal transformation, which officially freed the Confederate slaves and constitutionally guaranteed all citizens equal protection of the laws, may be described as one whereby the American political system began explicitly to acknowledge its responsibility in providing and maintaining the conditions for the ethical reproduction of citizens. That is, the Reconstruction Amendments are a first indication that the state explicitly recognizes a duty, however imperfectly, to engage in civic reproductive activity and to promote the conditions of a civic equality among its citizens. During this tumultuous time, moreover, all the necessary criteria of our definition of civic friendship were expressed, some even embodied in law (2.7).

For instance, awareness of the evils of the system of slavery (and the brutal Black Codes of the Jacksonian era), as well as sympathy with the downtrodden African American population, became widespread with the abolitionist movement; to this movement is even attributed the novel idea of an American people "unbounded by race," not to be found in the original 1787 Constitution.[36] As Angelina Grimké (daughter of a South Carolina slaveholder and a prominent abolitionist and feminist) wrote, the crusade against slavery was the nation's preeminent "school in which *human rights* . . . are investigated."[37] This period was marked by a widespread *awareness*, as well as a *desire* for the other (the slave) to be legally equal, backed by a committed *practical doing* (including the great fratricidal conflict known as the American Civil War), leading to one of the greatest extensions of the system of individual rights in American history. We can even glimpse an alternative conception of the state emerging as well. Union armies not only won the war, but in addition General Sherman's men entered the South to protect and enforce the rights of the newly emancipated slave; a Freedmen's Bureau was established in 1865 (and a Department of Education in 1867); Congress (at the behest of Thaddeus Stevens, Sumner, and other radical Republicans) even authorized the president to confiscate Rebel lands with plans of providing "forty acres and a mule" to every adult male freedman in order to begin life anew as an independent farmer. Indeed, more than 30,000 acres of farmland were set aside before the political and social reaction set in.[38]

Reconstruction is often viewed as the most radical, progressive, enlightened, corrupt, even "unconstitutional" time in American history, depending upon one's ultimate point of view. Here I note only that many of the actions taken (I exclude the atrocities committed by Sherman's army) do not sound radical from a feminist perspective—or at least not from a feminist perspective that stresses the value of ethical reproductive *praxis*. That the political state—after more than four score years of direct complicity in one of the worst crimes known to humanity (equaled only by the slaughter of America's native inhabitants) should seek redress for its nearly 4 million victims and actually *work* to establish the conditions for the possibility of just social relations free of prejudice and domination would appear merely the natural realization of the value of civic friendship. Depending upon one's conception of the state and its primary functions, it even becomes a critical *duty*. Despite the Reconstruction Amendments, of course, a genuine American civic friendship was not to be.

On our reading, American civic friendship failed to emerge from Reconstruction for two primary reasons. First, the model of "freedom" advocated by the Republican Party and many abolitionists (now applied to the circumstances of the slave as well) was still essentially the old Lockean *production model* of activity. For example, Abraham Lincoln wrote in 1857 with respect to the black woman slave: "In certain respects she is not my equal; but in her natural right to eat the bread she earns with her own hands without asking leave of any one else, she is my equal and the equal of all others."[39] Similarly, also echoing Locke, the Radical Republican Thaddeus Stevens in Congress urged guaranteeing the freedmen homesteads upon the very soil they had tilled because, like the recently emancipated serfs of Russia, "they have earned this, they have worked the land for ages, and they are entitled to it."[40] The Lockean image of owning the fruits of one's productive labor abounds in abolitionist literature and even becomes the standard of emancipation.

The right to the fruits of one's labor was legally implemented, however, without in the end securing the necessary background conditions we enumerated earlier: being recognized as an equal (to those who were male and white), possessing or having access to land, legally owning not only one's own body and labor, but a set of skills and the tools of a trade (1.2). On the Lockean model, moreover, labor alone is viewed as creating 99.99 one-hundredths of value; the earth supplies only "the almost worthless materials" (*ST*, para. 43). On this conception, legally owning one's own labor should be enough to bring freedom and value creation. In actual fact, however, the absence of these other background conditions—in combination with the revoking of land for the freed slaves under President Johnson, the withdrawal of northern troops from the South, and the whittling away of what political rights the ex-slaves had achieved—soon reduced the legally freed men and women in the South to a system of sharecropping and ultimately, once again, peonage. By the turn of the twentieth century, Jim Crow laws were firmly in place and remained so until the civil rights movement of the 1960s.

Thus, on the one hand, the necessary *civic reproductive labor* enabling the freed African American to attain genuine autonomy, although recognized by many and even begun, was never carried through during Reconstruction times. The freed slaves were released from bondage amid a hostile and resentful southern population humiliated by the war; they possessed few skills, lacked access to land, and received diminishing support and protection from the North. Paradoxically—and in direct contrast to the implications of the Lockean metaphor—in order for any individual (or citizen) to achieve true independence and autonomy (particularly if the citizen's earlier status was one of enslavement), a tremendous quantity and quality of social and civic reproductive labor is required. Genuine political autonomy—the ability to think up, pursue, and realize one's plans in the public sphere—requires not just the bare recognition of others, but the practical good will and support of fellow citizens. This is what feminists have begun calling "relational autonomy"; it cannot in the first instance be achieved on one's own.[41]

This fact points to a further reason for the failure of Reconstruction relevant to my thesis: the attempt after the Civil War to impose fairer social relations and a civic friendship on the South "from above"—that is, forcibly by way of northern armies and police. The Marxist W. E. B. DuBois famously argued that due to the shortcomings of liberalism (and American assumptions that the market will benefit everyone), the use of simple force was needed to overhaul the basis of the property system in the South.[42] In the view presented here, however, it remains doubtful that further forcible alterations of the "economic base" could have been successful (even if practically achievable). It is not clear how physical force alone could alleviate the continuing fact of deeply ingrained racism, and the question remains from whence a "good will" between citizens would ever emerge. We can never know for sure, but short of colonization elsewhere or of the total separation of the black population, the white South's anger, humiliation, and resentment after the Civil War might well have been directed in even greater measure at the freed men and women if a form of socialist collectivization had been sought.

In this respect the women's movement of this century may be more promising. Unlike the reigning paradigms of economic production or of military action—where imposing one's will by brute force is frequent and even characteristic—the model of ethical reproduction appears far more appropriate for long-lasting social change. A natural next step would be not only to stress the importance of such labor—as well as the importance of civic education and civic works generally—but to bring this attitude into government. Unlike in Reconstruction times, that is, the social "force" of the women's movement is not being imposed from elsewhere: from above or without, by government officials or armies. Women are everywhere in our midst and form the possibility of a peaceful social revolution "from within."

The growing awareness of the necessity of a civic friendship (the revolution from within, as it were) becomes even more obvious with that third great transformation of American constitutional law, the Revolution of 1937 commonly known as the New Deal. Although I leave a discussion of the necessity and dangers of the welfare state to the next chapter, I will make one point here. As scholars have generally indicated, the end of the Lochner era (the period from roughly the 1890s to 1937, during which the Supreme Court tended to strike down economic regulation of working conditions, wages, or working hours) and the turn to a national welfare state is often considered to begin with *Nebbia v. New York* (291 U.S. 502 [1934]), in which the Court cited the simple principle that "[n]either property rights nor contract rights are absolute; for government cannot exist if the citizen may at will use his property to the detriment of his fellows."

Beneath the surface of the American constitutional tradition and alongside the explicit values of liberty and equality, there lurks the necessary requirement of a minimal civic friendship between citizens as well. Moreover, a direct consciousness of this necessity appears to grow with each of the three major legal transformations. Civic friendship is a vaguely perceptible sub-theme of the U.S. constitutional tradition. The hope presented here is that it might become an explicit and even dominant theme, as women continue to gain their rightful place within the spheres of philosophy, politics, and law.

6.6 RECTIFYING THE LACUNA IN REPRESENTATION

What might be a concrete example of political reproductive *praxis*, or what I call the civic labor of democracy, an example perfectly in keeping with the U.S. Constitution? There are numerous institutions that may encourage and express a civic friendship to a greater or lesser degree. In chapter 5 we argued for a more demanding version of Rawls's difference principle—an economic principle Rawls calls "a principle of fraternity"—and for greater restrictions on the accumulation of ownership and private wealth (5.6). In this chapter we have indicated that a civic friendship would require some form of reparations for centuries of wrongs committed by the state against its citizens, whether those wrongs be centuries of black slavery or the extirpation of millions of America's original inhabitants and the outright theft of their land.[43] Similarly, in the following chapter I will argue for the value of a civil service where ethical reproductive (and not simple military or productive) labor would be more equally divided among all citizens (7.5). In all these cases, the argument rests on an appeal to the value of friendship as well as to women's historical labor in furthering it. Here I explore one further avenue of institutional embodiment that also appears to kill two birds with one stone; that is, it furthers women's participation in public life at the same time as it encourages a civic friendship among all citizens.

Recently the awareness is growing in the United States that there must be a better and more democratic electoral system than our present one. I do not refer simply to the call for more civil political discourse (which is far too weak), nor merely to the issue of campaign finance reform and the public funding of elections (which is clearly also important). Rather, I refer more generally to the American two-party system. Numerous thinkers in both England and the United States have by now argued carefully that a form of proportional representation is fairer and more just, encourages greater voter turnout and more substance-oriented campaigns, is more representative and inclusive of women and other minorities, as well as simply more democratic than our "winner take all" system.[44] Certainly, the evidence that connects women's greater representation in government with those countries practicing proportional representation is overwhelming.[45] Here I shall add one further argument of my own: in comparison with our present political system, a system of proportional representation appears far superior in terms of the value of civic friendship between citizens.

It is widely recognized that there are a number of different mechanisms by which a representative democratic system—while assuming the principle of "one person, one vote" as well as universal suffrage—can aggregate votes. Collective democratic decisions can be reached by the unanimity rule (where each has an absolute veto), by the stipulated majority rule (decision requires, say, 70 percent of votes), by the simple majority or plurality rule, by lot, or by different forms of proportional representation. It is generally held in our own tradition, from the Federalists up until the early work of Robert Dahl, that the simple majority rule is both the most effective and (considering that unanimity is unrealistic) the most democratic. But recently the problem of "the permanent minority" has surfaced. No matter how much a political minority succeeds in organizing its members (Dahl), no matter how much "log-rolling" and "vote-trading" takes place (Buchanan and Tullock), it is still possible, if not highly likely, that an ensconced majority will view certain decisions as nonnegotiable (particularly if they do not need minority support on a wide range of other social issues). While women can perhaps conceive of themselves as one day (in the far future) in the representative majority in Congress, this is hardly the case with blacks or other oppressed and truly permanent minorities. Thus we must ask: What are the background assumptions at work behind this critical rule, which gives the maximum payoff to one group and zero payoff to the other on issues that could be of fundamental importance to the latter?

The problem with the simple majority rule is not only that it assumes that the typical political conflict is an agonistic "winner take all" situation, while this is probably closer to the exception in most political contexts (where compromise is the rule). The situation is even worse. The simple majority procedure actually *transforms* many disagreements into the limiting case of zero-sum conflict. That is, by employing this rule, the system produces maximum payoff to the majority and zero payoff to the minority—actually *enhancing the inequality* between them—when there could have been any number of other options. The winners in this case need not consider the interests of the poor losers further, nor need they address the latter's arguments nor their situation (that is, at least until the next round of elections or some public eruption). But this, I want to claim, is a *failure of civic friendship*. The institutionalized procedure encourages not only inequality, but a systematic insolence, on the one hand, and hostility, anger, and resentment, on the other. It hardly encourages their amelioration.

If one assumes a competitive, adversarial model of politics, the simple majority rule is difficult to challenge in terms of the value of either freedom or equality. Its defenders simply answer that there must be some procedure, that unanimity is unrealistic, and that under this rule each individual and group is as free as any other to organize. Each has equal chances in trying to affect the outcome; all have the same opportunities to present their arguments and to persuade others, and so forth. Democracy does not entail equal influence on *outcome*, after all (which is impossible), and, surely, one must admit that there is something wrong with a minority imposing its views on the majority (the reason we fought the Revolution in the first place). What all these classic defenses of the two-party system overlook, however, is that there is another alternative: a system of proportional representation.

Let us compare this alternative, which is some form of institutional proportionality, say, in the decision by the electorate of who will represent them in government. Here the losers will, in proportion to the vote received, still gain representation (and here third and even fourth parties are likely). Thus, if three parties put forth candidates for representation and Party A receives 55 percent of the vote; Party B, 35 percent; and Party C, 10 percent, the parties will have 55 percent, 35 percent, and 10 percent of the seats in government, respectively. In this case, those who voted for B or C candidates have not "wasted" their votes; they still gain representation in government, although not to the extent they may have wanted. Similarly, the winning party A cannot claim a "sweeping mandate" for its views with barely half of the vote of the electorate. In contrast to "winner take all" (100 percent or zero), the result of this form of electoral system is far closer to a cooperative ruling. The debate between the parties will continue inside the halls of government, and further discussion and genuine deliberation are not foreclosed but become a necessity. Proportional representation not only reduces inequality, but also gives deliberative democracy a genuine chance while encouraging more participation among the population—all signs of a greater civic friendship.

Critics of the system, of course, frequently point to the "inefficiency" of such a system, priding themselves on the single-member plurality system's ability to make swift and forceful decisions, while European parliaments are often bogged down in negotiations and broken into myriad splinter groups. I believe such pride is misplaced, although I can hardly defend the system of proportional representation on this point here.[46] My aim lies elsewhere. It is to provide a further example of how a political institution—while continuing to respect both the freedom and equality of citizens—might *in addition* foster cooperation and political friendship between them, rather than impede it or encourage its opposite. The institution's superiority is proven in other terms than those of the old debate.

6.7 FRIENDSHIP AND DEMOCRACY

I believe we have before us a novel way of viewing the normative development (as well as lapses) of the U.S. constitutional tradition: as a growing awareness of the necessity, not only of the political values of liberty and equality, but of civic friendship also. This interpretation does no violence to the historical texts at the same time as it *centrally* includes women and their traditional activity in the constitutional evolution (women are no longer conceived as mere afterthoughts). So too, it offers a novel way (or at least a renewed way) of conceiving of democracy itself.[47] As noted earlier, most democratic theorists today account for the superiority of democracy in terms of the value of freedom or of equality or both (see preface). Stressing the critical value of civic friendship, by contrast, not only allows us a new perspective on such contemporary debates, but it even provides the tools to break through various impasses.

One such impasse concerns two dominant and competing senses of *equality*. Let us call the first "strategic equality of coordination," a conception that reaches back at least to Hobbes. On this conception, I grudgingly concede equality to you basically *because I must*; I am no more powerful than you. A second conception, stressed by Kant, refers to the recognition of a deeper *moral equality* and respect between persons, which I have a duty to uphold and further. These two competing conceptions have played off one another over and over again in the past few hundred years, right up until the present-day theories of a Gauthier, Dahl, or Rawls. By considerations of equality alone, however, it is difficult to decide between them; both appear to have their legitimate place.

If, however, we introduce and weigh the distinct value of friendship as well—and keep in mind the vast quantity of actual reproductive labor being performed—the balance, I believe, tips in favor of the latter conception. That is, the equality that truly does and ought to concern us is the moral respect and positive regard we have for persons; fear of them becomes a derivative mode. For (unlike certain other types of creatures) persons are not the sort of beings to which most of us can respond neutrally or simply in fear. Persons are creatures of reason and moral sensibility, and our most basic stance toward them characteristically remains one of *positive regard*.[48]

A similar point can be made with regard to the value of liberty. Many see the preeminent value of democracy as consisting in the freedom of individuals to decide regarding their own life; hence, by extension, all citizens possess the right in democracy to participate in political decision making. But among this group of freedom theorists we again find two distinct camps. On the one side, we find the libertarians and neo-conservatives who define freedom *negatively*, as nearly unlimited individual choice, and who tend to view political decision making as no different from simple market choices.[49] On the other extreme, we have those who stress the notion of *positive* freedom and who, as democrats, proclaim the right of each person not simply to choose but to be afforded the conditions of self-development.[50]

Here again, I believe the debate gets stalled because focusing on the concept of freedom by itself (or even in conjunction with that of equality) cannot resolve the difficulty between what appear to be two quite legitimate uses. If we introduce the value of friendship, however, embedding our understanding of freedom within the context of what is important to us in our everyday personal and political lives, the impasse begins to dissolve. We find that in some contexts the right to choose is paramount, that in others the background enabling conditions are critical, and at still other times we might willingly forgo our freedom altogether for the sake of the other person or of other values. Certainly in personal life we often freely limit our individual freedom for the sake of friendship; a similar self-restraint appears just as necessary in public, political life. The normative ideal of the flexible give-and-take of friendship may act as a guiding thread in political disputes for when asserting one's freedom is right and reasonable, and when such assertion amounts to nothing more than simple license.

In this manner, focusing on the political value of friendship may actually help reveal the limits of legitimate civic freedom and equality. In the best case, these values must be seen as *conditioned* by a civic friendship. That is, individual freedom (as in libertarian doctrine) or the demand for further equality (as in various dogmatic communist regimes) reach their limits when they erode, not personal friendship (people must be free to choose their closest friends) but civic friendship: that institutionalized basic trust and good will citizens must have for one another as a precondition for justice. If I am correct, as democratic theorists, we must go beyond the simple debate between freedom and equality, and include this third distinct value. At the same time, as feminists, our job is—consistent with the best of women's historical role—to elaborate this value both personally and politically, only now never leaving our hard-won freedom and equality behind.

In sum, I am not claiming that civic friendship is the only value in democracy; individual freedom and equality (and even efficiency) are clearly crucial as well. Rather, I argue that it is central and must enter into the philosophical and political debate. Democracy is *also* the political extension of the friendship between equals, and if democracy violates this central value, it fundamentally compromises its nature. In the final analysis, the reason is this: we can appeal to the freedom and equality of others (not just to our own) until the cows come home, but if no one cares for these others, if no one is motivated to help them when they are down or to check them when they grow arrogant, all appeals to freedom and equality—and particularly to justice—are in vain. Civic friendship points to that necessary prior motivation for democracy to begin with and to its ultimate source in satisfying and equal human relationships for their own sake. The U.S. constitutional tradition has skirted around this value for over two centuries—it is high time that it finally looks it squarely in the face.

7 THE STATE OF FEMINIST THEORY

The citizenship of women is more of a challenge,
a source and object of change than it is a fait accompli.
ETIENNE BALIBAR

7.1 THE STATE REVISITED

Theorizing the nature of the political state from a feminist point of view is still in its earliest stages. Despite a major transformation of consciousness occasioned by the women's movement—and on a scale that suggests powerful historical forces are at work—the state is perhaps the last and certainly among the most powerful of institutions that needs not only to be transformed, but in the first instance *reconceived.* In recent years, however, feminist political theorists have tended more toward exploring the realm of "civil society" and those many private associations, social movements, and forms of public communication that constitute it: whether in terms of the many forgotten voices of women of color (e.g., Maria Lugones, Lisa Lowe, and Uma Narayan), of "identity/ difference movements" more generally (Iris Young, Anne Phillips, Linda Alcoff, and Chandra Mohanty), of the "struggles for recognition" (Nancy Fraser, Jean Cohen), or of the "claims of culture" (Seyla Benhabib). This tendency to focus on civil society, however—and the propensity to view civil society as the primary locus of liberation—runs the risk of leaving the powerful state largely unattended and its nature only marginally placed into question.

The state has the dubious distinction of being perhaps the most "male" of all institutions. Particularly in the United States, it persists in signifying raw physical power and the monopoly of organized force (Weber's definition), retaining the power to legislate laws with the penalty of death (Locke). The state's primary functions are still conceived in terms of the male roles of "protection" against both external enemies (a powerful military and preparedness for war) and internal foes (a strong police and internal security force, an extensive prison system), coupled with the regulation and policing of economic competition (production). These crucial functions, moreover, are reflected in the duties expected of the individual citizen: the duties of soldiers in times of war and of producers (and taxpayers) in times of peace (with occasional voting and jury duty thrown in). Finally, the modern liberal political state is still justified primarily in terms of the values of the freedom and equality of all citizens—a freedom and equality originally granted to men in their fraternal capacity only (6.7). None of these roles belonged to women historically, and thus (not surprisingly), for the vast majority of the history of the state, both ancient and modern, women have characteristically remained "passive" citizens, residing outside the political state narrowly conceived (1.3).

Today, however, with the large-scale entry of women into various public spheres, we find not only the centuries-long demand that the liberal values of freedom and equality be granted to women, too, but also a call for the politicization of formerly insular "female" values. Numerous voices have called for a political articulation of the value of "care," for a public theory of the emotions, such as "compassion" or "sympathy," and I have argued here for the importance of a political conception of friendship (*philia*).[1] It has even been suggested that the magnitude of the transformation ushered in by the recent wave of the women's movement may be comparable to such historic developments as the emergence of the idea of personal freedom among a bonded European peasantry, or the spread of the idea of democratic rights among the small farmers of the American colonies.[2] Whatever the ultimate significance of this transformation—and I believe it is great—the question for us continues to be how best to conceive it, and what further practical guidelines (if any) we may draw. In this chapter, I distinguish my position on the nature of the political state from those of various leading feminist theorists of the present. I argue that it is the richer notion of friendship as *philia*—and not merely a political conception of "care" or "compassion"—that will help us determine the limits of legitimate freedom and equality in a genuine democracy.

7.2 EARLIER FEMINIST POSITIONS

I believe it is fair to claim that for much of the nineteenth and twentieth centuries, feminists focused on what ruling men historically possessed that women lacked: individual freedom from slavery and bondage, a right to property, a public voice and recognition, the vote, protection from violence in both private and public domains, decision making in family affairs, a profession, equal pay, and so on. In general, women sought equal political rights, as summed up in the (failed) Equal Rights Amendment of 1972, as well as the social respect and individual dignity they perceived as having been granted to the full-fledged citizen. Not surprisingly, therefore, when twentieth-century feminists first turned to an analysis of the distinctive nature of women's "reproductive labor" in the home, the value and importance of the male *productive* model of free labor remained a pervasive standard of liberation.

Many feminists of the 1960s and 1970s, for instance, spent a good deal of time showing that traditional women's work in child and family care (contrary to Karl Marx's own claims) is economically "productive": of great worth, a creator of use value and wealth, and thus also a central contributor to the exchange value and surplus profits of capitalists.[3] Even such careful thinkers as Ann Ferguson and Nancy Folbre—thinkers who explicitly criticize the focus on the economic role of women's labor in the home, in order to emphasize its sexual and affective side—continue to call such labor "sex/affective production," defined as the "labor devoted to bearing and rearing children and nurturing adult men."[4] Ferguson and Folbre explicitly intend "to emphasize that the term *production*—purposeful human behavior which creates use values—encompasses far more than the production of tangible goods such as food and clothing."[5] Although both broaden the category of "production" to include nonmaterial goods and services, they appear not to believe that women's activity is of an entirely different order. That is, in their view reproductive activity continues to be conceived as a form of *poiesis* (production) and not as a form of *praxis* in the best case and done for its own sake (2.5). As such, the issue becomes whether women should receive a wage for sex/affective production from a transitional socialist state or whether (consistent with radical Marxism) all work should be nonwaged and organized by councils of "associated producers," as Marx himself had envisioned (a debate known as "the domestic labor dispute").

Even MacKinnon's "radical feminist" rejection of orthodox Marxism tends to leave the category of productive labor untouched (including, in her case, the larger question of how the economic realm should be organized), for MacKinnon claims that "sexuality is to feminism what work is to Marxism."[6] In MacKinnon's analysis, sexuality becomes the central category of women's exploitation; our system is not simply one of capitalist exploitation, but of systematic sexual subordination as well. Significantly, MacKinnon (along with others) has directed our attention to issues of male violence and control over women, whether in the area of birth control, abortion, rape, incest, sterilization, domestic battery, lesbianism, sexual harassment, prostitution, or pornography. Women are revealed to be subject to "a double exploitation": exploited by capitalists insofar as they are wage workers, but also subordinated by men simply in virtue of their being women.[7] In so shifting our attention to the realm of sexuality and violence, however, we must note that MacKinnon leaves the original socialist account of productive labor and its value largely undisturbed (4.8).

It is not just socialist feminists (such as Ferguson, Folbre, or MacKinnon), who begin from within the Marxist tradition, who tend to assume this model as the standard of valuable laboring activity; liberal feminist theorists characteristically do so also. In her influential *Justice, Gender, and the Family,* Susan Okin argues for the value of what she calls "reproductive labor" (the labor of caring for children, the household, and the home), but she also continues to model such labor on production, that is, on labor worthy of a market wage. Okin's liberal solution to a fairer distribution between productive and reproductive labor is to propose a "redistribution," which now neither demands an end to the general system of wage-labor or to the market (as for classical Marxists), nor requires wage support for such labor by a transitional socialist state (the solution for many socialist feminists). On the contrary, Okin largely accepts the present market system with one proviso; she proffers the novel solution that the wife as caregiver in the home should receive a "co-pay check" from her husband's firm or employer for her efforts.[8] Although noting differences between women's work and other market-oriented activity, Okin argues that the simplest way for the value of domestic reproductive labor to be recognized and reimbursed—considering that in our society value and prestige are connected with monetary income—is to require the husband's employer to "split" the employee's paycheck, sending half the monies in a separate payment directly to his wife.

The difficulties with Okin's suggestion are numerous. For one, as Frazer points out, this scheme continues to make the wife's income depend *directly* on the individual husband's and hardly promotes her safety and independence from him.[9] Worse, the scheme affords no aid to those women who do not have husbands or male partners, or for those whose husbands or partners are unemployed, even though these women may have numerous children and often perform a great deal of care work. Further, the suggestion does little, if anything, to alter the perception that care giving in the home is "woman's work"; it is likely that just as few men would stay at home under Okin's scheme and choose care-giving work, as do so today. Finally, and perhaps most important, the split-paycheck suggestion leaves the marketplace and our present class and race structure pretty much as is. The woman of minority or working-class background, even if she is lucky enough to have an employed husband, will receive a relatively small paycheck from her partner's employer for what could be a great deal of work, while the upper-class woman would characteristically receive a bonanza as her half of her executive husband's salary.

In this latter case, the woman (typically white) might do almost no care work herself and simply hire another woman (frequently of color and from the Third World, who in turn would be compelled to leave her own children behind, thrust onto relatives, etc.) to do the nursing, housework, and childcare. The mistress of the household may go off, say, to play tennis. This new "redistribution" of the rewards of carework, although perhaps helpful to many middle-class women, hardly seems fairer and more just in general. The plan reinforces the position of traditional housewife and mother, of those who depend on high-market earners, while continuing to track and reduplicate injustices of class, race, and heterosexual orientation.

What these early Marxist, radical, and liberal feminists seem to have in common—despite very different analyses and conclusions—is a continuing awe of productive labor (and the wages it generates), as well as the need to justify the value of reproduction in terms of it. It is unclear to me whether even theorists of the "third wave" (women of color and the Third World), in their criticism of middle-class white feminist political theory, have analyzed the complexities of alternative conceptions of laboring activity, for they tend to focus more on issues of identity and "recognition" (of race, class, culture, and gender orientation).[10] All these strands and movements have thereby failed, however, to recognize how truly radical a transformation is under way in attempts to theorize the realm of women's historical activity. As I argued earlier, ethical reproduction is not simply a subset of production; to the contrary, the proper relation is best conceived as the other way around (2.5). We ought to produce things and services in order to enjoy flourishing relations and a good life for its own sake: not vice versa. This is not to say that production can never be performed for its own sake (it is then revealed as a form of *praxis*), nor that care work and reproductive labor should never receive a wage (even a very good one); my claim is only that we must rethink fundamentals and defetishize "production" as the reigning norm of laboring activity.

The more recent turn known as "care theory" goes some way toward such defetishizing of production, and I believe it contains radically new elements as well. As I shall argue, however, new dangers emerge here in turn (7.3 and 7.5). Many care theorists still tend to focus on "women's work" far too narrowly conceived; reproductive labor is often conceived as highly particular and culturally specific (e.g., as taking place in the private home), and it is characteristically still modeled on the activities surrounding biological motherhood (pregnancy, parturition, nursing, and infant care).[11] The danger here is that normative discussions of women's traditional *praxis* may become marginalized and relegated to the realm of childcare, nursing, or special "women's issues"; they soon lose their larger critical and political potential.

It is true that the economic realm of market production—as well as its unfailing consequences of poverty and inequality when this realm goes unfettered—is beginning to be confronted head on by care theorists and other feminists.[12] Everything depends, however, on *how* such alternative labor is conceived. Earlier, we argued that much of women's historical work, when properly conceived as ethical reproductive *praxis* and labor, has far-reaching implications for the general question of ownership in society (5.5). This alternative form of activity offers a glimpse of an alternative form of "owning"—one resembling a temporary guardianship or stewardship and not the private property model—for such labor entails a form of real world motivation *not* based on the vast unequal incentives presupposed and spawned by present market models. Similarly, in what follows, I ask the reader to keep in mind our earlier discussion of the possibility of the growing self-representation of women in government—whether gradually with time or more swiftly through a system of proportional representation or one of positive quotas (6.6). The feasibility of these alternative economic, legal, and political institutions becomes an important presupposition of (or at least lends support to) numerous other social transformations, to which we now turn.

7.3 CARE THEORY: MOTHERHOOD OR FRIENDSHIP?

Having first modeled much of women's reproductive labor on traditional production models, in recent decades feminist theorists began to pursue a new trend: the awareness of a differently structured "care" model of activity historically performed by women. According to most care theorists, the activity of caring for others is clearly different from production: genuine care work is other-directed and is focused on the needs not of the self, but of the particular *cared-for*. In turn, it requires special emotional abilities in *the carer*: capacities for listening, sympathy, patience, and so on, as well as a motivation for the other's good or for a transformed good or friendly relation with them. All this contrasts markedly with the goals of competitive production on the market, with a "mastering" of the physical and even social world and the surmounting of command hierarchies. Among care theorists themselves, however, one now finds numerous subspecies. I single out two tendencies in particular to warn against here, despite—or perhaps because of—their immense and persisting popularity.

The first tendency is that of continuing to conceive of care by focusing on *mothers* as the paradigm of carers. As numerous critics have noted, this can function as an oppressive ideology for women. Rather than encouraging women critically to reevaluate the traditional roles and burdens customarily (and thoughtlessly) thrust upon them—known as the "cult of domesticity"—this approach simply glorifies such roles and burdens.[13] Nonetheless, the focus on mothers—even when it comes to normative conceptions of the political person or citizen—persists in much recent feminist thought.

The second tendency, which applies even to theorists who reject mothering as the paradigm of care, is to conceive of care as not only central but as close to ubiquitous—as the *only* value of any real import.[14] Although the project of generating all other significant values from the value of care itself—developing "a care theory of value," as it were—is an interesting and perhaps even fruitful one, I believe it contains numerous confusions and must ultimately fail. What is missing, I shall argue, is a *normative* theory of care—a more thorough analysis of different *types* of care, when care is important and when not. For this, however, one must look beyond the category of care itself. Indeed, the ideal of friendship may here act as guiding norm (7.5). In the final analysis, care theory tends to remain parochial, and this makes developing a public civic analogue of ethical reproductive activity far more difficult to conceive.

In chapter 2, we argued that ethical reproductive activity, care, and friendship, as performed by human beings, are characteristically imbued with reason, or *logos*. These activities typically entail foresight, imagination, memory, principles of choice, and so forth (2.3). We thereby distinguished our position from those thinkers (such as Nel Noddings) who view care as "essentially non-rational." But among those who accept the reason-imbued nature of human caring activity, there exists a group of feminists who believe that the forgotten social, economic, and even political category is "the mother" (or to a lesser extent "the parent"). Virginia Held, for example, writes that what we need now is to "replace the paradigm of economic man with that of mother and child."[15] Similarly, Eva Kittay attempts to formulate a moral theory "grounded in the maternal relation, the paradigm of the relation of care," and she aims for a political model based on the "non-equalitarian, but caring relationship between mother and child" (*LL*, 19). In such cases, it is not simply that the dominant economic production model must be rejected, or that a careful analysis of motherhood has been neglected by political theorists, or merely that we need to explore the changing nature of the family as well as recognize publicly the value of caring for others. The claims are far stronger: we need to reconceive economic and political relations between citizens on the model of mother and child. Since I am here arguing for a political conception of friendship (*philia*)—in which motherhood emerged as a particularly "thick" instance (2.6)—the question becomes whether these two positions are compatible.

I believe they are not. Although the concept of "motherhood" must clearly be explored further (indeed, it has only just begun to be theorized philosophically), conceiving of citizenship in terms of motherhood (or even in terms of parenthood) has numerous reactionary consequences. The concept of friendship (*philia*) is far more appropriate, for several reasons and not just for feminists.

For one, the category of friendship is far more general, if not actually universal. Everyone (except perhaps the hermit) is profoundly motivated by the desire for friends (at least at times in their lives), while not everyone wants to be a mother or parent (nor should they have to be). Friendship, in its various forms, is a leading candidate for a universal desire and common need, while being a parent or a "mothering person" is not. It thus appears far too strong to demand politically that "everything be arranged in society to benefit children and the next generation" (as the novelist Charlotte Perkins Gilman claims) or that the "highest priority should be the future of children," as Held writes.[16] Persons have many other legitimate interests than the production of future human babies. Having noted this, let us recall that the friendship relation also necessarily reveals an "other-directedness," as well as a care and concern for particular persons (and animals, etc.)—characteristics that are absent from the dominant economic and political models.

This nonuniversal character of parenthood in contrast to friendship takes on added significance when viewed from a global perspective: we surely do not *want* more and more parents (with more children) inhabiting the globe. The earth is dangerously overpopulated as it is, with one-fourth of the human population hovering on the edge of starvation (8.4). By contrast, few of us wish to live in the world without more friends, nor is there any moral "ought" that we should so live. Indeed, *how to live together on the earth as political friends* is becoming the new global challenge. There is a general duty of friendship that binds us all, but there is hardly any longer a general duty to become a parent.

Friendship (as *philia*) is thus the more universal category; it encompasses the best parent–child relationships, while the reverse is not the case. Earlier we saw that the mother–child relation is a special subset of friendship; it is a particularly "thick" and extreme instance of it (2.6). This is not to claim, of course, that mothers should try to act like their teenage daughters, but that in the best parent–child relation (and when conceived over a complete life), parent and child reciprocally possess an awareness of each other as moral equals; wish each other well (including aiming at the other's autonomy and well-being); and practically do things for the other to whatever extent is possible and appropriate. These are also the three necessary characteristics of genuine friendship.

What is absent from many or most friendship relations, in contrast to typical parenting ones, is a biological link and the extreme inequality and dependency found in the material reproductive unit of birth, growth, and maturity. But these extreme dependencies and racial similarities, although they pervade the natural realm of biological offspring, ought to diminish in importance when we turn to the political domain of right, at least in the modern period. That is, the evolution of the modern liberal and democratic state—from Locke and Rousseau to Kant and Rawls—no longer views social unity as grounded on feudal blood ties or race, nor is extreme legal and political inequality any longer acceptable between citizens. The political realm is ideally conceived as the most sustained and reasonable attempt ever undertaken to *rectify* the inequalities and arbitrariness of the natural lottery. And we hardly want to reverse this aspect of liberal theory, do we?

For all these reasons, the paradigm of mother and child emerges as the wrong model for the relation of citizens to one another whether in the political or economic sphere. Most members of a democratic regime would be insulted at the thought of viewing other citizens as their parents or children, even if we were to replace our present patriarchy with a new enlightened "matriarchy." The oppressive possibilities of any parental relation (inherent in the great inequalities in and discrepancies of physical power and control, in realized abilities, status, and so forth), as well as the extreme partiality typical of the mother–child relation (characteristically grounded in a nonrational biology) should make us more than wary. And, again, this category simply does not include all citizens.

By contrast, there is nothing inherently repugnant in the idea of thinking of one's fellow citizens as "civic friends." The category covers *all* members of a political community, including the young (potential citizens), the old (retired citizens), the poor, and even the severely handicapped (who, despite not being productive, may contribute much emotionally, and so on). Here there is no biological (or racial, religious, or cultural) requirement, but rather a moral/political connection. Similarly, the "fact of dependency" that many feminists have recently stressed in the mother–child relation—that human infants are born into years of extreme dependency—is included in the concept of friendship, at least to a certain degree. If I do not attempt practically to help my friends when they are young, old, ill, or forsaken in hard times, I am simply not a friend. The degree to which a child may be dependent on its particular mother (especially considering the institution of the bourgeois family as organized at present) is surely greater than the degree of dependency found in other forms of *philia*. But glorification of such extreme dependency by some feminists—to the point of wishing it to be a political characteristic—strikes me as misguided. Mothers, as we all know, can do a great deal of damage to their children, and the safety, security, and health of any child might be far better served if she or he could be guaranteed *multiple* caring persons, guardians, or friends. And the same may be said for the civic relation between political persons.

What conceiving of citizens as civic friends nonetheless still adds to the liberal paradigm of citizen as free and equal persons is the explicit notion of a "shared responsibility" in each other's lives (at the same time as it avoids the pitfalls of the republican tradition of "fraternity").[17] Such responsible sharing is hardly a full responsibility for one's fellow citizens (the motherhood paradigm), but rather an explicit acknowledgment that fellow citizens—through a common constitution, set of social institutions, body of traditions and laws—will not be abandoned in hard times or fall below a certain minimum of well-being, and that all will share in the good times (and wealth) as well. This dimension of civic friendship is not only a requirement for genuine justice, as we have argued throughout (starting at 2.7), but it also makes explicit a *positive political concern* as crucial to free and equal democratic citizenship. But just as such a concern is not the independent and "indifferent" stance of the liberal citizen, so, too, it is not the intense, private, and inward-looking concern with "one's own" family members. On the contrary, the political concern I am interested in here is a natural and spontaneous concern for others (*philia*), which must nonetheless be trained and educated to operate outward—amid ever growing cultural diversity and complexity, and through principle and law—in the larger civic spheres of school, neighborhood, economy, and state. Such positive political concern for fellow citizens has remained largely submerged and forgotten in our official (particularly American) economic, state, and constitutional traditions (chapter 6)—even if it is still present in many neighborhood associations, farming communities, and local citizen practices.

Finally, I believe the dangers that result from theoretical focus on the private mothering person as the paradigm of care as a model of political personhood emerge most clearly when concrete policy suggestions are offered. We saw how Okin's suggestion that employers split the husband's paycheck between himself and his wife helps a small group of middle-class wives, but does little for the rest of us; in most cases this scheme would simply compound preexisting class, race, and gender injustices (7.2). Similarly, working to better the situation of "mothers" without simultaneous awareness of the legislation's effect on other women (or on men, for that matter) only brings a train of new injustices in its wake.

Consider the following example. Recently, practical attempts to realize a public ethics of care have been made in the field of law and social policy, respectively, by feminists Martha Fineman and Eva Kittay, among others.[18] Both Fineman and Kittay argue for adequate recognition and reimbursement of what both (independently) call "dependency work": that unpaid labor women perform in the home for those unable to care for themselves (such as children, the ill and infirm, the handicapped, or the elderly). Kittay writes, for example, that such dependency work should be recognized as work and "adequately compensated and given the same status and social standing as any legitimate employment"(*LL*, 545). She advocates a system whereby the taxpayer supports social programs that reimburse families and dependents, citing as justification that we have all benefited from the unpaid dependency labor of women in our lives and that such exploitation must be rectified:

> *Familial dependency workers must be permitted to devote themselves to caring for dependents, if that is their preference, without becoming impoverished and without irrevocably damaging their opportunities to engage in other labor if and when the period of intense dependency ends. Like other workers who are treated in an equitable manner, those doing familial dependency work should have available opportunities for retraining when the period of their charges' dependency is over; they also should have the equivalent of a paid vacation and time off for personal medical care, worker's compensation if they are injured, and so forth. Such monetary compensation and benefits must be universal (i.e., they should not be limited to those who are impoverished); otherwise, they quickly deteriorate into stingy and stigmatized assistance such as welfare, both as we knew it and as we now know it.* (LL, 544)

Let us contemplate this suggestion for a moment. Kittay here describes a universal social welfare "system of payment" for all dependency work. In theory, this would include the work not just of mothers, but of fathers, grandparents, and even friends and lovers; the suggestion seems to be a form of general voucher system for dependency labor. Beyond the practical difficulties of such a scheme (the bureaucratic nightmare, the cost, and the problems of defining "dependency labor" in specific instances and determining who is worthy and who not, etc.), it raises critical issues of fairness that I believe must also be addressed.

On the one hand, Kittay wants to grant dependency workers "the same status" and treat them just "like other workers." But which other workers, we may ask, are entitled to direct payment from the state? Street sweepers or administrative assistants also do labor from which we all benefit, labor that is valuable and necessary, often underpaid, but they are hardly entitled (as things stand now) to such a guaranteed reimbursement system. If we take this "treat just like other workers" strand of Kittay's argument seriously, either private dependency labor in the home should be reimbursed by the market (for which it would receive very little), or other forms of useful work (clerks and plumbers, and so on) should be state supported also (with paid vacations, subsidized retooling, etc.). If we follow this line of reasoning consistently, we soon arrive at the idea of a *guaranteed basic income* for all workers. If we push even further, why not guarantee a scheme of *basic income for all citizens* regardless of their ability to work (since not all are capable of it)? This scheme is not so wild as it may appear at first sight. On the contrary, not only is a guaranteed basic income for all an old socialist ideal, but the movement for one is again gaining ground in Europe (Basic Income Earth Network [BIEN]) and even in the United States (Basic Income Guarantee [BIG]).[19] A guaranteed minimal income for all citizens, however, is not the conclusion reached by Kittay.

For, on the other hand, Kittay wants to treat dependency labor and care-work as special. She seems to assume that administrative assistants, grocers, and street sweepers can be reimbursed by the market, but that unlike such market relations "the relationship between the dependency worker and the charge itself must be respected as nonfungible and of value, in and of itself" (*LL*, 543). This claim reveals that Kittay does not really have in mind "all dependency work," but rather a far more particular form. Hers is a politics "grounded in the maternal relation." And unlike the work of the mother, the work of the professional nurse, childcare provider, geriatric aide, and the like is typically not "nonfungible"; these latter types of work, although perhaps less fungible than many others, can and indeed often are replaceable and reimbursed by the market. The gist of Kittay's proposal can now be stated: the state should reimburse parents—typically the mother—for taking care of their own family members in the home: full-time *Kinder-* or *Pflegegeld,* as it were, with paid vacations and the like. To some extent this is already the case in Sweden and some other European countries.

At this point we are forced to ask, however, what happens to other women (or men) who do not have children (or relatives) and who perhaps do not even want children. On this scheme, an inordinate amount of money and special rights (to guaranteed income, vacations, and so on) flow in the direction of mothers or parents (and more so, presumably, the greater the number of their children). These parents stay at home and take care of their own family with little risk to their careers (for they are guaranteed a position on their return). In the mean time, the single woman who works long hours at the office or the man who packs goods for shipping or solders pipes must deal with the vicissitudes of the market, fearful of being laid off, struggling with his or her boss (or the union) for a raise, receiving little or no paid vacation time, and so on. This cannot help but cause resentment among (at least some) co-workers.[20] Far from rectifying the injustices of private dependency labor, Kittay's politics exalts maternal labor above all other forms of work, granting it unheard-of security and privileges.

A point overlooked in much of the literature on care and mothering is that there remains a difference in the final analysis between my taking care of my own child (or parents or friends) and caring for others—particularly for strangers. These two forms of activity cannot easily be equated even if they overlap in some instances (e.g., I often take care of my neighbor's child as if it were my own). So, again, what is it that distinguishes my caring for my own child or beloved as a form of *praxis* (done for its own sake) and for which I put out a great deal of effort?

In chapter 2, I answered with the general category of *philia*. There is an "unselfish satisfaction" in caring for others for their own sake; we witness a flourishing of abilities, a renewed hope and joy, a sense of well-being and rightness in the universe, and in the best case we have a new or deepened relationship as well. In trying to fathom why mature women continue to bear and raise children in today's Western world (women with some control over their lives, awareness of and access to birth control, with some inkling of the ideology of motherhood and all the work it involves), I can see no other legitimate reason. That is, once one clears away the cobwebs of suspect ideologies (it is in women's true "nature," her emotional fulfillment, necessary for physical health, for leaving her genes behind, to avoid loneliness, and so on), as well as historically necessary but ultimately socially contingent reasons (children as old-age insurance, needed as work hands on the farm, to secure property transmission, and so forth), it seems the only reason left. Children can be a joy to have and lovely to be with, for all their bother. Even to this idea of bringing children into the world as special, intimate, and unique friends (who will survive oneself), something suspect adheres: Can one acquire special and unique intimates in no other way?

Whatever the ultimate mysteries surrounding planned children, one question must be asked in regard to many of the suggestions made by feminists: Why exactly should people be paid or privately reimbursed for taking care of their *own* children? If the initial decision is truly the choice of an adult (and not the result of ignorance, rape, lack of access to abortion or contraception, etc.), where precisely lies the obligation on the part of others (and the state)? Feminists tend to pass over this point far too quickly. Kittay writes that children are "the next generation" and provide us with "necessary services." This is true, but there are plenty of children on the planet already to produce such services; why introduce more? A common response from within the wealthy developed world is that the birth rate of nearly all the industrial nations is declining. This does not satisfactorily answer the question; why not simply allow more immigration, unless one believes "one's own kind" alone can provide such necessary services (an idea bordering on racism)? After all, there are millions clamoring to enter the advanced industrial nations. One thinker notes that "unlike pets"—which benefit and provide pleasure mainly to the person owning them—children in addition "benefit the rest of us."[21] But, again, this is too quick. Not only can my neighbor's kittens or horses, say, bring great enjoyment to my own family, but other people's children can also clearly "harm us." The latter consume a great deal, they compete for resources, they pollute, and they might even develop into my enemies, white-collar thieves, or axe murderers. The answer is more complex.

My own sense is that we should all be concerned with the children of others (and not just with our "our own") for at least two important reasons. The first is that people, including most women, routinely underestimate the immense difficulties, pitfalls, and burdens that are typically a part of raising good children; it is simply too difficult to go it alone and without help (particularly in an indifferent or unsupportive public environment). Thus, what appears at first as reproductive *praxis*—done for its own sake, joyful, life enhancing, and so on—can quickly degenerate into a burdensome, desperate labor and even continue thus for twenty or so years. For, as numerous thinkers have pointed out by now, one common, distinguishing characteristic of personal reproductive labor is that one cannot typically, even when exhausted and abused, quit or go on strike; the needs of the other do not go away. Thus, given that our society still routinely throws up the expectations that it is natural and normal for everyone to have children (and often for women to care for their relatives as well), and considering at the same time the general lack of social support structures and institutions for such caretaking, we all (to this extent) become partly responsible for the surprises and pitfalls awaiting new parents and particularly most mothers. This we might call the *argument from individual fairness.*

I am here reminded of a remark made by Hegel in a slightly different context in his *Philosophy of Right.* Hegel speaks of the new obligations that the emerging modern state—with its burgeoning market and civil society—now has to the individual (male) worker, unlike in feudal and agricultural times. Early in the nineteenth century Hegel writes, "But civil society tears the individual from his family ties, estranges the members of the family from one another, and recognizes them as self-subsistent persons. Further, for the paternal soil and the external inorganic resources of nature from which the individual formerly derived his livelihood, it substitutes its own soil and subjects the permanent existence of even the entire family to dependence on itself and to contingency. Thus the individual becomes a son of civil society, which has as many claims upon him as he has rights against it."[22]

In an analogous manner, at the turn of the twenty-first century, in both the industrialized and industrializing nations, large numbers of *women* are being "torn" from their historically constituted families (where they were derivatively dependent on a male) and thrust out into developed market and even global structures. The changing nature of the family unit (from feudal extended household to nuclear unit and beyond), the new and demanding roles calling for women in public, coupled with a simultaneous lack (particularly in the United States) of existing societal supports (e.g., easily available, high-quality daycare), all contrive to make child rearing an especially burdensome task—if one is without major sources of outside income or help. As noted earlier, this trend is not all bad; the rate of population growth in the industrialized world is declining, and individual women have time to rethink the nature of their intense social conditioning. The other aspect of the trend, however, is simple unfairness (as Hegel intimates in the quoted passage). Those whose legitimate expectations to embark on a life of blissful motherhood are systematically and socially encouraged from their earliest days, can well find themselves thrust into unexpected insecurity, toil, and sacrifice for near twenty years or longer. Of course, one horn of this dilemma could be tackled by altering the fundamental social expectation that it is necessary for everyone to have children, but for this to happen, our present society's background basic structure would have to be changed as well.

The second critical reason we should be concerned with the children of others (despite their being competitors for scarce resources, possible enemies, and so on) is that we all can and will be benefited by other people's children if they become *good* children: if they are raised with care and grow into ethical and lawful, helpful and concerned others. That is, if they emerge as civic friends. This I shall call the argument *from reciprocity or civic friendship,* and it further supports the demand for a public (state) role in the care of everyone's children. We stress, however, that the nature and extent of such public support are still an open issue. The argument for reciprocity hardly supports the leap to the conclusion that mothers in the private home should be reimbursed for taking care of their own children. On the contrary, this second argument from civic friendship (as well as the first) might just as well support public subsidies for the establishment of high-quality daycare centers or, for that matter, public training programs for care workers and immigrants (female or male) or even a care-taking civil service itself. In fact, I would argue that these latter policies are actually far superior in terms of the value of both individual fairness *and* civic friendship. Nor do they violate anyone's individual liberty properly conceived, as I shall argue next.

7.4 THREE MODELS OF PUBLIC CARE

Let us be clear why the political state today must directly concern itself with—support, oversee, fund—a fairer distribution of caring and ethical reproductive labor. We have just seen that, for reasons of both individual fairness and civic reciprocity, care for the next generation must become a public concern—at least in part. While all reap the advantages of the good care of their fellow citizens (and suffer from the bad), the burdens of concrete physical and emotional caring tend to fall on individual women alone and disproportionately on women of color.[23] That having been said, the attribution of a new function of "caring" to the political state strikes many people as deeply suspect. Images come to mind of Plato's guardian state (where children are removed at birth from their parents) or of dark and gloomy, state-run orphanages with hundreds of cribs holding listless infants. "Public care" need hardly take these forms, however. Aristotle, as we saw, repeatedly urges his legislators to maintain a "common care" for all citizens, and yet he simultaneously advocated a form of private family (2.7). The real reason, I believe, why people still today are so afraid to link the modern state with the function of "caring" is because the business of care—for the political tradition of liberalism and for the last four centuries—has been considered the primary duty not only of women but of the "private" family (5.1). The nature of this modern Western institution of the private family is worthy of reflection.

Despite first appearances, the "family" is actually one of the most highly constructed legal and political entities.[24] In the American tradition, both common law and the narrowly political state (our particular political institutions, Constitution, and explicit laws) not only determine the family's contours—who can enter into its coveted status, when, by what means, under what circumstances, and so on—but also define the various social benefits and privileges, as well as the aspirations and duties, placed on the unit and its members (e.g., legitimacy, parental responsibility, care of infants, and so on). State and federal income tax advantages (deductions, exemptions, credits), property rights and inheritance, spousal support, award of child custody in case of divorce, and right to bring wrongful death action are just some of the privileges and benefits afforded to family units. The family thus is not a prepolitical natural institution, but rather one constituted by law in a deeper sense than most other social institutions (for instance, many religious institutions); the family's very definition is legal or political.[25]

This fact of political regulation—indeed, outright state constitution of what a legitimate family is—has been obscured by endless proclamations of the "naturalness" of the modern nuclear unit. Such claims are largely based on the tendency since the eighteenth century to cast the relationship between family and state as one of "separate spheres"; the family (the private sphere) and the state (the public) were perceived as largely independent of one another. State intervention in the family was considered the exception rather than the rule; it provided assistance only in the case of "default." This perception is very much with us still today, even though the older (extended) feudal household was just as "natural" as the modern nuclear form, and even though today in the United States an ever growing proportion of households with children are headed by women alone. The ideal of the male breadwinner independently supporting wife and child has become the exception rather than the rule.[26]

Let us here recall Hegel's words. In the modern period "civil society tears the individual from his family ties, estranges the members of the family from one another, and recognizes them as self-subsistent persons." Many male workers were torn from the land centuries ago—and in response society developed the needed supports of minimum wage, workman's insurance and Social Security, unemployment compensation, and so on. The social forces tearing masses of women from the bosom of the extended (patriarchal) family, although far more recent, are just as certain. As a result of industrialized and expanding markets, global forces of immigration, the modern women's movement, divorce, birth control, and safe abortion, individual women are ever more apt to find themselves standing on their own (without the help of close relatives or other family members), often as the sole provider for children and with little or no customary social support. Our state and our society as a whole have not yet responded with the much needed replacement structures and new supporting institutions.

Of course, conservatives yearn for the good old days and for the return of women to the dependency of the patriarchal nuclear unit. Feminists, however, not only note the altered (and irreversible) social and historical circumstances, but look forward to and prepare for a new and far more equal set of just family arrangements. So the question becomes: In which direction do we want to take our families? While feminists are united in their claim that a women can no longer shoulder the burden of family caretaking alone—the costs are simply too great—they divide (as we have seen) when it comes to proposals for a more equitable distribution of reproductive labor. At least three basic models are currently operating in contemporary feminist literature. Let us call these (1) the state-reimbursed private care model, (2) community-based care, and (3) a civil service devoted now, at least in part, to ethical reproductive labor. I shall briefly discuss these three models in turn.

A. PRIVATE OR STATE-REIMBURSED PRIVATE CARE

We have already discussed a number of versions of this model, but considering its present popularity among American feminists, I return for one final look. On this model, much personal care (for children, as well as for the aged, and so on) continues to be performed in the private home, but now is directly supported and/or reimbursed by various agencies: by a split paycheck from the partner's employer (Okin), direct support in the form of a government check (Kittay), or, as in another version proposed by Martha Fineman, by subsidies in the form of generous tax credits and privileges for dependency work. In fact, Fineman seeks to have the family unit legally redefined, in such a way that the line of familial privacy and privilege is drawn, not around heterosexual husband and wife (the present *form* of the family), but around those who do the actual caretaking and their dependent charges (what she considers to be the family *function*).[27] These newly reconstituted families Fineman calls "caretaking or dependency units," and they can take on a multitude many forms (care of children, of the elderly, care of an ill gay partner, etc.). The unifying idea behind all such new families, in her view, is the significance of the caretaker-dependent relationship, which necessarily entails not only encouragement by a supportive state, but also a certain autonomy and privacy with respect to it.[28] Fineman is particularly sensitive to the dangers of state intervention and the regulation of intimacy. She stresses that "collective responsibility for dependency labor," although requiring social subsidies, should not entail "collective control" or the imposition of conformity.

I have already indicated some of the drawbacks of this first type of privatized scheme, and I believe they apply to Fineman's version of the reconstructed family as well. In general, the criticisms may be summed up under three headings: doubts with regard to fairness, a return to the cult of domesticity, and finally also questions of feasibility and efficiency. First, regarding fairness, in Fineman's proposal (as in Kittay's) there remains the question of why the state should support—or privilege—this particular form of labor and not other types. As we saw, this is a difficulty that proponents of a basic guaranteed income do not have: the proposed guaranteed income is universal and applies to all (7.3). Moreover, in the case of a guaranteed basic income, a woman raising young children would have her own income supplemented by the income guaranteed to each of her children or wards; she would thus indirectly, through her dependent(s), be guaranteed more income than single persons. Short of this, however, I see unfairness, particularly when we consider that having and raising children is meant to be "optional" and that there is an overabundance of children on the planet. The state would be privileging, subsidizing, or supporting some workers and relations outright, while others would be left to struggle on the market for their basic necessities.

Second, regarding the return to the cult of domesticity, Fineman's proposal, like those of Okin and Kittay, perpetuates and even further legitimizes (through official state endorsement) the present gendered division of labor. In all these schemes, care for others is kept so private and individualized (and even focused on biology that it is doubtful that many men (educated for the public realm) would be motivated to perform it, despite any new privileges it might receive. At the same time, such official recognition and reimbursement works to stigmatize those women who do not so conform—those who wish to be physicists, say, or airline pilots. As Joan Williams notes, the thrust of the 1964 Title VII antidiscrimination clause was to protect women who want to perform *nontraditional* work.[29] At best, these schemes detract from the support and encouragement of women developing abilities and skills other than mothering; at worst, they legitimize women's traditional oppression.

I should note that none of these proposals is proffered as a necessary guarantee or safety net in times and places of crises, but rather as a state of affairs we should ideally move toward. However, even from the point of view of a single mother living in poverty, it is not clear that such private reimbursement schemes are necessarily the best—except as temporary measures. That is, state-backed support for private caretaking all too often allows a woman to continue (to borrow a phrase from Anita Allen) "to care herself into oblivion."[30] There lurks the danger that (again, primarily) women would be facilitated to devote their entire lives—supported now not only by custom, but by the political state as well—to the performance of such intensely private reproductive activity. To be sure, this is a superior arrangement to being forced to raise children in dire poverty, or to be dependent on a controlling or abusive partner, but it comes at the cost of developing other skills: for oneself, for the market, and for the larger community. And there *are* alternatives.

Part of what Allen means, I believe, by "caring oneself into oblivion" is that one's thoughts are always on concrete particular others, individual things and specific relations close to home; one becomes encapsulated in a world "of one's own" (*to idion*, or what the Greeks considered simple "idiocy"). Such a citizen not only develops little understanding of the more complex demands of the marketplace (the general system of needs), but also is never required to develop her abilities with regard to total strangers and thus to confront genuine (cultural, religious, ethnic, class) *difference* in others. This citizen can also escape any universal claims of the state or of the global community. Indeed, the possibility of such a thorough-going parochialism, I believe, remains the weak point of much recent care theory. The real challenge today lies not in advocating and supporting private caring for one's own (this comes closer to the historically unavoidable, at least for women), but in conceptualizing, realizing, and institutionalizing a more expanded care and concern for all—including for those well outside the small circle of "one's own" (2.7, 4.6, and chapter 8). This more expansive "care," however, requires an added effort, a new training and education, as well as public encouragement and institutional embodiment. And we have barely mentioned the benefits that accrue to the children of such widened social child-rearing arrangements.

Last but not least, these proposals for privatized care-giving reimbursement emerge as prohibitively expensive. The inefficiency of workers laboring in isolation (each under her own roof) has been recognized in other areas of work since the time of Adam Smith: there is little or no pooling of hours, resources, or materials; much unnecessary reduplication takes place; the isolation leads to enervation and fatigue. So, too, who is to determine whether a woman is doing real "dependency labor" and not just hanging out with friends? (Does my fifteen-year-old niece who visits for eleven months from San Francisco become my "dependent" for this amount of time?) A vast bureaucracy is once again needed to determine the "deserving" from the not-so-deserving dependency laborers (a central reason why a guaranteed basic income for all is so attractive).

The issue also arises of from where the funds needed for reimbursements will come. Just as support of private care in the home is today largely dependent on the productive labor of a breadwinner on the market, the proposed schemes of generalized private reimbursement remain fully dependent on existing market and state arrangements. It is difficult to see how women could make transformative inroads into state and market without a breakdown of the cult of domesticity, and we also know that liberal political government today is deeply dependent on successes of the market as well as subject to its fluctuations. Under present arrangements support for "welfare" programs is typically the first budget item to be eliminated in hard financial times. Thus, the precariousness of support and reimbursement for care-giving labor continues under these privatized schemes, only now in a new form.

For all these reasons, reimbursement by the state for private reproductive labor should be the exception and not the rule. It should be instituted for women who find themselves de facto alone, with children, and without adequate means of support, and then freely given. Or it should be the minimum guarantee for all those who suddenly must take care of elderly parents, children, or relatives, because there are no viable alternative social arrangements. But it should not be advocated as a general rule—and certainly not as an ideal—to which we aspire in the new state.

B. COMMUNITY-BASED CARE

On this second model of public care, state or city funding would go, not to individual private care providers (again, there should be exceptions for temporary or special cases) but primarily to local or community-based care centers. The many advantages of some form of flexible community-based care over private provision seem overwhelming. Generally, such centers are in the position to share both the burdens and the advantages of various forms of child, elderly, or other dependent care. Being community based, they can utilize the skills and abilities of many individuals, as well as pool materials, resources, and local knowledge; they thus emerge as far more efficient as well. So, too, significantly, such centers can already begin to elaborate in practice, not only wider ethical values (granted, often those of a particular ethnic group), but also an early education in various social and political virtues. Finally, there seems no reason why successful models that already exist in various educational settings today could not routinely be extended to the cases of early child, elderly, and even disabled care. Indeed, such reproductive *praxis* and organized caring activities seem natural extensions of a neighborhood's local public schools, its community and religious centers, even hospitals.

Let us consider one actual model of such community-based care: the Beacons program in New York City. In 1991, in response to community concerns that children were growing up in dangerous neighborhoods and had no place to go after school, the mayor of New York City allotted $10 million to establish ten school-based community centers.[31] These centers—known as Beacons—were geographically located within the neighborhood and soon came to provide youth with a mix of social services: educational, recreational, and vocational. There are now at least forty-one Beacon schools operating in thirty-two school districts throughout the five boroughs of New York City. The program is so successful that the cities of Oakland, Savannah, Denver, Minneapolis, and San Francisco are replicating it.

What distinguishes these programs is *community involvement*: a sharing of resources as well as the breaking down of the permanent distinction between professional caregivers or social workers, on the one hand, and informal caregivers and social welfare "recipients," on the other. Public funds are largely "handed over" to these community-based organizations, local school buildings are made available at off hours, and broad participation in decision-making processes is encouraged; there is a strong sense that the work of care and concern should be done as much as possible by members of the community for other members. Although originally developed predominantly for the care of older children (teenagers), a number of these programs are being extended to include early child daycare, as well as care for the elderly and the disabled. The advantages of such a system of community "mutual care giving"—not only over private caregiver reimbursement schemes, but over the more traditional bureaucratic and paternalistic welfare services—are numerous and striking.

1. ***Efficiency.*** As already noted, in this case local resources and skills are shared, and there is a marked efficiency of care giving in contrast to privatized models. Neighborhood schools, for instance, are kept open for extended hours (some up to 14 hours a day, 360 days a year). Perhaps most important, the vast and costly bureaucracy needed to determine the "deserving" from the "undeserving" poor, the "at risk" from the "not so at risk" becomes largely superfluous, for now much of the reproductive work is done by volunteers or by members of the neighborhood themselves. These members take on a wide range of roles, from assisting with security, tutoring, or leading workshops or neighborhood beautification projects, to developing plans for parks, public gardens, or even city budgeting.

2. ***Nonpaternalistic interpretation of needs.*** Similarly, the process of needs assessment is far less paternalistic. In care work and caring relations generally, a central locus of domination comes about in the course of defining needs; "experts" claim knowledge of what the other (community or individual members) "truly" needs. In the Beacons program, by contrast, community members themselves perform much of the self-assessment of needs, tapping a basic trust, loyalty, and reserve of local knowledge that community members have for one another. Neither a professional elite coming in from the outside, nor a single "mother knows best" model, has the last word in the interpretation of the community's or a single child's needs. Needs interpretation becomes more of a cooperative process.

3. ***Share in decision making.*** So too, there is a focus on inclusion in decision making and power; authority is widely distributed and relatively equal. Those who were at first most dependent and needy frequently later become resources for the identification and articulation of the needs of others. In appealing to their own experiences, moreover, they can help formulate strategies for need alleviation, becoming sources of strength and even experts of sorts. In such cases, the distinction between the carer and those cared for begins to crumble. In the vocabulary I have used here, the labor of ethical reproduction

becomes a form of *shared praxis* where people care and are cared for in turn. Personal friendships are also sure to emerge. Finally, that such caring and educative processes take place in and emerge out of a local community bodes well for those individuals and children who come from abusive or deprived homes; basic protection as well as mentoring is literally just around the corner. Thus the protection, safety, and basic freedom of such children, as well as the possibility of their exit from restrictive homes, is far more likely to be guaranteed, and before it is too late.

4. Social basis of self-worth. Particularly important for many women and minority groups, the pooling of community resources can often avoid two destructive poles of full-time private care and education. The first of these is the early inculcation of a society's dominant racist, sexist, religious, or ethnic societal values, which are often reproduced in the private home and can lead to self-hating and disrespectful images of a child's gender, class, race, or abilities and thus to a general lack of a sense of self-worth. If the child develops connections to numerous caretakers in the neighborhood, however, the likelihood increases of countering intense private conditioning. The second destructive aspect, which may be avoided as well, is the situation where (for whatever reasons) parents glorify their own race, religion, or ethnicity, leading the child to have an overly inflated or false sense of self-worth. Both extremes can be mitigated if the community takes greater responsibility in the care of all its children, for in this case the chances of exposure to different views are enhanced. In programs such as the Beacon schools, children are characteristically exposed to many instances of identification and sympathy with and support for their own particular gender, racial, or cultural identity. This is the case because the child is typically not the only token of its racial, ethnic, or religious type in the neighborhood, and in interacting with numerous adults or older individuals, children are presented with models of success by persons similar to themselves. This community involvement thus speaks not only to their intellectual yearnings but also to their emotional self-perceptions. Much recent literature by minority educators (whether Native American, black, or Hispanic) has stressed this twofold process in the successful education of minority children. For healthy learning as well as successful negotiation and integration into the larger political community, minority children need to be shown a sympathy with their particular cultural history at the same time as they are taught how to negotiate the "codes of power" leading to greater understanding and success in the majority culture and larger institutions of power.[32] Community programs such as Beacons aim to provide precisely this.

5. ***Men as carers.*** Finally, the likelihood that more men participate, not merely in early child education but in daycare and even elderly care, would seem to increase if the care is community based—even if only part-time. The labor and activity involved retain in this instance a public and organizational dimension, while few men would have been trained for (or would feel comfortable with) the purely private labors of the traditional housewife. To be sure, certain dominant groups (e.g., top-earning white men or various fundamentalist Christian sects) would be likely to resist these moves toward greater community funding of and responsibility for daycare and elderly centers (even though making use of such care centers could be purely voluntary). For, just as such groups often resist greater funding for public education—favoring a form of private support or voucher system—so, too, they are likely to resent the diversion of public funds into early care community centers. The exponential growth in the home-schooling trend in the United States (a choice that often expresses disappointment with the quality or perceived "secular humanism" of public schools) points to this likely resistance. Recent studies of home schooling (the education of children within the private home, apart from any campus-based school) estimate the number of home-schooled children in the United States at 350,000 in 1990, 750,000 in 1996, and as high as 1.9 million in 2000.[33]

From the standpoint of furthering a genuine civic friendship between citizens in a complex democratic society, however, the sheer number of home-schooled children in the United States may well constitute a serious threat. According to one U.S. Department of Education study in 2003, the top three reasons parents home-school their children is concern with the environment of other schools (31.2 percent), to provide religious or moral instruction (29.8 percent), and dissatisfaction with academic instruction (16.5 percent).[34] The tremendous effort involved in home-schooling one's own children, however, surely *withdraws* much effort from the public realm, from *bettering* our public and local schools, as well as from democratically having to work with others who are different or who disagree. In many countries home schooling is illegal (for example, in Germany). This is not to say that those who are home-schooled cannot be well schooled, or good citizens, or that (if the situation is desperate or singular) parents should not take on the education of their own children. The worry is more that as a growing norm our public schools are being abandoned and, in the worst case, not only may home-schooled children (in their isolation) lack the personal exposure to and interaction with children of other religions and cultures, but in their (near) full subjection to their parents' ways of thinking, they may also actively learn disdain for other groups. The difficulty then becomes one of later reestablishing, not merely some commonality between citizens in general (once it has been ruptured in the home), but a commonality that furthers civic good will in the concrete (versus merely getting along for instrumental reasons). Genuine good will and a democratic working together is difficult to learn as a habit in later life.

In any event, as various civic theorists have warned, public state regulation and oversight guaranteeing a minimal core of civic content and a minimal autonomy of children in these home schools appears a necessity.[35] I would go even further. If we are aiming to include, beyond the minimal values of equality and autonomy, the public value of civic friendship in the foundations of the new state, even greater restrictions will be required in any system of home schooling. If the necessity of a genuine civic friendship is a condition for the possibility of true justice (2.7), then state monies must not only flow toward public and a common civic education, but children must also be secured the right to interact with, play with, and be educated (for at least a certain number of hours per week) in public, supportive spaces with their fellow citizens of all varieties. In a free, open, and democratic society, that is, parents have no right to interfere with the spontaneous and open interaction of young citizens among themselves.

I will not pursue this argument further here, for our concern is with infant, child, and elderly care (not with formal education, properly speaking) and such early care in the policy proffered here remains largely optional. Nonetheless, I do not wish to gloss over the tension between this scheme and much of the home-schooling movement. Whatever the precise configuration of community care, anything resembling the Beacons programs will entail more state funding being channeled into and around our public schools, while such schools in turn move closer to being the heart and center of the community (replacing, say, the local shopping mall). In a society devoted to a civic friendship, this is as it should be.

C. A UNIVERSAL CIVIL SERVICE

Although far less prevalent than the first two, a third model of "public care" has begun to surface in contemporary feminist thought: the idea of a universal civil service now transformed to include the activity of care and reproductive *praxis*.[36] In the future state, for example, a certain amount of care and concern for fellow citizens (and reproductive *praxis* more generally) could become the obligation of each citizen across the board—much as defense of the nation has traditionally been the duty of the citizen-soldier since ancient times. With this suggestion, moreover, a number of the drawbacks that remain with the model of community care just discussed might be rectified. For instance, the cult of domesticity (where women continue to do the vast majority of hands-on care work) might well continue to flourish in many local community care centers (as might a racism or xenophobia, and so on). A universal care service, by contrast, would require ethical reproductive work of men as well as women, thus helping to deconstruct the cult of domesticity as well as other prejudices. In the final position presented here, the idea of a universal care service does not replace individual or community-based proposals, but rather supplements and completes them.

Traditional armies (whether the Spartan army of ancient times, the Continental Army under George Washington, or the modern Swiss army) have always been more than mere instruments in the defense of the homeland. They have been important means in the formation of a national civic identity as well. Armies have been central in the schooling of various communal virtues, in creating a "brotherhood" between men from different parts of the country, from different walks of life, and often from different races and cultures. Indeed, armies have even been perceived as a training ground for the virtues needed in civilian leadership—for an understanding of foreign policy, for schooling in the command of large numbers of men, an understanding of the limits of democratic government, and so forth—and a string of American presidents with distinguished military careers (from George Washington, Andrew Jackson, and Ulysses S. Grant, up to Dwight D. Eisenhower and John F. Kennedy) attests to this perception. Moreover, it is not coincidental that women were traditionally excluded from such armies and that the virtues and activities learned there were decidedly "male": a training in physical strength, endurance of hardship and deprivation, self-discipline and command, the production and use of weapons, strategic planning, and so forth.

But let us consider a possible alternative scenario. As women increasingly enter the armed forces along with men—indeed, as women enter all the public fields and professions, including government office—the need for public support and funding of women's historical care and reproductive work will only grow (there being few now left in the private home to do it, at least for long stretches of time). Surely, at some point during this historical movement, the demand will be raised that we begin to transform the aims and goals of our traditional armed forces. Why should we not divert at least a part of our exorbitant military budget and resources (the 2009 projected budget is at present $515.4 *billion*) toward a universal citizen *caring* service.[37]

A universal national service would require each citizen across the board (all classes and genders) to devote one year or more (some number of months) of service to public civic work between, say, their seventeenth and twenty-fifth year of life. Unlike other recent proposals for a civil service, the emphasis here would be on a different set of skills and abilities. The democratic theorist Benjamin Barber, for instance, in advocating a universal citizen service suggests that the first three months of basic training should be in "applied skills of general utility such as mechanics, agriculture, tools, and ecology, and in civic education, including parliamentary and electoral skills, community structure and organization, some elementary social science and perhaps American history."[38] Far from condemning any of those skills (all of which are important), one is nonetheless forced to ask: But who will now help with the children, the sick, the poor, and the infirm? In fact, under Barber's strong "participatory democratic" scheme, even *more* of society's reproductive labor and care burdens would be thrust onto fewer and fewer individual women (as well as onto those of the Third World)—that is, onto those who must now substitute for the young women performing their civil service.

By contrast, in the scheme I am proposing, the first months of service would indeed become a new type of training ground, but not primarily in physical and emotional hardship (although it might involve a nutrition and fitness aspect, given the growing obesity of Americans), the use of weapons or strategic planning, or even the use of mechanics, agriculture, and tools. First and foremost, the basic training would be in the identification, creation, and maintenance of what we have been calling the "conditions of a civic friendship." That is, all citizens would first be educated in and learn to debate the constitutional essentials of their land and its common problems (a civic education); in addition, they would get to know in greater depth their nation's diverse peoples, their history, geography, and their particular concerns. Significantly, such growing "awareness" of fellow citizens would include a "practical doing" for them as well: a practical learning how to identify and meet the fundamental needs of others, as well as how to encourage their equality and autonomous capacities (their good). This practical aspect might stress work in poorer neighborhoods, in hospitals and drug clinics, but also in the routine care of young children, the elderly, and the disabled. As Kant long ago noted, in order to develop our compassionate powers, we have an actual "duty not to avoid the places where the poor who lack most basic necessities are to be found but rather to seek them out."[39] Such an "army" of young workers could thus "seek out" those who need help, supplementing the community care centers, working with the poor and the elderly, but also with those individual women (or men) with dependents who—for whatever reason—remained confined to their homes.

Significantly, unlike the present training in the armed forces, where the skills and virtues of the soldier are learned, or the training in more traditional versions of civil service (such as Barber's), where citizens are schooled in the skills of production and management also (both these sets of skills could remain later options), my proposal of a civil service would stress first and foremost the skills and virtues of *democratic cooperation*: recognizing the needs of others and caring for them, respecting their persons and encouraging their autonomy, being able to work cooperatively with and for them, and so on. Above all, such service would explicitly now stress the emotional and perceptual competence we argued is central to *politike philia*: the capacity not only to perceive and to understand, but to *respond with good will* (both abstractly and in the concrete) to other persons who are very different from oneself (2.7). Earlier we called this "the art of respecting the person." Moreover, this art would now be cultivated through shared speech and activity in the safe and "artificially" created environment of a civil service: where all draftees would be treated equally, with identical freedoms, and without the inequalities of outside power, economic status, and competition. As such, what was once a part of the organization called the U.S. military could become a training ground for the multifaceted democratic citizen of the future.

7.5 REPLY TO OBJECTIONS

Objections to our proposal for a universal care service are sure to arise: just think of the bureaucratic nightmare, the extent of the state's intrusion into each individual's freedom and personal life, the move toward a "command society," the expense, and so forth. A number of these objections I find a bit disingenuous, however, for we have an even larger bureaucratic organization right now: it is called the U.S. military. Although not mandatory at the moment, military service could become so for eighteen-year-olds at nearly any moment (particularly considering the recent spate of wars the United States has undertaken, whether in Afghanistan, Iraq, or now possibly even Pakistan). Why should this largest and most extensive military in the history of the world not be turned, at least in part, into a civil service? To say that we need such a huge military force (the most recent excuse is "the war on terrorism"), or to argue that military defense and secure protection of its citizens and productive activity is the overwhelming duty of the state, begs the very issue at question. For the issue is why the rational organization of the political state should prioritize activities of production and military defense, rather than ethical reproductive concerns that have no military analogue. Perhaps we only believe we need such an exorbitant defense system because we can imagine no other secure and fruitful way of living with other peoples of the world. If this is the case, then a false assessment of the real nature of the dangers out there in the world might be caused by a simple failure of imagination (8.1 and 8.5).

If I am correct, many of the critical problems facing the advanced industrial nations today are decidedly not military problems nor primarily productive ones, but "reproductive" concerns: ever growing disparities in wealth and control over resources (both internally and globally), mounting violence and the retreat into racism and national recidivism, the need for an alternative and enlightened organization of a multicultural workforce, alterations in traditional family structures necessitating new provisions for care, the alleviation of a growing global poverty, as well as the looming environmental crisis (8.4). For solutions to such problems, however, the well-known "adversarial method" used in the armed forces and military academies (where first-year students are often designated as despicable "rats" and subjected to hazing by officers and upperclassmen, where privacy and individuality are largely eliminated, and so on) is not only unhelpful, it actually *constitutes a part of the problem*. Far from first teaching a friendly and judicious attitude toward all, such training has the pedagogical aim of producing precisely its opposite: an intense male (macho) bonding, a superior "us versus them" mentality, a blind and ignorant attachment to "one's own," as well as an unthinking and dangerous willingness to sacrifice oneself (and others) for one's country's purported good. To think (as the present administration argues) that by this method America is going to "bring democracy" to the Middle East is simply mind-boggling. From an ethical reproductive perspective, such militaristic and antidemocratic attitudes (and arrogance) have not only outlived their usefulness, they constitute the old habits and customs *to be overcome*. And this is not even yet to mention the brutality and death—the human, animal, and environmental destruction—produced by actual war.

A second set of objections to my proposal concerns the restriction on individual freedom of requiring a year or so from each citizen's life for a civil service; this is said to be far "too demanding" of the modern citizen.[40] Others argue that the idea of a civil service is a praiseworthy one, but such a service should remain "voluntary." One cannot legitimately force people "to care," after all, and trying to do so would entail the oppressive and suffocating use of state power.[41]

In response to the objection that my proposal places too heavy a demand on the citizen, we might note that as argued earlier (5.6), requiring restrictions on the accumulation of private wealth in the name of the worst off, as well as requiring performance of a minimal civil service for a year or so (now conceived primarily as ethical reproductive labor), appears demanding only because such requirements place added civic responsibilities largely on *well-to-do men*. In reality, the institution would *alleviate* the situation of the vast majority of women (not to mention the rest of the poor) by relieving them of many de facto demands and responsibilities with which they are unfairly burdened right now: the extreme demands of taking care of others in the private sphere, work that is largely unremunerated and leaves little time or room for anything else (including little time for participation in public political life), and so on. From a feminist perspective, that is, far from placing new burdens on "the citizen," the proposed arrangements actually work to "liberate" more than half the citizenry from drudgery. So, too, although certain new civic responsibilities (such as one year or more in civil service) may indeed be placed on some men, other burdens, such as a third tour of duty in Iraq or the burden of accumulating ever more wealth, would be reduced.

Similarly, I believe such a civil service must be mandatory as well as across the board (all classes and genders, no exceptions) for a very simple reason: *fairness*. As many democratic theorists have argued, neither a professional nor a volunteer army sits well with the duties of democratic citizenship. The former separates national defense from democratic responsibility, and the latter makes service a function of economic need: in reality, the poor, the undereducated, and the ill trained "volunteer" their services, primarily because they have no other alternatives.[42] But further, we began from the concern that women can no longer perform the vast majority of ethical reproductive labor alone (particularly women of color and from the poorer sectors), nor can we collectively do without this important form of necessary labor. Thus, the burdens of such activity in a democracy—like the burdens of defense—ought to be shared equally by all. The question becomes how to get men (especially from the well-to-do classes) to perform such socially necessary and valuable labor. The most elegant and fair solution is surely a mandatory civil service—perhaps one day possible, if women ever arrive in power.

The further claim that a mandatory civil service would entail the illegitimate use of state power is, again, to argue in a circle for it assumes a predetermined answer to the question of what proper functions belong to the state—precisely what is here at issue. We need only reflect on the traditional duties of the soldier to see how one-sided and biased our present state conception remains. In the case of protecting the homeland, for instance, the traditional citizen is required and trained by the state to risk his life and limb in order to kill distant and different others (as well as to destroy their things, children, and animals) if the need should so arise. This is no simple feat. Whatever reluctance the individual might feel in leaving the warmth of his home, whatever natural sympathy or commonality he might experience when confronted with fellow human beings on the battlefield (regardless of their origin), or whatever the personal horror he suffers in the actual killing of another or in personally being wounded or maimed, his physical, mental, and emotional being must be trained and carefully prepared, his behavior channeled and formed into something ideally approaching a war hero's action. The tremendous social resources, time, and cooperative effort involved in the production and training of such "fighters"—when viewed from a slight distance—is, once again, mind-boggling.

I am not here referring merely to the vast material resources or technological know-how required to teach a young person to maneuver, say, an F-16 fighter or a Stealth bomber. I am pointing to the extensive *emotional* training required as well. If such emotional education is acknowledged and considered legitimate, however—if the political state has the authority to require, in times of crisis, that its citizens actually risk their own lives for the defense of their fellow citizens (and even kill other human beings in the name of this goal), there can be no doubt that it also has the rightful authority to require that its members actively care for fellow citizens in their times of need. To deny this is to continue to operate with a gendered notion of the state.

7.6 A NOTE ON DISCOURSE ETHICS

A further criticism may be raised against my proposal, however, this time from the direction of the left and from many of those who call themselves deliberative democrats.[43] This criticism might grant the need and importance of a general schooling in civic friendship, but it would question whether such training would not better be performed in the everyday voluntary associations of civil society, and without bringing in the unwieldy (and dangerous) apparatus of the state. Public service and reproductive *praxis,* after all, are hardly "done for their own sake" if they are required by the state; a genuine civic friendship cannot be imposed from above or from without. Whatever ones hopes and wishes, the modern political state still retains the monopoly of organized force, and as such it is surely the wrong instrument to bring into being a friendship between citizens.

My response here must be that if it is possible to bring about a genuine civic friendship without state involvement—and simply through the free institutions of civil society—so much the better, but I cannot imagine it is. First, there is no question of the political state being the only instrument involved. Earlier we argued for certain new directives in the workplace and economy (chapter 5), in the self-representation of women (chapter 6), and in the community centers of civil society and in the family (7.4); in our final chapter we will touch on international relations as well (chapter 8). My position is only that the state must *also* be involved, and the issue becomes the nature and extent of such involvement. By contrast, deliberative democrats are surprisingly silent when it comes to visions of state reconfiguration. The opportunity thus presents itself to distinguish my position more generally from those who call themselves deliberative democrats, at least on a number of crucial issues.

Like nearly all contemporary democrats, this group justifies democracy primarily in terms of the values of freedom and equality. In contrast to older aggregative and interest-group models of democratic legitimacy, however, their aim (like mine) is to conceive of democracy as primarily a *cooperative enterprise*. More specifically, what distinguishes them as a group is their stress on viewing democracy as the result of a *fair and participatory deliberative process*. Thus, for example, Seyla Benhabib writes: "Democracy, in my view, is best understood as a model for organizing the collective and public exercise of power in the major institutions of a society on the basis of the principle that decisions affecting the well-being of a collectivity can be viewed as the outcome of a procedure of free and reasoned deliberation among individuals considered as moral and political equals" (*DD*, 105). Building on Habermas's discourse ethics, Benhabib puts forth an ideal of democracy that requires that we "create public practices, dialogues and spaces in civil society around controversial normative questions in which all those affected can participate" (*DD*, 165). To what extent does this notion of deliberative democracy diverge from our conception of civic friendship as a requirement of democracy? Not surprisingly, our concept diverges in that deliberation (a "talking with") is characteristically a crucial element of any genuine notion of human friendship (civic or otherwise), but in my view it is not the only crucial element or even necessarily always the central one (2.6). An awareness of the other as an equal, a reciprocal good will, and a practical doing for that other are just as central, and these elements may be revealed or performed in absolute silence. There will thus be important differences in the two ideals, with the discourse ethicist trying to create "civic discourses" or "public practices, dialogues and spaces in civil society around controversial normative questions affecting all," and my approach attempting to bring about a greater friendship among citizens and its institutional embodiment. What are some of these differences?

The principle of legitimate democracy cited by Benhabib tends to presuppose that citizens already de facto perceive themselves as free and equal to each other, that their deliberation is well intentioned, that they are law-abiding and will stick to the decisions reached in public deliberation, and so on. If this is not the case—if actual citizens deliberate in "bad faith," purely strategically or from a position of power and economic superiority—then such "discourses" will hardly have normative grounding force. But the question then becomes how we arrive at such a "friendly" debate between good-willed free-and-equals in the first place. It is not as if in practice we may presuppose this friendliness to be the case. On the contrary, we have noted its lack, particularly in the American context where much (perhaps most) friendship tends to be seen as merely instrumental. However, *this is the critical prior question of establishing a civic friendship,* and it is not clear that "more talk" or institutionalizing "discourses" can or will necessarily bring it about. In contrast, concrete actions of generosity or aid, the execution of public works, actual deeds establishing trust between different groups, or organized efforts of listening and official group recognition—in some cases even ostracism of, say, hate-filled groups—may be more effective and more just. In none of these latter cases, however, need there be norms agreed to in an actual universal discourse; the latter is not necessary.

By the same token, any suggestion of transforming a part of the U.S. military into a civil service must emphasize common and public deliberation about society's history and constitutional essentials, and about many other normative and practical issues of the land—that is, if such a civil service is to avoid degenerating into mere state propaganda and indoctrination. One might even claim that such a properly conceived universal care service would be one practical embodiment of a Habermasian discourse ethics; it could educate all to take on "the stand point of the concrete other," facilitate their listening to each other across differences, as well as encourage a dialogue where positions are justified in general terms that appeal to the public good of all. The point to be stressed here is that such a care service, although including a truly universal discourse ethic, must also entail more; it would neither begin nor stop at public debate.

That is, the proposed service must centrally also stress "hands on" practical work and shared action performed in the service of disadvantaged individuals or groups: rebuilding inner-city slums; getting to know and care for the young, disabled, or elderly; participating in environmental clean-ups, and so on. In such instances, citizens from all walks of life and cultural backgrounds will grow to know each other and the problems facing them or their groups, not simply through face-to-face discourse as a debate—an intimidating and potentially humiliating experience for the less articulate—but in learning and executing shared tasks with goals on which many or most are likely to agree (protecting the environment, rebuilding infrastructure, helping the sick, etc.). To the extent that such joint projects and activities are well organized and successfully executed—based on widely shared values, publicly accountable, and experienced as rewarding for their own sake—they not only are likely to enhance all who participate, but also are sure to encourage lasting and positive personal bonds between citizens. Such universal shared activities of *praxis* (what a privatized society lacks) could encourage positive bonds to a far greater extent than citizens facing each other only in "deliberative discourses," which tend to focus on normative points of *disagreement*. In general, the deliberative democratic vision remains far too heavily influenced by academic and legal models of intellectual debate; it tends to be *antagonistic* at its core.

Iris Young has also criticized standard deliberative democratic ideals as competitive and "agonistic." Young argues that such theorists operate with assertive modes of articulate speech (dispassionate, disembodied, general, and so on), and that such modes are typical of white, male-dominated Western institutions (for example, academic and scientific debates, modern parliaments, courts, and so on).[44] In her view, not only do these devalue silence or different forms of expression (e.g., the halting or circuitous speech often associated with those who are underprivileged), but also institutionalizing such discourses in practice merely operates as new forms of power over the dispossessed. Young's own solution is not to jettison discussion-based theories of democracy but to "broaden" the conception of discourse to include other than argumentative forms: in particular, she discusses greeting, rhetoric, and storytelling. Her suggestion is that we move to an ideal of "communicative democracy," which indicates "an equal privileging" of any form of communicative interaction where people "aim to reach understanding." Such communicative democracy maintains a "situated plurality of perspective, considers difference a resource (and not just an obstacle) to learning . . . [and such] perceiving and listening across differences of position and perspective causes the transformation in preference that deliberative theorists recommend."[45]

Although Young's conception of "communicative democracy" is surely an improvement over older deliberative models, in my view she does not go far enough. Young still operates with the paradigm of "speaking" across differences of culture and with the same Habermasian aim of "reaching understanding" only; she thus offers no suggestions for other forms of shared *praxis*. As we noted earlier, however, successfully *doing things together* on concrete issues about which nearly all agree would appear to have a far greater likelihood of producing positive or friendly bonds between diverse citizens than sitting in a room and focusing on everyone's vast differences. The former practices—and not the latter—would appear to have a greater likelihood of leading to "the enlightened mentality" and positive "transformation of preferences" deliberative democrats seek.[46]

This point leads to a final, central difference between our position on civic friendship here and the deliberative democrats: their tendency in recent years to *idealize* "civil society." While definitions of civil society—from earliest discussions in Hegel to the most recent ones of John Rawls—have always included both the realm of civil associations and the vast inequalities generated by the economic domain as part of the sphere of civil society, contemporary deliberative democrats tend to tiptoe around this economic domain in an interesting fashion. Many (including even Habermas now) simply define "civil society" so as to rule out the economic realm from the start. Thus Cohen and Arato define the "civil sphere" as "a sphere of social interaction between economy and state, composed above all of the intimate sphere (especially the family), the sphere of associations (especially voluntary ones), social movements, and forms of public communication."[47]

But how can the vast inequalities generated by corporate America *not* interfere with, and set strict limits upon, the furtherance of civic friendship (as well as of equality and freedom) in these arenas of civil society, no matter how "community spirited" such associations start out to be? And which institution, other than the political state, is ever going to take on the enormous concentrations of economic power and their influence, in order to aim for a truly *universal* doctrine of right? Theoretical analyses of different configurations of state power may not be sufficient, but they are necessary. In the end, it appears that Aristotle is correct once again; for a truly inclusive political friendship, such friendship must work, not merely through private and local civic associations, but necessarily *also* through the constitution and public laws of the land, and for this a central organizing principle is required.

7.7 THE NEW STATE: LIBERTY, EQUALITY, AND CIVIC FRIENDSHIP

Generally, we have argued that in response to various historical (and irreversible) trends, the central organizing principle of the liberal political state must move away from being primarily an instrument of military defense and of the regulation of property and productive competition (chapter 8). The new state once again—and in accordance with Aristotle's original insight—must incorporate the explicit and central function of a public common care (*koinon epimelia*) as well. Clearly, not just any conception of public care will do, however. We need a *normative* account of care, one that carefully analyzes and distinguishes legitimate from illegitimate (or better and worse) forms. This point has not been stressed nearly enough by care theorists themselves, and it leads me to my last set of criticisms of them. As mentioned earlier, not all care theorists rest their notions of care on the mother–child paradigm: a growing number of them explicitly reject it (7.3). However, in this case (freed from the private mothering model) a further difficulty emerges—what may be called the amorphous and ubiquitous nature of care, the problem of how to define it and how to contain its legitimate boundaries. Joan Tronto (perhaps the leading proponent for a political ethic of care) clearly separates care from the motherhood model, for instance, but she works with a broad definition indeed: "On the most general level caring is a species activity that includes everything we do to maintain, continue and repair our 'world' so that we can live in it as well as possible. That world includes our bodies, our selves, and our environment, all of which we seek to interweave into a complex, life-sustaining web."[48] Tronto's "definition" of care is surely too broad, however, for it excludes *nothing*. "Everything we do to maintain, continue, and repair our 'world'" includes the slaughter of beef cattle, Nazi death camps, as well as each of the military escapades of the United States. More promisingly, Tronto and Fischer describe four "stages" of the practice of care (4.6), but the difficulty of knowing when caring is appropriate and when not and to what extent remains—particularly in political circumstances.

The need for an explicitly normative theory of political care (to be filled by our notion of civic friendship) leads to another difficulty regarding care's ubiquitous and amorphous character. There is a tendency to incorporate numerous other values *within* the concept of care itself. Bubeck, for instance, has rightly argued that the concept of care entails some *harm minimization principle*; when one cares for someone (or something), one wishes to prevent harm to them or to rectify harm done to them.[49] But from this "first principle of care" she claims to derive another—*the principle of equal care*—and she goes on to discuss the case of a mother feeling pressed to spend equal time with her two children.

This further step strikes me as a simple non sequitur. There is nothing in the nature of care (or in harm minimization) itself that mandates equality also, whether between all persons or even for the same person at different times (although there is surely something about the modern bourgeois family that mandates equal care between children). And the history of the concept of care reveals this clearly. Care has frequently been (and continues to be) highly *paternalistic*; in feudal times the lord "cared for" his serfs, the southern plantation owner for his slaves, the paterfamilias for his family, and so on. Care has also been distributed most unequally (boy children still receive more attention and care than girls worldwide, for example). One might well try to construct a model of *reciprocal care among equals*, but here I would claim that we leave the realm of simple care and begin to enter that of friendship. As we have argued throughout, the ideal of genuine friendship—*unlike care*—has the reciprocal aim of equality at its heart (2.6). So, too, friendship *cannot* be one-sided. The idea of a moral equilibrium and a reciprocal, practical good as found in friendship can now begin to function as the norm for the democratic civic relationship itself.[50]

Finally, there is one last tendency in much care theory from which I wish to distance myself also: the avoidance of all "principle." Both Nel Noddings and Carol Gilligan speak of an ethic of care in contrast to one of justice or principle. According to Noddings, when considerations of care conflict (say, between a sick child and a husband's needs), a woman's "decision is right or wrong according to how faithfully it is rooted in caring." Noddings defines caring, recall, as "essentially non-rational in that it requires a constitutive engrossment and displacement of motivation."[51] Tronto is also dismissive of "principles,"[52] and the virtue theorist Michael Slote writes regarding them: "Anyone who needs to make use of some overarching principle or rule in order to act in a 'balanced' way toward his children can be suspected of an unloving, or at least a less than equally loving, attitude toward those children; and I am suggesting, by way of contrast, that equal concern for children by its very (unselfconscious) nature tends to lead a person to allot efforts and attention in a somewhat balanced way."[53] Is Slote really suggesting that if, at times, I weigh and reflect on whether I actually treat my two (very different) children "equally," I can be suspected of an "unloving attitude"? Do we not often find ourselves favoring one child over the other (say, the boy or the youngest) despite our best intentions, a point at which we (or a friend) must remind us that we show an unprincipled favoritism?

This onslaught against "principles" not only strikes me as seriously misguided but, more important, it spells doom for the political project of extending care or practices of *philia* into the public realm. When it comes time to construct new social institutions embodying relations of equal care in the larger political arena, we can hardly expect personal feelings to carry us very far (especially since no prior social customs exist). In such cases, rather, we must reflect deeply, confer with others, and theorize regarding what it means to incorporate greater practical friendship into public institutions and without violating other precious civic values (such as freedom or equality). Principles need hardly be conceived, moreover, as abstract, contextless formal entities, which one follows blindly or unthinkingly. As Dworkin has famously argued, principles (in contrast to rules) *incline* in a specific direction and in specific contexts. Unlike formal rules, principles suggest, they supply reasons, and these must always be counterbalanced by the possibility of counter-reasons or argument. Finally, the balancing and weighting of these different sets of reasons will be dependent on our background visions, here of free and equal and politically friendly (democratic) types. In sum, in current care theory there is still far too strong a tendency to believe that our obligations to other citizens, as well as to others worldwide, will end up resting—not on our reason, reasoned discourse, and principles, in addition to a habituated friendly response—but on *nothing more* than contingent (arbitrary, unprincipled), de facto personal "feelings" alone. This is fully unsatisfactory: a form of "emotional intuitionism," as it were.[54]

In sum, the new state must be one ideally based both on reasoned principle and on the educated emotional capacity for a flexible public care or civic friendship, nor is there any one ultimate, overriding principle or value embodied above all others (we reject even the value of friendship, as in a perfectionism), other than that needed for the practical purposes at hand (1.1 and 1.4). Thus, it becomes necessary for care theorists to go beyond the category of care itself and to compare and integrate it with other values—particularly with those reigning democratic values of freedom and equality. I have tried to do this, moreover, by providing the normative model of a civic friendship between democratic citizens. One could even formulate this normative ideal as a political test: *Would you allow a particular type of action to be done to a genuine friend* (e.g., allow your friend to be lied to, exploited, or left untended)? If not, then perhaps it is your duty to see that your government (through its laws, practices, and institutions) does not allow *any* of your fellow citizens to be treated thus either. Let us call this *the formal test of civic friendship.*

Similarly, in focusing not on motherhood but on friendship as *philia* (where the mother–child relationship becomes but one extreme instance), we simultaneously go beyond the biological, the merely "mine," and the near (7.3). I have argued that the aim for feminists is to extend early parochial practices of care *outward* toward others, toward nondependents, and ultimately toward total strangers. The goal is realistically and rationally to *construct friendly practices* among diverse but civic equals—to be embodied in public institutions and with the aim of transforming unnecessary antagonistic relations—but I have also tried to show how at this point the mother–child relation increasingly becomes of less help. Rather, as Kant already noticed, friendship is the true paradigm of a relationship based on natural needs and desires, but that requires morality for its continuance. Friendship leads us in the direction of a moral common life—one based on shared ends and adopted through reasonable principles. Unknown to many—and giving the lie to Kant as individualist—the relationship of friendship for Kant emerges as the most concrete and everyday example of the realm of ends (*Reich der Zweche*).[55]

In conclusion, the specific set of proposals for a "public care" given in this chapter—publicly funded private care in the exceptional case, with community care centers supplemented by a universal civil service as the norm—is to be considered part of a distinctively *feminist* conception of the state, and this for a number of reasons. First and foremost, it is feminist because it conceives of the state and its central responsibilities and functions to be as much a political extension of women's historical social roles of ethical reproductive *praxis,* labor, and care as of any traditional male pursuit (such as production or defense). If, as James Madison writes in the *Federalist Papers,* the political state is nothing other than "the greatest reflection on human nature," let the state finally become the reflection on those aspects of human nature historically expressed in these social roles. At the same time, the cult of domesticity, which adheres to all privatized models—as well as even to present European versions of the state—would largely be disrupted. This is the case because with a civil caring service, young men—for the first time in history and en masse—would be schooled in the intricate labor and *praxis* of caring for society's most vulnerable members and in the concrete. Even if such civic schooling and practice were for a relatively short period of time only (between the ages of eighteen and twenty-five), they could nonetheless be life transforming.

Taken together with the various other economic and representative measures discussed earlier in this work (chapters 4 and 5), the new state begins to move beyond its historical foundations in any gendered division of labor. Simultaneously, it moves beyond conceiving its justification in terms of the values of freedom and equality alone, and begins to incorporate and realize in its institutions the forgotten value of civic friendship as well. Finally, such a major restructuring of the central priorities of the modern political state could never occur without a simultaneous revolution in our conception of the political person or citizen. Most important, this new citizen will be conceived with a third fundamental moral power (3.5). The new political person will be one who from the start is carefully nurtured, respectfully educated, and thoroughly grounded in the ways of civic good will and democratic cooperation, long before they learn anything of the arts of war.

8

LOOKING OUTWARD
Beyond the National Security State

One may even observe in one's travels to distant countries, the feelings of recognition and affiliation that link every human being to every other.

ARISTOTLE

8.1 INTERNATIONAL *PHILIA*?

If reconceiving the fundamentals of the modern nation-state in the direction of a civic friendship is difficult enough, the task of rethinking the international system appears near impossible. In the larger arena, the inequalities in terms of natural resources, wealth, productivity, standard of living, and so forth are even more extreme than in the domestic case—with over one-quarter of the world population undernourished and starving—while the diversity in natural habitats, cultures, languages, and social structures are nearly endless. Many will think that our notion of a friendship "across differences" is surely here stretched beyond the breaking point. To make matters worse, for centuries now the sphere of international relations has been conceived in terms of a Hobbesian state of nature: as one governed by a self-interested realism or what neo-realists more recently term "structural anarchy." Under anarchic assumptions, states are unitary and rational actors seeking security and survival in an international system void of all law and Leviathan. This system is viewed primarily as one of *self-help*, whereby each state is solely responsible for its own security, and thus (as in the well-known prisoner's dilemma where cooperation with others is far too risky) it is only rational that each must consider other states as potential threats. Under structural anarchic assumptions, that is, states would be remiss if they did not aim to accumulate power (and military capabilities) for deterrence and defensive purposes.

The problem, of course, and as Hobbes noted long ago, is that such a diffident and anxious self-conception—if truly universal and absent all enforcement—quickly degenerates into a war of all against all. With each state trying to ensure its own security, the system as a whole becomes less secure, since other states can mistake defensive for offensive build-up efforts and may thus be inclined to strengthen their own military capabilities. Individual rational (state) actions here lead to a collectively irrational outcome. If active war does not break out, it nonetheless seethes beneath the surface. Even in the best of times we are left with a global arms race and a dangerous international "balancing of power."

Cracks are beginning to appear in this dominant picture, however, as the recent resurgence of neo-Kantianism and the new discourse on "global justice" bears witness.[1] As we shall see, however, even those partaking in this promising new discourse rarely (if ever) use the language of friendship. When it comes to the international domain—of all places—the concept of friendship appears not to have a home.

In this final chapter I reject (along with a growing number of others) the dominant neo-realist picture of the functioning of international relations, and for many of the same reasons we have discussed in the civic realm. This model (despite claims of being objective, purely descriptive, etc.) provides an inaccurate description of the true state of things; it focuses exclusively (again) on traditional "male" activity, conceived as either production or military action, to the near total exclusion of ethical reproductive labor. It thereby emerges as unnecessarily pessimistic. Analogous to the domestic case, the neo-realist here again projects an understanding and self-conception that belongs to relatively few of us—only this time outward onto the peoples of the world. Even more important, the projection leads to a particular set of prescriptions regarding how states ought to behave in the international domain, prescriptions that all too often lead to a dangerous escalation of the arms race. Finally, unlike the vast majority of contemporary global justice theorists, I argue in this chapter that the concept of friendship plays a valuable role even in the international realm—the role of *guiding norm,* only adapted now to the new and changed (international) terrain. Before turning to our account of where friendship might fit into the present interstate system, however, allow me to summarize our position thus far.

Until this point the argument of this book has stressed the necessity of relations of *philia* for the civic realm. What we have called the new state will centrally protect and further the conditions for the possibility of a civic friendship among its citizens (in addition to their individual freedom and equality), and this in the name of genuine justice (as its necessary condition). We saw that such a turn toward friendship would lead to changes in the economy limiting inequalities (chapter 5), to transformations in political representation and in our (particularly American) self-conception (chapter 6), as well as to the reevaluation, increased funding, and public protection of activities of education, public care, and civic reproductive *praxis* in the form of a civil service (chapter 7). The new funding would derive from the streamlining of military expenditures—from the deconstruction of a bloated U.S. military far more worthy of an imperialist empire than of a modern democratic state—as the military would be transformed in large part into a civil service. These changes are all grounded, moreover, in the acknowledgment by the new state of the critical role women have always played, as well as in the independent value of ethical reproductive *praxis* itself.

If we hold this vision of the state before us, one thing surely follows from what has gone before: any state that views the value and duty of civic friendship as central to its self-conception will quite naturally build this value into its foreign relations as well, that is, if its conception of *philia* is a truly civic one. By a civic conception, recall, I intend a political friendship incorporating universal principles, individual rights, and the rule of law (3.1). In thus focusing on one form of friendship, we are led naturally to focus on and explore the other (1.3).

An international *philia* is here to be contrasted with the idea of an international war of all against all, or with a system of states each pursuing only its self-interest, or with a global system of a mere indifference between states. Such interstate friendship would surely require even greater recognition of the autonomy and diversity among peoples than a civic conception would—the global diversity and differences being themselves that much greater. So, too, any attempt at a global political friendship would surely entail attempts to strengthen certain international laws, support an evolving dialogue on international human rights, maintain a world court, establish rules of fair trade, and so on. There are many intermediate stages (and intermediate entities) to be explored before we jump to "one world government"—a goal that, for various reasons, is not particularly appealing at present (8.3).

In any event, if a form of friendship is recognized as central to the notion of the just state (both internally and externally), then our old conception of the nation-state begins to "loosen up," as it were. Its absolute sovereignty is brought into question (whether absolute over its own people or over its own land), boundaries between states become more fluid (more easily incorporating foreigners, immigrants, and outside ideas), a large military buildup becomes less necessary as "national security" comes to be envisaged in other terms than those of military power (8.5), and so forth. Even problems of membership, or of when succession is justified and when not, might fruitfully be illuminated in terms of this new vocabulary: in terms of when the conditions for the possibility of a civic friendship exist or when such conditions have irretrievably broken down, and why.

Similarly, an international friendship between peoples will clearly distinguish itself from any particular civic conception, for the latter necessarily acknowledges and feels an affinity for a people's particular natural and social geography, its political principles, and its concrete historical traditions within which its citizens are born, educated, or find themselves living. But this need not be conceived as a problem, unless one persists in conceiving friendship in terms of "fraternity": in terms of (male) likeness and similarity (2.6–7). It does not seem arbitrary to me (always with the stipulation, "other things being equal") that an individual should typically know more about, be more concerned with, and indebted to—as well as held responsible for—persons in her own family over people in her city, say, or people in her own country over those of foreign countries; in the former cases I characteristically understand, know, care, and can *practically do* more. Let us call this a "practical argument" for the primacy of concern for one's fellow citizens in terms of their basic rights to freedom, a safe and healthful environment, work, and education. These are social and political conditions for which we are all *in part* responsible (chapter 6).

This practical argument, however, is decidedly not an argument for the moral primacy of "the nation" (or of my cultural group, religion, and so on), as in various defenses of "nationalism."[2] On the contrary, I refer to the duties owed fellow citizens and to those advantages conferred by the new state (and not some cultural group), assuming all along that the state is multicultural, and acknowledges the dignity of each individual and the fact of modern pluralism (5.1). Of course, one might claim that my "practical argument" would be largely mitigated today through the explosion of new technologies and communications around the world, bringing others far away into our homes and us into theirs.[3] If we continue to stress the role and importance of actual hands-on ethical reproductive labor and *praxis* (4.5–6), however, the new temporal and spatial concentrations of communications and technologies will inevitably—no matter how powerful—have their practical limits. For many activities (from back massages to the changing of diapers, from taking temperatures to soothing cries and concerns of those in the last moments of life) there is no replacement for a particular set of hands, and new technologies will never reduce that distance to zero. No pair of hands can be in two different places at once.

But although, other things being equal, we may have a greater practical duty toward those near to us (or toward those who are more immediately affected by our actions), this is hardly a theoretical recognition that they are somehow more "valuable," objectively speaking. Quite to the contrary, we have begun from the modern perspective that criticizes the ancient world of hierarchically ordered value: from the axiom that all persons are ends in themselves and—morally speaking—equal. To this extent, the present position finds itself among those who call themselves "moral cosmopolitans"; the moral cosmopolitan assumes that every human being has global stature as an ultimate unit of moral concern.[4] What is needed to recognize such equal moral value of all in practice, however—given that psychologically no one can experience and practice it directly—will be the rational construction of new global social and political institutions—institutions today still in their infancy. Again, that the new state has a priority of responsibility for its own citizens, both as things stand now and in the near future, appears justified, given the characteristic knowledge, practical avenues of access, common language and patterns of familiar behavior, shared institutions and culture, etc. that most citizens have in a functional state. Particularly, we would hope, this is the case in a functioning democracy.

It thus strikes me as somewhat hypocritical when Americans express outrage at the destitute lives of poor children in Africa, yet neglect similar destitution in quarters of their own cities. Any genuine civic friendship (except, perhaps, for a few genuine "world citizens") characteristically entails a belonging to some particular political community (with a specific physical geography, a set of common laws, a constitution, political culture, and so forth) in which an individual lives, and this entails special duties owed civic others—only this is hardly the end of the story. For one, as political philosophers have stressed since ancient times, we always retain our "natural duties" to others whom we encounter even in distant lands (duties of refraining from lying and deception, of keeping one's word, of not harming others, or of giving basic aid if it causes minimal disadvantage to ourselves). Second, more and more of us are emerging today as "dual" (or more) citizens with serious ties to more than one land and people; certainly many of us have grown up in more than one "pure" culture, with ancestors hearkening from different locations on the earth. Finally, as Kant also argued long ago, increasing international social and economic cooperation does create a new basis for an international or global morality, although it hardly by itself determines that morality. Considering not only the increasingly global nature of modern scientific, technological, environmental, economic, and social exchange, it becomes quite clear that our obligations cannot end at the historical (often fully arbitrary) borders of our present nation-states. We are also, slowly, all becoming denizens of one planet, whether we like it or not. Thus, although a sincere ethical and political reflective equilibrium must begin from within a particular set of social and political traditions and institutions (1.4)—and so must assume a specific culture, state, or local community—no adequate philosophical reflection on the value of *philia* can remain there. At the same time, we must not jump too swiftly into talk of a global morality (all too often a mask for hegemonic interests) as if we were able to leap over our own shadows.

8.2 INTERNATIONAL RELATIONS AND STRUCTURAL ANARCHY

The call for relations of political *philia*, particularly in the interstate domain, will strike many as hopelessly naïve. This is at least partly because one dominant conception of international relations has reigned supreme in our collective imagination, particularly in the last sixty years or so, and other alternatives have been lost from view. Let us now look more closely at this realist conception of international relations, versions of which (both in its classical and neoclassical form) characteristically contain a number of assumptions. First, the Peace of Westphalia (1648) is typically considered the constitutive event of this new world order, having codified the principles of tolerance and peaceful coexistence between Catholic and Protestant (European) states, as well as legitimized the existence of religious self-sufficient states (in contrast to the Roman emperor and pope) as independent and equal actors in the international arena.

Second, the new nation-states are not only assumed to be rational actors seeking survival and security, but also considered to be politically sovereign; there is no higher court of earthly political appeal. Recall the Hobbesian position; once all political persons of a given territory have entered the social contract—and the state has been constituted by handing over all power to an absolute sovereign—the sovereign itself remains in a state of nature and is bound by no juridical law whatsoever. While a legal order arises within the boundaries of the state, the sovereign itself inhabits an uncertain environment populated only by other sovereigns (anarchy). With no authority above states to ensure rule enforcement between them, and as a result of the problems of cooperation already noted, the possibility of a war of all against all exists just beneath the surface of this international order, whenever and wherever it does not actively break out.

Of course, some kind of order, security, and predictability must be sustained—even on the structural anarchistic view—and this is accomplished by forming leagues, creating alliances, and, finally, distinguishing "one's friends from one's enemies." Since one cannot rely too much on such political alliances and friends, however (because states cannot fully trust each other when compliance with rules is not guaranteed), the declaration of war and the making of peace become exclusive powers belonging to sovereignty. Thus, Hobbes writes in *De Cive* (1651): "no Subject can privately determine who is a publique friend, who an enemy, when Warre, when Peace, when Truce is to be made; nor yet what Subjects, what authority, and of what men, are commodious, or prejudiciall to the safety of the Commonweale. These, and all like matters therefore are to be learned, if need be, from the City, that is, from the Soveraign powers."[5]

Three centuries later, Carl Schmidt will emphasize again this feature of sovereignty which stipulates an enemy, arguing that the declaration of war and the decision of the state in times of emergency and chaos are precisely what constitutes sovereignty itself. Schmidt writes in *The Concept of the Political*:

> *The state as the decisive political entity possesses an enormous power: the possibility of waging war and thereby publicly disposing of the lives of men. Thus* jus belli *contains such a disposition. It implies a double possibility: the right to demand from its own members the readiness to die and unhesitantly to kill enemies. . . . As long as the state is a political entity this requirement for internal peace compels it in critical situations to decide also upon the domestic enemy . . . the aim is always the same, namely to declare an enemy.*[6]

In this quotation, we have a critical further piece of the international realist position: even *internal* state unity is maintained by the existence of a common enemy. The enemy—whether external or from within—becomes a "requirement for internal peace."

A conception of friend thus lies at the heart of the realist worldview, after all. Let us call this form of friendship and cooperation with others—hardly a friendship for its own sake but a cooperation formed under the necessity of confronting a common threat—*negative friendship*. And it soon becomes apparent that Schmidt, in all his writings and despite the importance of the friend–enemy distinction in his thought, has no other conception. Schmidt's model of friendship is the simple one of being held together by a common menace—like two soldiers bonding under fire. No doubt such camaraderie may produce strong and longstanding emotional attachments, as anyone who has attended a veterans' group knows. Still, it is hardly an adequate notion of friendship in general—even for the explanation of political states.

Throughout this work we have elaborated a positive conception of friendship as *philia*, one performed for its own sake, as in those friendships where persons "delight in each other's presence" and do many things for one another. Such may be the case between parents and children, between siblings, or between lovers. Moreover, in these (far more common) everyday cases, having an "enemy" is largely irrelevant. It sounds decidedly odd, for instance, to say that I fell in love with Martin *because* I hate Peter. If I marry a man, say, because doing so allows me to escape my father, we tend to think this a rather poor reason—at least not an instance of genuine love. It is relatively late in the life of a healthy child, after all, that the concept of an enemy is even learned (in contrast to "Mommy," "Baba," "Aya"). Are modern states—particularly the new state—incapable of this positive form of "friendly" relation with other states? Again, why should only the negative form of attachments operate in international affairs?

What the dominant realist view (following the likes of Schmidt) fails to acknowledge is that a principle of friendship already operates internationally—it even began to do so during the seventeenth century—and not just in its negative sense.[7] The new world order of the sixteenth and seventeenth centuries not only distinguished itself from the *respublica christiana* of medieval times (associated with figures of pope and emperor), but it did so in terms of discussions of *public friendship*. Recent scholarship has revealed, for instance, that the Latin concept *amicitia* (amity or friendship) was a rare concept in the Middle Ages, at least when it concerned the relations between princes within Christian Europe.[8] The idea of a public friendship functioned predominantly in the *vertical* dimension of the medieval political order—requiring princes to have some friends among their subjects (thus mediating relations of subordination) as a requirement of peace and stability—but it rarely functioned between principalities themselves. With the age of discovery, reformation, religious wars, and the final emergence of the sovereign nation-state, however, the *horizontal* dimension became the main domain for the realization of political friendship.

Not only does Thomas More's *Utopia* (like other works in the same genre) already in 1516 use the term *friendship* in regard to external relations of abstract political entities (such as England),[9] but with the rediscovery of Roman law (and the influence of the ancient republican tradition) the sixteenth century saw a relative boom in concluding "friendship treaties" among European sovereigns.[10] Similarly, in the seventeenth-century writings of the political theorist Edward Coke or in those of the jurist Hugo Grotius (often considered the first thinker of international relations), the concept of "amity" contrasts with a public and authorized enemy (*hostis*): both refer to political entities of equal status.[11] Indeed, amity (or public friendship) is viewed as a prerogative of the king, and perceiving other (at least European) states as a potential friend could just be a way out of religious massacres and could lay the foundation of civilized interstate conduct (codified in the Peace of Westphalia in 1648). In 1871 Thomas Starkey still claims friendship with surrounding nations is one of the three main requirements for a commonwealth to exist and to prosper (the other two being number of people and good laws and order).[12] Finally, with the slow emergence of the European Union (EU), and despite all its recent problems, few people today continue to think that the unity of Spain, say, will persist only if it remains enemies with France or Italy.

What these early modern theorists, who tried to adapt Roman law to the reality of a new international order, meant by "amity" differs significantly from what I intend by an international *politike philia* in this work. Nonetheless, it is clear that many such thinkers did not think state unity is attained only in the face of an enemy, or that relations outward among neighboring states are based merely on calculations of self-interest or "marriages of convenience." Friendship between nations may be sought positively as an end in itself. Just as for individuals, for states also at least two incentives can operate, which differ in both motivation and effects: (1) the desire to meet an external threat by cooperative effort where the cooperation is predicated on the continuance of the threat, and (2) cooperation from a desire to improve relations within the cooperating group itself.[13] Friendship, like so many other human activities, proceeds in stages.

Finally, a number of important changes since World War II only reinforce this evolving conception of the role of states toward one another. Among these are: the slow demise of colonial rule; increasing international recognition of human rights (and a "culture of rights"); the view that war is legitimate for self-defense only or, in extreme cases, to protect human rights; and the establishment and development of the United Nations and other supranational organizations. All of these developments entail a new evaluation of the old international relations picture. Of course, the neo-realist does not claim that the second state motivation (for improved relations) is impossible, only that the former (the desire to meet external threats) proves far more potent and reliable. Again, we have the cynical Hobbes pitted against the more idealistic Kant (6.7).

And once again, I believe, theorizing the overlooked category of ethical reproductive labor, *praxis,* and *philia*—now applied to the domain of relations between states—can help break ties *in the direction of Kant.* As we have seen, such labor and activity is that type which helps build confidence, mutual trust, and improved social relations (2.3–5). Moreover, far more people de facto operate on this reproductive model of activity than Hobbes in his wildest dreams imagined (not only most women have been socialized for it, but many others from noncapitalist societies around the world as well). Finally, an increasing number of international relations scholars are coming to recognize that relations comparable to those of friendship have grown in certain regions of the world where the condition of anarchy has taken a very different turn from what realism predicted.[14] Echoing our argument in chapter 1, Alexander Wendt writes, for instance: "Relative to 'enemy,' the concept of 'friend' is under theorized in social theory, and especially in IR [international relations], where substantial literature exists on enemy images but little on friend images, on enduring rivalries but little on enduring friendships, on the causes of war but little on the causes of peace, and so on."[15]

And Andrea Oelsner, basing her work on the "securitization approach" developed by Barry Buzan, Ole Waever, and their colleagues of the so-called Copenhagen School, argues that the maintenance of stable regional peace is connected with domestic processes of *desecuritization* taking place at the regional level.[16] That is, states can surmount—and indeed have surmounted—the Hobbesian "security" dilemma externally, without resort to a global enforcer, on the one hand, and without resort to threats and shifting alliances, on the other. Allow me to summarize some of the findings of this new approach.

By "securitization" (or "the logic of security"), Waever intends the process by which issues come to be seen as security matters.[17] Building upon Austin's speech act theory, Waever argues that the mere invocation of something using the word *security* can declare its existential threatening nature to some referent subject, justifying in turn the use of extraordinary measures (read: competition or violence) to counter it. Security is the realm where emergency measures beyond ordinary political procedures become permissible. By contrast, "the logic of desecuritization" is the process of moving issues out of the emergency mode and into the normal bargaining processes of the political sphere.[18] In this case, for instance, violence ceases to be a legitimate option. One can thus identify not just two but *three* states (or conditions) of security: (1) *insecurity,* when one feels one lacks adequate defenses to counter perceived threats; (2) *security,* when sufficient counter-measures are felt to be available; and (3) *asecurity,* the slow erosion of the perception of threat until neither security nor insecurity language applies (8.5).

What Oelsner adds to this securitization debate (which tends to focus on internal state processes) is the extension of its central concepts to regional peace between states: to the establishment of pluralistic security communities—where war becomes unthinkable—and which she argues are comparable to genuine friendship relations.[19] That is, theorists have long placed stages of peace on a continuum (fragile, unstable, cold, or conditional peace) and have distinguished between negative and positive forms.[20] While negative peace might range anywhere from the recent cessation of war, perhaps with troops remaining on the borders but with continued antipathy between two societies, to the beginnings of diplomatic visits, the move to a positive peace entails a different type of relation altogether. In positive peace—defined by the presence of mutual confidence and trust—states do not prepare for war at all, nor do they frame issues between them in security language, and disputes are resolved by negotiation and agreement. Here scholars have distinguished at least two further stages: *stable peace* and *pluralistic security communities*.[21]

While all pluralistic security communities are zones of stable peace, the reverse is not the case. The idea of a pluralistic security community is important for our purposes because the phenomenon most closely exhibits traits of genuine friendship. It is a "consolidated" zone of stable peace whereby states reciprocally observe at least two rules: nonviolence and the rule of mutual aid.[22] Moreover, such observance is not narrowly self-interested but more "participatory" in that the societies involved have developed links, mutual sympathies, and various types of common identifications that make members perceive themselves as members of similar or even of the same communities.[23] The two (or more) states typically possess similar political systems (or even common ones) and have considerable cultural exchange and economic interdependence. In short, envisaging the option of advancing rapprochement with a former rival need not be merely instrumental, but may already have value for its own sake. While members of the European Union, as well as Canada and the United States, are clear examples of pluralistic security communities, relations between members of the Association of Southeast Asian Nations (ASEAN) since the late 1970s are frequently cited as examples of stable peace.

What allows two states (even those that were once bitter rivals) to step outside "the security dilemma" and progress to a pluralist security community where war (or resolution of issues by force) has been taken "off the table"? Traditional international relations might stress shifting circumstances such that two states suddenly find themselves with growing common "material interests." But such an account could never describe more than a contingent (or the coalescence of material forces), calculating relationship, while recent scholarship stresses something further and deeper: a changing self-image, transformed rhetoric, construction of common projects, and an *altered perception of the other*. In her study of the evolving relations between the once bitter rivals Argentina and Brazil, for instance, Oelsner notes how in the 1970s a cold peace still prevailed: both countries were under military rule, there were serious water disputes, each pursued its own nuclear development program, and negative perceptions abounded.[24] To be sure, in the late 1970s U.S. pressure on nuclear arms development led both countries to cooperate (and President Carter's pressure on rights violations punished both), but simultaneous with international pressure there was a regional *abertura* (liberalization of politics) and changing domestic circumstances where leaders in both countries (military, scientific, economic) began to adopt more positive images. By 1979 Argentina, Brazil, and Paraguay had signed the Tripartite Agreement, their presidents visited each other's countries, documents were signed ending competition (e.g., Brazil and Argentina established joint hydroelectric enterprises), and Brazil went on to support Argentina's claim to the Malvinas against Britain at the United Nations.

What appears to have happened (although Oelsner calls the relation between Argentina and Brazil at present an "incipient" security community only) is that through new interactions and ideas, identifications and perceptions are transformed, in turn opening up new possibilities of policy actions (removal of troops from borders, for instance), as well as a growing confidence and trust. Analogous to the individual who is tired of fighting and suddenly realizes it is also unnecessary, a country's "interest" may be redefined in such a way that mutual peace and regional friendship become a part of it. Such evolving "interstate amity"—in direct contrast to realist claims—tends to promote *emotional* friendship as well: the experience of successful common effort (say, a bilateral common market), positive rhetoric and favorable image of the other (in which government typically plays a role), increasing communication and ties among civil societies (facilitation of mobility or cross-country recognition of degrees), and, finally, social and cultural exchange in art, music, languages, and festivals.

Thawing traditionally chilly interstate relationships, however, need hardly always work "from above." As one author notes, municipalities themselves can initiate friendly relations with other cross-border cities in the phenomenon that has come to be called "town twinning": the intentional creation of new practices establishing a friendship bond between towns or cities in two different countries.[25] Foremost among such practices are official ceremonies (a mix of solemnity and enjoyment, with flags, sprays of flowers, rhetorical speeches, exchange of city keys), the celebrations of ritual (always music, with dancing, traditional costumes, sports competitions, and so forth), and, of course, feasts (the enjoyment and tasting of local foods, wine, and drink, including frequent bouts of drunkenness). Containing vestiges of the medieval communes, town twinning makes an interesting study of how friendship bonds are actually forged and maintained through the civilization of habits, even over long distances and times, and with the participation of large numbers of people. They reveal that achieving friendship—even on the international level—is not a matter of mere "discourse" or discursive speech, but that emotional and aesthetic experiences (as well as outright "fun") are critical parts of the process. Similarly, such rituals between two cities exemplify not merely local, state, or regional diplomacy, but the communal autonomy of each city or region and its inhabitants. The independence of each, far from being relinquished in the celebration of their relationship, is exemplified.

The phenomenon of town twinning involves widespread participation in the construction of compatible identities, mutual sympathies, and the sense of a shared transnational (at least transregional) security community with a common future and destiny. In this way the conditions for the possibility of a genuine political friendship between larger states emerge as well and from the "bottom up," as it were. Not just material forces are transformed, but cognitive structures, emotions, and identities, too, and in such a way that disputes are resolved by negotiation and discussion—*as if* between two friends. War between former rivals slowly becomes unthinkable, but this is only because a great deal of ethical reproductive work and *praxis* have been performed on both sides and become deeply embedded in the history of the relationship.

Indeed, in direct contrast to Schmidt's claim that it is a sign and right of sovereignty to declare war in the name of state interest, *we here deny there is any longer such a right.* On the contrary, what appears to be emerging over time is the awareness of a *duty* among states to pursue a positive friendship. Except for instances of genuine self-defense (instances in actual fact growing ever rarer), the declaration of war need no longer be perceived as part of our new conception of state sovereignty. Just as I no longer see myself physically "fighting" to resolve disputes with my family members, colleagues, or fellow citizens (something many of us still did as children), the time is arriving when the political state matures to that point where military methods are revealed for what they characteristically are: the egoistic utilization of brute force (typically with base ulterior motives), which will increasingly win only the world's condemnation. Certainly, women in general are less enamored of the macho show of military muscle and beginning to speak out.[26] There is an alternative ideal of reconciliation and wisdom, moreover, which could become our ideal—say, of a Nelson Mandela, who not only experienced lifelong humiliation and injustice, but who could have helped unleash a wide genocide against the white elites of South Africa had he so chosen, but who refused to do so.

In direct contrast to the neo-realists, from the ethical reproductive perspective, government has the primary duty of *a positive peace*: of a civic friendship not only among its own citizens but with its neighbors as well. Such is the reconceived nature of the feminist political state; military force is increasingly viewed as suspect and illegitimate. This positive duty, moreover, must include the rhetoric and images of good will and friendship, backed by practical actions and sustained funding, as well as by the construction of common projects, cultural exchanges, festivities, and simple fun. All of these result in the changed perceptions and motives of a state's own (as well as of the other's) citizens.

Of course, the case of Brazil and Argentina may be distinguished by the fact that both are large, industrializing countries of the Southern Hemisphere, with contiguous borders, each rich in natural resources, independent, with vast populations. What if we turn our attention to the relations between North and South in general, however, or between the United States and, say, Niger? It is at this point that Rawls's difference principle becomes relevant again (5.2)—only now on the international level.

8.3 A GLOBAL DIFFERENCE PRINCIPLE?

Scholars tend to agree that the modern nation-state is undergoing profound transformations, but they hardly agree in which direction. Unfortunately, much of the recent debate on global justice proceeds in terms of global "integration" or its absence—a conception and vocabulary that remain far too simple. On the one extreme, we find the many moral and political cosmopolitans (Charles Beitz, Carol Gould, Martha Nussbaum, Thomas Pogge, Henry Shue, Peter Singer, and others) who argue that we are all world citizens now due to the growing "internationalization" of both legal and economic structures. Internationalization means that the functions of the nation-state are increasingly being replaced by new, "horizontally" dispersed agencies and/or world agents (e.g., the United Nations, International Monetary Fund, World Trade Organization [WTO], World Bank, and so on). Such integration is assumed by this group to be not only inevitable, but for the most part a good thing; global interaction is revealing our dependencies and need for one another, including our "shared humanity." Although most cosmopolitans do not advocate a world government, some of them do argue for global political democracy (David Held or Kai Neilson), on the one hand, or for some version of a global economic difference principle, on the other (most famously, Beitz and Pogge).

In the opposite camp, we find critics of globalization who claim any and all moves toward greater integration inevitably favor the most powerful states, such as the United States or those of Europe—hegemonic states that can set the rules of the game to their own advantage. This group of theorists advocates some form of continued local sovereignty or even "deglobalization." Omar Dahbour, for example, argues against "a world of common concern" and claims that a system of "mutual indifference" is actually preferable. Building upon the work of Herman Daly and John Cobb, in part (and also, we might assume, the 1999 Seattle protests against the WTO), Dahbour concludes that the ideal global community is one of autonomous, ecologically sustainable communities that are "disengaged" and "self-absorbed."[27]

The issue, in our view, is not so much whether there should be "integration," or how much, but the quality of the relations between what at present still count as nation-states. For this purpose, the model of an international *philia* becomes of help once more in its role as normative guide; it may help distinguish undesirable "integration" (domination, oppression, exploitation, etc.) from the more enabling and positive sorts of interactions between peoples. Since we argued earlier for a reconception of Rawls's difference principle on the domestic level—not as a principle of male "fraternity" but in terms of a thicker *praxis* of civic friendship (5.6)—the question now becomes what our analysis suggests regarding this principle at the international level. In this section, I turn to an analysis of one prominent argument for an international difference principle: Pogge's call for a Global Resource Dividend (GRD), or tax on the earth's resource use by the wealthy nations (roughly 1 percent of the global product), as that which rightfully belongs to the poorer peoples of the earth.[28] I focus on Pogge's view, not only because his proposal has garnered much attention of late, but also because it broaches the important issue of environmental responsibility.

Famously, John Rawls himself denies that his difference principle (conceived as a "principle of fraternity") should be applied worldwide, on the grounds that one people should not have to bear the costs of decisions made by another.[29] Beyond a guarantee of minimal universal rights, general fair trade practices and laws, and a transitional "duty of assistance" to help "burdened societies" (societies where the conditions are so dismal that just institutions are impossible) until such point as they can manage their own affairs justly, there is no further economic "target," such as reducing vast inequalities in wealth for its own sake. This is the case, according to Rawls, because the "crucial element" in how a society fares in establishing just institutions—the ultimate political goal—is its "political culture" and not the level of its resources. "The arbitrariness of the distribution of natural resources causes no difficulty," the later Rawls writes.[30] Not only would a global difference principle require some form of "world government" for its implementation—and hence in his view a dangerous concentration of power—but every society (except for the burdened ones) has within its own population a sufficient array of human capabilities and resources to realize just institutions. Rawls's "law of peoples" concerns itself with "the justice of societies" or "peoples" and is not a cosmopolitan view concerned with the "well being of individuals."

By now numerous thinkers have argued that Rawls's own arguments justifying a domestic difference principle continue to hold for the international domain; Rawls fails to give adequate justification for "the separation of contexts." Most important, both Beitz and Pogge point to an ever more integrated global "basic structure"—a more or less common background of international economic, political, and social institutions and a shared and extensive history of European colonialism. Although less tightly structured than their domestic counterparts, such modern global institutions include increasing global trade with a general set of rules, an ever growing body of internationally recognized law, and a developing language of universal human rights norms. Further, just as in the domestic case, this common "system of cooperation" morally demands (through a similar method of choice, now from within a higher level, global, original position) that those who gain most by this global system do so *only if* they also benefit its worst off members. This is particularly important when one acknowledges that the inequality between states (and between Northern and Southern Hemispheres) in terms of wealth and advantages is not only what Tom Nagel calls "radical" (the worst-off countries are so both relatively and absolutely, the inequality is pervasive, and it is difficult or impossible for these countries to better their lot on their own), but has been radically expanding in recent decades.

The income gap between the fifth of the world's people living in the richest countries and the fifth living in the poorest is far from diminishing. Rather, it is growing at an astonishing rate. According to the 1999 *United Nations Development Report*, in 1820 this gap was 3 to 1; by 1913, it was 7 to 1; in 1960, 30 to 1; and in 1997, 74 to 1.[31] Similarly, one-quarter of the people alive on the earth today (roughly 1.5 billion out of 6 billion) subsist below the international poverty line (the level of income required for basic nutrition and necessities, pegged by the World Bank in 2000 at $2 a day purchasing power), while one-third of all human deaths on the planet can be traced to hunger-related causes.[32] This means global hunger causes approximately 18 million person deaths per year—15 million of which are children. Finally, Pogge stresses that such radical inequality is fully avoidable. Effective reduction of hunger and severe poverty worldwide, it is generally estimated, would require an effort costing perhaps as much as $230 billion annually for several years: an enormous sounding amount, until one realizes that it is only 1 percent of the affluent countries' gross national product.[33] The fact that we can help with so little cost to ourselves underscores the fact that we *should*.

Pogge labels his approach to global justice "ecumenical"; he uses different arguments appealing to the diverse assumptions of his readers.[34] Thus, in the face of those (such as Nozick) who defend historical-entitlement conceptions of justice, Pogge points out that the actual historical path leading to the present inequality arose by way of grievous wrong. There is a historical, causal connection between present inequalities and the past practices of the wealthier nations: in particular, the ugly and violent history of European colonialism with its bitter legacy of exploited peoples, destruction of local institutions, and theft of natural resources.

To the libertarian of a different stripe (one who does not believe that the actual historical process is relevant for today), Pogge argues that the richer nations also violate their purely negative duties not to harm the global poor *now*; they do so by continuing to uphold and exploit the global system for their own advantage.[35] Whether through unilateral appropriations (often by way of the military) or through institutional arrangements, such as the imposition of radically nonequalitarian property regimes, the rich nations are hardly leaving "enough and as good" natural resources of the globe to the poor (Locke's criterion of the state of nature baseline [3.3]). Finally, to those of a broadly consequentialist persuasion, Pogge argues that there exists a feasible alternative under which such extensive and extreme poverty would not persist: one where as little as 1 percent of the global world product would be considered the right of the poor, as compensation for their exclusion from adequate access to natural resources. This 1 percent Pogge calls a Global Resource Dividend (GRD)—a tax on the use of the world's resources by the wealthy, which is not only due the poor but rightly belongs to them (as their right to the earth itself) (*WPHR*, 196–215). In sum, the present state of affairs, where social and economic human rights are unfulfilled on a massive scale, is morally unacceptable whichever way one looks at it. Denizens of rich countries all share in responsibility for such nonfulfillment insofar as we participate in—and continue to support—the existing global institutional imposition of this order.

Not surprisingly, many of Pogge's critics have attacked his empirical, causal claims. Thus, they stress the frequent corruption and incompetence of many Third World local officials and the latter's responsibility for the poverty of their own people, and so on. Even if this is so, however, it does not follow (as Pogge points out) that the advantaged nations therefore have no responsibility; poverty typically has multiple causes. (Rawls himself commits a version of this fallacy when he writes that "the crucial element" in poverty is a people's "political culture"—including their religious, philosophical, and moral traditions—but then goes on to treat these as the *only* relevant factors.)[36] Pogge elaborates nicely how the present global system of trade and property rights sets the agenda and many of the incentives for local corruption: for instance, by granting international legal recognition and ownership rights of national resources to every two-bit tyrant—what Pogge calls a "resource and borrowing privilege"—which in turn encourages further coups attempts by illegitimate others to plunder their nation's wealth.[37]

Even if we acknowledge the critical importance of a background global structure, however, others argue that by Pogge's own criteria we are responsible only for those who partake in our "shared system of cooperation"; this hardly amounts to each and every impoverished person in every far-flung corner of the disconnected earth.[38] Pogge appears to leave himself open to such criticism when he writes, rather ambiguously: "we are concerned about avoidably unfulfilled human rights not simply insofar as they exist at all, but only insofar as they are produced by coercive social institutions in whose imposition we are involved" (*WPHR*, 172). Nonetheless, critics such as Mathias Risse overlook that the causal argument is only one strand of Pogge's overall ecumenical approach.

In the view proffered here, all such criticisms miss the central thrust of Rawls's original (economic) difference principle: it is a political interpretation of "fraternity" (5.2). Thus, even if some of

Pogge's causal claims break down (as I believe they do), it is still the case that a significant portion of world poverty is due to the legacies of colonialism. More important, it is still true that world hunger and poverty are avoidable through a better global institutional order. Finally, on the view argued here, there exists a political duty of friendship: a positive duty we attract simply by being alive and human. This duty not only cuts across the traditional negative/positive duty distinction, but it is a necessary precondition for justice *überhaupt* (2.7). Thus, going beyond Pogge, we have a prima facie duty (other things being equal) to befriend even those we might discover on Venus (so long as they don't directly attack us) and to help them should they be in trouble. This duty of *philia,* moreover, is an expression of our giving nature—just as fundamental as our "taking" side—and it is a part of our nature grounded and expressed in traditional reproductive activity. The question now becomes whether Pogge's Global Resource Dividend is the best way to pursue this international duty.

I offer three criticisms of Pogge's GRD principle, which track our earlier criticisms of Rawls's domestic difference principle itself (5.2–4).[39] First, and most important, Pogge's proposal does little to dislodge the reigning Lockean paradigm of labor as production: the dominant model of "mixing one's labor" with the natural physical world and with the aim of private acquisition. Although Pogge explicitly criticizes the ideal type *Homo economicus,*[40] he fails to delineate any plausible alternative conception. On the contrary, Pogge (like Rawls) accepts a number of rather questionable tenets of neo-classical economics. We find scattered throughout his texts, for instance, references to "economic growth" (as if this were an unmitigated good), to percentages of gross national product (which environmentalists increasingly emphasize is the wrong measure, and a highly destructive one), and Pogge leaves ownership rights of the developed nations pretty much as they are (but for the 1 percent resource tax in the name of the poorer nations). There is, for instance, no attempt to restructure the firm or economic corporation itself (5.5). Pogge even sees his closeness to standard economic theory as a virtue; he writes that it is possible "without major changes to our global economic order . . . to eradicate world hunger within a few years" (*WPHR,* 205–6). From the perspective of this book, this last claim is mere wishful thinking. Not only does Pogge minimize the environmental destructiveness of the production model, but also, in lacking any alternative conception of ethical reproductive labor, he ignores the activity of millions of people (most of them women) who still perform such work. As a consequence—and this is my second criticism—the motivation for the richer countries to give up even 1 percent of their GNP remains problematic on Pogge's account. If the primary goal of individual economic labor (and of the nation-state) remains private "economic growth," then the moral "ought" that the individual should also think of others emerges as a bit weak—like blowing into a strong headwind. Pogge acknowledges this difficulty when he writes, "There remains the problem of generating this good will, especially on the part of the rich and mighty" (*WPHR*, 210–11). Nonetheless, he claims it is still a duty to protect any victims of injustice, and perhaps it is not so "unrealistic" after all; moral convictions can have real effects, even in international politics (*WPHR*, 211). On Pogge's view, following one's duty is at least *not impossible*.

In the final analysis, Pogge (like Rawls) wishes to presuppose nothing further about political persons than the possession of the two moral powers of personality: the capacity to pursue a conception of the good, and the capacity for justice or the ability to act from universal laws and principles.[41] These two powers by themselves, however, as we have argued, are insufficient to account for a deep awareness of others and for genuine good will toward them (3.5). For such behavior, which not only allows the rejection of extreme acquisitiveness in the realm of labor, but also grounds the possibility of an alternative motivation, a third moral power, not reducible to the other two, must be acknowledged in everyone. This third moral power we have called the abstract capacity for friendship (3.6).

Indeed, on this point, Pogge is between a rock and a hard place, for his main proposal for a GRD has frequently been criticized as "unrealistic" by others.[42] Let us emphasize that this is *not* our criticism. Pogge's proposals are hardly far-fetched if one rejects the acquisitive self in the realm of labor (as a false description of persons in general) and acknowledges and delineates an alternative model—labor whose ultimate aim, in the best case, is the reproduction of relations of *philia*. (Nor can this conception so easily be co-opted by the more powerful nations, for genuine friendship must include the recognition and free response of both parties.) So, too, Pogge's proposal is not far-fetched when the (nearly all male) United Nations not long ago called on the wealthy member nations to give 0.7 percent of their GNP to end world hunger. Granted, such a call remains "voluntary," but it seems clear that many peoples of the world desire to move in this direction and think it fully plausible. Finally, it is hard to imagine that women *as a group* would not support a global policy so clearly an extension of their traditional line of work, were they only allowed entry into our international organizations en masse and on equal terms. Pogge's principle is thus not entirely unrealistic or unrealizable, but his own theory has insufficiently rid itself of old assumptions regarding motivation and labor, assumptions that keep this principle from being plausible to many developed nations, much less realized by them.

This last point leads to our third and final criticism of Pogge's principle. Again, like Rawls's domestic principle, the Global Resource Principle (GRP) operates from the top down (5.6). In Rawls's theory, the difference principle is to be implemented by one of the four main branches of domestic government—the branch that implements "the principle of need" (*TJ*, 274–84). But as we have seen, if the acquisitive self remains primary in the realm of labor, there is little possibility that the difference principle will become an actual directive of our representatives in government. This is the problem of *theoretical acceptance*; what motivates the average individual, atomized and self-absorbed in the marketplace, to emerge other-directed in the voting booth? Even if the principle should be accepted by government "from above," who is to implement it? Who will do the actual, hands-on, other-directed work of caring for the worst off in the concrete? This we called the problem of *the practical implementation* of Rawls's principle (5.6).

The same difficulty plagues Pogge's view. His GRP is to be applied by the United Nations or by some analogous global economic agency. The problem is that even if we could somehow manage to get the rich and powerful nations to decide upon when and how to extract dividends and redistribute them—sending money to where it is presumably needed most on the planet—these are merely the first steps in the far larger project of ending world hunger. These two steps (acknowledging need and beginning to take responsibility) emerge as only the first half (out of four stages) of an actual, integrated act of political caring (4.6). That is, even if we could motivate the wealthier nations to part with 1 percent of their collective GNP for allotment to the poorer nations, this is still a far cry from de facto feeding the starving, much less from actually bringing about an end to world poverty. These two steps are hardly sufficient, although (to Pogge's credit) they well may be necessary.

Recall that of the four characteristic stages in an accomplished act of care or friendship, the first two (following Tronto) are *noticing the existence of a need* and *beginning to take responsibility* for its fulfillment (4.6). The completion of a genuine act of friendship or care, however, requires two further stages: the *hands-on reproductive labor* of acting to satisfy the need, and *listening and obtaining feedback* from the worst off regarding their position. Pogge speaks nowhere about either of these final stages. But what is sending money abroad if not a way of getting other people to do the actual hands-on ethical reproductive labor all people (but especially the starving) need?

Concern about precisely this top-down implementation of the GRP has led to a further set of criticisms of Pogge's proposal. Risse, for example, has pointed out that such freely moving "monies" from the advanced nations present numerous problems: outside assistance from the world's wealthy is often ineffective (one can't import what is most needed to end hunger, that is, local institutions built up from within); funds are spent inefficiently (often going to special and corrupt interests rather than to the poor); there is the paternalism concern (outsider help from above is inevitably shaped according to the giver's understanding); lack of responsibility on the part of givers (after their failures, they simply move on); and the risk of undermining the stability of local institutions (by continued support from without).[43]

Similarly, Dale Jamieson advocates "extreme caution" in the face of such a global principle (DD, 154). Jamieson points to what he calls the "Live Aid conception" of humanitarian aid that emerged from the celebrity-driven, media-centered projects of the 1970s and 1980s. This conception models humanitarian aid (reflected in Singer's analogy of plucking a drowning child from the pond) as a response to immediate needs of innocent, passive victims (primarily women and children), whose lives are threatened by some natural disaster (such as a drought or an earthquake). Jamieson argues that the real world is far more complex. Famine is increasing being revealed as linked to war, vulnerability (frequently due to ecological degradation), systematic violations of human rights, and radically unequal power relations.[44] If we are concerned with world hunger, perhaps our primary goal should be aimed at hindering wars and ecological destruction in the first place—at the very least, at ceasing to instigate and perpetuate them—and a decrease in poverty and starvation may just follow.

So, too, humanitarian assistance (or development aid; I am not distinguishing between them here) has become a self-serving industry. As the United States Agency for International Development (USAID) has itself acknowledged, of the billions of U.S. dollars spent on foreign aid in the late 1990s (actually a tiny fraction of 1 percent of American GDP), 77 percent went to suppliers within the United States (DD, 159). Aid is not distributed on the basis of need, but largely for political reasons. While the United States spends more than 20 percent of its development aid on the relatively well-off nations of Russia and Israel (and lately increasingly on Bosnia and Iraq), the far larger needs of Africa continue to be ignored (DD, 160, 164). Finally, Jamieson points to the serious new dangers that accompany the use of military intervention in the name of peace-keeping and aid. Not only are armies trained to kill people and to smash things (they are not humanitarian organizations), but many an empire (e.g., the British empire) enriched the mother nation in the name of "doing good" to others (for the British, ostensibly to abolish the slave trade and spread civilization) (DD, 165).

Many of these dangers could be avoided, I believe, if our primary aim in helping the worst off is not simply to send dollars, but to reconceive the fundamentals of our own laboring arrangements (5.5). Not only must we criticize the production model of activity, along with its destructive consumption—the old ideal of *Homo economicus*—far more ruthlessly than Pogge does, but also we must acknowledge a type of laboring activity (and millions of laboring peoples) that the ideal actually obscures: those still operating on an ethical reproductive model. What is needed today, above all else, is a profound change in the awareness and structure of dominant motivation in the wealthy nations first of all. I have argued, moreover, that such a widespread change in motivation is hardly utopian once we begin to factor in (finally) the alternative structure of labor and motivation operating right before our eyes, but which has until now been eclipsed by reigning metaphors and theories. In chapter 7, we argued that in the new state, where ethical reproductive labor and *praxis* will be acknowledged at the highest levels of government, at least half of our exorbitant military budget could be turned into a mandatory civil service, in which ethical reproductive labor (and not productive and military skills) would be more fairly distributed among all (7.4). Similarly here, at the international level and in the name of international *philia,* why not send, in addition to dollars, and instead of weapons and military support, our idealistic and unarmed youth, in what could be an expanded Peace Corps, as it were? As a partial fulfillment of their mandatory civic duties, the eighteen- to twenty-five-year-olds of the wealthy nations could be sent to foreign and exotic lands for six months or up to a year, not to exploit or control the inhabitants, but *to learn from them and be of service.* Carefully supervised and trained by local indigenous organizations themselves (the youth could become a part of the current global justice movement), such crews of strong and healthy young men and women could be sent to where they are needed most: to build roads, to transport medicines, to help bring in the harvest, to watch the children, to supply the most elementary food and care, and so forth. In this way, the young of the richer (often emotionally impoverished) nations could learn of how the other half lives—their needs, work and family life, festivals and growing seasons, sacred rites, and way of life generally. For the wealthy nation's privileged youth, this would be an opportunity to see beyond the endless materialism of elite culture (the vacuous bubble of country clubs or debutante gatherings). For the less well off (of the wealthier nations), this could be the only opportunity to travel and experience foreign lands that their lives afford. In this manner all citizens will have at some point left their home countries, and all will surely be transformed by the experience. What these young people lack in expertise and knowhow, moreover, they will surely make up amply by their energy, curiosity, and enthusiasm—above all, by their often still intact ethical idealism. Such experiences will surely result in many strong and lasting personal friendships as well.

8.4 BACK TO THE DRAWING BOARD: ECOLOGICAL CONCERNS

On the other extreme of the globalization debates lies the position of those who argue that we should generally "leave things as they are," but for an adjustment here or there (the later Rawls), or else we should actually "ease down" on global trade, strengthen national borders in the name of economic self-sufficiency (Daly), and even, in the extreme case, become "disengaged" and "self-absorbed" as an ideal stance (Dahbour). We have seen that for Rawls, beyond a guarantee of minimal universal rights, maintenance of general "fair trade" practices and laws, and a transitional "duty of assistance" to help "burdened societies," wealthy nations have no further duty toward the poorer ones (8.3). We found this claim unconvincing, however, for (as Pogge argues) much of the "political culture" and corruption of poorer nations is induced by the more powerful states and continues to work to the latter's advantage.

Historically, the wealthy nations have been reluctant to allow Third World nations to develop autonomously. Instead, they have intervened in many ways: through the legacy of Western colonialism (which typically divided local populations in order to conquer them and extract their natural resources), the common practice of corporations bribing national officials (a perfectly legal practice until recently), the exploitation of lax environmental or labor standards of poorer nations, or the granting of legal recognition to corrupt local tyrants who do the more powerful country's bidding. Even worse, "global" economic agencies, such as the World Bank and the International Monetary Fund, have succeeded in drawing into the market Third World nations, which are often self-sufficient even though materially poor, with the result, in many cases, of fostering their dependency and ballooning debt.[45] To the extent that Rawls's theory accepts this basic economic state of things—seems unaware of it, much less critical—the theory accepts a blatantly unjust global "basic structure."

Finally, in looking away from the de facto interdependencies existing between nations at present, Rawls's noncosmopolitan position (as I shall call it) also looks away from all global ecological concerns (to this extent Pogge's position is a clear improvement). Do not the industrialized nations have a clear duty *not* to continue pouring emissions from their smokestacks and automobiles into the (ever warming) atmosphere, which all the earth's inhabitants have in common? And must there not, at some point soon, be a global agreement and universal laws to protect our fragile environment as a whole from the rapacious use that has swept the earth in the last few centuries? The move toward far stronger, universal *ecological laws* than Rawls envisions—including regulation and enforcement mechanisms, say, through the United Nations or other global institutions—appears inevitable, but may still be of an entirely different order than the autocratic "one world government" he fears.

What some of the "localists" or "nationalists" nonetheless seem to have right (at least from the ethical reproductive perspective presented here) is that various legitimate functions that the nation-state traditionally possesses are in danger of being lost today. Among these are the traditional duty of the state to preserve and protect its populace and territory, not merely from bombs and enemy soldiers (in reality, an ever diminishing threat for most), certainly not from peaceful intellectual or cultural exchange with others, but from exploitative economic dependency on and direction by foreign powers. This economic dependency may be in regard to other nations (in terms of a huge foreign debt, trade deficits, and so forth) or, as is frequently the case today, in regard to international corporate and financial entities. Hegel stressed two centuries ago that the nation-state's responsibility is as much to *break up* concentrations of monopolistic property power in the name of individual freedom as to protect its citizens' legitimate property from others and from the state as a whole. Indeed, there remain at least two powerful reasons to stress an "economic localism" (a form of nationalism, if you will) today in the face of globalization, despite working simultaneously to strengthen international laws, agencies, and institutions of human (including women's) rights.

The first reason concerns the relation between economic dependency and democratic autonomy. Not only Hegel but many others—including John Maynard Keynes—point to the loss of control that dependency on international trade, world markets, and international finance produces. As Keynes notes, "Ideas, knowledge, art, hospitality, travel—these are the things which should of their nature be international. But let goods be homespun whenever it is reasonably and conveniently possible; and above all, let finance be primarily national."[46]

Any people that must depend on far-away places for the reproduction of their basic daily necessities (whether food, clothing, heat, or housing) open themselves to myriad forms of disruption beyond their control—a loss of control often just as threatening to "national security" as foreign armies. This simple truth seems to have been forgotten in the recent onslaught of free-trade propaganda, with its ideals of capital mobility, efficient specialization, raised productivity and standard of living (measured by average rise in GNP). Free international trade, after all, hardly means trade in the name of the whole community; to the contrary, the lowering of national trade barriers, import duties, and so on usually allows some individuals to profit handsomely while other citizens feel no effect or find that their situation worsens. In what way do local family farming communities remain independent and autonomous, for instance, when they are forced to compete in milk production with international agribusiness? Indeed, nothing reveals the ideology of production—and its false equation of market production with independence (3.4)—more thoroughly than free-trade tendencies that lead to the actual *forsaking* of autonomous local decisions and stable, healthful relations with neighbors, for the sake of a few cents cheaper tomato or unnecessary products from halfway around the world.

And this claim, especially as theorists of the Third World point out, applies to vast numbers of subsistence farmers in developing nations even if such farmers exist at relatively low levels of material well-being. Many subsistence farmers (the majority of them still women) continue to satisfy their family's basic needs by a customary "self-provisioning of nature"; they gather food from the land, forest, or jungle; they make their own decisions; they know what to expect and where to turn; and many live relatively healthful and long lives. As Vandana Shiva emphasizes, there is a critical difference between poverty as subsistence and poverty as genuine material deprivation.[47] The subsistence farmer seems poor to Western materialistic eyes, because subsistence living has no financial resources to buy television sets or other commodities; but this is often a culturally perceived poverty, for basic needs (in terms of use value) are typically satisfied and the quality of life itself is anything but poor. Genuine deprivation and poverty, in contrast, frequently emerge when economic "development" and market forces deny local people access to their old means of subsistence. Their traditional land is enclosed and resources diverted to intensive commodity production, at the same time as the most elementary vital needs of these people can no longer be met, now due to a lack of income on their part (exchange value).

Shiva illustrates this critical point with the example of *bathua*, a leafy green vegetable that Indian women traditionally collected for their families when weeding local wheat fields. This nutritive plant grows well in association with wheat, but when "enhanced productivity" for export became the norm, chemical fertilizers were introduced and *bathua* was relegated to a "weed" and eradicated. As a direct consequence of "economic development" (and the introduction of the institution of private property), local women were not only denied their traditional land-use rights (the land having been enclosed, bought out from under them, or outright stolen), but also were deprived of work (men characteristically being the first to enter the new factories or plantations) at the same time as they and their families lost an important source of nutrition. The centuries-old food cycle is abruptly broken in this manner, and far too many people fall into genuine material deprivation—a state far worse than their traditional subsistence life. Recall that 15 million children die each year from hunger-related causes, and the number if anything (contrary to what many believe) is going up (8.3).

Many recent economic trade policies, moreover, do little more than dash madly toward dependence on international trade and overseas resources. Dominant policies (e.g., those expressed in the Uruguay Round of GATT or in NAFTA) increase dependence on trade by working for specialization of production on a global scale; they increase dependence on global resources by advocating increased quantitative "throughput" as the measure of economic growth (essentially what GNP measures). In this manner (and by a twisted sort of logic) our present economic accounting practices portray subsistence farmers as "unproductive" and "unemployed" (they remain outside the market), while the clean-up efforts of the *Exxon Valdez* oil spill are calculated as part of the "growing" GNP (a sign of "success"). As Daly argues, the more these policies succeed, the less any nation (including our own) is able to feed and clothe itself out of its own resources. "Even a temporary disruption of supply lines will become increasingly disastrous," Daly predicted, well before the most recent war in Iraq and the spike in oil prices.[48]

To the extent that ideals of regional or national economic self-sufficiency and enhancement of a people's political autonomy are seen as valuable—as well as necessary for a participatory democracy—the goal becomes restriction of trade in the interest of a people's well-being and community, to lessen dependency on international markets, to strengthen borders against adverse international capital and labor flow, and to reassert a nation's control over its own labor policies and environmental standards—including enforcement. The importance of this becomes clear when we consider that a relative autonomy between trading partners—and a balance in trade—appears to be a precondition for a mature and lasting relationship of political friendship (2.7). Whatever shortfall in physical quantity of goods and services might arise by this alternative approach (primarily in luxuries and for a minority) will be more than offset by a greater security of basic necessities produced and reproduced out of a country's own resources, and by a focus on healthy interpersonal relations, safer working conditions, and a sustainable local environment—in short, by greater communal security and a guaranteed well-being for all.

The second important reason for advocating a national localism (at the same time as the old Lockean production model is dethroned from power) is for straightforward ecological reasons, reasons that loom larger each day. Locke considered nature the "almost worthless condition" for the creation of value, at least 99 percent of which was due to human labor (3.2). Today such arrogance is being exposed as simple ignorance. The tremendous wealth, complexity, and resourcefulness of the natural world (if not abused)—its regenerative powers, the richness and diversity of its animal species and flora, its healing capacities (both mental and physical), and its spectacular beauty—have been revealed and emphasized over and over again in the scientific and environmental literature. Most of this beauty and richness, however, falls outside our mainstream economic reckonings—and outside the wise control of its national populations—at the same time as the world economy (measured a century ago in billions of dollars, but today in trillions) is rapidly outstripping its natural base.[49]

Let us here note a few statistics. Between 1960 and 2000, the world population doubled, from 3 billion to nearly 6 billion, and it is estimated the global economy increased more than sixfold.[50] North Americans, of course, are the largest consumers. If all people on earth were to live like Americans, the *2005 Millennium Assessment Report* estimates, the global economy would have to increase at least sevenfold. There is growing scientific consensus, however, that a fourfold quantitative growth factor is already impossible. For example, the human economy at present preempts one-fourth of the world's net primary product of photosynthesis (NPP); we cannot go beyond 100 percent. Our fossil fuel–based, automobile-centered, throwaway economy, moreover, is still *reducing* NPP. It thus appears that not even the present world population of 5.8 billion—much less the 10 billion expected by 2040—can hope to achieve North America's material standard of living without destroying the ecosphere and precipitating its own collapse.[51] Everywhere we see failures of the quantitative growth economy to respect the biophysical limits of its earthly host: in the form not merely of toxic waste, acid rain, and climate modification (global warming), but also nutrient loading (causing algal blooms), fisheries and coral reef collapse (expanding dead zones in the oceans), devastation of rainforests, precipitous loss of species, and destruction of ecosystem services resulting from wars and aggression. The rich natural world is being plundered and the explosion of "global trade" is only hastening the process.

Consider something as lowly as the banana, one of the cheapest of all fruits. Many of us love our morning banana with cereal, but must we really eat bananas all year long? And might not the experience of eating a banana actually be better tasting and far more memorable when the fruit is plucked ripe from a tropical tree or presented as a gift on a special occasion? The banana ("little finger" in Arabic) is perhaps the most popular fruit in the world. Originally from Southeast Asia, the 500 different types of banana are grown today mostly near the Equator on vast mono-crop plantations and on land that was originally tropical rainforest (highly evolved, complex, and diverse in both flora and fauna). Routinely sprayed with pesticides, fungicides, herbicides, nematocides, and other chemicals by the big three U.S. growers (Chiquita, Dole, and Del Monte), bananas are shipped across the world while still green in vast refrigeration ships and trucks—all of which economic activity takes a heavy toll on the natural world.

Further, in 1995 several thousand workers sued the big three fruit companies for medical and reproductive injuries suffered on the job; the suit was settled out of court for $41 million.[52] Despite all this human and environmental destruction, the U.S. companies complained only a few years later to the World Trade Organization about European "protectionism": the Europeans wished to purchase bananas from their former colonies (Jamaica, Surinam, Dominica, and so on) where working conditions were better, wages were higher, and far less chemicals were used. The WTO ruled in favor of the U.S. companies. Nowhere is the triumph of a detached "product" (here, the banana) and its profit maximization over all ethical reproductive concerns (regarding how, where, and by whom it is produced, etc.) clearer than in this decision—a decision that is clearly *wrong*. Not only will the economy of these small islands suffer, while forests, rivers, and workers will be further degraded on the huge plantations, but it is hard to tell who is truly being "enriched" now other than the corporations themselves. The deceptively "cheap" banana one eats each morning for breakfast emerges as exorbitantly "costly" in terms of human damage and "ecological footprint."[53]

Or consider another debate that bedeviled the WTO and became one cause of the 1999 Seattle riots. In the early 1990s, when the European Union tried to ban the import of all fur taken from animals caught in steel leg traps—on grounds of cruelty to animals—the major fur-producing countries (the United States, Canada, and Russia) lodged complaints before an international GATT panel. In the face of their accusations that the EU restrictions violated "free and fair trade" practices—that its attempt to regulate the *process* of fur production impinged on the internal national sovereignty of the fur-producing countries, whose fur *products* were as good as any other—the European Union was forced to relent. Here again, the notion of an abstracted "product"—no matter how cruelly produced or morally repugnant and no matter how many people wished the practice stopped anywhere in their region—triumphed in the global race to the bottom: to the lowest and meanest standards of production. Since when, we might ask, is there a "national sovereign" *right* of imposing one nation's products (and practices) on another?

Four hundred years of theoretical and practical reliance on the production model of activity as the ideal of laboring activity—while surely benefiting an elite minority—is today leaving mammoth suffering and destruction in its wake. In abstracting from its background conditions, its sustaining social institutions, and the munificence of the natural world, the creed of production and "growth" perpetuates a thoughtlessness and callousness toward its de facto surroundings, as well as an ignorance of its own human, animal, and environmental presuppositions. In drawing attention to its failures not only for our central question of furthering human community, but for a sustainable communion with other creatures on the planet and even with the earth itself, ethical reproductive labor and *praxis* emerges as by far the more appropriate model of future action.

Needed first is *a shift in vision*—particularly concerning our own motivations and laboring conditions, but now also with regard to the natural world; a shift from an arrogant production (with its underlying destructive consumption) to an ideal of respectful cooperation. We need to move away from the violent extraction and dirty burning of fossil fuels (or nuclear power with all its dangers and waste) back to an economy powered by smaller, diverse, widely dispersed, renewable sources, such as wind, solar, geothermal, hydropower, and certain bio-fuels. (In the last few hundred years we have in fact been moving *away* from a solar based economy—where agriculture mimicked the land and the cycles of the sun—to one heavily reliant on fertilizers, that is, fossil fuels.) Now we must switch from a society centered on the combustion engine and automobile to one with varied transportation systems widely employing light rail, hybrid (gas-electric) buses or other vehicles, and even bicycles. As one author notes, the goal now is to maximize mobility, not automobile ownership.[54] Similarly, the mass (quantitative) production of throwaway things must yield to a qualitative and comprehensive reuse/recycle economy; consumer products from cars to computers must be designed for complete recycling, phasing out single-use items once and for all. In short, for ecological reasons *too* we must move from a production to a *reproduction* model of activity.

By advocating an economic and ecological localism, I do not intend that the new state should avoid its international or global obligations in general (whether to the poor, to other states and human rights institutions, or to the global environment). On the contrary, I intend only that each people—or better yet, each ecological region—should strive to grow and reproduce its own basic necessities wherever possible: its own food, clothing, and housing. In chapter 5, we argued for greater government restrictions on the market or for a form of market socialism; now we see that the greater restrictions must apply to the land as well. Rather than madly crisscrossing the globe, peoples, containers, and goods will have to leave less of an impact on the fragile earth. Reversing the present tendency of things, however, reversing the destruction of our common life and common lands, oceans, and now even our atmosphere, will require collective awareness as well as much collective concerted action. Here is a worthy "enemy" that may indeed bring a commonality to our goals (if Schmidt turns out to be correct after all and an external enemy is needed for unity)—but the enemy, in the final analysis, is ourselves.

It is precisely for this reason, the need to solve the collective action or coordination problem, that the political state remains of such importance today. By the coordination problem, I refer to that situation where each of us may want a certain result, which depends on the cooperation of others, but each may be insufficiently motivated to cooperate unless he or she can be assured that the others will too (5.2). Just as in earlier centuries newly freed productive labor needed to find some solution to the coordination problem, isolated individual reproductive action must do so today. To combat the destruction of our communities and of our common environment, there needs to be an overarching organizing principle: a democratically responsive government required to ensure and coordinate positive action. As one thinker suggests, if the United States could mobilize its vast resources within a matter of months on entering World War II, we can surely "mobilize" to restructure our economy in the face of environmental collapse, growing world hunger, and a planet under stress.[55] If only people could see the danger and the need.

In this manner, what might be called the hesitant universalism discussed earlier may be paired with an economic and environmental regionalism advocated here. Leave to the international community those things that are genuinely of universal and global scope: help build or strengthen those institutions that protect and further human rights generally, that help combat world hunger, and so forth, but act hesitantly and with humility. This hesitant approach is also critically important when it comes to women's human rights. As MacKinnon has shown, there is much international critique of practices of torture today and of combating world terrorism, but when it comes time to protecting against the concrete battering, torture, and terrorization of women in their own homes in every country (as well as their systematic rape in war), suddenly the issue seems of less import to male legislators.[56] The evolving structure of international human (and women's) rights and institutions must not be modeled on the economically insecure and community-impoverished set of individual rights put forth in constitutions such as that of the United States (6.2).

At the same time, in order to combat global warming, species and habitat loss, and the starvation of millions, it remains critical for us all in the wealthier nations to rein in our own gluttonous practices and not to spread them worldwide. In this way, through an economic and environmental localism, the concrete and particular (the specific food we eat, the local rivers from which we drink and in which we swim, the plant and animal life that surrounds us) will be given their legitimate recognition. Moving between these two tendencies, the new state becomes part of a hesitant and differentiated approach toward the world beyond its borders, but one that hardly entails the "self-absorption," "disengagement," or "mutual indifference" that some antiglobalists advocate.

It is now time to sum up what is distinctive about our model of ethical reproduction and *praxis* over against the classical model. I have argued throughout that such labor and activity is hardly utopian: over half the human population have performed modifications of it throughout the centuries, not only in the home, but in neighborhoods, civil societies, in times of war, and even still today in the center of the wealthy nations. Nor is such labor mysterious; it seeks to help humans and their relationships flourish, in the best case those of a friendship between equals and as ends in themselves. If we look at the world through the lens of ethical reproduction—of our lives, our relations, and our planet—ethical reproduction labor and *praxis* may now be said necessarily to entail the following.

1. Taking a wider view of the whole. Rather than focusing on the narrow product produced (the designer jeans or juicy hamburger) one looks behind them, as it were, to the process that brought the thing into being. One becomes aware of the set of human and animal relations (hierarchical, exploitative, equal, etc.) that brought the object into existence, the reason it was produced, by whom it was produced, its proposed use, what need it supplies, and its true cost. Taking this wider relational view, we should note, is basically again to see the wisdom in knowing all four of the Aristotelian "causes" (*aitia*): formal, efficient, material, and final (2.4). It is to move from a blind short-term rationality of the present consumer society to a greater depth of reasonableness or what Herman Daly has called "a wisdom economy." The concern necessarily again includes the good of the whole.

2. Retaining a cyclical notion of time. This larger perspective entails not only a long-term view but possession of a cyclical view of time as well. In ethical reproductive labor, the focus is not characteristically on weeks, quarterly reports, or even years, but rather on life stages, a complete life, and even generations upon generations. At the same time, as *praxis,* the focus remains (to use a term from Hegel) firmly planted in "the rose of the present." Such activity celebrates the present and particular, but with an eye ever to what lies ahead and not forgetful of the distant past: the maturity of a child or grandchild, the continuance or rejection of tradition spanning centuries, the memories of crimes committed and indignations experienced years ago but still active in the here and now (and which must be laid to rest). It is little wonder that many peoples of old conceived time as primarily cyclical, for such a perception is far more appropriate to the ebb and flow of the natural world and the return of the seasons, and also to the birth and death of humans and their particular relationships. Life and the natural world rarely proceed in a straight line. Taking the wider and cyclical view thus contrasts with the linear directed profit motive as well as with the irrational up and down motions of consumer markets with their fickle tastes, and short-term goals.

3. Focusing on use value and the person. Similarly, the focus is again on those concrete values (including time) that satisfy particular human (animal, ecological) individual and social needs. Unlike the artificial and abstract needs created by a market society, tending toward the inexhaustible (needs for money, for ever more possessions, larger houses, and so on), concrete human needs have natural limits. There is only so much food or so many pairs of shoes that a healthy person can eat or wear. Unlike exchange value, that is, use value is limited and concrete; it has a distinct physical dimension and the need for which it was originally designed can be objectively satisfied. Here there is such a thing as *enough*. After all our labors, we arrive back at Aristotle's notion of *oikonomia* or "the household management of true wealth" (2.5). Rather than the obsession with *chrematistics* (the manipulation of money and exchange value) extending into the infinite (for the ancient Greeks, a sign of the irrational), use value is necessarily concrete and finite, with particular qualities of sight and sound: the smell of fresh coffee, the screech of a horned owl, the cathedral bells tolling. It is only in the concrete here and now, moreover, that we genuinely feel "at home."

4. Reestablishing praxis as the aim. Finally, unlike in market production where the goal is the product and the motives of the individual person are largely irrelevant (the motive can even be pure greed), in reproductive *praxis* the aim is constitutive of the action, and this action itself is worth doing for its own sake. Focusing on such activity returns the awareness and sensitivities toward individual persons, and not just the specific needs of others, but reflectively back on those of the self as well: new capacities are elicited and brought to flourish, and old ones put to bed. In the best case, as we have argued, the distinctive aim and need in reproductive *praxis* is to create, maintain, and further particular relations of *philia*, whether personal or civic. Deep friendliness becomes an educated habit, a disposition or general stance outward surmounting attitudes of fear or hostility, of planned exploitation or of simple indifference. The virtue of *philia* spills over in our attitudes toward strangers, even to the animal kingdom and the natural world. From within the ethical reproductive paradigm, that is, animals and the natural world are no longer there to be feared or used merely as a means (or even simply ignored). On the contrary, they become partners of the earthly voyage.

Here many will object: How can one possibly be a genuine friend of a tiger, say (a fierce predator that may eat you), or of an ecological niche filled with mosquitoes carrying malaria? And yet the metaphor of mixing one's labor with the aim of enhancing one's relationships with others—of noting and listening, of responding with practical good will, of doing things for them and observing their responses—is hardly here stretched beyond recognition. There are many people working desperately to prevent the extinction of the large carnivores (threatened primarily by loss of jungle habitat), and their reward is hardly the profit motive (or else they would work elsewhere); it is nothing more than to see these magnificent beasts continue to flourish in their native homes. Indeed, I would argue (although this is the proper subject of another book) that such an ethical reproductive shift in perspective—now focused on the animal and natural world—comes close to what is being advocated by many environmental thinkers today.

One such theorist, for instance, sums up his legal approach to the natural world as "the guardianship approach." In this approach, friends of a natural object (such as a river or mountain range) apply to the courts for creation of a stewardship protecting the object's interests, much like the legal guardians of those humans who cannot take care of themselves (3.3).[57] The corporate entity Friends of the Hudson, for example, aims to keep the Hudson River (and its riparian inhabitants) clear of pollution and destructive commercial development and to return the river to its more or less natural state. Another thinker asks: "Why do we love the land?" and concludes it is because the land has intrinsically lovable properties, much like a friend.[58] There is nothing surprising here, only a relation of *philia* to the natural world: a love by humans for a particular place, a rock, or a specific bird or animal species that happens to have crossed our paths. And it is clear that these loved objects (the animal or river) can "respond" to our efforts; they do so by "befriending" us, as the eagle chicks rescued from a fallen nest return again each spring, or as the river and mountain range retain and reproduce their beauty over the years.

8.5 A FINAL NOTE ON TERRORISM

If the promise of developing alternative models of civic behavior opens doors to changing conceptions of ourselves, of our international relations, and of our environmental priorities, this work would be remiss if it did not take into account perhaps the most powerful objection of all: that the ethical reproductive approach advocated here is not only naïve and unrealistic—due to its overly optimistic account of human motivation in general—but actually *dangerous* to a political community's national security. There are many people in the world, after all, who wish ill toward us (the industrialized nations). They do not want to be our friends, but on the contrary sincerely hate us; they actively resent our wealth while envying our lifestyles, and so on. How can we maintain good will in the face of another's malicious intent?

It is in full recognition of the destruction and hostility endemic to our modern world, and of the deep and violent tendencies in all of us, that it becomes so critical that our social and political institutions be intelligently designed: that they elicit the best in us without unleashing the worst. But a part of the problem of violence, hatred, and enemies surely derives from how we envision ourselves and the other to begin with (8.2). Nothing struck me as more disgraceful in the Bush administration's response to the attack on the World Trade Center on September 11, 2001, than its successive depictions of "the terrorists" (the enemy). Ignoring the fact that fifteen out of the nineteen hijackers of the four U.S. passenger planes were from Saudi Arabia—a corrupt, despotic religious kingdom, which nonetheless supplies the United States with much of its oil—the United States attacked the impoverished country of Afghanistan and its religious Taliban. Granted, the Taliban are a mean, fanatical group, who served as a hatching ground for al-Qaeda (and who ostensibly hid Osama bin Laden, the real culprit). But it was the United States *itself* that had supplied these religious fanatics with weapons only a decade or two earlier while praising them as "freedom fighters" against the Soviet Union.

If, as I have argued throughout, there is a duty of political friendship for both citizens and states, not simply allowing but actually *furthering* the production and sale of weapons whenever it appears instrumentally expedient can hardly be a way of fulfilling this duty. On the contrary, the proliferation of weapons becomes one of the most grievous violations. More than half the weapons sold anywhere in the world are sold by the United States.[59] It should hardly come as a great surprise that many of these weapons will, in the not too distant future, find themselves pointed in our direction.

Having apparently not had enough of war and destruction, and still far from securing Afghanistan against religious fanaticism, civil war, and rule by vast drug cartels, the administration next proceeds to attack neighboring Iraq and its blustering tyrant—a country and tyrant who had no connection with the September 11 terrorist attacks, or with their religious fervor, but who sits on top of further reserves of oil. Squandering the world's good will directed toward it after the September 11 terrorist attacks, the largely unilateral, unprovoked attack on Iraq by the United States will surely be viewed in the light of history not as the carefully reasoned actions and explanations of an intelligent, civilized country defending itself, but as the dangerous, erratic movements of a wounded and voracious dragon:

a giant Fafner that thrashes its tail and shakes the earth's floor in response to the mosquito-like pinpricks of a Siegfried. Worst of all, as a result of the human, cultural, and environmental destruction the U.S. bombs and forces have caused in the most recent "war on terrorism," the movements of the giant beast appear to have produced only one thing: greater worldwide fear, rage, and terror, and in particular an enhanced global distrust of and contempt for *itself*.

The alternative approach to security advocated here is, first, to acknowledge an insight from the Cold War: that the high-tech arms race and the reckless proliferation of weapons around the globe actually make everyone less secure; they are collectively *irrational*. So too, the present U.S. bias toward expensive and complex weapon systems overlooks many more probable threats. What are the true dangers facing the United States today? With two major oceans between us and most of the rest of the world, the true *military* danger is the possibility of a random nuclear attack; here the solution appears to be to maintain a nuclear arsenal sufficient only for deterrence (estimated at roughly three hundred bombs and far below present numbers) while simultaneously working to reduce and clean up nuclear arsenals elsewhere (as in the former Soviet Union). It seems to have been overlooked that, with all our high-tech weapons, we were attacked on September 11, 2001, with box cutters and our own passenger planes; a low-tech solution may just be what is now called for.

Second, as recent feminist work has stressed, military security is hardly synonymous with *genuine* security; indeed, it is not only a narrow but a "gendered" notion of "being secure."[60] For one, a military "solution" is rarely an actual political solution, as all the killing and bombing and destruction in the Middle East in the last decades reveal. Rather than resignation and acceptance, rage and hatred are the far more probable response to bombings. So too, risk of military attack is hardly the biggest risk facing us. Far more people in the world die of hunger and preventable disease than by direct military action. According to the World Health Organization (WHO), in 1999 there were some 588,000 human deaths due to war, while starvation and preventable diseases claimed close to 18 million.[61] Similarly, while nearly 3,000 people died in the crumbling of the World Trade Center towers, far more are killed each year due to drought, desertification, hurricanes, landslides, and tsunamis. It is now estimated that the heat wave that crossed Europe in 2003 caused close to 45,000 deaths.[62] Security in the broader sense—in the *genuine* sense—entails not simply reducing the risk of military attack, but also securing basic material well-being, a sustaining and healthful environment, and supportive and just civic relations for all. Each of these latter forms of genuine security, moreover, is a traditional goal of ethical reproductive labor and *praxis*.

Let us take as a final example the present state of the economy in the United States. As noted, the autonomy and self-directedness of a people are directly linked to its ability to sustain itself, at least with regard to basic necessities, but the United States is headed in the opposite direction (8.3). At the beginning of 2006, the U.S. federal budget deficit again exceeded $400 billion.[63] The dubious distinction of being the world's largest debtor nation entails that we continue to borrow heavily, while our assets are being rapidly sold off and we (the people) are increasingly less able to make decisions over our own economy. But the downward spiral continues; our heavy reliance on trade and imports, and particularly heavy dependence on oil from the Middle East, necessitates even greater military expenditure in order to protect those same oil fields, production and supply lines, the extensive international trade routes, and so on. At the same time the present war in Iraq alone costs U.S. taxpayers billions per year. It would make far more sense, and produce far greater genuine security for all, if instead of pumping money into our bloated military-industrial complex, we invested that sum in developing alternative and far more localized energy sources (such as small-scale solar plants), efficient transportation, and environmentally sound homes. In this way, small acts of sabotage (against oil fields, an extensive electric grid, large refineries, etc.) would not bring the whole country to a halt. As one prescient study in the late 1980s concluded: "In fact, if we spent as much to make buildings heat-tight as we spent in *one year* on the military forces meant to protect the Middle Eastern oil fields, we could eliminate the need to import oil from the Middle East."[64]

If genuine security is our concern, then active *reduction* of the size of the U.S. military, together with the scaling back of trade and reduction of dependence on foreign oil (as well as healing and transforming our relations with other nations) emerges as closer to the solution. This would not only allow resources to be shifted to where they are needed most (such as into a civilian or foreign service devoted to individual need satisfaction, environmental preservation, and local energy concerns [7.4]), but would also allow us, by folding back into ourselves and reestablishing our own economic independence, to begin to make our nation all the more secure in the genuine sense of the term.

Indeed, I believe the heavy toll on the environment of the triumvirate of economic growth, explosive trade, and our ever expanding military should be viewed as the *greatest threat* to our national security—taking *security* now in its true sense of health and well-being, a long life, and stable friendships for all. Not only are all three heavily dependent on oil (or other combustible resources) and thus among the majors contributors to rapid climate change and depletion of the world's resources, but, not surprisingly, each in its own way is constantly exceeding the limits required for sound health and environmental policy. Whether it is the spent uranium from U.S. weapons now scattered across southern Iraq and linked to soaring cancer rates in Iraqi children,[65] or the detonation of underwater sonic explosions that leads the U.S. Navy to exempt itself from the Mammalian Sea Act, or simply the "dumbing down" of all human and environmental laws in the name of free trade and a slightly cheaper banana, the present system actually *thrives* upon the destruction of its social and environmental conditions. And such destructive practices hardly end once we arrive inside U.S. borders, as witnessed by the impetus for opening up the Gulf Coast or the Alaskan wilderness to further oil exploration, falling water tables and the depletion of non-replenishable aquifers, or the accumulation of chemicals from agricultural (and golf-course) run-off. Which people, after all, can truly be secure if the earth's climate alters abruptly and violently, causing deadly hurricanes and tsunamis, heat-induced algae blooms, and the collapse of whole fisheries, while epidemiologists warn of new diseases transported around the globe, liable to cause pandemics more deadly than the influenza and AIDS epidemics of the twentieth century? Again, if a common enemy is really needed to end the interstate squabbles (and Schmidt is right), we have a common enemy in the rapid destruction of planet earth.

Finally, and perhaps most important, nations can collapse from within: from the weight of their own indifference, greed, and corruption as well as from the neglect of their citizens and neighbors. Such become "failed states," and they are the hatching ground of a new lawlessness and terror. We have argued that continuing to view the world through the Lockean production metaphor, including its various presuppositions and assumptions, leads to such indifference: to others, to the land, and to all its inhabitants (3.2). This model of labor and activity (always backed up by the older warrior model) looks away from the positive relations between persons as well as from our love and cherishing of the land. It leaves to others the responsibility of checking our rapacious activities, instead of disciplining ourselves. It is thus time to dethrone and displace this model, if not rid ourselves of it altogether, and shift to an ethical reproductive stance instead. In the end, the greatest crime of the present U.S. administration is its repeated violation of the political duty of friendship—not maintaining the conditions for the possibility of a civic friendship among its own citizens, and violating the duty of amity or a positive peace between states as well. It has squandered the good will of the world, engaged in war under false pretenses, and all in order to further its own crude and narrow interests.

Marxist, feminist, postmodern, cosmopolitan, and other calls for the growing insignificance of, or even end to, the modern nation-state are a bit premature. While clearly the modern state's absolute sovereignty has come to an end—it is no longer considered legitimate to make war in the name of plunder or self-interest, for instance, or to kill members of its own citizenry (as in the death penalty, which most civilized lands have abolished)—the whole of its role is by no means expendable. Indeed, the state's actions today are restricted by an evolving doctrine of universal human rights, and its legitimate unity (in the face of a growing multiculturalism worldwide) is ever less to be found in the "nation": in birth, blood, or ethnic identity. Nonetheless, while certain traditional functions are being given over, on the one hand, to global institutions (such as the United Nations or WHO) and, on the other, to local ecological and civic groups of civil society, there still remains much for the democratic, representative state to achieve before it takes its bow on the stage of history and transforms itself into something else. Among these central functions are to realize a reasonable democratic control over its own economy and working conditions, over its ecological territory, as well as over the creation and maintenance of a civic friendship, not only between its citizens, but also with its neighbors. And the new state in this way only realizes a promise vaguely expressed already in the Peace of Westphalia in 1648 (8.2): the duty of amity or of both a civic and an international friendship. International *amity*, perceiving other sovereign peoples as potential friends, takes a good deal of preparation and work back on the home territory. Still, it must become an explicit demand of the women's (and global justice) movement, and may just be the surest way out of a new round of religious and other massacres.

NOTES

PREFACE

1. See, for example, Elizabeth Anderson, "What is the Point of Equality?" *Ethics* 109 (1990): 287–337; Josh Cohen and Joel Rogers, *On Democracy* (New York: Penguin, 1983); David Copp, Jean Hampton, and John Roemer, eds., *The Idea of Democracy* (Cambridge: Cambridge University Press, 1993); Robert Dahl, *Democracy and Its Critics* (New Haven, Conn.: Yale University Press, 1989); Carol Gould, *Rethinking Democracy: Freedom, and Social Cooperation in Politics, Economy, and Society* (Cambridge: Cambridge University Press, 1988); and Creighton Peden and James Sterba, *Freedom, Equality, and Social Change* (New York: Edwin Mellen Press, 1989), to name but a few. There are, of course, some exceptions, most notably John Rawls's *A Theory of Justice* (Cambridge, Mass.: Harvard University Press, 1971), whose famous difference principle Rawls calls an "interpretation of fraternity." See my 5.2.
2. Ian Shapiro, *Democracy's Place* (Ithaca, N.Y.: Cornell University Press, 1996); Gould, *Rethinking Democracy.* For writings of various deliberative democrats, see, for example, Amy Gutmann and Dennis Thompson, *Democracy and Disagreement* (Cambridge, Mass.: Harvard University Press, 1996); Cass Sunstein, *The Partial Constitution* (Cambridge, Mass.: Harvard University Press, 1993); or James Bohman and William Rehg, *Deliberative Democracy* (Cambridge, Mass.: MIT Press, 1997).

1. INTRODUCTION

1. John Rawls, *Political Liberalism* (New York: Columbia University Press, 1993), xviii (hereafter cited as *PL*).
2. Michael Sandel, *Liberalism and the Limits of Justice* (Cambridge: Cambridge University Press, 1982), 175.
3. John Rawls, *A Theory of Justice* (Cambridge, Mass.: Harvard University Press, 1971), 105 (hereafter cited as *TJ*). I am not here deciding the issue of whether it is something "essential" to liberalism that leads to a neglect of issues of community,

I am only registering the fact that historically the tradition has tended to do so. See chapter 5.

4. Ronald Dworkin, "Liberal Community," *California Law Review* 77 (1989): 479–504.
5. See, for example, Will Kymlicka, *Liberalism, Community and Culture* (Oxford: Clarendon Press, 1989); Stephen Macedo, *Liberal Virtues: Citizenship, Virtue, and Community in Liberal Constitutionalism* (Oxford: Clarendon Press, 1990); William Galston, *Liberal Purposes: Goods, Virtues, and Diversity in the Liberal State* (Cambridge: Cambridge University Press, 1991); and Richard Dagger, *Civic Virtues: Rights, Citizenship, and Republican Liberalism* (Oxford: Oxford University Press, 1997).
6. The number of authors now working on "care" is far too large to list (see chapter 7). Pioneering works include Sara Ruddick, "Maternal Thinking," *Feminist Studies* 6 (1980): 342–67; Carol Gilligan, *In a Different Voice: Psychological Theory and Women's Development* (Cambridge, Mass.: Harvard University Press, 1982); Nel Nodding, *Caring: A Feminine Approach to Ethics and Moral Education* (Berkeley: University of California Press, 1986); and Joan C. Tronto, *Moral Boundaries: A Political Argument for an Ethic of Care* (New York: Routledge, 1993).
7. Thomas Hobbes, *Leviathan*, 2.17; John Locke, *The Second Treatise of Government*, in *Two Treatises of Government*, ed. Peter Laslett (Cambridge: Cambridge University Press, 1970), chaps. 7–9 (hereafter cited as *ST*, followed by paragraph number).
8. See, for example, David Hume, *Essays Moral, Political and Literary* (Indianapolis: Liberty Fund, 1987).
9. See *TJ*, chap. 8; John Rawls, "Social Unity and Primary Goods," in *Utilitarianism and Beyond*, ed. Amartya Sen and Bernard Williams (Cambridge: Cambridge University Press, 1982), 159–86; and my discussion in chapter 5.
10. Jürgen Habermas, "Appendix II: Citizenship and National Identity (1990)," in *Facts and Norms*, trans. William Rehg (Cambridge, Mass.: MIT Press, 1996), 491–515.
11. All references to Aristotle's works are to the revised Oxford translation, *The Complete Works of Aristotle*, ed. J. Barnes, 2 vols. (Princeton, N.J.: Princeton University Press, 1984), and will be noted by abbreviated title and line numbers of the Greek text: *De Anima* (*De An*), *Economics* (*Eco*), *Eudemian Ethics* (*EE*), *Generation of Animals* (*GA*), *History of Animals* (*HA*), *Metaphysics* (*Met*), *Nicomachean Ethics* (*NE*), *On Generation and Corruption* (*On Gen*), *Physics* (*Phy*), *Poetics* (*Poe*), *Politics* (*Pol*), and *Rhetoric* (*Rhet*).
12. G. W. F. Hegel, *The Philosophy of Right*, ed. T. M. Knox (Oxford: Clarendon Press, 1967), para. 158A.
13. Karl Marx's disdain for the notion of individual rights and of the state is legendary. See, for example, "On the Jewish Question," in *Collected Works of Marx and Engels*, vol. 3, *1843–1844* (New York: International Publishers, 1976), 146–75. More recently, the communitarian Alasdair MacIntyre writes that the belief in individual rights is

on a par with the belief in witches, in *After Virtue: A Study in Moral Theory* (Notre Dame, Ind.: University of Notre Dame Press, 1984), 67. A number of feminists in the tradition of Carol Gilligan also assume an exclusive either/or stance with regard to issues of care and community, on the one hand, and issues of individual rights and justice, on the other. See, for example, Elizabeth Fox-Genovese, *Feminism Without Illusions: A Critique of Individualism* (Chapel Hill: University of North Carolina Press, 1991).

14. Carl Schmidt, *The Concept of the Political* (Chicago: University of Chicago Press, 1996), 26. See also chapter 8.
15. Donald Schoen, "Generative Metaphor: A Perspective on Problem-Setting in Social Policy," in *Metaphor and Thought*, ed. Andrew Ortony (Cambridge: Cambridge University Press, 1979), 254–83.
16. Max Black, "More About Metaphor," in *Metaphor and Thought*, ed. Ortony, 31.
17. Nelson Goodman, *Ways of World-Making* (Indianapolis: Hackett, 1978), 104–5.
18. Richard Rorty, "Philosophy as Science, as Metaphor, and as Politics," in *Essays on Heidegger and Others: Philosophical Papers* (Cambridge: Cambridge University Press, 1991), 2:13.
19. Richard Schlatter, *Private Property: The History of an Idea* (New Brunswick, N.J.: Rutgers University Press, 1951), 156. Schlatter cites the year 1690, the traditional dating of the composition of *The Second Treatise*, although more recently Laslett has argued that the text was actually written a decade earlier, between 1679 and 1681, which makes it a radical call for revolution ("Introduction," in *ST*).
20. Richard Ashcraft, *Revolutionary Politics and Locke's Two Treatises of Government* (Princeton, N.J.: Princeton University Press, 1986), 250.
21. G. E. M. de Ste. Croix, *Class Struggle in the Ancient Greek World* (Ithaca, N.Y.: Cornell University Press, 1981), 133.
22. Hannah Arendt, *The Human Condition* (Chicago: University of Chicago Press, 1958), 96.
23. For a more extended discussion of this point, see Sibyl Schwarzenbach, "Towards a New Conception of Ownership" (Ph.D. diss., Harvard University, 1985), chap. 1.
24. Marylynn Salmon, *Women and the Law of Property in Early America* (Chapel Hill: University of North Carolina Press, 1986).
25. H. M. Honoré, "Ownership," in *Oxford Essays in Jurisprudence*, ed. A. G. Guest (Oxford: Clarendon Press, 1961), 107–47. That this form of ownership was hardly the dominant form of property in the medieval world is clear from the fact that in feudal society land was not alienable (there was no market for it). The feudal manor was largely self-subsistent, and land (like many of the goods that accompanied it) descended from father to eldest son via the institution of primogeniture.
26. In contrast to one point in Roman law where the paterfamilias possessed the legal right to maim or kill his wife, children, and slaves if he so chose. See Sir Henry Maine, *Ancient Law* (London: Holt, 1884). The great exception to this growing

awareness of the political freedom of all persons was, of course, the continued existence of slavery in the United States.

27. One must add to this list "being white" as well. See Rogers M. Smith, *Civic Ideals* (New Haven, Conn.: Yale University Press, 1997); and my 6.5.
28. Compare the discussion in Eva Kittay, *Metaphor: Its Cognitive Force and Linguistic Structure* (Oxford: Oxford University Press, 1987), 2.
29. It should be noted that the term *model* is here being used in its more ordinary sense, denoting an abstractive representation of some object or state of affairs, and not as used by logicians, for whom a model is the interpretation or embodiment of a formal calculus in which the relation of isomorphism holds between the structure of the formal system and that of its interpretation. In the more ordinary sense of the term, anything can be taken as a model of anything else—if we can sort out the relevant respects in which one entity is like another (e.g., a grouping of ping-pong balls can model the universe). For something to be a model in this more ordinary sense, it appears to suffice that the model as representation must be some form of abstraction, less rich in the range of relevant properties than its object or reference, and that it cannot thus be a model of itself or of something identical to it. One way of classifying models might be according to their degree of existential commitment, with those operating at the limits of our rational belief (such as many metaphors) commanding at the same time the greatest degree of belief. See Marx Wartofsky, "The Model Muddle," in *Models* (Boston: Reidel, 1979), 1–11.
30. *TJ*, 20, 46–53, 130–35. Nelson Goodman was the first to introduce the notion of reflective equilibrium, in *Fact, Fiction and Forecast* (Cambridge, Mass.: Harvard University Press, 1955), a method then applied to ethics and the political domain by Rawls.
31. Compare *PL*, lecture 1; and see my 6.3.
32. See, for example, Thomas Pogge, *Realizing Rawls* (Ithaca, N.Y.: Cornell University Press, 1989); John Rawls, *The Law of Peoples* (Cambridge, Mass.: Harvard University Press, 1999); and chapter 8.
33. For an early criticism of the idea that ethics can be justified by appeal to divine commands, see Plato's *Euthyphro*. See also Rawls's reference to Aristotle's *aporetic* method (*TJ*, 577).
34. This formulation occurs in "Justice as Fairness: Political Not Metaphysical," in *John Rawls: Collected Papers*, ed. Samuel Freeman (Cambridge, Mass.: Harvard University Press, 1999), 388–414.
35. John Rawls, "Kantian Constructivism in Moral Theory," 303–58, and "The Idea of an Overlapping Consensus," 421–49, both in *John Rawls*, ed. Freeman. In the latter, Rawls again takes up the debate with the rational intuitionist.
36. On this point, see Rawls's recognition of his indebtedness to Willard V. O. Quine and the German Idealist tradition (*TJ*, 577–79). See also my comparison of the

method of reflective equilibrium with Hegel's notion of dialectic, in Sibyl Schwarzenbach, "Rawls, Hegel and Communitarianism," *Political Theory* 19, no. 4 (1991): 539–71.

37. For a discussion of this point, see Salmon, *Women and the Law of Property in Early America.*
38. At least since Mary Wollstonecraft's *Vindication of the Rights of Women* (1792), women have depicted such theoretical (and not just practical) bias.
39. *TJ*, 303. For a more extensive discussion, see Sibyl Schwarzenbach, "Valuing Ideal Theory: Reflections on Virginia Held's Critique of Rawls," *Metaphilosophy* 21, nos. 1–2 (1990): 173–78.
40. For those who remain suspicious of such a transfer of concepts from personal to political domain, consider the economic notion of "efficiency." This term surely first referred to something like "Person X produced a pair of shoes for particular person Y in time Z," before it was elaborated, generalized, and eventually came to mean something like Pareto optimality. Many, if not all, of our economic and political concepts originally derived from concrete particular contexts and specific practices, which were then generalized and applied to larger institutional and public domains. The issue is thus not *whether* such an extension from private to public is generally possible, but whether or not it is a good extrapolation in a particular case.
41. Hegel, *Philosophy of Right*, paras. 267, 274.
42. See, for example, *TJ*, 87; Rawls, "Justice as Fairness"; Ronald Dworkin, *Law's Empire* (Cambridge, Mass.: Harvard University Press, 1986), chap. 1; and chapter 6.

2. THE FORGOTTEN CATEGORY OF ETHICAL REPRODUCTION

1. Feminist secondary literature on Aristotle remained highly negative for many years, focusing on Aristotle's hierarchical worldview, his subordination of classes of people, his defense of slavery, and his general misogyny. More recently, however, feminists have moved toward a more nuanced reading and are bringing into focus aspects important to feminism but previously ignored: for example, Aristotle's rejection of "abstract" universals, his elaborate account of the emotions, and his stress on "situated perception" in ethical reasoning. See, for example, Cynthia Freeland, ed., *Feminist Interpretations of Aristotle* (University Park: Pennsylvania State University Press, 1998).
2. In the *Nicomachean Ethics*, we should note, Aristotle reveals a "moral bipartite" psychology, which is to be distinguished from (and not easily reconciled with) the "biological tripartite" psychology typical of the *De Anima*. In the latter work, Aristotle speaks exclusively of the three souls (vegetable, animal, and human) and their

respective faculties. See W. W. Fortenbaugh, *Aristotle on Emotion* (London: Duckworth, 1975), chap. 2.

3. F. E. Peter, *Greek Philosophical Terms: A Historical Lexicon* (New York: New York University Press, 1967), 166.
4. At numerous points Aristotle claims that heavenly bodies and the Unmoved Mover are "alive," but he does not wish to attribute to either nutrition and growth (*De An* 2.413a22). I here leave this difficulty aside, however, for nutrition and growth are surely necessary conditions for the activity of thinking in us embodied *mortals*.
5. G. W. F. Hegel, *Lectures in the History of Philosophy*, trans. E. S. Haldane and Frances H. Simpson, 3 vols. (London, 1894, 1955), 2:184.
6. For a review of the relevant literature, see Martha Nussbaum, "Aristotle on Human Nature and the Foundations of Ethics," in *World, Mind, and Ethics: Essays on the Ethical Philosophy of Bernard Williams*, ed. J. E. J. Altham and Ross Harrison (Cambridge: Cambridge University Press, 1995), 86–131. The following discussion is indebted to Nussbaum's account.
7. Numerous passages in Aristotle support the intellectualist interpretation, the most famous being *NE* 10.6–8, where Aristotle appears to defend the superiority of a life of contemplative wisdom over a life of practice.
8. See, for instance, *Summa Contra Gentiles* 3.25.37, where Aquinas writes that happiness consists "solely" in the contemplation of God and "this operation alone is proper to man."
9. Hegel, *Lectures on the History of Philosophy*, 2:180–84. More recent intellectualist interpretations include, among many others, John M. Cooper, *Reason and Human Good in Aristotle* (Indianapolis: Hackett, 1986); Richard Kraut, *Aristotle on the Human Good* (Princeton, N.J.: Princeton University Press, 1989); and Thomas Nagel, "Aristotle on *Eudaimonia*," in *Essays on Aristotle's Ethics*, ed. Amelie Rorty (Berkeley: University of California Press, 1980), 7–15.
10. Nagel, "Aristotle on *Eudaimonia*," 12.
11. Karl Marx gives such a reading of Aristotle in his *1844 Manuscripts*. See chapter 4. See also, among others, John Cooper, "Contemplation and Happiness," *Synthèse* 72 (1987): 187–216; T. H. Irwin, "The Metaphysical and Psychological Basis of Aristotle's Ethics," in *Essays on Aristotle's Ethics*, ed. Rorty, 35–54; Nussbaum, "Aristotle on Human Nature"; and Nancy Sherman, *The Fabric of Character* (Oxford: Oxford University Press, 1989), 94–106.
12. Passages supporting the inclusive interpretation include those where Aristotle claims that the activities of perceiving and hearing are intrinsically valuable (e.g., *Met* 980a24), where he insists human nature is fundamentally composite (e.g., *NE* 1119a9, 1177b27), as well as those where he identifies the human self with *nous*, but where it is clearly practical *nous* that he has in mind (*NE* 9.4.1166a22–23, 9.8.1168b29–1169a2; *Pol* 1333a25–27).

13. For my reply to the objection that Aristotle would consider the biological processes of the *threptikon* as those that truly fall under the activities of the first soul (and to which ethical distinctions do not apply), while the activities just cited already fall under *aesthetikon* (the sensitive and perceptive soul), see Sibyl Schwarzenbach, "A Political Reading of the Reproductive Soul in Aristotle," *History of Philosophy Quarterly* 9, no. 3 (1992): 260–63.

14. One might here object that "permanent coupling" is not only *not* a feature of the human (consider our present-day divorce rates), but it is also a feature of many animal species (Canada geese, for instance, mate for life). Still, I think Aristotle's point holds that humans distinguish themselves in this respect. Canada geese do not tell their grandchildren about themselves or about their great-grandparents. It is important to remember that when Aristotle speaks of "permanent coupling," he does not merely have male–female relationships in mind. Friends are said to "live together" if they spend their days together and share in discussion and thought (even if they sleep in different houses), and most mothers are permanently "coupled" with their children even if the children have moved away, provided that the mothers continue to spend time with them and share thoughts. See my 2.6.

15. Numerous commentators have found the distinction so confusing and unhelpful as to suggest discarding it altogether. See, for example, J. L. Ackrill, "Aristotle on Action," in *Essays on Aristotle's Ethics*, ed. Rorty, 93, where the author stresses how many actions at least appear to be "productions" and various productions "actions," as well as further unclarities surrounding Aristotle's notion of *praxis*. My own view is that the distinction Aristotle is getting at here is not clearly made until Kant, with the latter's distinction between the *Bewegungsgrund* of an action (the motive, reason, or subjective principle of the action) and the *Zweck* (the goal or purpose of the action). Although Aristotle did not, of course, use Kant's language, he clearly did think (like Kant) that the motive or "moving ground" is what determines the virtuousness of an action: not so much what is brought about, or how it is brought about, but *why*.

16. At this point, in order to avoid confusion, we must distinguish between reproductive *action*, or *praxis*, which is done for its own sake (e.g., the mother happily bathing and playing with her children), and reproductive *labor*, which is done largely for reasons beyond merely reproducing the relationship itself (the case of domestic or child-care provider where the primary aim is usually a wage). This distinction between labor and *praxis* will grow in importance as we proceed. Unlike in reproductive labor, in reproductive action or *praxis* the motive (*Bewegungsgrund*) and goal (*Zweck*) mesh fully. Many concrete activities, of course, will be a greater or lesser mixture of these two categories. See my 5.4.

17. All persons, that is, normally take part in ethical reproduction (except perhaps the hermit). It might be added that I here move away from a recent tendency in femi-

nist literature, which proffers the mother–child relationship as the paradigm of a new politics, while at the same time I find myself at odds with those feminists who wish to reject all appeal to care as a mere outgrowth of subservience under patriarchy. On my reading, care and reproductive activity are an important (if neglected) *universal* human attribute. See my 7.2 and note 40.

18. The term *person* derives from the Latin *persona*, which originally referred to the masks worn by actors in Greek tragedy: by extension, the term comes to include anyone who plays a "publicly recognized role." See *PL*, 18. In contrast to that of human being, the concept of a person is notoriously absent in Aristotle's discussion in the *De Anima*, although it does seem to be implied throughout much of his ethical writings. See *Aristotle's De Anima, Books II and III*, trans. D. W. Hamlyn (Oxford: Clarendon Press, 1968), 95. In these writings, Aristotle distinguishes between those more fully realized humans (who hold important public roles) and private non-persons, such as natural slaves (who lack the deliberative intellect) and women (whose reasoning faculty remains "defective") (*Pol* 1260a12–15).
19. That an entity is a human being does not automatically imply that it is a person. On the one hand, it is not obvious that fetuses, the mentally deranged, or the irreversibly senile have all the rights accorded persons (it may be more correct to call them moral patients rather than agents). On the other hand, corporations have been considered legal persons in our tradition for over a century now, and as some environmentalists today argue, perhaps some animals and even some natural objects should be granted the legal status of personhood. See, for example, C. D. Stone, "Should Trees Have Standing? Toward Legal Rights for Natural Objects," in *Environmental Ethics: Concepts, Policy, Theory*, ed. Joseph DesJardins (Mountain View, Calif.: Mayfield, 1999), 203–14.
20. A brief note on Aristotle's notion of nature (*phusis*) is in order here, if only so as not to conflate it with our modern conception of "nature" (and the latter's biological, genetic, unconscious, or automatic implications). In the *Physics*, Aristotle defines *phusis* as "the principle [*arche*] and cause [*aitios*] of motion and rest for the things in which it is immediately present" (*Phys* 2.192b). *Phusis* is primarily *form* (*eidos*, *Phys* 2.193a), and it works toward an end (*telos*, *Phys* 2.194a). So, too, living "ensouled" things have within them both the principle of movement and the initiator of movement; they thus differ from inanimate objects (*Phys* 8.255b–256a). In things that come about by art, by contrast, the "source of its production" lies "outside" the object itself, while in natural processes it lies "within" (*Phys* 2.192b).
21. See, for example, David Keyt, "Three Fundamental Theorems in Aristotle's *Politics*," *Phronesis* 32, no. 1 (1987): 54–79. That the state is essentially a human construct or "artifice," and hence a product of *techne*, is, of course, the position generally taken by modern political thinkers. See Hobbes's introduction to *Leviathan*, "For by Art is created that great Leviathan called a Commonwealth, or State." See also my 3.2.

22. See David Depew's response to Keyt in "Does Aristotle's Political Philosophy Rest on a Contradiction?" (manuscript, Society for Ancient Greek Philosophy, 1990).

23. "Care" is given as *epimeleia*'s primary meaning in Henry George Liddell and Robert Scott, comps., *A Greek–English Lexicon* (Oxford: Clarendon Press, 1968), but the many occurrences of the term in Aristotle's ethical writings are almost *never* translated as such. See note 40.

24. Richard Sorabji, "Aristotle on the Role of Intellect in Virtue," in *Essays on Aristotle's Ethics*, ed. Rorty, 206.

25. John Cooper, "Aristotle on Friendship," in *Essays on Aristotle's Ethics*, ed. Rorty, 323.

26. This point is carefully argued in ibid., 308–15.

27. Aristotle is not above attributing relations of *philia* between certain animals and humans, however, and even between animals of different species; he notes, for instance, Herodotus' mention of "the friendship between the sandpiper and the crocodile" as an instance of advantage friendship (*EE* 1236b).

28. For instance, C. S. Lewis claims that "friendship must be *about* something" (other than the parties themselves) and this is why "we picture lovers face to face but friends side by side" (*The Four Loves* [London: Fontana, 1963], 63). More recently, Thomas Spragens still agrees, in *Civic Liberalism: Reflections on Our Democratic Ideals* (Lanham, Md.: Rowman & Littlefield, 1999), 182.

29. I am not suggesting that fathers cannot play a similar (or even ethically identical) role in regard to their children; traditionally, of course, they have done so far more rarely.

30. For a classic account of Aristotle's sexism, see Susan Moller Okin, *Women in Western Political Thought* (Princeton, N.J.: Princeton University Press, 1979), chap. 2.

31. The belief that friendship must presuppose de facto equality (in class, age, race, and so forth) has become a near axiomatic truth of the modern Western (male) tradition. Thus Descartes writes, "Affection is felt for an object considered lesser than ourselves, friendship for an object equal to ourselves, and devotion for an object that is greater than ourselves" (*Passions of the Soul*, book 2, no. 79, CSM 1:356). I thank Amy Schmitter for this quote.

32. See, for example, A. W. Price, *Love and Friendship in Plato and Aristotle* (Oxford: Oxford University Press, 1989), chap. 5. Price suggests that for Aristotle the most genuine friendship takes place not only between two men of the same class, age, and intellectual abilities, but between identical twins! See also notes 28 and 31.

33. Jacques Derrida calls the paradigm "homogeneous" friendship, and he discusses numerous authors in Western thought who hold it, in *Politics of Friendship*, trans. George Collins (London: Verso, 1997), esp. chap. 10.

34. Examples abound in the literature: Lewis's claim that friends are never depicted "face to face" (*Four Loves*), Descartes's claim that friendship entails strict equality (*Passions of the Soul*), and Price's view that the ideal of friendship is the relationship between near identical individuals (*Love and Friendship*). For an even more recent

example, see Christopher Wellman, "Friends, Compatriots, and Special Political Obligations," *Political Theory* 29, no. 2 (2001): 217–36, where the author still analyzes only the friendship between two autonomous and similar males.

35. At moments, Aristotle admits women must be included as part of the state taken in the wide sense (e.g., *Pol* 1260b22). For the distinction between a "wider" and a "narrower" conception of the state, see my 1.4 and 5.1.
36. Carl Schmidt, *The Concept of the Political*, trans. Tracy Strong (Chicago: University of Chicago Press, 1996), 35. See also my discussion in 8.2.
37. John Cooper, "Political Animals and Civic Friendship," in *Aristotle's "Politik,"* ed. Gunther Patzig (Friedrichshafen: Vandenhoeck and Ruprecht, 1990), 220–41. Once again, I am indebted to Cooper's interpretation.
38. Evelin G. Lindner, *Making Enemies: Humiliation and International Conflict* (Westport, Conn.: Greenwood Press, 2006), xii.
39. In contrast to Hannah Arendt's claim that one finds "time and again in political philosophy since Democritus and Plato that politics is a *techne*" (*The Human Condition* [Chicago: University of Chicago Press, 1958], 185).
40. For a discussion of "common care," see my 7.4. As noted in note 23, English translations of the Greek *epimeleia* (for at least the past two centuries) never seem to translate the Greek term *epimeleias* as "care," which remains the primary meaning. Thus, at the end of the *Nicomachean Ethics* where Aristotle urges the legislator to secure by way of good laws "right nurture and care [*trophes kai epimeleias tuxein orthos*]" to all citizens, Harold H. Joachim (1951) translates the phrase "right nurture and attention," as does W. D. Ross (1908). H. Rackham (1967) translates it "right nurture and discipline," and J. E. C. Welldon (1892) "right nurture and control." (A recent exception is in *The Politics of Aristotle*, trans. Peter L. Phillips Simpson [Chapel Hill: University of North Carolina Press, 1997], but this was only due to my insistence.) Nor is *epimeleia* to be found in any of the indexes of modern translations of Aristotle's two *Ethics* or of his *Politics*, despite the term's many occurrences. (By contrast, the entry "masturbation" occurs in *all* of the indexes of the *Politics* that I could find, although it is mentioned only once by Aristotle. Apparently, even our scholarly indexes are gendered.) The important reference at *NE* 10.9 is not even cited in the *Bonitz Index Aristotelicas* (Berlin: Akademie Verlag, 1955), which is supposed to contain every occurrence of central terms. Clearly, the political use of the term *care* causes the vast majority of *modern* political thinkers discomfort—in explicit contrast to Aristotle himself, for whom the concept presents no such difficulties.

3. THE LIBERAL PRODUCTION MODEL

1. G. W. F. Hegel, *The Philosophy of Right*, ed. T. M. Knox (Oxford: Clarendon Press, 1967), para. 158A.
2. At first sight, a number of modern thinkers may appear to be exceptions to this gen-

eral rule, Rousseau being the most obvious, along with Karl Marx and even John Rawls. None of these thinkers, however, uses the language of friendship per se. See chapters 4 and 5.

3. Jane Mansbridge's highly influential study, *Beyond Adversary Democracy* (Chicago: University of Chicago Press, 1983), for example, conflates the phenomenon of political friendship with the requirement that all citizens can "gather under one roof" of face-to-face-assembly (10).
4. Christopher Wellman, "Friends, Compatriots, and Special Political Obligations," *Political Theory* 29, no. 2 (2001): 231.
5. Oleg Kharkhordin raised the latter concern at the European Consortium of Political Research (ECPR), Joint Sessions, Granada, Spain, April 19, 2005.
6. *PL*, xxii–xxvi.
7. Again, see Karl Marx, "On the Jewish Question," in *Collected Works of Marx and Engels*, vol. 3, *1843–1844* (New York: International Publishers, 1976), 146–75; and Alasdair MacIntyre's account in *After Virtue: A Study in Moral Theory* (Notre Dame, Ind.: University of Notre Dame Press, 1984), 67.
8. The classic work is Carol Gilligan, *In a Different Voice: Psychological Theory and Women's Development* (Cambridge, Mass.: Harvard University Press, 1982), but see also Elizabeth Fox-Genovese, *Feminism Without Illusions: A Critique of Individualism* (Chapel Hill: University of North Carolina Press, 1991).
9. The dominance of a production model of activity in the modern era has been noted by various thinkers (each drawing their own conclusions): for example, Hannah Arendt, *The Human Condition* (Chicago: University of Chicago Press, 1958), chap. 3; Jürgen Habermas, "Excursus on the Obsolescence of the Production Paradigm," in *The Philosophical Discourse of Modernity* (Cambridge, Mass.: MIT Press, 1987); and Ian Shapiro, "Resources, Capacities, and Ownership: The Workmanship Ideal and Distributive Justice," *Political Theory* 19, no. 1 (1991): 47–72.
10. Immanuel Kant, *The Metaphysics of Morals*, para. 46. By contrast, Aristotle explicitly excluded farmers and artisans from full citizenship on the grounds that they lack the leisure time (*schole*) required for *praxis* and the development of practical wisdom (*phronesis*) (*Pol* 2).
11. Adam Smith, *An Inquiry into the Nature and Causes of the Wealth of Nations*, ed. R. H. Campbell and A. S. Skinner, 2 vols. (Indianapolis: Liberty Press, 1981), 1: book 2, 330–31.
12. Thomas Hobbes, *Leviathan*, book 2, chap. 17; *ST*, chap. 9, para. 123; Kant, *Metaphysics of Morals*, para. 43.
13. This point is stressed in both John Cooper, "Political Animals and Civic Friendship," in *Aristotle's "Politik,"* ed. Gunther Patzig (Friedrichshafen: Vandenhoeck and Ruprecht, 1990), 220–41; and Michael Pakaluk, "Political Friendship, Ancient and Modern," in *The Changing Face of Friendship*, ed. Leroy S. Rouner, Boston University Studies in Philosophy and Religion 15 (Notre Dame, Ind.: University of Notre Dame Press, 1994), 197–214.

14. See, for example, William Galston, *Liberal Purposes* (Cambridge: Cambridge University Press, 1991), chaps. 1–5; Stephen Macedo, *Liberal Virtue: Citizenship, Virtue, and Community in Liberal Constitutionalism* (Oxford: Clarendon Press, 1990); Richard Dagger, *Civic Virtues: Rights, Citizenship and Republican Liberalism* (Oxford: Oxford University Press, 1997), among others.
15. Wellman, "Friends, Compatriots," 225.
16. Marx, "On the Jewish Question"; MacIntyre, *After Virtue*; Gilligan, *In a Different Voice*; Fox-Genovese, *Feminism Without Illusions*.
17. In "Political Friendship," Pakaluk argues that by securing fundamental human rights within its borders, a state may be interpreted as expressing a regard or love for humanity generally. My own conception of civic friendship is not based solely on a citizen's "common humanity," however; the civic spirit must also acknowledge (and feel an affinity for) a people's particular traditions and political principles. See chapter 8.
18. Kant, *Metaphysics of Morals*, para. 399.
19. I here follow Thomas Pogge, *World Poverty and Human Rights* (Cambridge: Polity Press, 2002), 43–48. The institutional view of individual rights is associated with Hegel as well as F. H. Bradley.
20. See the discussion in Neal Wood, *John Locke and Agrarian Capitalism* (Berkeley: University of California Press, 1984).
21. James Tully, *A Discourse on Property: John Locke and His Adversaries* (Cambridge: Cambridge University Press, 1980), 118.
22. John Locke, *Essays on the Law of Nature*, ed. W. von Leyden (Oxford: Clarendon Press, 1970), 185.
23. Sibyl Schwarzenbach, "Locke's Two Conceptions of Property," *Social Theory and Practice* 14, no. 2 (1988): 141–71.
24. The following discussion is indebted to Paul F. Camenisch, "Gift and Gratitude in Ethics," *Journal of Religious Ethics* 9 (1981): 1–34.
25. That gift-exchange requires interpretation and creativity (and in this respect also stands opposed to contract) may be seen by the fact that too precise repayment of a gift (giving you, say, the same gift as you gave me last year) reduces not only the flexibility and openness of the gift relation, but also its durability. My relation to you begins to resemble the tit-for-tat contract in which indebtedness can be paid off and the relation brought to a neat conclusion.
26. A. Gurevich, "Representations of Property During the High Middle Ages," *Economy and Society* 6 (1977): 1–30.
27. H. M. Honoré claims, for instance, that the institution of ownership is still today best studied against the background of "the basic model of a single human being owning a single material object" ("Ownership," in *Oxford Essays in Jurisprudence*, ed. A. G. Guest [Oxford: Clarendon Press, 1961], 114).

28. Schwarzenbach, "Locke's Two Conceptions," 148–56.
29. Locke's ideas that the earth is almost "worthless" and that human labor puts ninety-nine one-hundredths of the value on things are assumptions, of course, which modern environmental science has shown to be not only false, but arrogant and ideological. See my 8.4.
30. For instance, Robert Nozick, *State, Anarchy, and Utopia* (New York: Basic Books, 1974), 174. Jeremy Waldron also falls into this naturalistic trap in *The Right to Private Property* (Oxford: Oxford University Press, 1988), 184, 140, 186.
31. C. B. Macpherson, *The Political Theory of Possessive Individualism: From Hobbes to Locke* (London: Oxford University Press, 1962), 203.
32. For a discussion of Mill's view, see Sibyl Schwarzenbach, "Towards a New Conception of Ownership" (Ph.D. diss., Harvard University, 1985), esp. 145–51.
33. Richard Ashcraft, *Revolutionary Politics and Locke's Two Treatises of Government* (Princeton, N.J.: Princeton University Press, 1986), 278.
34. John Rawls (lectures presented at Harvard University, spring 1984) has formulated Locke's criterion thus: a form of institution is legitimate if and only if it is such that it has been (or could have been) contracted into as part of a rightly conducted process of historical change (where everyone acts rationally and in accord with the fundamental law of nature) beginning from a state of nature as a state of equal political right.
35. To this extent Locke's theory contains an early version of Rawls's difference principle. Compare my 5.2.
36. See, for example, David Wiggens, "Deliberation and Practical Reason," *Proceedings of the Aristotelian Society* 76 (1975–1976): 29–51; or Martha Nussbaum, *The Fragility of Goodness* (Cambridge: Cambridge University Press, 1986), chap. 10.
37. James Madison, "The Federalist No. 49," in Alexander Hamilton, James Madison, and John Jay, *The Federalist Papers*, ed. Clinton Rossiter (New York: Penguin, 1961), 317.
38. The differences between friendship and care—and the reasons why I prefer considering this capacity one of *philia*, or friendship, and not merely "care"—are discussed in chapter 7.
39. This claim should be refined somewhat. In times of war the modern state has traditionally required *women*, for example, to be nurses and to care for wounded soldiers. What it cannot seem to do is to require *men* (other than those who are already doctors or nurses by profession) to do the same, and certainly not in the normal course of events.
40. David Hume, *A Treatise of Human Nature*, book 2, part 3, sec. 3, para. 4.
41. See Rawls's famous account, as well as criticism, of utilitarian doctrine in *TJ*, secs. 27–30.

42. Paul Gombürg, "Friendship in the Context of a Consequentialist Life," *Ethics* 102 (1992): 552–54.
43. Neera Badhwar Kapur, "Why It Is Wrong to Be Always Guided by the Best: Consequentialism and Friendship," in *Ethics* 101 (1991): 483–504.
44. Barbara Herman, *The Practice of Moral Judgment* (Cambridge, Mass.: Harvard University Press, 1993), 94–112. Although Herman defends a Kantian view, I view Kant as attempting to reawaken the notion of *praxis*, or moral action, for its own sake (see my 2.4) within the horizon of the modern period.

4. THE SOCIALIST TURN

1. Ernst Block was among the first to propose this thesis, in *Das Prinzip Hoffnung*, 2 vols. (Frankfurt am Main: Suhrkamp, 1970), 2:479, 546. See also Alfred Schmidt, *The Concept of Nature in Marx* (London: New Left Books 1971); David J. Depew, "Aristotle's *De Anima* and Marx's Theory of Man," *New School Graduate Faculty Philosophy Journal* 8 (1982): 133–87; and George E. McCarthy, ed., *Marx and Aristotle: Nineteenth-Century German Social Theory and Classical Antiquity* (New York: Rowman & Littlefield, 1992).
2. G. E. M de Ste. Croix, *Class Struggle in the Ancient World* (Ithaca, N.Y.: Cornell University Press, 1981), 5–6.
3. For Marx's translation, see Karl Marx and Friedrich Engels, *Historische-Kritische Gesamtausgabe*, vol. 1 (Berlin: Dietz-Verlag, 1927). Generally, in citing Marx's works in the text, I use the following abbreviations: *MECW* for *Collected Works of Marx and Engels*, 50 vols. (New York: International Publishers, 1975–2004); *EP* for *The Economic and Philosophical Manuscripts of 1844*, in *MECW*, vol. 3, *1843–1844*; *GI* for *The German Ideology*, in *MECW*, vol. 5, *1845–1847*; *Gr* for *Grundrisse: Foundations of the Critique of Political Economy*, trans. M. Nicolaus (New York: Random House, 1973); *C* 1 for *Capital*, vol. 1, trans. B. Fowkes (Harmondsworth: Penguin, 1976); *C* 2 and *C* 3 for *Capital*, vols. 2 and 3 (New York: International Publishers, 1967); and *TSV* for *Theories of Surplus Value* (vol. 4 of *Capital*), 3 vols. (Moscow: Progress Publishers, 1969).
4. Depew, "Aristotle's *De Anima* and Marx's Theory of Man."
5. Ibid., 159; George L. Kline, "The Myth of Marx's Materialism," *Annals of Scholarship* 3, no. 2 (1984).
6. The concept "species-being" is usually associated with Feuerbach, but according to Feuerbach himself, the idea derives from Kant's *Idea for a Universal History from a Cosmopolitan Point of View*. See Marx Wartofsky, *Feuerbach* (Cambridge: Cambridge University Press, 1977). In this essay, Kant argues that all man's "natural capacities" can be realized only in the society between men and ultimately only in the history of the race taken as a whole. See my 4.3.

7. Sibyl Schwarzenbach, "Towards a New Conception of Ownership" (Ph.D. diss., Harvard University, 1985), chap. 3. See also Depew, "Aristotle's *De Anima* and Marx's Theory of Man."
8. Richard Miller, "Marx and Aristotle: A Kind of Consequentialism," *Canadian Journal of Philosophy* 7 (1981): 326.
9. Not only in the *Gr*, 87, 705, but still in *Capital*, one finds the distinction between a narrower (economic) sense of appropriation and a wider, cultural one. Marx writes, for example, "But 'capitalist' appropriation and 'personal' appropriation, whether of science or material wealth, are totally different things. Dr. Ure himself deplores the gross ignorance of mechanical science which exists among his beloved machinery-exploiting manufacturers, and Liebling can tell us about the astounding ignorance of chemistry displayed by English Chemical manufacturers" (*C* 1:58).
10. Schwarzenbach, "Towards a New Conception of Ownership," chap. 4.
11. G. W. F. Hegel, *Phenomenology of Spirit*, trans. A. V. Miller (Oxford: Oxford University Press, 1979), 115, and *Philosophy of Right*, no. 54.
12. For the lowly status accorded nearly all forms of labor by the ancients, see Hannah Arendt, *The Human Condition* (Chicago: University of Chicago Press, 1958), chap. 3.
13. The standard reading interprets Marx's notion of "production" in a narrowly economic or technological sense. See, for example, G. A. Cohen, *Karl Marx's Theory of History* (Princeton, N.J.: Princeton University Press, 1978); or Jürgen Habermas, *Knowledge and Human Interests*, trans. Jeremy J. Shapiro (Boston: Beacon Press, 1971), chap. 3.
14. See, for example, the debate surrounding "the capability approach" pioneered by Amartya Sen, "Capabilities and Well Being," in *The Quality of Life*, ed. Martha C. Nussbaum and Amartya Sen (Oxford: Clarendon Press, 1994), 30–53. See also Martha Nussbaum, "Non-Relative Virtues: An Aristotelian Approach," in *Quality of Life*, ed. Nussbaum and Sen, 242–69.
15. See, for example, Miller, "Marx and Aristotle."
16. An unregenerate defender of Marx will claim that it was not part of his agenda to provide such an account; Marx's was a "scientific" analysis of the exploitative relations of capitalism and not a normative recipe for the future. My own view is that such a defense excuses what should be criticized. Marx says many things about the "future communist society," "immanent in the present," and so on, and to omit a discussion of the subjective conditions for its possibility emerges as a weak point indeed. See my 4.8.
17. See, for instance, Karl Marx, *Origins of the Family, Private Property, and the State* (New York: International Publishers, 1972), 71, and *GI*, 41–42.
18. Susan Himmelweit, "Reproduction and the Materialist Conception of History: A Feminist Critique," in *The Cambridge Companion to Marx*, ed. Terrell Carver (Cambridge: Cambridge University Press, 1991), 196–221.

19. I am particularly indebted to Ronald de Sousa, *The Rationality of Emotion* (Cambridge, Mass.: MIT Press, 1987) (hereafter cited as *Rat*), but see also Nancy Sherman, *The Fabric of Character* (Oxford: Oxford University, 1989); W. W. Fortenbaugh, *Aristotle on Emotion* (London: Duckworth, 1975); Martha Nussbaum, *Love's Knowledge* (New York: Oxford University Press, 1990); and Henry Richardson, *Practical Reasoning About Final Ends* (Cambridge: Cambridge University Press, 1997).
20. Richardson, *Practical Reasoning*, 178.
21. For instance, Nel Noddings defines care as "essentially nonrational in that it requires a constitutive engrossment and displacement of motivation" (*Caring: A Feminine Approach to Ethics and Moral Education* [Berkeley: University of California Press, 1986], 25). See also chapter 7.
22. Gerhard Wahrig, ed., *Wahrig Deutsches Wörterbuch* (Berlin: Bertelsmann Lexikon Verlag, 1975), s.v. *Pflicht*.
23. Sibyl Schwarzenbach, "On Civic Friendship," *Ethics* 107 (1996): 119–20.
24. See my discussion and response to Wellman (and Michael Stocker) in 3.1, and my critique of various feminists who tend to hold this view, in chapter 7.
25. Allen Wood, *Kant's Ethical Thought* (Cambridge: Cambridge University Press, 1999), 26.
26. Immanuel Kant, *Groundwork of the Metaphysics of Morals*, trans. H. J. Paton (New York: Harper & Row, 1964), 97n. Paton mistranslates *Liebespflichten* as "duties of kindness."
27. The following discussion is indebted to Joan Tronto, *Moral Boundaries: A Political Argument for an Ethic of Care* (New York: Routledge, 1993), chap. 4.
28. Ibid., 106.
29. The first stages are more "abstract" and often duties of the powerful; men *take care of* their families and doctors *care about* their patients, while nurses or aides do the actual care work. See ibid., 114.
30. David Hume, *A Treatise of Human Nature*, book 2, part 3, sec. 3, para. 4.
31. Annette Baier, *A Progress of Sentiments: Reflections on Hume's Treatise* (Cambridge, Mass.: Harvard University Press, 1991), chap. 12.
32. For convincing evidence that Marx's materialism is primarily a methodological principle of social investigation and not an ontological doctrine, see, among others, Karl Korsch, *Marxism and Philosophy*, trans. Fred Halliday (Boston: Monthly Review Press, 1970); Marx Wartofsky, "Lectures at Boston University" (1979); and Alfred Schmidt, *The Concept of Nature in Marx*, trans. Ben Fowkes (London: NLB, 1971), and *History and Structure: An Essay in Hegelian, Marxist, and Structuralist Theories of History*, trans. Jeffrey Herf (Cambridge, Mass.: MIT Press, 1983). These writers have shown that while it is one thing to accuse Hegel of "ontologizing grammar," it stretches things too far to accuse Marx of the same.

33. It is the fundamental weakness of Cohen's "technological interpretation," in my view, that he reduces Marx's notion of "productive forces" to instruments, raw materials, and labor-power, excluding all relations between individuals (*Karl Marx's Theory of History*, 28). Cohen thereby fails to account for all those passages where Marx explicitly claims that a "certain mode of co-operation" can itself be a "productive force" (e.g., *GI*, 43).
34. Schmidt, *History and Structure*, 38.
35. Immanuel Kant, *Critique of Pure Reason*, trans. N. Smith (New York: St. Martin's Press, 1965), Bxvi (hereafter cited as *CPR*, followed by the line number of the B edition).
36. Dieter Henrich, "Lectures at Harvard" (1984), and *Between Kant and Hegel: Lectures on German Idealism* (Cambridge, Mass.: Harvard University Press, 2003).
37. Schwarzenbach, "Towards a New Conception of Ownership," 122–30.
38. Earlier we saw how Locke's conception of private property as primarily the "fruit" of individual labor already presupposes the institution of private property that it is meant to justify (see my 1.2 and 3.2). Marx's practical project, parallel to Kant's in the theoretical realm, may be described as an analysis of the "conditions for the possibility" of different types of social practice and resulting ownership. See ibid., chap. 4.
39. Stanley Cavell, "Genteel Responses to Kant," *Raritan* 3 (1983): 49.
40. Joachim Ritter, ed., *Historische Wörterbuch der Philosophie*, vol. 1 (Basel: Schwabe Verlag, 1971), s. v. *Bedingung*.
41. Supporting Marx's point, Steve Marglin argues that capitalism's productivity was due primarily to three factors: the enlargement of the labor force (including women, children, paupers, slaves); the intensification of labor (tight supervision in large work places, forced labor in poor houses, longer workdays); and political measures taken against noncapitalist types of production ("What Do Bosses Do?: Part I," *Review of Radical Political Economics* 6 [1974]: 60–112).
42. Jürgen Habermas, *Towards a Rational Society*, trans. Jeremy J. Shapiro (Boston: Beacon Press, 1970), 118.
43. See, for example, Josh Cohen and Joel Rogers, *On Democracy* (New York: Penguin Books, 1983); Robert Dahl, *A Preface to Economic Democracy* (Berkeley: University of California Press, 1985); and Carol Gould, *Rethinking Democracy* (Cambridge: Cambridge University Press, 1988).
44. See, for example, Paul Q. Hirst, *On Law and Ideology* (New York: Macmillan, 1979), 130.
45. Hirst himself concludes Marxists must give up the persistent dogma that law is merely "super-structural" and instead demand positive legal enactment, especially in the realm of corporate law (ibid., 143). His particular proposal is to call for legislative action restricting shareholder rights in respect to governance of a company—and hence the stock market as a source of control—in turn encouraging worker management.

5. THE POSSIBILITY OF A MODERN CIVIC FRIENDSHIP

1. John Rawls, *Justice as Fairness: A Restatement* (Cambridge, Mass.: Harvard University Press, 2001), 48–49.
2. I here use Rawls's later formulation of the social primary goods in "Kantian Constructivism in Moral Theory," in *John Rawls: Collected Papers*, ed. Samuel Freeman (Cambridge, Mass.: Harvard Univ–ersity Press, 1999), 313. See also Rawls, "Social Unity and Primary Goods," in *John Rawls*, ed. Freeman, 359–87 (hereafter cited as SU).
3. Sibyl Schwarzenbach, "Rawls and Ownership: The Forgotten Category of Reproductive Labor," *Canadian Journal of Philosophy*, supp. 13 (1987): 142–50.
4. A. Esheté, "Contractarianism and the Scope of Justice," *Ethics* 85 (1974): 38–49; G. A. Cohen, *If You're an Equalitarian, How Come You're So Rich?* (Cambridge, Mass.: Harvard University Press, 2000), chap. 8.
5. John Rawls, "Fairness to Goodness," in *John Rawls*, ed. Freeman, 271.
6. See, for example, Robert Nozick, *Anarchy, State, and Utopia* (New York: Basic Books, 1974), chap. 4.
7. For similarities between the thought of Rawls and Hegel, see Sibyl Schwarzenbach, "Rawls, Hegel and Communitarianism," *Political Theory* 19 (1991): 539–71.
8. Indeed, one way of characterizing the turn from the "early" to the "later" Rawls is by noting an increasing concern with the moral purposeful self, together with a change in Rawls's account of the primary goods. See SU.
9. Rawls's Aristotelian principle states that (other things being equal) humans enjoy the exercise of their distinctive capacities, and this enjoyment increases the more the capacity is realized or the greater the complexity (*TJ*, 426).
10. For a fuller discussion of this distinction, see James E. Meade, *Efficiency, Equality and the Ownership of Property* (London: George Allen and Unwin, 1964); A. DiQuattro, "The Market and Liberal Values," *Political Theory* 8 (1980): 183–202; or Herman E. Daly and John B. Cobb, Jr., *For the Common Good* (Boston: Beacon Press, 1994), 58–61.
11. Hegel was among the first to make this point. In both *Phenomenology of Mind* and *Philosophy of Right*, Hegel argues that the relation of any subject to a given physical object already presupposes—or is mediated by—a particular pattern of relations between subjects themselves. See Sibyl Schwarzenbach, "Towards a New Conception of Ownership" (Ph.D. diss., Harvard University, 1985), chap. 3.
12. This appears to be a significant discovery of twentieth-century anthropology. See, for example, Rayna R. Reiter, ed., *Toward an Anthropology of Women* (New York: Monthly Review Press, 1975). A second "fact of difference" is the differential role the genders play in war. See Joshua S. Goldstein, *War and Gender: How Gender Shapes the War System and Vice Versa* (Cambridge: Cambridge University Press, 2001), 21; and my 7.7.

13. See, for example, Martha Fineman, *The Neutered Mother, the Sexual Family, and Other Twentieth Century Tragedies* (New York: Routledge, 1995); or Eva Feder Kittay, *Love's Labor: Essays on Women, Equality, and Dependency* (New York: Routledge, 1999).
14. It may seem strained to speak of tending to the "good" of a mineral, but one may well "befriend" the soil (against dangerous chemicals), a beautiful rock (against destruction), or a river and its inhabitant (from pollution). See my 8.4.
15. For the notion of "communicative action," see Jürgen Habermas's early "Labor and Interaction," in *Theory and Praxis* (Boston: Beacon Press, 1973), 142–69, and *Knowledge and Human Interest* (Boston: Beacon Press, 1971), chap. 3, where he distinguishes between *technical labor or instrumental action* and *praxis, interactive or communicative action*—a distinction that remains fundamental throughout his later works. We must note, however, that the form of labor we are elaborating undercuts the very dichotomy Habermas established. Ethical reproductive labor does so because it is labor (a production of use value) and essentially communicative, *both at once*. Even Habermas, it turns out, continues to view laboring activity on the production model.
16. Other respects in which a mother's caring for her own children differs from the professions (such as doctor, nurse, and so forth) have been explored in recent feminist literature. The professional, for instance, is typically viewed as needing specialized training, the work entails a significant "intellectual" component, the service is important to the community, and the nature of the work tends to be "interventionist" (versus continuous and sustaining). See Kittay, *Love's Labor*, 38.
17. Martha Nussbaum and Amartya Sen, eds., *The Quality of Life* (Oxford: Clarendon Press, 1994).
18. See, for example, Nancy Folbre, *The Invisible Heart: Economics and Family Values* (New York: New Press, 2001); Martha Fineman and Terence Dougherty, eds., *Feminism Confronts Homo Economicus: Gender, Law, and Society* (Ithaca, N.Y.: Cornell University Press, 2005); and Joan Williams, *Unbending Gender: Why Family and Work Conflict and What to Do About It* (Oxford: Oxford University Press, 2000). None of these works, however, questions the institution of private ownership in the major means of production per se.
19. H. M. Honoré, "Ownership," in *Oxford Essays in Jurisprudence*, ed. A. G. Guest (Oxford: Clarendon Press, 1961), 114.
20. Lewis Hyde, *The Gift* (New York: Vintage Books, 1983), chap. 6.
21. See M. Mauss's classic, *The Gift: Forms and Functions of Exchange in Archaic Societies* (New York: Newton Library, 1967); and Sandra Harding, "The Curious Coincidence of Feminine and African Moralities: Challenges for Feminist Theory," in *Women and Moral Theory*, ed. Eva Feder Kittay and Diana T. Meyers (Totowa, N.J.: Rowman & Littlefield, 1987), 296–315.
22. Hilda Hein, "Woman and Morality," *Ms. Magazine*, 1979.

23. Some have argued that given woman's sexual and biological reproductive functions (penetration, pregnancy, parturition, lactation, and so forth), the suppression of the boundaries between body and world has been far more easily experienced in her case. This is not to claim that woman's biology "determines" her personality, just that historically it may have facilitated it. See Nancy Chodorow's arguments against the cruder interpretation in *The Reproduction of Mothering* (Berkeley: University of California Press, 1978). On the contrary, the relative "ease of sliding from self to other" is characteristic of male personality in many other cultures and historical periods. See, for example, A. Gurevich's discussion of the medieval personality in "Representations of Property During the High Middle Ages," *Economy and Society* 6 (1977): 1–30.
24. Meade, *Efficiency, Equality and the Ownership of Property*; DiQuattro, "Market and Liberal Values"; Daly and Cobb, *For the Common Good*; Gar Alperovitz, *America Beyond Capitalism* (New York: Wiley, 2005); Robert Dahl, *A Preface to Economic Democracy* (Berkeley: University of California Press, 1985); Michael Howard, *Self-Management and the Crisis of Socialism* (Lanham, Md.: Rowman & Littlefield, 2000); Carol Gould, *Rethinking Democracy: Freedom, and Social Cooperation in Politics, Economy, and Society* (Cambridge: Cambridge University Press, 1988), to name but a few.
25. Seyla Benhabib, "The Generalized and the Concrete Other," in *Feminism as Critique*, ed. Seyla Benhabib and Drucilla Cornell (Minneapolis: University of Minnesota Press, 1987), 77–95.
26. See, for example, Williams, *Unbending Gender*; and Fineman, *Neutered Mother*.
27. Chodorow, *Reproduction of Mothering*; Dorothy Dinnerstein, *The Mermaid and the Minotaur: Sexual Arrangements and Human Malaise* (New York: Harper & Row, 1977); my 7.3. For an account of the backlash against the women's movement, see Susan Faludi, *Backlash: The Undeclared War Against American Women* (New York: Doubleday, 1991).
28. J. S. Mill already argued many of these points in *The Principles of Political Economy* (Toronto: University of Toronto Press, 1968), book 2, as do Meade, *Efficiency, Equality and the Ownership of Property*; DiQuattro, "Market and Liberal Values"; Daly and Cobb, *For the Common Good*; Alperovitz, *America Beyond Capitalism*; Dahl, *Preface to Economic Democracy*; Howard, *Self-Management*; and Gould, *Rethinking Democracy*. For an overview, see Bertell Olman, ed., *Market Socialism: The Debate Among Socialists* (New York: Routledge, 1998).
29. Gar Alperovitz, "The New Ownership Society," *The Nation*, June 27, 2005, 31, and *America Beyond Capitalism*.
30. Indeed, as Alperovitz shows, present inequalities are even greater when it comes to the ownership of wealth (in contrast to income); in 2003 the richest 1 percent of American households were estimated to own half of all outstanding stock, financial securities, trust equity, and business equity (*America Beyond Capitalism*, 5).

31. For the objection that my proposal violates certain "liberties" of others, and response, see 7.7.
32. Mill, *Principles of Political Economy*, 204.
33. Alperovitz, "New Ownership Society," 30.
34. Nozick, *Anarchy, State, and Utopia*, chap. 7; Michael Sandel also points to a version of this difficulty in *Liberalism and the Limits of Justice* (Cambridge: Cambridge University Press, 1982), chap. 4.

6. WOMEN, DEMOCRACY, AND THE U.S. CONSTITUTION

1. See, for instance, *TJ*, sec. 42.
2. See "PR [Proportional Representation] for Women," Accurate Democracy, http://accuratedemocracy.com/d_dataw.htm; and Anne Phillips, "The Representation of Women," in *The Democracy Sourcebook*, ed. Robert Dahl, Ian Shapiro, and Jose Antonio Cheibub (Cambridge, Mass.: MIT Press, 2003), 354–61.
3. See, for example, Robert Dahl, *How Democratic Is the American Constitution?* (New Haven, Conn.: Yale University Press, 2001); or Daniel Lazare, *The Frozen Republic: How the Constitution Is Paralyzing Democracy* (New York: Harcourt, Brace, 1996).
4. See, for example, Andrea Dworkin, "Against the Male Flood: Censorship, Pornography, and Equality," in *Feminist Jurisprudence*, ed. Patricia Smith (Oxford: Oxford University Press, 1993), 449–66; or Catharine MacKinnon, *Toward a New Theory of the State* (Cambridge, Mass.: Harvard University Press, 1989).
5. See, for example, Sylvia Law, "Rethinking Sex and the Constitution," *University of Pennsylvania Law Review* 132 (1984): 987–1013.
6. For some exceptions to this general rule, see Robin West, *Progressive Constitutionalism: Restructuring the Fourteenth Amendment* (Durham, N.C.: Duke University Press, 1994); and Suzanna Sherry, "The Founders' Unwritten Constitution," *University of Chicago Law Review* 54, no. 4 (1987): 1127–77.
7. See, for example, Smith, ed., *Feminist Jurisprudence*; Virginia Held, *Feminist Morality* (Chicago: University of Chicago Press, 1993); Carole Pateman, *The Sexual Contract* (Stanford, Calif.: Stanford University Press, 1988); Nancy Hirschmann, "Toward a Feminist Theory of Freedom," *Political Theory* 24, no. 1 (1996): 46–67; and, in constitutional theory, West, *Progressive Constitutionalism*; or Tracy E. Higgins, "Democracy and Feminism," *Harvard Law Review* 110, no. 8 (1997): 1657–1703.
8. Shulamith Firestone, *The Dialectic of Sex* (New York: Morrow, 1970); Catharine MacKinnon, *Feminism Unmodified* (Cambridge, Mass.: Harvard University Press, 1988); Andrea Dworkin, *Intercourse* (London: Secker and Warburg, 1987); Robin West, *Caring for Justice* (New York: New York University Press, 1997) (hereafter cited as *CJ*).

9. See, for instance, Sandra Harding's studies on African society in "The Curious Coincidence of Feminine and African Moralities: Challenges for Feminist Theory," in *Women and Moral Theory*, ed. Eva Feder Kittay and Diana T. Meyers (Totowa, N.J.: Rowman & Littlefield, 1987), 296–315; and A. Gurevich, "Representations of Property During the High Middle Ages," *Economy and Society* 6 (1977): 1–30, where the author discusses the medieval personality.
10. Nancy Chodorow, *The Reproduction of Mothering* (Berkeley: University of California Press, 1978); Sara Ruddick, *Maternal Thinking* (Boston: Beacon Press, 1989).
11. Even in West's more recent *Caring for Justice*, she nowhere attempts an explicit definition of the word *care*.
12. Higgins, "Democracy and Feminism," 1694.
13. Ibid., 1693.
14. Chodorow, *Reproduction of Mothering*; Ruddick, *Maternal Thinking*; Joan Tronto, *Moral Boundaries: A Political Argument for an Ethic of Care* (New York: Routledge, 1993), where the author stresses that care work is typically relegated in our society, not just to women but to the lower classes generally and to people of color (e.g., our grounds caretakers, medics, nurses, and so forth).
15. David Richards, *Foundations of American Constitutionalism* (Oxford: Oxford University Press, 1989), chap. 1.
16. An example of this approach is John Hart Ely, *Democracy and Distrust: A Theory of Judicial Review* (Cambridge, Mass.: Harvard University Press, 1980). See also Richards, *Foundations of American Constitutionalism*, 12.
17. See, for example, Ronald Dworkin, *Taking Rights Seriously* (Cambridge, Mass.: Harvard University Press, 1979), chap. 5, and *Law's Empire* (Cambridge, Mass.: Harvard University Press, 1986); Richards, *Foundations of American Constitutionalism*, chap. 2; and Cass Sunstein, *The Partial Constitution* (Cambridge, Mass.: Harvard University Press, 1993), chap. 4.
18. *TJ*, 20, 46–53, 130–35. See also Dworkin, *Taking Rights Seriously*, chap. 5.
19. *PL*, lecture 1.
20. Sunstein, *Partial Constitution*, 93.
21. Dworkin, *Taking Rights Seriously*, chap. 5.
22. Richards, *Foundations of American Constitutionalism*, 14.
23. Again, see Eleanor Flexner, *Century of Struggle* (Cambridge, Mass.: Belknap Press, 1959), 62–65; and Marylynn Salmon, *Women and the Law of Property* (Chapel Hill: University of North Carolina Press, 1986).
24. Bruce Ackerman, *We the People: Foundations* (Cambridge, Mass.: Harvard University Press, 1991), 81–103.
25. The Articles of Confederation aimed to create a "firm league of friendship" between the separate state republics for purposes of "defense, the security of their Liberties, and their mutual and general welfare" (Article III).

26. The 1787 Constitution left the matter of defining who was to be a citizen to the individual states. Accordingly, as one study notes, "when restrictions on voting rights, naturalization and immigration are taken into account, it turns out that [not just at the Founding, but] for over 80 percent of U.S. history, American laws declared most people in the world legally ineligible to become full U.S. citizens solely because of their race, original nationality or gender" (Rogers M. Smith, *Civic Ideals* [New Haven, Conn.: Yale University Press, 1997], 15).
27. For the notion of a "republic of reasons," see Sunstein, *Partial Constitution*, chap. 1.
28. James Madison, "The Federalist No. 10," in *The Federalist Papers: Hamilton, Madison, Jay*, ed. Clinton Rossiter (New York: Penguin, 1961) (hereafter cited as Fed, followed by paper number).
29. Brutus 18 (October 1787), 270; Cato, Letter 5, 320–21; Federal Farmer 8 (October 1787), 264; and DeWitt, "Essay 1," 190, all in *The Anti-Federalist Papers, and the Constitutional Convention Debates*, ed. Ralph Ketcham (New York: Penguin, 1986).
30. Although statistics vary, all agree that U.S. executive compensation rose sharply throughout the 1980s, the 1990s, and into the new millennium (peaking around 2003). According to one in-depth study, in 1980 the ratio of average executive compensation to average production worker compensation was 40 to 1. By 2003, the ratio was 400 to 1, an increase by a factor of 10 over the course of two decades. See Laraine S. Rothenberg and Todd S. McCafferty "'Say-on-Pay': Linking Executive Pay to Performance," *New York Law Journal*, September 24, 2008, http://www.law.com/jsp/ihc/PubArticleIHC.jsp?id=1202424735938. See also Gar Alperovitz, *America Beyond Capitalism* (New York: Wiley, 2005), 5; David Cay Johnston, "More Get Rich and Pay Less in Taxes," *New York Times*, February 7, 2002; and U.S. Bureau of Labor Statistics, http://www.bls.gov/.
31. Kate Jennings, "The Hypocrisy of Wall Street Culture," *New York Times*, July 14, 2002.
32. Douglas J. Amy, *Real Choices, New Voices: The Case for Proportional Elections in the United States* (New York: Columbia University Press, 1993), 5.
33. J. D. Salant, "Corrections Census Reaches Record High," *Times Union*, August 26, 2002. In June 2007, there were a record 1,528,041 sentenced prisoners in the United States under state or federal jurisdiction (roughly five times the number in 1980) and over 4 million people on parole (more than four times the number in 1980). See U.S. Bureau of Justice Statistics, http://www.ojp.usdoj.gov/bjs/glance/corrtyp.htm.
34. Linda Gordon, ed., *Women, the State, and Welfare* (Madison: University of Wisconsin Press, 1990); Patricia Smith, "The Silent Constitution: Affirmative Obligation and the Feminization of Poverty," 108–24, and Judith Resnik, "Federalism(s), Feminism, Families, and the Constitution," 127–52, both in *Women and the United States Constitution: History, Interpretation, and Practice*, ed. Sibyl A. Schwarzenbach and Patricia Smith (New York: Columbia University Press, 2003).

35. J. Kahn and T. Weiner, "World Leaders Rethinking Strategy on Aid to Poor," *New York Times,* March 18, 2002. See also Thomas Pogge, "Priorities of Global Justice" in *Global Justice,* ed. Thomas Pogge (Oxford: Blackwell, 2003), 9, where the author cites statistics from the United States Agency for International Development (USAID).
36. Eric Foner, "The Strange Career of the Reconstruction Amendments," *Yale Law Journal* 108 (1999): 2003.
37. Quoted in ibid., 2004–5.
38. Ibid.; Adjoa Aiyetero, "The Unkept Promise of the Thirteenth Amendment: A Call for Reparations," in *Women and the United States Constitution,* ed. Schwarzenbach and Smith, 70–89.
39. Abraham Lincoln, "The Dred Scott Speech," June 26, 1857, in *The Writings of Abraham Lincoln,* ed. A. B. Lapsley (New York: Lamb, 1906), 2:299.
40. Quoted in Kenneth Stampp, *The Era of Reconstruction, 1865–1877* (New York: Knopf, 1965), 122.
41. See, for example, Catriona Mackenzie and Natalie Stoljar, eds., *Relational Autonomy: Feminist Perspectives on Autonomy, Agency, and the Social Self* (Oxford: Oxford University Press, 2000).
42. W. E. B. DuBois, *Black Reconstruction,* quoted in Smith, *Civic Ideals,* 287.
43. Contrary to traditional accounts that minimize the number of native inhabitants in the Americas before the arrival of the Europeans (the Smithsonian Institution puts the number at 2 million), scholarship in recent decades has revealed the native population as closer to 100 million, while two centuries later the number had decreased by 90 percent. See Ward Churchill, *A Little Matter of Genocide* (San Francisco: City Lights Books, 1997), 289.
44. See, among others, Arend Lijphart, *Patterns of Democracy* (New Haven, Conn.: Yale University Press, 1999); Josh Cohen and Joel Rogers, *On Democracy* (New York: Penguin, 1983); Anne Phillips, *Engendering Democracy* (Cambridge: Polity Press, 1991); Amy, *Real Choices, New Voices*; Lani Guinier, *The Tyranny of the Majority: Fundamental Fairness in Representative Democracy* (New York: Free Press, 1994); J. L. Hyland, *Democratic Theory* (Manchester: University of Manchester Press, 1995); and Dahl, *How Democratic?* chap. 5.
45. All the top-ranking democracies in terms of the self-representation of women have systems of proportional representation. In various Nordic countries (led by Norway, Sweden, and Finland), the percentage of legislative seats won by women hovers around 36 to 43 percent, compared with only 13 percent in the United States after more than eighty-five years. Even Switzerland—where women received the vote only in 1971—by now has at least 21 percent of its legislative seats occupied by women. Many attribute such discrepancies to the institution of proportional representation, in which it is far easier for outsiders (minorities) to gain at least some representative seats in contrast to winning in the single-member, winner-take-all

system. See Amy, *Real Choices, Real Voices*, chap. 6; and "PR [Proportional Representation] for Women."

46. Regarding the criticism that proportional representation necessarily leads to myriad splinter parties (the case of Israel is usually invoked), the fear seems misplaced. If this becomes a danger, the solution is simply to raise the percentage of the vote required to establish a new party (say from 2 or 3 percent of the electorate to 4 percent or higher.)

47. Of course, not only Aristotle saw friendship as central to democracy, but so do many "premodern" equalitarian peoples; notions of friendship (including ancestral spirits, healers and sorcerers, lineages and clans, competitive feasting, etc.) play a central political role, incorporating responsive, face-to-face assembly; the right to speak out; commitment to the community; flexible and undogmatic decision making, and so on. The Iroquois come to mind (as noted by Engels), but so do many African and South Pacific nations. See Glenn Peterson, "The Small-Republic Argument in Modern Micronesia," *Philosophical Forum* 21, no. 4 (1990): 393–411; or Kwame Gyeke, *Tradition and Modernity: Philosophical Reflections on the African Experience* (New York: Oxford University Press, 1997).

48. This we earlier called the third fundamental moral power of personality, or *philia* (Kant's *Menschenliebe*), which is a necessary *subjective* condition for the possibility of responding to moral notions in the first place. See my 3.5.

49. Some classic examples are Milton Friedman, *Capitalism and Freedom* (Chicago: University of Chicago Press, 1962); Robert Nozick, *Anarchy, State and Utopia* (New York: Basic Books, 1974); and David Gauthier, *Morals by Agreement* (Oxford: Oxford University Press, 1986).

50. See, for instance, C. F. MacPherson, *Democratic Theory: Essays in Retrieval* (Oxford: Oxford University Press, 1973); Charles Taylor, "What's Wrong with Negative Liberty," in *The Idea of Liberty*, ed. Alan Ryan (Oxford University Press, 1979), 175–93; and Carol Gould, *Rethinking Democracy: Freedom, and Social Cooperation in Politics, Economy, and Society* (Cambridge: Cambridge University Press, 1988).

7. THE STATE OF FEMINIST THEORY

1. Regarding calls for a public conception of care, see, for example, Joan Tronto, *Moral Boundaries: A Political Argument for an Ethic of Care* (New York: Routledge, 1993); Diemut Bubeck, *Care, Gender and Justice* (Oxford: Clarendon Press, 1995); Eva Feder Kittay, *Love's Labor: Essays on Women, Equality, and Dependency* (New York: Routledge, 1999) (hereafter cited as *LL*); and Julie Anne White, *Democracy, Justice, and the Welfare State* (University Park: Pennsylvania State University Press, 2000). Similarly, Martha Nussbaum argues for a political form of "compassion" in *Frontiers of Justice* (Cambridge, Mass.: Harvard University Press, 2006), and Barbara Koziak

argues for a political theory of the emotions in general, in *Retrieving Political Emotion* (University Park: Pennsylvania State University Press, 2000).

2. Frances Fox Piven, "Ideology and the State," in *Women, the State, and Welfare,* ed. Linda Gordon (Madison: University of Wisconsin Press, 1990), 251–52.
3. See, for example, Heidi Hartmann, "The Unhappy Marriage of Marxism and Feminism," in *Women and Revolution,* ed. Lydia Sargent (Boston: South End Press, 1981), 1–41, as well as other essays in this volume; and Paddy Quick, "The Class Nature of Women's Oppression," *Review of Radical Political Economics* 9, no. 3 (1971): 42–53.
4. Ann Ferguson and Nancy Folbre, "The Unhappy Marriage of Patriarchy and Capitalism," in *Women and Revolution,* ed. Sargent, 317. Recently, Folbre moved away from this model, in *The Invisible Heart: Economics and Family Values* (New York: New Press, 2001). See also my 7.3.
5. Ferguson and Folbre, "Unhappy Marriage of Patriarchy and Capitalism," 318.
6. Catharine MacKinnon, "Feminism, Marxism, Method, and the State," *Signs* (1982): 68. See also MacKinnon, *Toward a Feminist Theory of the State* (Cambridge, Mass.: Harvard University Press, 1989), 3.
7. MacKinnon, "Feminism, Marxism," 68.
8. Susan Okin, *Justice, Gender, and the Family* (New York: Basic Books, 1989), chap. 8.
9. Nancy Frazer, *Justice Interruptus* (New York: Routledge, 1997), 66.
10. See, for example, bell hooks, *Feminist Theory: From Margin to Center* (Boston: South End Press, 1984); Lisa Lowe, *Immigrant Acts* (Durham, N.C.: Duke University Press, 1996); Maria Lugones and Elisabeth Spellman, "Have We Got a Theory for You!" *Women's International Forum* 6 (1986): 573–81; Chandra Mohanty, *Feminism Without Borders* (Durham, N.C.: Duke University Press, 2003); Paula Moya, *Learning from Experience* (Ithaca, N.Y.: Cornell University Press, 1998); and Uma Narayan, *Dislocating Cultures* (New York: Routledge, 1997). There are some clear exceptions to this rule, notably Maria Mies, *Patriarchy and Accumulation on a World Scale: Women in the International Division of Labor* (London: Zed Books, 1986); and Maria Mies and Vandana Shiva, *Ecofeminism* (London: Zed Books, 1993).
11. See, for example, Elizabeth Anderson, "Is Women's Labor a Commodity?" *Philosophy and Public Affairs* 19, no. 1 (1990): 71–92; Debra Satz, "Markets in Women's Reproductive Labor," *Philosophy and Public Affairs* 21, no. 2 (1992): 107–31; or Susan Okin, "A Critique of Pregnancy Contracts," *Politics and the Life Sciences* 8 (1990): 205–10.
12. See, for example, the journal *Feminist Economics,* founded in 1995.
13. See, for example, Mary Dietz, "Citizenship with a Feminist Face," *Political Theory* 13 (1985): 19–37; Bubeck, *Care, Gender and Justice,* chap. 4; and Koziak, *Retrieving Political Emotion,* chap. 1.
14. I believe that Tronto, *Moral Boundaries*; Bubeck, *Care, Gender and Justice*; Michael Slote, *Morals from Motives* (Oxford: Oxford University Press, 2001); and Virginia

Held, *The Ethics of Care* (New York: Routledge, 2007), all fall into this error. See my 7.6.

15. Virginia Held, *Feminist Morality* (Chicago: University of Chicago Press, 1993), 195.
16. Ibid., 225.
17. By the republican tradition, I intend that other main tradition of political thought, which reaches back at least to Rousseau and is represented today by such thinkers as Michael Sandel, *Democracy and Its Discontents* (Cambridge, Mass.: Harvard University Press, 1996), and Phillip Pettit, *Republicanism* (Oxford: Clarendon Press, 1997). Republicans tend to hold such beliefs as "political activity is the most meaningful of all activities" (a form of perfectionism), and "the state should embody the value of 'fraternity'"—still conceived, I am afraid, as a relation *between similar males.*
18. Martha Fineman, *The Neutered Mother* (New York: New Press, 1995); and Kittay, *Love's Labor.*
19. Both BIEN and BIG propose a system of social security that periodically provides each citizen with a sum of money that is sufficient to live on. Except for citizenship, a basic income is entirely unconditional. For numerous arguments for a guaranteed basic income, see Philippe van Parijs, ed., *What's Wrong with a Free Lunch?* (Boston: Beacon Press, 2000); and Guy Standing, ed., *Justifying Guaranteed Basic Income in Europe and North America* (London: Anthem Press, 2004). See also Sibyl Schwarzenbach, "The Limits of Production: Justifying Guaranteed Basic Income," in *Justifying Guaranteed Basic Income,* ed. Standing, 107–14.
20. Such resentment is already well under way. See Elinor Burkett, *The Baby Boon: How Family Friendly America Cheats the Childless* (New York: Free Press, 2000). That mothers receive *more* from the state because they are raising children, Burkett notes, parallels older arguments that men should receive more than single women because men typically have a family to support—a historical inequity that the feminist movement has long tried to rectify.
21. Folbre, *Invisible Heart,* 109. Folbre later acknowledges, however, that the real issue is the *quality* of care (153).
22. G. W. F. Hegel, *The Philosophy of Right,* para. 238A.
23. Tronto, *Moral Boundaries,* 112.
24. My discussion is indebted to Martha Minow, "All in the Family and in All Families," in *Sex, Preference, and the Family,* ed. David Estlund and Martha Nussbaum (New York: Oxford University Press, 1997), 249–76.
25. The term *family* derives from the Latin *familia,* which originally referred in Roman law to a man's property: his wife, children, and slaves (those over whom he had the legal right of life and death). See Sir Henry Maine, *Ancient Law* (London: Holt, 1884).
26. Judith Bruce, Cynthia B. Lloyd, and Ann Leonard, with Patrice L. Engle and Niev Duffy, *Families in Focus: New Perspectives on Mothers, Fathers, and Children* (New

York: Population Council, 1995). In 1870, 14 percent of American women worked outside the home, but by 1992, 60 percent did so. The number of households headed by women grew from 7 percent of all families with children in 1960 to 25 percent in 1992. This trend, moreover, is happening around the world.

27. Martha Fineman, "What Place for Family Privacy?" in *Women and the United States Constitution: History, Interpretation, and Practice*, ed. Sibyl A. Schwarzenbach and Patricia Smith (New York: Columbia University Press, 2003), 236–54.
28. Ibid., 246.
29. Joan Williams, *Unbending Gender: Why Family and Work Conflict and What to Do About It* (Oxford: Oxford University Press, 2000), 105.
30. Anita Allen, "Privacy at Home: The Twofold Problem," in *Revisioning the Political*, ed. Nancy J. Hirschmann and Christine Di Stefano (Boulder, Colo.: Westview Press, 1996), 205.
31. I am indebted to White's account of the Beacons program, in *Democracy, Justice, and the Welfare State*, chap. 2. For more on this program, see http://www.ncjrs.org/txtfiles/beacons.txt.
32. See, for example, Moya, *Learning from Experience*, chap. 4.
33. Rob Reich, *Bridging Liberalism and Multiculturalism in American Education* (Chicago: University of Chicago Press, 2002), chap. 6. Other studies cite the number at 1,096,000 in the spring of 2003, a figure that still represents a 29 percent increase from the estimated 850,000 students who were being homeschooled in 1999. See U.S. Department of Education, National Center for Education Statistics, "Homeschooling in the United States: 2003," http://nces.ed.gov/pubs2006/homeschool/TableDisplay.asp?TablePath=TablesHTML/table_4.asp.
34. Department of Education, "Homeschooling in the United States: 2003."
35. See, for example, Reich, *Bridging Liberalism*; William Galston, *Liberal Purposes: Goods, Virtues and Diversity in the Liberal State* (Cambridge: Cambridge University Press, 1991); Amy Gutmann, *Democratic Education* (Cambridge, Mass.: Harvard University Press, 1989); and Stephen Macedo, *Diversity and Distrust: Civic Education in a Multicultural Democracy* (Cambridge, Mass.: Harvard University Press, 2000).
36. See, for example, Bubeck, *Care, Justice and Gender*, 259–61; and Sibyl Schwarzenbach, "On Civic Friendship," *Ethics* 107 (1996): 126–28.
37. Thom Shanker, "Proposed Military Spending Is Highest Since WWII," *New York Times*, February 4, 2008, A10. As noted earlier, U.S. expenditure on military forces already outstrips that of the rest of the world *combined*.
38. Benjamin Barber, *Strong Democracy* (Berkeley: University of California Press, 1984), 300. To be fair, Barber does mention that "child care" could be a later area of specialization; but why only "later" and why not for all?
39. Immanuel Kant, *Metaphysics of Morals*, sec. 34.

40. See, for example, Jason Scorza, "Liberal Citizenship and Civic Friendship," *Political Theory* 32, no. 1 (2004): 88.

41. Immediately after the September 11, 2001, attack on the World Trade Center, there were patriotic calls for "voluntary" civil service from conservatives. President Bush suggested that each citizen strive to contribute the equivalent of two years of voluntary service to the country (AmeriCorps), and figures such as Ross Perot waxed eloquent on the rewards of volunteering to teach inner-city children, as on *Larry King Live*, CNN, February 20, 2002.

42. See, for example, Barber, *Strong Democracy*, 299.

43. For the writings of various deliberative democrats, see, for example, Amy Gutmann and Dennis Thompson, *Democracy and Disagreement* (Cambridge, Mass.: Harvard University Press, 1996); Jean Cohen and Andrew Arato, *Civil Society and Political Theory* (Cambridge, Mass.: MIT Press, 1999); James Bohman and William Rehg, eds., *Deliberative Democracy* (Cambridge, Mass.: MIT Press, 1997); and Stephen Macedo, ed., *Deliberative Politics* (Oxford: Oxford University Press, 1999). For deliberative democrats who see their positions as connected with their feminism, see Frazer, *Justice Interruptus*; Seyla Benhabib, *Deliberative Democracy and Multicultural Dilemmas* (Princeton, N.J.: Princeton University Press, 2002) (hereafter cited as *DD*); and Iris Young, *Inclusion and Democracy* (Oxford: Oxford University Press, 2000).

44. Iris Young, "Communication and the Other," in *Democracy and Difference: Contesting the Boundaries of the Political*, ed. Seyla Benhabib (Princeton, N.J.: Princeton University Press, 1996), 125–35.

45. Ibid., 129.

46. Again, an important reason why so many deliberative democrats stop at the ideal of "reaching understanding" (and do not delineate a form of shared *praxis* as well) is that Habermas (in whose footsteps most follow) himself so sharply divides *communicative action* (aimed at reaching understanding) from *technical labor* (strategic action in the world) (see my 2.4–5). These two forms of action tend to divvy up the practical world in the Habermasian universe—mistakenly, in my view.

47. Cohen and Arato, *Civil Society*, ix.

48. Tronto, *Moral Boundaries*, 103. This definition is still found in her later work, such as "Care as the Work of Citizens" (working paper, Yale Political Theory Workshop, April 15, 2003), 1.

49. Bubeck, *Care, Gender, and Justice*, 202.

50. A similar critique, we might note, pertains to the widely used notion of "solidarity" (see preface); it, too, has amorphous boundaries. One may normatively *stipulate* a certain conception of what solidarity means, in order to exclude such unsavory groups as the KKK, say, or in order to emphasize an equality and reciprocity between members. See *Journal of Social Philosophy* 38, no. 1 (2007), special issue on

"Solidarity." The advantage of our ideal of civic friendship, however, is that friendship already entails these characteristics *inherently.*

51. Nel Noddings, *Caring: A Feminine Approach to Ethics and Moral Education* (Berkeley: University of California Press, 1984), 53, 25.
52. Tronto, *Moral Boundaries,* 148.
53. Slote, *Morals from Motives,* 68.
54. By an "emotional intuitionism," I intend the position that certain emotions (such as care) are viewed as rock-bottom and untouchable, and that they mostly trump other emotions or values, but with no priority rules given and no higher order background norms to be specified, and so forth. See my 1.4 and (by analogy) Rawls's critique of rational intuitionism: the doctrine that there is an irreducible family of moral first principles and we can only vaguely "weigh" one against the other in our judgments by intuition (*TJ,* 34–40).
55. Immanuel Kant, *Doctrine of Virtue,* sec. 46. Kant also claims that the ideal of friendship makes us "worthy of happiness"; hence we have a *duty* of friendship (sec. 45).

8. LOOKING OUTWARD

1. See, among others, Charles Beitz, *Political Theory and International Relations* (Princeton, N.J.: Princeton University Press, 1979); Carol Gould, *Globalizing Democracy and Human Rights* (Cambridge: Cambridge University Press, 2004); Onora O'Neil, *Bounds of Justice* (Cambridge: Cambridge University Press, 2000); Thomas Pogge, *World Poverty and Human Rights* (Cambridge: Polity Press, 2002) (hereafter cited as *WPHR*); Thomas Pogge, ed., *Global Justice* (Oxford: Blackwell, 2001); John Rawls, *The Law of Peoples* (Cambridge, Mass.: Harvard University Press, 1997); and Gillian Brock and Darrel Möllendorf, eds., *Current Debates in Global Justice* (Dordrecht: Springer Verlag, 2005).
2. See, for example, Alasdair MacIntyre, "Is Patriotism a Virtue?" in *Theorizing Citizenship,* ed. Ronald Beiner (New York: State University of New York Press, 1995), 209–28; David Miller, *On Nationality* (Oxford: Oxford University Press, 1995); or Michael Walzer, "The Distribution of Membership," in *Boundaries: National Autonomy and Its Limits,* ed. Peter G. Brown and Henry Shue (Totowa, N.J.: Rowman & Littlefield, 1981), 1–35.
3. Peter Singer, *One World: The Ethics of Globalization* (New Haven, Conn.: Yale University Press, 2002).
4. *WPHR,* 169.
5. Thomas Hobbes, *De Cive* (London: Printed by J. C. for R. Royston, at Angel in Ivielane, 1651), chap. 17, xi.

6. Carl Schmidt, *The Concept of the Political*, trans George Schwab (Chicago: University of Chicago Press, 1996), 46–47.
7. I here rely on Evgeny Roshchin, "The Concept of Friendship: From Princes to States," *European Journal of International Relations* 12, no. 4 (2006): 599–624.
8. Gerd Althoff, "Friendship and Political Order," in *Friendship in Medieval Europe*, ed. Julian Haseldine (Phoenix Mill, Eng.: Stroud, 1999), 94.
9. Thomas More writes, "The Utopians call those nations that come and ask magistrates from them, neighbors; but those to whom they have been of more particular service, friends" (*Utopia*, ed. Timothy O'Hagan [London: Dent, 1991], 89).
10. Randall Lesaffer, "*Amicitia* in Renaissance Peace and Alliance Treatises," *Journal of the History of International Law* 4 (2002): 95–96. Granted, such were often entered into with what were considered "inferior" peoples.
11. Thus Coke, in 1608, writes, "And all Aliens that are within the Realme of England, and *whose Soveraignes are in amity with the King of England*, are within the protection of the King." Grotius, in 1625, said of the political stranger (*hostis*) that he is the person "who possesses the civil and military powers of the state [and who has] power to conclude treaties of peace and amity" (quoted in Roshchin, "Concept of Friendship," 609).
12. Thomas Starkey (1871), quoted in Roschin, "Concept of Friendship," 606.
13. Arnold Wolfers, "Amity and Enmity Among Nations," in *Discord and Collaboration: Essays on International Politics* (Baltimore: Johns Hopkins University Press, 1962), 25–27.
14. See, for example, Andrea Oelsner, "Friendship, Mutual Trust, and the Evolution of Regional Peace in the International System," in "Friendship in Politics" (special issue), ed. G.raham Smith and Preston King, *Critical Review of International Social and Political Philosophy* 10, no. 2 (2007): 257–79; Karl Deutsch, Sidney A. Burrell, and Robert A. Kann, *Political Community and the North Atlantic Area: International Organization in the Light of Historical Experience* (Princeton, N.J.: Princeton University Press, 1957); Emanuel Adler and Michael Barnett, eds., *Security Communities* (Cambridge: Cambridge University Press, 1998); Alexander Wendt, *Social Theory and International Politics* (Cambridge: Cambridge University Press, 1999); and Arie M. Kacowicz, Yaacov Bar-Siman-Tov, Ole Elgström, and Magnus Jerneck, eds., *Stable Peace Among Nations* (Lanham, Md.: Rowman & Littlefield, 2000).
15. Wendt, *Social Theory*, 298.
16. The securitization approach is elaborated in Ole Waever, "Securitization and Desecuritization," in *On Security*, ed. Ronny Lipschutz (New York: Columbia University Press, 1995), 46–86; and in Barry Buzan, Ole Waever, and Jaap de Wilde, *Security: A New Framework for Analysis* (Boulder, Colo.: Rienner, 1998). My account is heavily indebted to Oelsner, "Friendship, Mutual Trust."
17. Waever, "Securitization and Desecuritization," 61.

18. Buzan, Waever, and de Wilde, *Security*, 4.
19. Oelsner, "Friendship, Mutual Trust," 276.
20. The distinction between negative and positive peace is commonly attributed to Kenneth Boulding, who claimed the former implies an absence of tension and war, while the latter refers to "good management, orderly resolution of conflict, harmony associated with mature relationships" (*Stable Peace* [Austin: University of Texas Press, 1978], 3). See also Alexander L. George's discussion of "stages of peace" in "Foreword," in *Stable Peace Among Nations*, ed. Kacowicz et al., 8.
21. Arie M. Kacowicz and Yacov Bar-Siman-Tov, "Stable Peace: A Conceptual Framework," in *Stable Peace Among Nations*, ed. Kacowicz et al., 22.
22. Wendt, *Social Theory*, 299.
23. Buzan, Waever, and de Wilde, *Security*, 4.
24. Oelsner, "Friendship, Mutual Trust," 269.
25. Antoine Vion discusses the twinning relation, for example, between Rennes, France, and Rochester, New York, during the Cold War (1948–1990), in "The Institutionalization of International Friendship," in "Friendship in Politics" (special issue), ed. G.raham Smith and Preston King, *Critical Review of International Social and Political Philosophy* 10, no. 2 (2007): 290.
26. For an account of recent culturally comparative studies, which reveal that nowhere in the world are women as physically aggressive as men, see Helen E. Fischer, *The First Sex: The Natural Talents of Women and How They Are Changing the World* (New York: Random House, 1999), 155–58. As I was writing this in July 2006, Hezbollah was lobbing missiles into northern Israel from Lebanon, while Israel retaliated with the direct bombing of Beirut, its airport, bridges, roads, neighboring power plants, and population. It is difficult to see how the latter's overwhelming retaliation and disproportionate use of military force could cause anything throughout the world but greater condemnation of Israel itself. Do such actions truly make Israel and its borders safer? Hardly. How much better it would be to put all those billions of dollars of U.S. aid to this tiny country into town twinnings with its Arab villages, transforming its relationships with its native Palestinian peoples and neighbors into genuine friendships. See my 8.5.
27. Omar Dahbour, "Three Models of Global Community," in *Current Debates in Global Justice*, ed. Brock and Möllendorf, 217–18. See also the doubts expressed in Jean L. Cohen, "Whose Sovereignty? Empire versus International Law," in *Global Institutions and Responsibilities: Achieving Global Justice*, ed. Christian Barry and Thomas Pogge (Malden Mass.: Blackwell, 2005), 159–89.
28. *WPHR*, chap. 8.
29. Rawls, *Law of Peoples*, 116.
30. Ibid., 119. As illustrative of his point, Rawls cites Japan, which is flourishing despite its scanty natural resources.
31. Thomas Pogge, "Priorities of Global Justice," in *Global Justice*, ed. Pogge, 13.

32. Statistics are from the World Bank, the United Nations Development Report, and the World Health Organization, as quoted in Pogge, "Priorities of Global Justice," 7–8.
33. Ibid., 14. See also *WPHR*, 199.
34. *WPHR*, 199; Pogge, "Real World Justice," in *Current Debates in Global Justice*, ed. Brock and Möllendorf, 36.
35. *WPHR*, 201. In later works, Pogge refines his analysis to include a third category of "intermediate duties," which have been violated (not so much "negative" ones), but this distinction need not concern us here.
36. Rawls, *Law of Peoples*, 117.
37. See also the chilling insider account of corruption and deception in developed countries, aimed at Third World economic dependence, in John Perkins, *Confessions of an Economic Hit Man* (San Francisco: Berret-Koehler, 2004).
38. Mathias Risse raises this objection in "What We Owe to the Global Poor," in *Current Debates in Global Justice*, ed. Brock and Möllendorf, 81–117.
39. In chapter 5 we argued that Rawls's difference principle (despite his Kantian conception of the person) continues to presuppose a Lockean acquisitive self *in the realm of labor* (5.3), leading to the problem we identified as that of the theoretical and practical *acceptance of the difference principle*: especially the well-to-do will not buy it, and have not bought it (5.6). If we reject this fundamental assumption of modern economic theory, however, and begin instead from the model of ethical reproduction (again, empirical studies confirm that on average women are still alternatively motivated [Fischer, *First Sex*, 29–40]), the possibility of acknowledgment and motivation to realize this principle is far easier to conceive. Of course, it is then no longer a principle of "fraternity" (between male household heads), but an economic principle of "civic friendship," which holds between all citizens (including all women), and the inequalities in primary goods needed to motivate the laboring self, as well as those allowed by the principle, are far less than Rawls envisioned. See my 5.6.
40. Pogge, "Real World Justice," 29.
41. Thomas Pogge, *Realizing Rawls* (Ithaca, N.Y.: Cornell University Press, 1989), chap. 2, sec. 9.
42. For example, Dale Jamieson, "Duties to the Distant," in *Current Debates in Global Justice*, ed. Brock and Möllendorf, 161 (hereafter cited as DD).
43. Mathias Risse, "What We Owe to the Global Poor," in *Current Debates in Global Justice*, ed. Brock and Möllendorf, 91.
44. From 1990 to 2000, for instance, 2 million children died in wars, three times the total number of American soldiers killed throughout history. See DD, 155.
45. Again, see the disturbing insider account by Perkins, *Confessions*.
46. Quoted in Herman E. Daly and John B. Cobb, Jr., *For the Common Good* (Boston: Beacon Press, 1994), 209.

47. Vandana Shiva, "The Impoverishment of the Environment," in Maria Mies and Vandana Shiva, *Ecofeminism* (London: Zed Books, 1993), 72.
48. Daly and Cobb, *For the Common Good*, 343.
49. For alternative economic accounts seeking to include the value of our environment and our communities, see, among others, Herman E. Daly and Kenneth N. Townsend, eds., *Valuing the Earth: Economics, Ecology, Ethics* (Cambridge, Mass.: MIT Press, 1993); Lester Brown, *Plan B 2.0* (New York: Norton, 2006); and Andrew Dobson, ed., *Fairness and Futurity* (Oxford: Oxford University Press, 1999).
50. United Nations, *2005 Millennium Assessment Report*, is the result of the considered opinion of 1,360 leading scientists from 95 countries around the world and is available at http://www.millenniumassessment.org/en/index.aspx. See also Steve Connor, "The State of the World?" *Independent*, March 30, 2005.
51. Mathis Wackernagel and William Rees, *Our Ecological Footprint* (Gabriela Island, B.C.: New Society Publishers, 1996), 90.
52. See the discussion in Fred Kaufman, *Foundations of Environmental Philosophy* (New York: McGraw-Hill, 2002), 2–3.
53. "Ecological footprint" is a measure current among many environmentalists. In one formulation, it is defined as the use or occupation of "ecological space" (expressed in global hectares), "which is the aggregated amount of biologically productive land and water area required to produce the resources consumed and to assimilate the waste products generated using prevailing technology" (Tom Hayward, "Global Justice and the Distribution of Natural Resources," *Political Studies* 54, no. 2 [2006]: 349–69).
54. Brown, *Plan B 2.0*, 4.
55. Ibid., 253. In early 1942, President Franklin Roosevelt met with American automobile industry leaders (the largest concentration of industrial power in the world at the time) and simply ordered them to convert to armaments production. From April 1942 until the end of 1944, there were no private cars produced in the United States, and the mobilization included a halt on residential and highway construction, a ban on driving for pleasure, and the rationing of all sorts of goods (cutting back on consumption).
56. Catharine MacKinnon, *Are Women Human?* (Cambridge, Mass.: Harvard University Press, 2006).
57. Christopher Stone, "Should Trees Have Standing?" in *Environmental Ethics*, ed. Joseph DesJardin (Belmont, Calif.: Wadsworth, 2000), 203–13.
58. Paul Schollmeier, "Why We Love the Land," *Ethics and the Environment* 2, no. 1 (1997): 53–66.
59. After the United States, Russia, France, Germany, and the United Kingdom are the next largest arms dealers, with 37 percent of total sales. See Congressional Research Service, *Conventional Arms Transfers to Developing Nations*, in *WPHR*, 219.

60. See, for example, Mary Daly, ed., *Care Work: The Quest for Security* (Geneva: International Labor Office, 2001).
61. Quoted in Pogge, "Priorities of Global Justice," 8.
62. Brown, *Plan B 2.0*, 251.
63. Edmund L. Andrews, "Budget Deficit Will Climb in 2006, White House Says," *New York Times*, January 13, 2006, A14. As of October 2008, the U.S. economy finds itself shaken to the core; major banks have failed, the stock market has plummeted, and President George W. Bush is proposing a $700 billion "bailout" package to try to rescue the economy.
64. Amory B. Lovins and L. Hunter Lovins, "Energy: The Avoidable Oil Crisis," *Atlantic*, December 22, 1987, 27.
65. In areas with heavy firing of U.S. ammunition, cancer rates of Iraqi children are as high as 71.8 per 100,000, as compared with a regional average of 3.9. See Augustus R. Norton, "Pity the Region," *Nation*, February 6, 2006, 29.

INDEX